THE CONTEMPORARY APPLICATIONS OF A SYSTEMS APPROACH TO EDUCATION

Models for Effective Reform

Kerry Dunn
John Scileppi
Leslie Averna
Vanessa Zerillo
Mark Skelding

University Press of America,® Inc.
Lanham · Boulder · New York · Toronto · Plymouth, UK

Copyright © 2007 by
University Press of America,® Inc.
4501 Forbes Boulevard
Suite 200
Lanham, Maryland 20706
UPA Acquisitions Department (301) 459-3366

Estover Road
Plymouth PL6 7PY
United Kingdom

Library of Congress Control Number: 2007930453
ISBN-13: 978-0-7618-3827-2 (paperback : alk. paper)
ISBN-10: 0-7618-3827-9 (paperback : alk. paper)

Table of Contents

The problem is that if our teaching is to be an art, we need an ongoing vision that brings together all these separate components into something graceful and vital and significant. It is not the number of good ideas that turns our work into art, but the selection, balance, coherence and design of those ideas. Calkins, 2001 in The Art of Teaching Reading

Preface

OVERVIEW

In this book, a systems approach to education is presented along with significant contemporary applications. The systems approach enables the reader to understand the degree to which all aspects of the school work together to enhance student learning.

Through this approach, educational leaders have the conceptual tools necessary to create meaningful, effective and long-lasting changes. Educators are often frustrated by the relatively minor effect interventions have created thus far, even though great effort went into these innovative programs. Frequently potential innovators have utilized a linear or piecemeal approach to change. They have targeted an isolated factor and attempted to increase student learning by changing this one aspect. Rarely does this work. Usually the one component is embedded in the entire educational system, and attempting to modify only this element will result in disruption and lower efficiency throughout the system. The isolated intervention is thus doomed to fail.

Through a systems approach, the interactions among all components are considered, and a more holistic innovation is conceived, planned and implemented. This book explores what a systems approach entails, and then investigates a number of significant contemporary issues in education from this approach. The book is intended for those who are currently—or aspire to become —educational leaders. The authors hope that these readers will become more knowledgeable about this approach and use it to create effective and persistent reforms that will truly improve student learning.

ORGANZIZATION OF THE BOOK

The book is divided into three sections.

Part 1 includes two chapters that introduce the systems approach and how to conduct meaningful action oriented research within this approach. Educational change agents need to demonstrate the need for new programs, assess community attitudes and evaluate the effectiveness of programs in the local school or community, and this research should have a direct bearing on what programs are proposed or revised.

Chapter 1 - Introduction to a Systems Approach to Education
The systems approach is an effective framework both for understanding the interaction among factors affecting learning, and for creating meaningful reform. Educators can benefit from conceptualizing the synergy that can exist within the educational system from the realization that any prospective change impacts the values and behaviors of all stakeholders in the community. The basic principles of systems theory, the levels of factors affecting learning, the context surrounding education and the diverse goals and views of socialization are explored.

Chapter 2 - Action Research and Educational Reform: Partners in a Process
When reviewing educational research studies located in scholarly journals, educators need to know whether the findings reported elsewhere will apply to their own district schools. Different cultures require different interventions, since students, teachers and community members vary from one school or district to another: they are unique systems unto themselves. Action research is a vehicle for inquiry and improvement that assists local educators and school teams in taking actions that match the needs of their stakeholders. It is a process that promotes change based on valid and reliable assessment of all the elements of the specific system as well as their relationships. In this way, any changes made are

longer lasting, creating a more proactive and accountable means for on going school improvement.

Part 2 includes seven chapters and focuses on contemporary topics of interest to current educators, and to those planning to enter teaching as a profession. Understanding the purposes of assessment and evaluation and the respective feedback they provide for stakeholders at all levels within education is discussed first. In a systems perspective these processes have a far more meaningful role than the isolated student-oriented one they have traditionally been assigned. The next topic concerns cultural diversity, a theme that permeates all levels of the system. In this chapter the myths and misconceptions of diversity are confronted, and examples of how to teach students from diverse backgrounds are presented. Closely parallel to the issue of cultural diversity is the topic of inclusion. In this chapter, the requirement of schools to help each student realize their fullest learning potential is described, and the history of special education presented—from both a systems approach. Parental involvement in education is the theme of the following chapter. Parent–teacher communication is seen as a two way process since a true dialog between the two can favorably impact the learning of the students. Parents become more knowledgeable about the teacher's instructional goals and teachers become more aware of the parents' concerns, expectations and values. The next two chapters discuss the role technology can play in education. Learning through technology considers the benefits and flaws in adopting electronic aids in teaching. Again the systems approach is evident as issues such as the digital divide are discussed. Related to the use of technology is the next chapter, distance learning. Teacher and students do not need to be in the same classroom—or even in the same state—for learning to take place. Removing the requirement of one location for holding a class enables educators to think literally 'out of the box' creating opportunities for new approaches to learning. The final chapter in this section concerns mental health and the schools. Students in today's society encounter many stressors in their lives, and the schools can offer programs that help them to deal effectively with these challenges to their psychological health. Furthermore, a student who is preoccupied or overly anxious is unable to attend to learning activities and enhancing the mental health of students can improve their academic performance as well.

Chapter 3 - Assessment vs. Evaluation: A Systems View

Educational assessment and evaluation is, and has been since the early days of formal testing, a perennial "hot" topic in education. Discourse over the differences between assessment and evaluation and their respective place and purpose in education is clearly divided along philosophical lines, fueled by differing understandings of the term accountability and differing levels of trust in quantitative data.

Although often used interchangeably, the terms assessment and evaluation are not synonyms. This is especially evident when the two are viewed from a systems perspective. True assessment is inherent in the dynamics and sustainability of any system. It is a natural, organic process. In education, it is assessment that sustains student learning, in turn creating a constructive ripple effect that permeates the educational system as a whole. The impact of evaluation, due to it non-systemic nature, is very different. The contrast between assessment and evaluation and their respective place and purpose in education is particularly salient when one explores formative assessment versus evaluation at the classroom level.

Chapter 4 - Cultural Diversity

Perhaps one of the most significant topics in American education today involves the need to enhance cultural diversity in a pluralistic society. Frequently, students of color perceive the school system as an institution alien to their culture. The majority of teachers, school administrators, and school board members seem to look different and to espouse values different than those of their own family. As demographic changes occur in many states and districts, which increase the proportion of people of color, school personnel need to enhance cultural diversity in the classroom. Cultural amplifiers which are more inviting to minority children and which increase the likelihood that they will perceive a familiar place in which to learn are desperately needed in schools. The interventions developed in a school in New Jersey which has students whose parents are United Nations staff members are described with the hope that they might stimulate parallel innovations in the readers' home districts. This issue is very systems—oriented. The school's activities must be tuned to the cultural perspectives of the group of students in the district while still reflecting the norms of society and the standards of the state and national educational systems.

Chapter 5 - Inclusion, Reform and Learning Organizations

The U.S. Congress passed Public Law 94-142 in 1975, mandating a free and appropriate public education for every child, regardless of his/her disability. This legislation challenged school administrators, teachers and related services providers to meet the requirements of this law in most cost-effective manner, while meeting the needs of all students at the same time. Prior to 1975, many districts either did not provide any education for these students or expelled them if they could not keep up with their classmates or if their behavior was disruptive to other students. Parents would then have to find an appropriate learning situation for their children and pay for this by themselves. If this was not possible, the children were often institutionalized, and the likelihood that they could lead a normalized life was decreased dramatically. Now, many of these students are being 'included' in regular classrooms. Again a systems perspective is needed to study all the aspects of this trend, and solutions must ensure that all the stakeholders are accommodated. The learning of both the special needs and typical student must be considered. Resources available to teachers, special services personnel and teacher aides have to be assessed. The curriculum of teacher training programs must be evaluated and modified, if necessary, with a focus on inclusion. The effect of the relevant laws on learning must be studied, and if unintended or unfavorable outcomes result, the legislation must be modified in the political arena or alternative systems developed and supported in local schools for the benefit of all children.

Chapter 6 - Parent Communication

A variety of studies have found that student learning is enhanced when parents become actively involved in their children's education. This involvement takes many forms, but the interaction between a student's teacher and parent is perhaps the most significant. As was mentioned earlier, Murrell (1973) found that the consistency in value between a child's school and family enhances the degree to which the student is likely to accept these values. The synergy of the educational experience favorably impacts on learning. If parents and teachers communicate with each other, this synergy is likely to result. Both parent and teacher learn from each other in this interaction. The teacher becomes more aware of the values and circumstances of the student's family and the parent becomes better informed about the teacher's learning objectives and the child's progress in class. The content and amount of homework is a topic that frequently arises in teacher / parent contacts. This communication is occurring more commonly now by e-mail.

While there are benefits to increasing parent/ teacher interaction, educators need to discover empirically whether there can be too much of a good thing. How much time is consumed, is the time spread evenly across all the parents of students in a class or do some parents need more than their fair share of the teacher's time, is the student's privacy unnecessarily violated? Should parental involvement be a requirement for having new programs funded by the federal or state governments? These questions need system wide input in arriving at accurate and acceptable answers.

Chapter 7 - Technology: The World of Wonder

The entire world community entered the Information Age in the final decade of the twentieth century. Information technology has pervaded just about every aspect of life. Students at home use computers in countless activities—from playing games and e-mailing friends to surfing the web and visiting sites of interest and joining chat rooms discussing common hobbies. The computer has become a major component of their lives just as television, radio, and books were to earlier generations. Educators need to keep abreast of developments in information technology, as the computer can become an electronic resource if properly exploited. Word processing, locating the appropriate web-site to find relevant information on subjects covered in class and posting discussion questions or problems of the week electronically for the students to debate and solve are just a few ways in which classroom learning can be enhanced through technology. In addition, technology exists to allow students to learn at their own pace and to individualize the content of the learning. Finally, technology can provide the teacher with an efficient information management system to track students' progress throughout the year. Just as earlier teachers would be at a terrible loss without access to chalkboards, today's educators need to be able to develop PowerPoint presentations and show students how to word-process and navigate the web effectively.

However, the computer is not a panacea, and educational researchers need to investigate how technology in the classroom affects writing style, interpersonal interaction, and the likelihood of cheating and plagiarizing. Finally, keeping current with information technology hardware and software is very expensive and not every family and school district can afford all the latest bells and whistles. The effect on educational equality and relative deprivation needs also to be investigated, and solutions at the political and economic levels of the system need to be proposed, implemented and evaluated.

Chapter 8 - Distance Learning: Flexibility in Education

Another recent phenomenon in education is distance learning in which a teacher in one location instructs students located elsewhere. This opportunity is particularly beneficial if there are not enough students in one school to justify a certain subject being taught, but through distance learning, a small number of students in each of a few schools would provide the 'critical mass' to support the subject offering. The flexibility provided through distance learning transcends not only space but also time. It is possible for a student who must work during the day to access in the evening the same learning that the rest of the class encountered during the day. There are many variations on this distance-learning theme, some of which involve hybrid approaches in which some learning may occur in real classrooms in which teachers and students interact face to face and other aspects of the learning occur electronically. Some distance learning utilizes the World Wide Web and the Internet while other forms use interactive audio-video contact over telephone lines. As with other forms of technology discussed in Chapter 7, distance learning is not effective for all students and teachers. Research needs to be conducted to determine which students in which subjects with which teachers and under what circumstances benefit from distance learning. As with technology, the decision to utilize distance learning does not rest solely with one individual. Teachers, administrators, superintendents, school boards, community residents and voters and representatives from the high technology business sector must all come together to agree on distance learning and forge a collaborative relationship to develop an effective system.

Chapter 9 - The School and the Mental Health System

The schools of course are an essential component of the educational system. It is also true however that the schools can be a significant element in the mental health system. Historically, leaders in the public physical as well as mental health field have realized that schools provide access to the vast majority of children. During the early twentieth century when large groups of immigrants were arriving in the major cities in the United States, not only school nurses but medical doctors as well had offices in schools and provided usually free health care to the students. Even today, many states have passed legislation that requires children to be vaccinated against common childhood diseases and to receive physical examinations prior to entering school as a way of preventing epidemics and improving the physical health of the children (Kamins, 1992). Mental health professionals also realize the benefits of using the school as a place to provide preventive interventions and treatment.

As is described in the chapter, promoting mental health also results in higher academic achievement. A child preoccupied by anxiety or experiencing symptoms of mental illness or difficulties in living is less likely to be able to concentrate on learning. Preventive workshops in coping skills, problem solving, stress management and social skills can help the students deal with challenging situations. School counselors can anticipate common developmental crises and offer interventions to prepare the children about to experience them. Also, educators and mental health professionals can collaborate together to create a school value climate that encourages character development, value clarification and affective learning, objectives that relate both to psychological well being and learning.

Finally, the schools can be used to foster community mental health and well being. Conflict resolution and assertiveness skills can be taught to students as alternatives to aggression and violence. In this way, the schools can help to promote good citizenship, a commonly accepted goal of education.

As with all the other topics in education, those advocating activities to promote mental health and prevent illness must be sensitive to the systems approach. School personnel, mental health professionals, parents, the school board and the entire community should collaborate in discussing, developing and implementing workshops and other interventions. The federal and state governments frequently support such cooperative ventures as the FAST (Families and Schools Together) Program.

Part 3 includes two chapters and offers a conclusion to the systems approach. The chapter on change identifies strategies educators can use to create meaningful interventions. Using the systems perspective, both global perspectives on the theory of change and practical techniques to accomplish reform—including grant writing—are included. The final concluding chapter focuses on magnet schools, a successful large-scale reform applying the systems approach. Magnet schools, the result of national and state initiatives to reform education, were established with a great deal of community, teacher, administrator, parent and student involvement. The magnet school concept is a fitting topic with which to conclude the book, as these schools embody the principles of systemic change and employ the best of educational practices, which have resulted in improved academic achievement, one of the primary goals of education.

Chapter 10 - Strategies for Educational Change

It is hoped that after reviewing the topics discussed in this book, educators may reflect on ways to improve student learning and decide to propose worthwhile innovations. This chapter presents both the theory of change and specific strategies and techniques to implement new programs. The theory of change focuses on the politics of change. Even the way a problem is stated is a political issue, and will affect the range of solutions debated. A child might not learn effectively because of a personal problem or disability, or because of a classroom or school level factor, or because of a societal, economic or regulatory concern. Assuming the problem exists at the wrong level will result in an ineffective and usually expensive solution creating a game without end. Conceptualizing the problem correctly creates the context for developing appropriate and effective interventions.

Once a solution is developed, various stakeholders in the school system need to be convinced that the program will remedy an existing problem effectively and with few unfavorable side effects. Techniques of promoting change are presented with the objective of providing a range of methods of benefit to the potential educational reformer.

Hopefully by the time the reader reviews this chapter, various ideas for change will have been imagined. To transform these ideas into concrete interventions, funding will be needed. This chapter concludes with a description of how to write grant proposals to support financially the proposed program.

Chapter 11 - The Magnet School as a Model System for Educational Reform

The courts initially conceived magnet schools in the early 1950s, as a solution to the problem of segregation of students in schools. Magnet schools offer a unique, specialized curriculum as the focal point of their existence, which serves as a "magnet" to attract students from different racial, economic and ethnic backgrounds. The mission of the school is delineated early during the inception process, and all components revolve around, and are related to, this mission. Through the years, the concept has expanded to provide an enriching teaching and learning environment which attracts a variety of students to learning communities by satisfying their learning styles, needs and interests and promising improved achievement in an atmosphere of diversity. The concept has been so successful that the number of schools is increasing, as is both state and federal support for their implementation. This chapter discusses this success in relation to the operation of its components and its adoption of best practices, both of which combine to provide a mechanism for systemic reform.   The theory behind the contemporary issues in education described earlier in the book (inclusion, parental involvement, technology, assessment and diversity, etc.) is applied within the magnet school. This is intended to give the reader the opportunity to witness theory in action and to determine those components of the magnet school worth replicating in the general education environment.

THE AUTHORS

To write this systems oriented book, a community of scholars and professionals who perform different roles in education were assembled. Among us, in alphabetical order, are Leslie Averna, 6th year in Education Administration, an education consultant, educator, and recently retired from the position of Associate Commissioner of the Connecticut State Department of Education; Kerry Dunn, Ed.D., also a former teacher and currently an Assistant Professor of Education; John Scileppi, Ph.D., an author of books on systems theory and community psychology and a Professor of Psychology; Mark Skelding, M.Ed, an academic coordinator in a graduate teacher education programand an expert on assessment and evaluation; and Vanessa Zerillo, Ed.D., former speech-language pathologist and administrator for special services and curriculum, and currently director and Associate Professor of Education of a university graduate program for educators. Many of us are also parents of students, and thus we can also utilize that perspective in our work; and finally, of course, all of us were students and are aware of both the successes and the failures encountered in our own education.

While the professors are expert in theory, the practitioners and administrators have a wealth of practical experience from which to draw upon when describing the educational system. We all agree on basic philosophy and orientation; however the reader may find occasional times when two of us may support opposing viewpoints. Let these instances themselves be good training for creating reform in the educational system. We assure you, it will not be the last time you encounter contradictory recommendations given by various stakeholders in the system!

All the authors have read and commented upon the material in each chapter, but individual authors had primary responsibility in writing various chapters. Kerry Dunn wrote the chapters on cultural diversity, parent—teacher communication, learning through technology and distance learning. John Scileppi prepared the chapters on the introduction to the systems analysis of education, mental health and the schools, and strategies for change. Vanessa Zerillo authored the chapters on action research and inclusion. Leslie Averna prepared the chapter on magnet schools, and Mark Skelding wrote the chapter on assessment and evaluation. We invite you to learn about the systems approach and the various possibilities for creating effective educational reform using this approach.

ACHNOWLEDGEMENTS

We give special thanks to Michelle Wojtaszek and Lauren Richmond, Marist graduate students for their professional assistance in editing, proofreading and formatting the textbook, and in developing the two indexes. Their capable and competent work was truly invaluable.

As we explain throughout this book, none of us learns in a vacuum; rather we live in a social system, a human ecology of family, colleagues, friends and acquaintances. We thank our spouses, our parents and our children for their support and encouragement.

Chapter 1: Introduction to a Systems Approach to Education

OBJECTIVES

After studying this chapter, the reader will be able to describe, analyze and apply the tenets of:

1. The components of a system;

2. Soft-systems methodology;

3. Community psychological approaches to education;

4. The factors that impact learning;

5. Research approaches on factors influencing student achievement and their benefits;

6. The goals of a social system and the difference between system maintenance and task productivity;

7. System inputs, throughputs and outputs as they relate to an educational system;

8. The role of goals in systems analysis; and

9. The goals of education as they relate to the socialization of the child.

OVERVIEW

Why can't Johnny learn? Too often, we are satisfied with labeling the student as a "slow learner" or as a "disadvantaged child". Yet there are too many "Johnnys" in America who are not learning to their fullest potentials. Many would rephrase the question "What is wrong with our schools?" Perhaps this too is inadequate, as it shifts the blame entirely to the educational institutions themselves. It is of the utmost importance that we arrive at some unified conceptualization as to what has gone wrong with our national educational system, and then what can be done about it.

Presently, education is one of the greatest concerns in America, and this concern can be seen from many perspectives. Across the country, educators are frustrated that achievement scores have not been improving. While vast sums of money have been expended on education, taxpayers concerned with the inefficiency and lack of effectiveness of their schools have been voting down school budgets. Citizens have even sued school districts for negligence in the performance of their educational function. Parents blame teachers and teachers blame parents. The students themselves are often caught in the crossfire.

Many groups previously unconcerned about education are becoming involved, each complaining about some aspect of the learning system. Business leaders in communities throughout the nation are unhappy that they must establish long and expensive programs to teach high school graduates how to read and write and perform basic mathematical operations before they can be trained in the specific job skills needed by their companies. Legislatures are mandating that the state education departments establish basic competency tests that all elementary and high school students must pass before graduation. The federal government has also created standards that schools must meet in order for funding to be continued. Colleges have instituted proficiency exams in writing and other basic competency areas partly out of fear that their graduates might embarrass these scholarly institutions by preparing less than literate resumes and letters of application for jobs. From just about every sector of the population—educators, parents, business leaders, voters, taxpayers, residents, politicians, and others—expressions of concern about education are being voiced. All are searching for a process that will produce significant improvement in student learning.

To create meaningful, effective educational reform, a more complete understanding of education as a social system and how to apply it is needed. Most of the earlier innovations have been piecemeal approaches to change, and have failed to truly impact the learning of students in schools. Over the past twenty years, educational leaders have learned about the systems approach as presented by Scileppi (1988), Fullan (1993) and Senge (1994); however most have not utilized the approach when attempting to improve learning. The goal of this book is to explore how significant contemporary issues in education can be approached from a systems perspective to develop effective reform.

The problems of education can not be solved by focusing on only one level of the system, say students, parents, teachers, administrators, school boards, the community, state or nation. Ultimately each contemporary issue affects every level of the system, and for interventions regarding these issues to be effective, the change agent must develop an awareness of how the reform affects every level. We need to view the learning process as a holistic phenomenon which is multidimensional and in which all the factors are interactive and not isolated. No one factor works in a vacuum and changing some component will have tandem effects on other components. Failing to realize this interaction can increase the risk of unintended effects occurring at other levels that negate any favorable effects of the change.

The alternative to applying the systems approach to create educational reform is what Watzlawick, Weakland & Fisch (1974) call "innovation without change"—narrowly focused interventions at one level which are buffered or absorbed by the rest of the system so that the intended effect is never realized. The systems approach allows for a holistic but detailed diagnosis of the specific components of education within a community that can then point to a prescription for enhancing the quality of learning. In this way, the synergy, or effective smooth functioning of the system in meeting its goals, is increased.

Also to be considered is the perspective that any individual student's learning is embedded in a particular social context. Thus, while there may be general principles affecting learning, each community's educational system has unique characteristics that must be considered when diagnosing and prescribing for the system. Thus the values of accepting diversity, and focusing on the goodness of fit between the learner's needs and abilities, cultural strengths and traditions on the one hand and the learning resources available within a community on the other must be included in any concrete intervention in schools.

Thus, one can view the problems of American education from either a linear, piecemeal perspective, or from a more holistic, systematic orientation. The first approach attempts to isolate the problem as occurring in one small component of the entire process. For example, in the piecemeal approach, a reformer might seek to remove a certain teacher, to change a particular textbook, or to impose a new form of teaching. Such an approach was very prevalent during the last decades of the twentieth century, a time of great turmoil in American education. Yet the main effect of these interventions was small at best, and typically the innovations tended to cancel each other out or to fade from existence. Many educators became frustrated and began to believe that changing the status quo in education was not possible. Deal (1990) noted that the history of effective change in education is poor. Previous efforts have not made significant lasting improvements perhaps because they were isolated and non-systemic attempts. Now veteran teachers are lukewarm to reform as they recall similar failed interventions decades earlier.

THE SOCIAL SYSTEMS APPROACH

There is hope. Effective educational leaders along with social scientists have come to take a different approach to the problems of American education. They observe that education, similar to other institutions, can be viewed as a social system. A system, according to Hearn (1969), is a set of elements together with the relationships between the elements. When people and material are brought together to achieve an organizational purpose such as in schools, a system is created (Patterson, 1993).

Checkland (1997) noted that the elements of a system link together to form a complex whole. At higher levels of organization the parts combine to exhibit emergent properties not seen by investigating the pieces separately. That is parts are not just a random collection of elements but that they are ordered in some way. The order can be seen only when viewing the system as a whole. The systems theorists truly believe that one can lose the forest through the trees, as significant principles that appear when viewing the larger system are not observable when focusing only on the smaller unit.

Social scientists began to use a systems approach following World War II. One of the originators of the perspective Ludwig Von Bertalanffy (1968) called this approach General Systems Theory (GST). GST is a multi-disciplinary approach that studies how a system achieves its goals in its environment. Systems act as whole organisms that exchange resources, energies and outputs with the setting in which it adapts. Systematic interventions are more likely to be successful than changes that focus only on an isolated element separate from the other parts.

In order for an entity to be considered an adaptive system, four aspects must be present. First, the elements must be linked together and not simply be grouped as a collection of parts. Emergent properties only appear in a true system. Second, the system contains parts, which are themselves, sub-systems or smaller wholes. In the human body, the organism is composed of linked organ systems such as the lungs or the brain, and these organ systems are composed of tissues which in turn are composed of cells and so on. Third, the entity has a hierarchical structure of layers in which the smaller sub-systems work together to form the larger system. Lastly, the system which adapts successfully to its setting must have effective processes of communication and control. The system must sense environmental change and respond. Also, the system must monitor its response to determine whether it is achieving its goal.

In an organization, systems thinking allows decision makers to see the whole picture as an ongoing activity—processes, interrelationships and patterns—and not just a static snapshot of events (Senge, 1990). He noted that in a 'learning organization', that is one that grows as the result of experience, systems thinking is the fifth discipline. To contribute fully to the well-being and effectiveness of the organization, critical staff members need to understand all five disciplines: a) personal mastery of the skills needed to do one's job, b) an awareness of the effect of mental models—the paradigms believed—which can either enable staff to understand their work better, or serve as blinders preventing individuals from attending to important information, c) the methods of building shared vision or consensus in the group, d) techniques to create team learning or the ability of all the members of the organization to work together, maximizing the use of each person's resources and energies and preventing defensiveness, and finally, e) systems thinking.

The purpose of systems thinking is not only to understand how systems work, but also to intervene to improve them. Applications exist in biological ecological studies of natural systems, engineering research on man manufactured mechanical systems, and social analyses of organizations such as the educational and mental health systems in the community. This last application area is known as soft systems methodology (SSM) (Checkland, 1997). In SSM, a social system is assessed according to how well it is performing. The same performance however, could be evaluated differently depending on various worldviews. Each "stakeholder" could have a unique perspective and the resulting expectations of what purpose a system should serve can be very diverse. In the educational system, teachers, students, administrators, parents, taxpayers, and others each view the purpose of schools differently to some degree, and the SSM interventionist needs to understand how to deal with these conflicting "stakeholders". As compared to systems analysts in the ecological and engineering areas, SSM researchers deal with objectives that are harder to define and are more political in nature.

Using SSM, educators can understand why various attempts at change in education have failed. The most basic concept of this approach is that no one element exists in a vacuum, but that each always relates to other components of the system. Kelly (1966) describes this property of social systems as the principle of interdependence. Thus, if one element is altered, the relationships between it and the other factors are potentially affected. This modification places a stress on the entire system. If all the interrelated components can be made consistent with the reformed element, the change is accepted, the system restabilizes, and a type of synergy, or effectively directed smooth functioning of the system, results. Engineers have long known that in building a bridge, supports can be placed in a number of ways, but if they are placed synergistically, the total support will be greater than the sum of each factor separately. Similarly in a social system, if the factors that affect learning are all interconnected and supporting each other the resulting effect will be greater than the sum of each factor separately. If however, the reform in one element of the system is inconsistent with all the other components of the system, the change is rejected as the system strives to regulate itself to reestablish a steady state following the disruption. This feature of social systems is often called equifinality (Hearn, 1969). That is, there is a tendency within a social system to produce identical results, even though some of the components within the system have been altered. Thus, the systems interpretation of the failure of educational reforms of the last few decades is that these reforms were piecemeal, and the change agents had not considered the effects their innovations would have on the remainder of the educational system. As Cromwell and Scileppi (1996) noted, "it takes a village" working together cooperatively to educate children. Reformers must be knowledgeable about interdependence to avoid equifinality when planning innovations.

The need for the members of the "village" to work together has received support at the highest levels of the educational system. In 1994, Congress passed and then President Bill Clinton signed PL 103-382: The Improving America's Schools Act (U.S. Department of Education, 1997). This Act required schools to develop with parents a compact or partnership agreement outlining how parents, the entire school staff, and students will share responsibility for improving student achievement. The resulting "Compacts for Learning" encouraged the entire community to work together to strengthen education. This law also emphasized the need for ongoing communication between parents and teachers. Many school districts continue to develop and implement their compacts.

Without the sharing of decision-making and sense of ongoing partnership among all those involved, reforms in the schools are not likely to succeed. Consider the example of a failed intervention. A teacher decided to alter her teaching style to allow a greater degree of student freedom within the classroom. However, administrators, hearing students talking and perhaps laughing while in small learning groups, might interpret the change as disruptive and not appreciate the new method. Parents might complain that their children are not receiving regular homework assignments. Other teachers might complain that their students are less obedient in class periods following the reformed class session. Perhaps some in the community might become annoyed at the drop in standardized test scores (as these tests were probably more consistent with the old teaching method). Even the students might complain that they no longer know what is expected of them. All in all, the innovation was probably doomed from the start, not because it was a non-productive idea, but because it was begun without a systems approach. Because of the lack of synergy, this new teaching style reform will probably be short lived and the actual learning of students might be decreased. Had the teacher considered all the potential consequences the change of teaching method may cause, she could have targeted each one prior to making the change and encouraged the other participants in the system to share their concerns and together work out a feasible strategy to deal satisfactorily with the issues. All aspects of the innovation need to be coordinated, including the core components such as school organization, curriculum, instructional methods, assessment and professional development (Jasparro, 1998). The change would then have been more systemic, and more likely to succeed.

Goodlad (1984), following a similar perspective, noted that controversial reform proposals, such as extending the school day or giving teachers merit pay, offer at best only a quick fix if these innovations are not incorporated into a total systematic reform of the schools. Some educational researchers have noted that most school-based reforms are poorly conceived and not well integrated into the rest of the system. Smith (1995) stated that education currently is not a "system" as a system requires that the entity be organized, integrated, orderly, predictable and functional. He perceived the schools to be disorganized, disorderly, unplanned and perhaps dysfunctional. Using a systems approach can help to make the components of education more synergistic and systematic. In addition, such an approach helps to organize and simplify the process of change and how it can be assessed accurately (Senge, 1990).

SYSTEMS ANALYSIS APPROACH AND COMMUNITY PSYCHOLOGY

Community psychology attempts to conceptualize how an individual's behavior is affected by the social setting. This view is more encompassing than the individualistic approaches of traditional psychology. In education, community psychology offers the opportunity to create a variety of interventions to enhance student achievement at many levels of the system. Community psychology views the social systems approach as the most accurate and appropriate way to understand human behavior (Scileppi, Teed & Torres, 2000). Community psychology in its emphasis on social ecology, diversity, empowerment and maximizing human strengths and resources looks beyond the individual and toward social systems and social change (Tebes, Kaufman & Watts, 2002). This ecological approach posits that behavior is best conceptualized as the interaction of the needs, interests and abilities of the person and the resources and the demands of the setting. Lewin (1951), the originator of this approach, described the ecological perspective on behavior as the person-environment fit. In an educational setting, if the school resources available and the teaching style utilized match the students' goals and learning style, learning will be enhanced. If the match is not good, less learning and greater frustration will result.

Note the effect on learning of the quality of the fit in the following example. If a curious child who likes to explore in a free-style approach is placed in a highly structured school, that student is likely to fail. The same student placed in an open school which values creativity and individual initiative will succeed. Similarly, the opposite learning outcomes would result if a more compliant student eager to follow the directives of the teacher were to be placed in either type of school. The compliant student will thrive in the highly structured setting and feel overwhelmed in the free style learning situation. If either student failed, it would be inappropriate to label the student as a poor learner. It would be just as inappropriate to label the school as a bad learning environment. The lack of learning resulted from the poor fit between the child and the school, and not because the child or the school was inferior. Thus, the best vantage point for understanding the child's degree of learning is the person-environment fit. This ecological conceptualization enables educators to develop effective interventions. Rather than providing intensive individual tutoring to change the child's learning style (an individual level correction which includes the implicit message that the student is somehow inferior), placing the child in a school where the teaching method is consistent with the student's learning style will resolve the concern. Another effective solution would be for school administrators to encourage teachers to assess the learning styles of the students and provide diverse activities, which capitalize on the learning styles present in the class.

LEVELS OF FACTORS IN THE EDUCATIONAL SYSTEM

In order to see how a systems theorist would design an intervention and plan for a more productive change in education, it is useful to map the elements and their interrelationships within the system. By adopting such a conceptualization the effects of each factor in meeting the system's goals can be studied.

There are many levels of elements that influence the learning in children in school. Boocock (1980) identified these levels of factors as follows:

1. The attributes of the individual child;
2. The qualities of the classroom;
3. The factors of the school itself;
4. The interface between the school and the community; and
5. The forces operating at the level of the state and national educational system.

At the most molecular level, a systems analyst investigates the characteristics of the individual learner. These factors are set to some degree even before the child enters a classroom. The child is a member of a family and such variables as family size, birth order, parental education, parenting practices, ethnic values and social status affect learning. At this level of conceptualization, the child's genetic and biological make up including sex differences, innate intellectual types and levels, genetic disorders and nutritional qualities influence the child's ability to function as a learner. Finally, psychological aspects such as self-attitudes, achievement motivation, personal developmental stage and degree of mental health affect how well a child does in class.

The child then enters a classroom and confronts a new level of factors that affect learning. At the classroom level, teacher characteristics, student body factors, classroom role structure and curriculum issues impact on learning. Teacher expectations, qualifications and experience, and the match between the student's preferred learning style and the teacher's method of teaching influence learning. Regarding the composition of the students in the classroom, issues such as homogeneous versus heterogeneous ability grouping, mainstreaming and inclusion, social, ethnic and racial diversity are all important variables affecting learning. Some classroom level factors result from the interaction of the teacher and students. Classroom or value climate—the social atmosphere of the classroom—including whether academic learning is emphasized affects student achievement. The classroom role structure, which encourages either an authoritarian or participative style, also influences whether students are productive students as does classroom management techniques and curriculum issues.

The classroom does not exist in isolation, but is embedded within a school, and school level factors including school role structure, physical facilities and available human resources, and type of school affect learning either directly or indirectly. Regarding role structure, the degree of bureaucracy can be studied. Is the principal perceived as an academic leader or as an administrator concerned about many non-academic issues? How well do students, teachers, parents and administrators relate to each other? These are questions of interest at this level of factor. Physical facilities such as the size of the school and the library, the quality of the science and language laboratories, level of technological equipment, and human learning resources such as the number and quality of counselors and other student services staff influence learning. Finally at this level, the size and type of school—magnet, academic versus vocational/technical, or comprehensive—affect learning.

The school exists within a community and the interface between the school and local community has a significant impact on the opportunity for students to learn. Community factors such as economic and ethnic composition, age and education demographics, the attitudes of the police, business leaders, members of civic and faith based groups toward the school and youth influence how residents are likely to vote on school district budgets and whether the "town-gown" barrier is raised or lowered. Finally characteristics of the school board, and how the school board interacts with the district superintendent, influence learning.

School districts are not fully autonomous but are part of the state and nation. The education department in each state mandates such policies as teacher certification requirements, curriculum content, and student learning requirements. Sometimes state education departments choose textbooks and set standards regarding the length of the scholastic year. In addition both a formal and informal national education system exists. The formal component consists of federal legislation affecting education and governmental funding of specific learning programs. The informal national system includes the mass media that can persuade the public to accept a particular educational philosophy and publishing companies that limit the type of textbooks, which will be available.

For a review of the empirical findings regarding how each factor affects student learning, consult Scileppi (1988). The effects of the various factors however are likely to be localized and time sensitive. Gergin (1973) noted that many social psychological empirical results are embedded in a social context. For example, historical trends and world events can shape educational priorities. In 1957, the Soviets launched 'Sputnik', the first man-made earth satellite. This shocked Americans who had assumed that the U.S. was technologically superior to the rest of the world. Many blamed the schools for the failure to train enough competent scientists. The federal government—and private foundations—increased funding for schools and colleges to upgrade their science facilities in order to 'close the gap' in the race toward space. Today, news of ethical violations by big business and some American military personnel, and concerns of increasing violence in schools and communities

are causing some to charge that the schools are not attending sufficiently to character education. Similar concerns ranging from the
lack of cultural sensitivity to the need for accountability form the
context that shapes how the public perceives the schools. While
some of these issues are national in scope, local events can also
exert unique effects on individual school districts. The results of
empirical studies are both time and space bound. As a perceived
educational deficit is remedied, enhancing that factor further has
little additional effect. As the culture changes, the priorities of its
members fluctuate and the relative influence of each variable on
learning changes. This is a major reason for systems oriented interventionists to conduct local studies—called action research—
prior to implementing large-scale change.

Table 1.1 outlines the factors affecting learning at each level of
analysis. The child is the smallest level of analysis. The child becomes the student and is affected by classroom level factors. The
classroom is embedded in the school, the school exists within the
community and the community is part of the state and nation. The
list is indicative but not exhaustive and readers can add other factors. It is important to note that all factors interrelate, and when one
variable is modified, the change agent must consider the effects of
this change on all the other elements of the system.

As can be seen, the educational system consists of increasing levels of complexity spanning the range from the individual
learner to the nation as a whole. One can conceptualize all the factors operating at each level and their interactions, and then explore
the relationships among levels of factors. Inconsistencies among
factors, which result in a lack of synergy, can be quickly detected.

TABLE 1.1: A SYSTEMS MODEL OF EDUCATION
Examples of Factors Affecting Learning at Each Level of Analysis

LEVEL OF ANALYSIS	FACTORS AFFECTING LEARNING	VARIABLES
The child	Biological	Genetic disorders Nutrition Illness having consequences on the brain or nervous system Sex differences Innate intellectual ability Temperament Learning style
	Psychological	Self attitudes Achievement motivation, Developmental level, Degree of mental health.
	Family Characteristics	Family size and composition Birth order Parental level of education Ethnic and family values Socioeconomic status.
The student	Teacher Characteristics	Teacher expectations Qualifications, Attitudes toward students Experiences Degree of stress
	Student Factors	Student body composition including homogeneous versus heterogeneous ability grouping, Inclusion issues Level of diversity Number of students in each classroom

	Teacher-Student Factors	Classroom climate Role structure Classroom management style Consistency between teaching style and preferred student learning style
The school	School Role Structure Physical and Human Resources School Characteristics	Degree of bureaucracy Communication networks among administrators, teachers, parents and students Quality of facilities such as computer, language and science laboratories The library Opportunities for athletic, social and artistic activities The number, types and quality of the support staff Teacher-student ratio Type of school (magnet, vocational-technical, academic, comprehensive) Size of the school Location of the school
The Community	School Board Characteristics	Composition Superintendent's leadership style Role of board as advocate or 'rubber stamp'
	Community Characteristics	Political, socio-economic, racial and ethnic composition Age and educational level demographics Attitudes toward learning School budget

		Taxation issues
The State and Nation	State Education Department National Educational System	Legislation Policies Funding Level of local control allowed Textbook selection Teacher certification Academic requirements Formal Components - Federal legislation - Department of Education grants and priorities Informal Components - Mass media - Textbook publishers - Politics
	Cross-cultural Comparisons of Educational Achievement	

The systems analyst depends heavily on the empirical research describing the influence of each factor on learning. While there has been extensive "linear" research (i.e., the effect of a single factor on learning), there is far less research of a more systematic nature. That is, research assessing the contextual relationship of factors embedded in larger or more complex conceptualizations of the system, and definitive research involving the effects of many factors simultaneously is greatly needed. Sizer (in O Neill, 1995) noted, for example, that each component of a school's operation is connected with every other one, and thus, any conceptualization that does not consider the pattern of factors is incomplete and distorting. While some of this systems analysis research has been done, far more must be conducted for us to fully understand the educational system.

EXAMPLES OF EMPIRICAL RESEARCH UTIL-IZING A SYSTEMS APPROACH

Some educators have questioned whether empirical studies can be conducted using a systems approach. These are studies that investigate patterns of factors and their interactions simultaneously rather than isolating only one variable at a time. Such studies, while they frequently are costly to conduct, are possible and do provide information useful in planning specific interventions which will enhance student learning. Coleman (1964, 1982), Burkhead (1967), and Clauset and Gaynor (1982), for example have conducted well-designed systems oriented studies, and these are described in Scileppi (1988). Two studies are presented below which demonstrate very different research approaches using a systems orientation. The first (Summers & Wolfe, 1975) studied the factors influencing student achievement in the schools of a large metropolitan area. The second study (Mayer, Mullins & Moore, 2001) reviewed data collected by the National Center for Education Statistics and assessed the factors affecting achievement throughout the country. Later in this book, the strategies and methods of conducting research are covered. At this point examples of studies are described in order to demonstrate that systems based studies are feasible and useful.

SUMMERS AND WOLFE'S PHILADELPHIA SCHOOLS STUDY

Summers and Wolfe (1975) investigated the pattern of factors associated with student achievement in the Philadelphia public schools. The Federal Reserve Bank of Philadelphia commissioned this study, as education is a great economic concern. The researchers reported that public education at that time consumed 8 percent of the United States gross national product and represented 30 percent of Philadelphia's total governmental expenditures. Thus for education, like any business or organization, determining which resources might result in greater productivity is an important question to investigate.

Summers and Wolfe measured students' growth in achievement based on the results of standardized reading, writing and mathematics tests. Students in elementary and junior and senior high schools in Philadelphia public schools were sampled. The individual level factors investigated included student social class, ethnic/racial background and achievement level. School level factors consisted of class and school size, years of teaching experience, racial mix of students, physical plant factors, and the relative ability levels of fellow students. These researchers analyzed the data relative to various categories of students. Thus, even if a factor did not result in significant differences in achievement for *all* students, the factor might have influenced the learning of *some* students. Indeed, Summers and Wolfe found that many school resources had opposing effects on different groups of students. By studying the specific (rather than global) effects of each school factor, a school system can reallocate its limited resources so they can be targeted to those students who would benefit most from the resource. This will increase the efficiency and productivity of the school and promote student learning without necessarily costing more money.

The major findings of this study were as follows: with respect to class size, low achieving students in elementary school achieved best when class size was smaller than 28 students. Other groups of elementary school students were not affected by this factor until class size reached 34 students. Beyond this level, all groups of students performed less well. In junior high school, academic growth decreased in classes with more than 32 students. This decline was greater for low-income students. In senior high schools, classes smaller than 26 students helped high achievers the most.

In terms of school size, smaller schools resulted in more learning for elementary and senior high school students. African American elementary school children and low achieving senior high school students performed best in small schools. School size did not affect the achievement of junior high school students.

A third variable that affected academic achievement was teacher experience. In elementary schools, high achievers performed best with experienced teachers, but low achievers showed more growth with less experienced teachers. These researchers reasoned that less experienced teachers have "undampened enthusiasm" for the slower learners. Perhaps also the newer teachers have not developed a lowered expectation for the learning ability of these students. At the high school level, all groups of students gained from experienced teachers.

A final set of variables that affected student achievement consisted of school climate factors such as the racial and achievement mix of the student body. With regard to the racial balance within the school, all elementary students performed better academically when the proportion of African American students ranged from 40-60 percent. In junior high school, a student body consisting of up to 50 percent African Americans benefited all students, and African American students performed better in schools where more than 50 percent of the students were Black. No conclusions were possible for senior high school students as the range of data with respect to racial mix was insufficient. The authors reported that the proportion of African American students in Philadelphia high schools ranged from 55 percent to 99 percent. This lack of variability in the range of data is a limitation of studies based on the results of student achievement in only one city. Research based on national samples remedy this concern but the findings of national studies are not necessarily applicable to local school districts.

The variable "achievement mixture" refers to the proportion of high, average and low achievers in each school. Summers and Wolfe found that in elementary school, low and high achievers performed better academically when more high achievers are present. High achievers tended not to be affected by the presence of low achievers. Thus in elementary schools, heterogeneous ability grouping was found to be effective in enhancing learning. A similar pattern was found in junior high school. In senior high school, schools with large numbers of dropouts hurt the high achievers. The researchers recommended that school desegregation be based on achievement level and not only on the racial mix of the school.

Other school level factors that did not affect academic achievement in this study included: physical facility characteristics, such as the age of the school or playground size; school principal characteristics, such as experience or education beyond the master's degree; and teacher characteristics, such as race or education beyond the bachelor's degree. In addition, expenditures for counseling and availability of remedial education did not affect student achievement.

Although it is likely that the results of this study are limited to the achievement of students thirty years ago in this one city, the method used by Summers and Wolfe could be replicated in other communities currently. The recommendations of these researchers led to specific interventions in Philadelphia that did enhance student learning at that time. The value of local and frequent replications of this type of research is that they enable school districts to allocate resources to maximize learning. As these reforms are put in place, the system evolves and the study needs to be repeated every decade or so to reallocate funds to meet new needs.

MONITORING SCHOOL QUALITY USING THE NATIONAL CENTER FOR EDUCATION STATISTICS INDICTORS

Whereas Summers and Wolfe focused on student performance in one metropolitan area, Mayer, Mullins and Moore (2001) conducted a systems analysis utilizing nationwide data available through the National Center for Education Statistics (NCES). Congress in 1991 mandated that NCES empirically monitor the health of the nation's schools. Mayer, Mullins and Moore reviewed 13 indicators collected through the NCES to discover which characteristics are related to student learning. These researchers divided the indicators into three categories: teacher characteristics, classroom factors, and school contextual/organizational variables. The authors evaluated the degree to which each indicator accurately and reliably assessed the quality of the characteristic investigated and their findings reflected this judgment. These researchers found the following patterns:

1. Students learned more from teachers with strong (rather than weak) academic skill backgrounds and from teachers who have more than three years experience in the classroom. Also, students in middle and secondary school performed better in those classes taught by teachers who have degrees in the subject area in which they are teaching;

2. Students who take higher-level academic courses in mathematics and science tend to learn more than those who graduate high school with only lower level courses (for example calculus versus algebra). The authors noted that compared to students who graduated twenty years earlier, today's students are enrolling in more challenging subjects but that this trend does not hold for all ethnic and income groups;

3. Students learned more when computers are used to teach discrete skills. Availability to technology has increased dramatically, and by 1999, 95 percent of all public schools had internet access;

4. Class size affected student achievement and the greatest increase in achievement occurred in classes of 13 to 20 students compared to larger size classes. The class size effect was more pronounced in the primary grades and for disadvantaged and minority students. The authors noted however that class size interacts with teacher qualifications. If a district reduces class size by hiring less qualified teachers, student learning suffers; and

5. School climates that emphasize discipline, though more difficult to assess by current NCES indicators, were associated with enhanced student learning. Severe punishment for drug offences and the presence of programs aimed at reducing school related violence and other criminal behavior are effective policies that create a social atmosphere favorable to academic learning. The authors also reported that learning is enhanced in schools that emphasize high academic expectation, perhaps because such an academic climate influences the student-student and student-teacher interactions.

Mayer, Mullins and Moore (2001) noted that these findings may change over time due to cultural movement, and the improvement of the social indicators utilized by NCES. As additional factors are added, more comprehensive systems analyses can be accomplished. Furthermore, research similar to the above systems analysis is more likely to happen now that there is widespread acceptance of the National Assessment of Educational Progress

(NAEP), a type of report card for education in the United States (Dillow, 2001).

EDUCATIONAL RESEARCH AND CULTURAL ASSUMPTIONS

Before leaving the issue of educational research, it is necessary to realize that any study is embedded in a particular paradigm that has specific goals and intentions in the research design.

There are two major inferences to be drawn from this statement. The first inference is that no researcher is truly objective, and, to at least some degree, scientists are products of their culture and will design research-incorporating assumptions common to the culture (Gergin, 1973). These assumptions are never tested; instead, they often lead to unnoticed design flaws. Since other scientists share the same cultural expectations, these flawed research designs are rarely critically evaluated.

For example, Kamin (1979) reported that in the early part of this century, many Americans were highly prejudiced against non-English speaking immigrants. Many laws were passed placing quotas on the number of individuals entering the United States. Partially to limit immigration, intelligence tests were administered to these immigrants, and they achieved lower IQ scores than the average native-born American. The scientists sharing the same cultural beliefs as the dominant society frequently interpreted the lower IQ scores of such immigrants as being the result of their inferior innate intelligence level rather than the result of language difficulties or culturally biased tests. Often times, such flawed interpretations were not challenged by the other scientists of the day who accepted the same basic assumptions. It is perhaps an intrinsic aspect of human nature not to critically review any research conclusion with which the person agrees. Thus, it is necessary to apply a special effort to critique educational research studies before attempting to apply them in classrooms across the nation.

A second meaning of the statement that each study is embedded in a paradigm with specific goals is that it is necessary to relate to research findings to the desired educational goals. Basically, the term "learning in school" in the research literature refers to a change in cognitive achievement test scores. Thus, more of the studies cited in the education literature implicitly assume that schools should be primarily concerned with cognitive learning. Frequently, educational experts believe that other goals are appropriate. Good and Weinstein (1986) argued that schools should be accountable for developing the emotional, social and moral capabilities of students as well as more cognitive skills. Gardner (1983) has identified many types of intelligence that typically are not stressed in schools and are currently not assessed. Measures of these abilities either do not exist or are not universally accepted, and thus far few researchers evaluate school effectiveness on these alternative student outcome criteria. Even though the bias is present, it is not intrinsic to the empirical method, and researchers should strive to develop accurate and appropriate measures of these goals.

EDUCATIONAL GOALS

The second task of the systems analyst is to understand the goals of the system and to determine who sets these goals and makes critical decisions regarding educational policy and practice. All systems have goals; some are expressed and others are less overt. Yet the elements of all social systems are designed to further these goals.

There are many ways to conceptualize the goals of a social system. One approach is to divide the goals into two general types: system maintenance and task productivity. System maintenance refers to the value placed on perpetuating the institution. If too much emphasis is placed on this goal, less system energy is available for the system to perform its function for the society in which the system is embedded. If system maintenance is given too little emphasis, the institution may destabilize and disappear.

Task productivity, the second type of goal, is the work of a system in achieving its purpose. The task productivity goals of the educational system have been a source of controversy in recent years. Numerous authors have attempted to persuade society to adopt diverse views of what good education should be about. Changing the values and goals upon which a system rests has a great influence on the structure and processes of education. Some social scientists, such as Bateson (1972) and Watzlawick, Weakland and Fisch (1974), believed that altering the goals of a system such as education results in true social change, as the rules of the institution change with each goal change. They distinguish between first order change, which is merely innovation without change, such as the example of altering a teaching method while keeping the remainder of the system intact, and true second order change, which alters the basic fabric and purpose of the system. By changing the goals, all the elements of the system are readjusted and the thermostat governing the operation of the system is reset to monitor different outputs of the institution. For example, if a school chooses to alter its goals to enhance parental participation, teachers will be encouraged to communicate more fully with parents, administrators will seek out parental input and the parents themselves will be surveyed about the degree to which the school is supporting their involvement.

Modifying the goals of the system is not easy, but it is also not impossible. In education, such change requires convincing all the major decision makers within the school system that the change in emphasis is desirable. Also, the change agent must persuade parents, students, and others in the local community that these changes will benefit themselves, as society needs to have graduates with certain qualities. Finally, the interventionist must convince the forces within the national educational system, such as the mass media, testing corporations, textbook publishers, and government legislators and funding sources, of the value of the change.

The process of changing values and goals, whether intentional or not, occurred in the final quarter of the twentieth century. After a period of recognizing a need for more creative, self-disciplined students who were encouraged to participate in designing their own educational curriculum, society began to perceive a need for educators to return to the basic academic skills. Then Secretary of Education, William Bennett (National Commission on Excellence in Education, 1983) emphasized this need in his landmark report, *A Nation at Risk*. The mass media began to preach that the major problem in American education was not a lack of freedom in the classroom but rather that students were falling behind in the basic writing, reading, and arithmetic skills. State governments began to establish norms in these academic areas that the graduates of each school had to meet in order to maintain state funding. Testing firms began to alter the relative proportion of the types of testing instruments away from measures of creativity and toward monitoring the basics. Parents started to demand that teachers assign more homework in the basic areas. Businesses complained that high school graduates needed to be trained extensively in the ability to read work manuals and follow written instructions. At all levels of the system, educators were being pressured to move "back to the basics", and slowly but consistently the system changed, and innovations furthering this movement were encouraged.

THE ROLE OF GOALS IN A SYSTEMS ANALYSIS

An effective system uses its goals as a basis for assessing its performance. This process describes another aspect of systems. That is, a system seeks feedback on the quality of its functioning. Typically, each system can be viewed as having an input, throughput, and output component. The input refers to the raw materials available to the system. In the case of education, the input includes the children before they enter the school, and the types of educational needs the community perceives. The throughput describes the basic processes within the system. In education, the throughput refers largely to the factors within the school itself, including teachers and other human resources, the buildings, facilities, books, and other teaching methods. The output consists of the system's products. In this case the academic qualities of the graduates comprise the output of the educational system. The system assesses its output, and on the basis of this monitoring, the throughput is fine-tuned. Note that Summers and Wolfe's Philadelphia public schools study utilized this input—throughput—output approach.

As stated before, the goals of the system determine the nature of the type of feedback the system searches for, and thus, the goals of the system greatly influence the process of education. For example, if society required that high school graduates are competent in basic academic skills, then schools are going to place great emphasis on standardized achievement tests in these fields. Decisions regarding teaching methods will be based on the degree to which the new method will produce students who score high on these tests. If, on the other hand, society indicates that schools are to produce open minded, non-prejudiced graduated who desire to celebrate cultural differences, other types of attitudinal, behavioral, and cultural information tests will be created to assess these graduates, and schools will modify their teaching methods and curriculum to enhance the probability that their graduates will succeed on these measures. Thus, change will result by analyzing and altering the goals of education and then by bonding specific innovations to these goals.

CONTROVERSY OVER EDUICATIONAL GOALS

The issue of which goals are appropriate for the educational system has been a political controversy for some time. Various commissions and many educational professionals have attempted to formulate and to promulgate their positions on these issues. In 1918, a national commission on education established the "Seven Cardinal Principles" as the goals of education. These goals included health, command of fundamental processes, worthy home membership, vocational training, citizenship, worthy use of leisure time, and ethical characteristics. These goals, which were influenced by Dewey (1916), stressed process, good citizenship, and a commitment to the students' needs and experience. This "progressive" view of educational goals has been at odds with the "back to basics" goal orientation which periodically is restated. A similar commission in 1973, named the National Commission on the Reform of Secondary Education, listed twelve goals which were divided into two categories: content and process goals. The content goals included communication skills, computation skills, critical and objective thinking, occupational competence, a clear perception of nature and the environment, economic understanding, and responsible citizenship. The process goal category included knowledge of self, appreciation of others, the ability to adjust to change, respect for law and authority, clarification of values, and the appreciation of the achievements of humanity. As can be seen, there is a great similarity between the two lists, yet there are some differences. The 1973 list attempts to incorporate the liberal values of that decade in its goals. Thus, values clarification, self-knowledge, acceptance of others, critical thinking skills, and environmental concern are included. These goals have tended to be de-emphasized in the past thirty years with the "back to basics" movement.

Individual authors have also expressed opposing views on the goals of education. Robert Ebel (1974) supported a back to basics approach. He posited that education should emphasize cognitive learning and knowledge, as opposed to affective or feeling-oriented learning. Students, according to Ebel, should become more aware of their social duties and not individual liberties and personal growth. These other learnings, while useful, should be the responsibility of institutions other than schools. To attempt to do all things, schools will dilute their effect and do nothing well.

Others disagreed strongly with Ebel. Harold Bessell (1972) believed that the prime responsibility of schools should be to foster personal development. Schools should develop greater self-awareness in students, more self-confidence and a deeper understanding of personal relationships. James Banks (1972) held that since American students will grow up in a nation of cultural diversity, schools should teach students about ethnic minority cultures, and help all students to understand racial conflict. Sidney Marland (1974) believed that schools should primarily prepare students for the world of work. Career education, or the developing of well functioning, vocationally competent citizens of society, should be the main goal of education. Finally, Thomas Lickona (1991, 2001) considers that public schools should include a focus on character development. The graduates of our schools should be moral individuals who respect one another's rights and uphold societal values.

In recent years, the federal government has become more directly involved in establishing the goals of the nation, and legislators have passed laws, which attempt to state the goals in such a way that the degree to which goals have been reached can be measured. In 1990 the National Educational Goals Panel (NEGP), formed by a bipartisan group, was composed of President G. H. Bush and the governors of the 50 states. Their purpose was to construct goals which the nation's school should try to reach, and then to identify educational indicators to allow the states to monitor their progress in attaining these objectives (Wurtz, 2000). In 1992 the NEGP developed the National Assessment of Educational Progress discussed earlier to monitor gains in student achievement throughout the nation. In 1994 President Clinton signed into law the Education of America Act (Hobbie, 2001), also called the Goals 2000: Educate America Act which established National Educational Goals. The eight goals identified in this 1994 bill were follows. By the year 2000:

1. All children in America will start school ready to learn;
2. The high school graduation rate will increase to at least 90 percent;
3. All students will leave grades 4, 8 and 12 having demonstrated competency in English, mathematics, science, modern languages, civics and government, economics, arts, history and geography;
4. All students will be prepared for responsible citizenship, further learning and productive employment;
5. All teachers will have access to continuing professional education enhancing their ability to teach challenging subject matter to an increasingly diverse student population;
6. All students will be the first in the world in science and mathematics achievement;
7. Every adult American will be literate and have the knowledge and skills needed to compete in a global economy and to practice good citizenship;
8. Every school will be free of drugs, violence, and the unauthorized presence of firearms and alcohol and will offer a disciplined environment conducive to learning; and
9. Every school will promote parental involvement and participation in encouraging the social, emotional and academic growth of children.

Hobbie (2001) noted that the intention of the above legislation was to create higher academic standards and to increase accountability through regular assessment. While the law may have stimulated activities in many states to improve student learning, she questioned whether any of the goals as stated could be reached in the foreseeable future. Hobbie studied the progress made on Goal 1, which required that all children would enter school ready to learn. While the goal seems non-controversial and straightforward, Hobbie found that the concepts involved are actually ambiguous and unable to be measured. The states do not agree on the age at which children should start school. Readiness to learn is not defined adequately in the law. Experts describe five areas necessary for a child to learn academic skills: "health and physical development, emotional well-being and competence, approaches to learning, communicative skills, and cognition and knowledge." Screening preschoolers regarding these characteristics tend to be unreliable and to lack predictive validity as children grow rapidly during this developmental stage and a task not mastered on the day of the testing could be met a short time later. Hobbie believed that the only way this goal could ever be met is for schools to become flexible in allowing for different multiage groups in each instructional area based on learning readiness, interests and needs. The schools must abandon the industrial model with its graded, lock step structure.

While the above paper focused only on the first of the eight goals, other researchers noted parallel concerns with some of the remaining goals and by 2001, the Education Act of 1994: Goals 2000 was replaced with the No Child Left Behind Act (NCLB), signed into law by President G. W. Bush. Congress dissolved the NEGP at the same time. The stated intent of this law was "to close the achievement gap between disadvantaged and minority students and their peers" (U.S. Department of Education, 2002, p.1). The NCLB Act was based on four principles: stronger accountability for results, expanded flexibility and local control, expanded options for parents of children 'trapped' in failing schools and an emphasis on teaching methods that have been proven to work. In addition, the bill sought to increase the funding of reading instruction programs and to support English proficiency programs to enable all limited English proficiency students to learn the language effectively. Perhaps the best known aspect of this legislation is that schools must show measurable adequate yearly progress (AYP) in meeting these student achievement goals. Parents of students in schools that consistently fail to meet these standards will be issued vouchers allowing them to send their children to other schools.

Linn, Baker and Betebenner (2002) noted concerns with the accountability standards of the NCLB Act. In order to maintain the local control principle, the states are given the right to establish their own AYP objectives and to design the tests to assess meeting these objectives. This eliminates the ability to make state-to-state comparisons of the percentage of students who meet proficiency levels of achievement. Those states which choose to set challenging standards may be penalized as a higher percentage of their schools will be identified as failing. Perhaps to balance this variability in standards among the states, the NCLB Act also requires that a sample of students disaggregated by social class and ethnic background be tested in mathematics and reading in grades 4 and 8 using the National Assessment of Educational Progress (NAEP). The law requires that schools demonstrate steady student achievement gains (AYP) for each group of students in each subject area and that the achievement gap between disadvantaged and minority students and their peers be narrowed. According to the NCLB regulations, all students must meet NAEP proficiency level within 12 years. Linn et al. note that this requirement as stated is "extraordinarily ambitious" (p. 8) given that in 2001, on the Grade 8 NAEP mathematics test, only 39 percent of students in Mississippi and 7 percent of students in Louisiana met the required proficiency level. Nationally, in 2000, the percentage of students who scored at or above the proficiency level on the NAEP at Grade 4 was 28 percent in mathematics and 32 percent in reading. Setting goals so high that they are unobtainable no matter how hard teachers try is very demoralizing. Even huge increases in the funding available to education will not prevent a large proportion of schools to be listed as failing. These researchers identify numerous strategies that could be taken to make the NCLB more realistic so that its desirable objectives can be realized.

As can be seen from both the 1994 and 2002 laws, establishing national goals for education has become an important part of the political process. Encouraging high achievement in academic content areas, and demonstrating accountability that these goals are met has taken "center stage."

In addition to the accountability initiatives undertaken by the federal government, another form of curriculum assessment and student progress monitoring is gathering momentum in school districts across the country. Heidi Hayes Jacobs has developed and refined a process of electronic "curriculum mapping" (Perkins-Gough, 2004; Jacobs, 1997). Curriculum mapping is a tool in which educators can swiftly determine what actually is being taught in the classroom. Teachers can find out what content students were taught in prior years, and with this knowledge, they can design relevant instructional plans to build on the students' previous learning. As this is done electronically, curriculum maps can be individualized for each student and appropriate instruction to fill gaps or extend learning can be planned. The curriculum maps provide what was actually taught, and not that which was intended to be taught. Learning can be assessed more accurately as student progress is monitored regarding the content that was actually covered.

As a result of consulting to many school districts on the use of curriculum mapping, Jacobs has a broad perspective on curricular goals and their achievement in classrooms across the country. In a recent interview (Perkins-Gough, 2004), Jacobs noted the following current practices and what tomorrow's curriculum should include. She noted that curriculum mapping enables educators to see what gaps exist in academic content. She found that schools do a relatively good job of covering the 'timeless' content, but tend to omit the more timely content. In many schools current events are not covered. For example, nearly every K-12 grade classroom covers the same events in U.S. history, and in each academic year, time runs out and the events of the past ten years are not adequately discussed. Furthermore, in most social studies curricula, students are not exposed to current world events and global issues. In science, Jacobs believes that students should be provided with more opportunities for conducting independent research, and be taught the ethical implications of scientific activities. Mathematics curricula tend to emphasize operations and techniques and not conceptual understanding. She believes that students should be required to state how they solved a mathematical problem and why they chose a particular strategy. In reviewing language arts, curricular objectives should include media literacy and criticism—not only of the books but of current mass media as well. The fine arts should include not only an appreciation of classic art, music and sculpture but also the opportunity for creative self-expression and original work. Finally throughout the curriculum, the basic skills of reading, writing, speaking and note taking should be taught, as these are essential tools for all the above learning to occur. In a sense, Heidi Hayes Jacobs insights provide an overview of the optimal school curriculum for use throughout the nation.

These are only a few of the positions regarding the goals of education. As society changes, different perspectives will become ascendant. One of the roles of a change agent in education is to analyze the goal structure of schools and then to modify the goals to enable specific interventions to succeed.

GOAL ACCEPTANCE AND SYNERGY

In addition, the change agent might find that within a school system, the administrators and staff do not have a clear or unified perspective regarding educational goals. In such a situation, decisions regarding teaching methods and the need for specific resources are often inconsistent. This reduces the total synergy of the system and student learning is adversely affected. Apparently, this lack of agreement regarding goals is fairly widespread. Goodlad (1984), in an eight year long study of 38 schools in 13 communities, found that state education officials and school administrators were often ambivalent about the goals for the schools under their jurisdiction. The change agent can create meaningful change in such situations by making the staff more aware of the lack of consensus and its effect on students' learning, and then persuading them to develop consensus around a specific educational philosophy.

Synergy can be created not only by ensuring all the staff accepts the same goals but also by encouraging all participants in the system to do so. The school district's compact for learning, described earlier in the chapter might provide a mechanism for encouraging parents and school personnel to decide on common educational goals and share in the strategies to achieve them.

Including all community residents in these compacts enhances synergy. Bronfenbrenner (1979) noted that children live in three microsystems or settings: the family, peer group and school. Murrell (1973) observed that when the members of these three spheres hold consistent values, the child's values are likely to conform to these goals. If parents, friends and teachers frequently discuss how important it is to attend a good college and land a quality job, the youth will also aspire to do so. If the peer group supports engaging in illegal behavior or drug use, the values of the teachers and parents will have less influence on the student. Consider that synergy among the members of the three micro-systems is more likely to occur when teachers, friends and family all some from the same culture. If the school staff and neighborhood friends express conflicting values, the student will be pulled in opposite directions and will become more ambivalent regarding goals. This will reduce academic achievement.

HIDDEN CURRICULUM GOALS

A final consideration concerning goals is one that is not explicitly expressed by the school. In most educational systems there are covert purposes, sometimes called the "hidden curriculum." For example, aside from the more noble goals mentioned above, schools also serve as a means of preventing children and young adolescents from entering the work force thus reducing competition for jobs for adults.

In addition, schools often teach (or perhaps preach) a specific political or religious ideology. One such non-expressed ideology is the belief that children have fewer rights than adults. Philip Jackson (1968) discussed life in classrooms, and he compared the conditions under which students are expected to learn to those in the typical adult work setting. Jackson described, for example, that approximately 25 students are required to sit in specific seats for long periods of time. They can speak only under certain conditions, and they are expected to obey every order of the teacher. If this situation occurred in an office or factory, the workers would surely strike. While today's classrooms offer more student freedom of activity than those of forty years ago, they are still more restrictive than typical settings for adults.

Another hidden curriculum goal of most school systems is the emphasis placed on time. We value those students who learn quickly and frown on those who take longer to accomplish academic tasks. Time periods have become a type of implicit criteria of success in schools. Educators frequently use timed tests to evaluate student progress. Accomplishing a specific task or arriving at the correct solution is less important than the time it took to perform these activities. Across the nation, the minimum number of hours and days comprising a scholastic year is prescribed. In most schools class periods extend for a fixed time period. Poor achievers are known as slow learners or perhaps as mentally retarded. While such "time consciousness" is consistent with the middle class orientation of teachers and with the fast paced lifestyle of the dominant culture, it is often alien to the "event consciousness" of many ethnic minority cultures.

Finally, a purpose of schools not often expressed openly is to provide jobs for teachers and administrators. All these hidden goals affect educational structure and practices, and thus, they also need to be understood in order to fully conceptualize the purposes of the educational system. Just as a social system uses its expressed goals for measuring performance, the institution will often informally monitor these hidden criteria when evaluating its policies and procedures.

VIEWS OF SOCIALIZATION

A final overriding concept about goals is that they (like all components of a social system) are embedded in a larger societal perspective. Each individual and each subculture has a viewpoint on how a child is socialized into a culture.

Zigler and Child (1969) have presented two opposing views as to the child's participation in the socialization process. These two positions define the endpoints of a continuum of possible approaches to the issue. As education is at least partially a socialization attempt, the goals we choose for education will relate, intentionally or not, to the socialization issue. Zigler and Child described the two views as positive and negative. These terms refer to the perceived degree to which the child helps or hinders the socialization process. The negative view is similar to the theories of Calvin and Freud, and reflects the viewpoint of the book, *Lord of the Flies* (Golding, 1978). This view holds that basic human nature is evil, and a person is essentially selfish, being motivated only by biological and antisocial drives. The only innate goal state is hedonism, and involves the reduction of the tension due to these drives. The positive view, on the other hand, is similar to the views of Rousseau, Dewey, and Rogers. In this view, the person's basic nature is good and the child is essentially sympathetic, being motivated by social interest. The person's goal states include the production or creation of something, and the achievement of self-actualization or of one's existential project.

In the negative view, the task of socialization is rather difficult, as the socializing agent must counter the child's innate destructive desire. The child must be curbed; his or her biological drives must be bridled and channeled into the needs and values of society. Drive reduction must be prevented or curtailed in the interests of society, and the socializing agent must impose a strict conformity on the child.

In the positive view, the task of socialization is an easier process, as the child desires to become a productive member of society. The child is perceived as being socially motivated and to be deficient only in the knowledge of the proper behavior allowed in a particular culture. The child is not to be imposed upon but is encouraged to be self-directed, as the child's own unique personality and sense of purpose in life must be allowed to develop unencumbered by others. The child seeks many diverse adult models and chooses the ones which relate most closely to the child's own individual life ethic.

While few educators accept either extreme view, there are a great variety of positions held by members of society who have impact on educational practice. The type of traditional classroom structure described earlier by Philip Jackson seems to take the more negative view, whereas the supporters of the more freestyle open classroom agree more with the positive view of socialization. Perhaps many of the controversies regarding which goals are appropriate for education might be understood in light of this socialization issue.

Throughout this chapter, the systems perspective and its various components have been discussed. Each of the following chapters explores the opportunities for applying this approach to research and contemporary issues in the field of education. Hopefully, implementation of the reforms generated through this framework will significantly enhance the learning of students in our schools.

DISCUSSION QUESTIONS

1. What are the benefits of using a systems approach to reform education? Is it likely that this approach will be used to effect widespread change in the teaching and learning process? If not, what are the impediments?

2. How would a systems theorist plan, design and implement a change in education?

3. Table I outlines factors affecting each level of analysis of a systems model of education. What is the effect of each factor? Which factors can be easily changed? Which cannot? Which would be the best to target to enhance student learning?

4. What are the strengths and weaknesses of the Summers and Wolfe study; the Mayer, Mullins and Moore study? In what paradigm is each study embedded?

5. What are the primary goals of education, in your view? How should the curriculum relate to these goals?

6. With which piecemeal approaches to educational reform are you familiar? Have they impacted student achievement?

7. What is the impact of Federal education laws (Goals 2000, No Child Left Behind Act, etc.)?

Chapter 2:
Action Research and Educational Reform: Partners in a Process

OBJECTIVES

After studying this chapter, the reader will be able to describe, analyze and apply the tenets of:

1. Action research from the perspective of the teacher(s), school and district;

2. The steps of action research;
   - Defining the problem;
   - Reviewing the literature;
   - Developing-determining assessment tools;
   - Analyzing the data;
   - Developing the actions/strategies to implement change; and

3. The benefits of action research.

OVERVIEW

The concept of educational reform and change is certainly not a new one. Beginning in the 1960s, large-scale curriculum efforts at the federal level began. Educational reform—or the apparent cure for all the problems in education—became synonymous with governmental dictates, policy mandates and multiple regulations at the local state levels. A *Nation at Risk* (National Commission on Excellence in Education, 1983) became controversial and a part of the most discussions at local community staff meetings as well as department of education sessions. The rhetoric concerning our 'poor schools, low test scores and ill-trained teachers' simply sparked more mandates through the creation of even greater numbers of new policies. Unfortunately, the reforms in the 1980s and 1990s were rarely organized around changing classroom practice, supporting curriculum and teaching models through staff development and accepting the importance of relationships in local communities (Levin & Wiens, 2003). It is no wonder that many who have been a part of the field of education for years had become somewhat cynical and frustrated at the great number of mandates with minimal support for implementation efforts. Why bother? There would simply be another change with a different direction dictated.

The cynicism was understandable, since the mandates never included strategies that were focused on processes that would make a difference for kids. The fact is that social systems—education being one of them—are complex. The mandates, both before and current (including the new nemesis No Child Left Behind) ignore the fact that education is simply a microcosm of society. The systems and the changes within that society are very complex in their own right. Unfortunately, complex systems give rise to simple behavior (Gleick, 1987), hence the large number and variety of reform movements or "quick fixes" and ultimately, the failure of those movements. An attempt is made to address superficial issues for short periods of time; the results of the reforms are therefore short-lived or lead to no reform at all (Eisner, 2003). Teaching driven by short-term results such as test scores only, oftentimes the measurement used within major reform movements, are not the kind of teaching that teachers want to do (Hargreaves and Fink, 2003).

Educational reform of the past as well as the present has greatly contradicted what we currently know about organizational change and leadership. There should be a creative tension in any change process: a juxtaposition of vision—or what we want—and a clear picture of current reality—or where we are relative to what we want (Senge, 1990). It is the "clear picture of current reality" that is oftentimes ignored when educational reform or change is recommended and subsequently instituted. Such change is not black and white, right or wrong. It has many shades of gray simply because it is a process, a lifelong discipline—there can never be mastery. Those in leadership positions should know that this ambiguity is simply a part of the process of change as well as a part of the process of building capacity and success on behalf of those that matter in the front lines: children, students, families and local communities. Organizational as well as personal missions are never nor should they ever be achieved. If the mindset is to "fix" a problem and think that it will be non-existent as a result, then naivete and ignorance are clearly the principles that are in effect. Change is a journey—not a blueprint (Fullan, 2000) and those who believe in this concept have the benefit of learning and implementing processes that are of benefit to local schools, kids and communities. Action research is a true partner in this journey of change.

WHAT IS ACTION RESEARCH—AND WHAT IS IT NOT?

Action research as a process is not a new one. Kurt Lewin, a social psychologist, developed its principles.

> Action Research is a three-step spiral process of (1) planning which involves reconnaissance; (2) taking actions; and (3) fact-finding about the results of the action. (Lewin, 1947)

Although there are many other definitions, this one does provide the full array of the distinct components of action research. First, there needs to be investigation or exploration regarding an issue (or "reconnaissance"). That examination should occur in multiple ways, including the investigation of information from others that have some degree of expertise in the chosen topic as well as inquiry within one's own setting. Secondly, as the name implies, one cannot have 'action research' without action or purposeful change that is directly linked to real data. Last but certainly not least, on-going assessment of the results of the action to determine its effectiveness and the possible need to 'tweak' the action is a necessary component.

There are many different kinds of research, all with their distinct advantages and disadvantages. Any research process needs to be matched with its overall purpose or goal. If there is no match, the process used will simply be a waste of time. When this happens in schools, we are not able to simply discard the product, since that product is our children and their education and not 'widgets' from an assembly line. If schools are truly serious about creating better accountability systems, we must understand the realities of schools and include, encourage and support teachers in the overall effort of improvement. With this in mind, a focus on the action research process as a reliable component in educational reform makes sense. The following criteria provide a set of baseline prerequisites within this process:

1. Direct and active involvement of teachers and front-line educators;
2. Use of the local environment (classroom, school, district) as the field or the 'research laboratory';
3. Focus on teaching and learning for all (teachers, students, administrators);
4. Use of expertise of others as only one part of the process;
5. Use of sound assessment tools; and
6. Action planning and implementation, based on a direct connection to local assessments and evaluation.

With these criteria in mind, we are better able to define what Action Research is as well as what action research is not.

Within a District

Action Research is: a School Board asking its administration and teachers to examine the current national and state initiatives and determine which initiatives 'match' their district's own needs and priorities. Based on those assessments, recommendations would then be made for an action plan and its implementation, with on-going professional development and support.

Action Research is not: a school board stating that the research completed as a part of a state or national initiative indicates that a valid indicator of student learning is that student's score on a national test. That same board then mandates that the administration and teaching staff will raise all test scores an average of 10 percentage points in one year.

Within a School Building

Action Research is: a building principal working with teachers to determine the degree to which "basic skills" are being taught in classrooms. The teachers study together and examine their classroom practices and assessment data. An analysis of the data occurs and together teachers and the principal as a collaborative team plan and begin implementation efforts. That data and subsequent implementation efforts are then shared with community members, asking for their involvement.

Action Research is *not*: a building principal mandating the use of a basal text by all classroom teachers that is based on current research because there is a "back to basics" community group in the neighborhood putting pressure on the principal.

For Individual Teachers or Teacher Teams

Action Research is: a university professor working with individuals, teams of teachers or the entire school community over a period of time to teach and facilitate the process of action research specific to a need (or needs) that exist in a particular classroom, grade level or school.

Action Research is not: having a university professor come into a school to gather raw data about a "hot" topic in education and then writing about it.

The action research process is one that can be applied to all educational environments. Applicable research laboratories can be one individual classroom, teams of teachers with their respective classrooms and/or professional teams; an entire school or a full school district. Knowing the process, however, is key.

Defining a Problem

"Problems are our friends" when seriously implementing organizational change strategies (Fullan, 2000). In this same regard, the first step in the action research process is identifying a particular problem or challenge that an individual teacher, team or school might have. It is important for the problem to be clear and focused. Who is involved with this problem? When or where is the problem occurring? What kind of a problem is it? What does the problem "look like" and how is it manifested? Clarity of the problem itself is important since the questions to be answered (that is, the action research questions) must have a direct connection to the problem definition itself.

When defining the problem, the individual or team also needs to be sure that the problem is something that they are able to control, both during the initial phases of the action research process as well as when the evaluation is complete and action planning is brainstormed and subsequently implemented. What is, therefore, necessary is a checkpoint that is known as "the three I's" (Zerillo, 1999):

1. Is the problem truly something that needs Improvement?
2. Is the problem Interesting enough for an individual, team or a district committee to focus their time? and
3. Is the problem within the individual's or the team's Influence?

Although all of these "I's" have importance, the last is perhaps the most significant. The ability for a team or committee to have influence over the results and recommendations of their action research is of primary importance. It is therefore invaluable for an individual, team or committee to work closely with those who are asking for this work to be done, whether that is an immediate supervisor, principal, superintendent or school board. Researching a problem with a group, both through the expertise of others as well as through local school assessments, takes a great deal of time, especially if it is to be done well. Communicating with and involving all is of absolute necessity if action research is to be seen as a valuable process. If action research begins without this communication and collaboration—and action planning based on the results is outside of a team's influence—the action research process will be looked upon as broken and unreliable. Support of the process as well as the outcomes of the process is of prime importance. Therefore, understanding and modifying the area of influence to insure control over the planning cannot be overestimated.

Conceptually, the action research process can well be defined and described. Examples of the variety of educational circumstances in which it can be used are of equal importance. The following are therefore examples of real problems in real schools, each with their accompanying action research questions:

Problem: We feel that we as well as our students in our fourth grade classrooms are having difficulties effectively communicating with parents about learning growth and process. Our students seem to lack skills in being self-reflective and independent thinkers about their own learning progress.

Questions: What skills do our students have or lack in communicating and/or being self-reflective about their learning progress? What activities or skills will foster better student self-reflection and communication about their learning growth? How are those activities used—or not used—within our own classrooms?

In the above case, this team of two teachers in a small rural school in northeast Vermont then began to increase their own knowledge about instructional methods and classroom environments that support and foster students' involvement in learning (which is the next phase of the action research process).

The following is another example of a problem that an entire school in rural New England faced, with related questions:

Problem: We believe that teachers at our school feel entrapped in positions due to economic constraints and position seniority. As a result, instructional and systematic change as well as collegial collaboration is minimized.

Questions: What factors influence our teachers' abilities to 'take risks' and change—or not change—their present status? What factors influence our teachers feeling encouraged in their profession?

It is important to note that these problem statements and questions are personalized to a specific group of students in a specific set of classrooms as well as a specific group of teachers in a specific school. Matching the research to the environment or culture is crucial to positive and long-lasting change. This is literally at the heart of action research.

Use of the Expertise of Others—Literature Reviews

The purpose of reviewing literature and the expertise from others is to expand one's thinking—not to direct the plan of action and tell one what to do. Using the knowledge of those who are well known in a particular field is a prompt to ask questions as it relates to the chosen problem. For example, if early elementary teachers are looking at the literature about developmentally appropriate classrooms, the following questions might be asked:

1. Do I have a range of materials and resources in my classroom that allows children a variety of ways to meet a particular goal?
2. Do I provide a variety of choices of activities for the children in my classroom so that I can meet their different learner styles?
3. Do I see children working individually, in small groups as well as in large groups?
4. How do I as a teacher elicit language understanding and use of appropriate language with my children? and
5. How am I as a teacher focusing on the cognitive, fine motor, gross motor and social-emotional areas of the children in my classroom?

The list can certainly go on. As educational researchers learn more about their chosen action research problem, they are forced to think about their own practice and instruction as it relates to the problem.

Using the previous example cited about a Vermont school, it may be helpful to see how those same teacher researchers used literature to assist them as they began to think about their original identified problem:

> We feel as well as our students in our fourth grade classrooms are having difficulties effectively communicating with parents about learning growth and process. Our students seem to lack skills in being self-reflective about their own progress.

This team of teachers worked hard between themselves and in collaboration with a university professor to increase their understanding about motivation and processes involved in developing better self-reflection. They put aside time to discuss and share information as they read articles from a variety of periodicals and chapters from books, attended workshops and interviewed experts. As they did so, they continually kept their original questions available and close by to them:

> What skills do our students have or lack in communicating and/or being self-reflective about their learning progress? What activities or skills will foster better student self-reflection and communication about their learning growth? How are those activities used—or not used— within our own classrooms?

As they gained more knowledge, they began by focusing on several instructional strategies that were of great interest to them, including but not limited to: learning logs, concept mapping, questioning techniques, negotiated learning and self-assessment rubrics and checklists. They studied these instructional strategies and concepts and how they were used in classrooms. Most importantly, after their innumerable discussion sessions, each member of the team had the same understanding of each concept as well as the range of other strategies that fostered independent and reflective learners. Through this process, they were developing a greater in-depth understanding of knowledge they had not known before.

Relating New Knowledge to the Development of Assessment Tools

The highest priority for dedicated educators is to improve the learning for their students. In order for this to happen, the focus must constantly be on teaching and learning, both for educators as well as students. Putting student learning first therefore takes precedence to front-line teachers: everyone else's learning is then directed toward supporting that goal (Hargreaves & Fink, 2003).

As this previously mentioned team of two Vermont teachers read the expertise of others, they progressively gained an in-depth understanding of new concepts and instructional methodologies that had previously been unknown. They then developed a series of assessment tools that would assist them in answering their original action research questions based on the new learning they has ac-quired through their reading and information gathering. The first was a Tool Documentation Form, a teacher self-assessment that identified the tools that fostered independent and reflective learners (learning logs, concept mapping, questioning techniques, negoti-ated learning and self-assessment checklists). They then developed a listing to document the evidence of the use of the tool and exam-ples of their use in each of their respective classrooms.

Through their reading, they also made note of other innumer-able curriculum and instructional strategies that helped to foster independent and reflective learning. As a result, they then created a Checklist of Curriculum Strategies Form that they used during their observations of each other. Were these strategies observed in their teammates' classrooms—and if so, how? Observing each other through the use of this assessment was an excellent source of professional support as well as a way to develop a sense of trust, confidence and honest communication for all, true foundations for effective school cultures (Saphier and King, 1985). Lastly, they developed a Teacher Report Card Form, citing those same cur-riculum strategies but putting them in question forms for their stu-dents. For example, in the Checklist of Curriculum Strategies Form for each teacher's self-assessment, one strategy noted for observa-tion was "I provide instructional choices." On the Teacher Report

Card, the same concept was modified by stating: "My teacher gives me choices about how I will learn something." Results were then be cross-referenced and compared.

Why Multiple Assessments? A Note about Reliability and Validity

Unfortunately, many of us either as individuals or as members of educational systems, are not reporting the right kind of data to be seen as accountable in the public eye. We might also be somewhat remiss in assessing our actions accurately, reliably and with validity. Within the action research process, it is therefore very important to insure that reliability and validity are maximized.

The concept of reliability means that the same results will be achieved with similar measurements, no matter what the circumstances. Simplifying the concept, a person's height and weight are said to be reliable if the same number of feet, inches and pounds are designated, no matter who measures that person. The results are consistent. Validity, on the other hand, is a measure of legitimacy. Is the tool being used measuring what it is supposed to be measuring? The assessment must be achieving its purpose in order to be considered valid. Using the analogy of height and weight, the reliable results of consistently having a height of 5'7" and a weight of 130 pounds is not necessarily valid if one's goal or purpose is to determine the exact dress size this person might need. Assessment by measuring the hips, waist and chest may be more appropriate or valid.

We argue about these same concepts of reliability and validity in our educational debates regarding testing and its relationship to student learning outcomes. Is one test only a reliable source of determining what a child knows? The fact that it is only one form of measurement makes it of questionable reliability, since there is no proof of consistency through multiple assessments or of students having that knowledge in different circumstances over time. The validity is also questionable, since one provides the answer to only one question: how well that child can perform on that one test. If the purpose of assessment is to provide a full picture of what students' strengths and weaknesses may be in order to provide the best possible instruction, then having multiple assessments to insure reliability of the information is necessary. Knowing how to incorporate these techniques within one's own action research as well as being able to assess others' research in this same regard assists any professional educator in being objective and knowledgeable, and therefore more responsible in the public eye in local communities.

We must have the same accountability standards when using the process of action research. Therefore, we must access or create assessment instruments that are measuring what we want them to measure (validity) as well as use multiple assessments to insure we are getting a full picture of our topic area (reliability). Triangulating the assessment data (Sagor, 1992) means that we are using a minimum of three forms of assessments to insure cross-comparisons. Following through on the example of the previous team's work with the students who were not involved in their learning, they then triangulated their assessments, as shown in Chart 2.1.

CHART 2.1: EXAMPLE OF ASSESSMENT TRIANGULATION

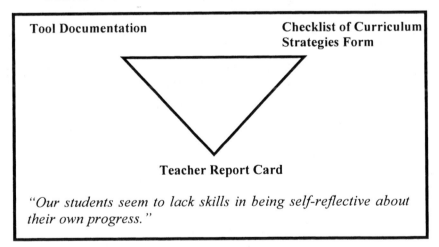

Tool Documentation   **Checklist of Curriculum Strategies Form**

Teacher Report Card

"Our students seem to lack skills in being self-reflective about their own progress."

Having a strong understanding of assessment processes is therefore essential as one uses the action research process. The insurance that accountability of the process is in place by maximizing both the reliability as well as the validity of the instruments being used cannot be underestimated. By doing so, there is greater insurance that the action research will have a greater and longer-lasting impact.

TAKING ACTION

The 'action' in action research occurs multiple times throughout the process. When a team has increased their knowledge base about their identified problem and determined the assessments that they will conduct, this is one of those times to literally "take action." The assessments or data collectors need to be implemented and the data or assessment information acquired needs to be analyzed. As the analysis of the assessments occurs, there may be discoveries that were neither anticipated nor expected. This is the beauty of action research—although the trend(s) may not have been predicted, these results are authentic and truly representative of viable and long-term solutions to the problem. The data then creates the accountability.

This same team of teacher researchers in rural Vermont referred to earlier compared the data on their Teacher Report Card, Tool Documentation Form and Checklist of Curriculum Strategies together. They looked at their teaching strategies as individuals as well as the results from the individual cultures in each of their respective classes. Through one team member's analysis, she noted that she was clearly not giving her students a voice in what they learned and how they learned it. She was providing the answers, doing a great deal of direct teaching and making the decisions regarding the students' final evaluations. The students felt they had high expectations for themselves yet were not involved in setting their own learning goals and subsequently assessing their progress toward those goals. She therefore decided to focus upon the process of Negotiated Learning with her students during that period of time. After six months, she re-assessed her instruction and strategies, the students' perceptions of their learning as well as her role in that process by implementing once again all of the original tools developed. Through another analysis, she found the most significant change to be the students' view on the decision-making power that they had achieved in their own learning. They had even begun the process of student-led parent conferences. Goal setting, reflection and self-assessment were now a rule in their classroom rather than an exception.

Action researchers need to understand that the up-front organization and preparation in planning, reading and developing valid and reliable assessment tools assists in creating less questionable results in the end, something that is true of any research model. Action researchers are able to use both qualitative as well as quantitative research techniques, dependent on the actual problem or topic that is chosen. Statistics are generally more commonly used in action research models that involve larger numbers of cases. In all instances, however, the results of the data or assessments must be quantifiable and objectified in some way.

After analyzing the data, the need to develop the strategy or the action or set of actions to implement change is necessary. The data must be presented objectively and honestly, especially if the results were unanticipated; in this way, that authenticity then convinces others to become more involved in the change process. As ideas for change are brainstormed, there is frequently the need to read and investigate more possible solutions from others that have had similar experiences, including more review of applicable reading and tapping upon the expertise of others. As this is done, alternatives for action and changes are generated.

The use of Chart 2.2 may facilitate the creative brainstorming process and discussion.

CHART 2.2: STRATEGY BRAINSTORMING

Possible Actions:

a. _____

b. _____

c. _____

Description of Action A:

_____

_____

_____

Advantages of Action A	Disadvantages of Action A

This exercise continues to involve others' experiences, expertise and involvement in a change process in which they have investment in the results. Learning communities are then naturally developed by choice, since the goals for improvement become more collective. Action research can "transform . . . a multitude of unrelated individuals frequently opposed in their outlook and their interests, into cooperative teams, not on the basis of sweetness but on the basis of readiness to face difficulties realistically, to apply honest fact-finding and to work together to overcome them" (Lewin, 1945). Instead of a mandate from up above (federal government, state department of education regulation or local school board) the focus is on the principle of teaching and learning, respecting all with the same principle and building leadership capacity for a school community.

VARIATIONS TO THE THEME

The beauty of action research is that its flexibility allows a number of variations to occur within the process while still maintaining the same original criteria. For example, a district-wide curriculum committee may be considering the possible adoption of a reading series in their kindergarten through grade 5 building. A group of teachers, each representative of all five grade levels, volunteer to pilot the series while continuing to meet as a collaborative group regularly. They may invite an early literacy expert in to some of their meetings to be a part of discussion regarding "best practice" in reading instruction as they determine the on-going assessments that they will use as they progress. In this situation, the processes in action research still exist but in a different sequence. Perhaps the original problem was that there were inconsistencies in this school's reading program: different teachers focused on different components of reading in each of their respective classrooms. This action research study would be to determine which parts of this particular program might assist in achieving greater consistency in teaching reading across all grades in this elementary school. The educators involved are still increasing their knowledge about best practice in reading; they are still instituting multiple assessments as they progress to determine what components appear to be positive and which do not. As they are reviewing their data, they are making recommendations for modifications, additions and deletions to the program itself in order to serve the needs of their children at their particular school. The process simply continues using the same criteria as identified earlier:

1. There is direct and active involvement of teachers and front-line educators;
2. The local environment, in this case kindergarten through grade 5 classrooms, is being used as the field in which the study is occurring or the 'research laboratory';
3. The focus is on teaching reading and on-going learning for these educators, their students and others, as the pilot expands and implementation for all classrooms occurs;

4. The use of a reading expert is only one part of this process to pilot this reading program; and
5. Sound assessment tools in the area of reading are utilized throughout the pilot study to determine the program's strengths as well as its weaknesses.

Although the sequence of the processes within action research may vary, the original criteria as well as the use of the action research processes themselves do not.

A PROCESS FOR POSITIVE CHANGE

As educators, we do not have the luxury of time to create new reforms, experiment with change, search for new fads or obtain simple answers from "experts from afar." Schools must be learning organizations, with the capacity for individuals as well as teams to think and work independently and collaboratively, in order for true educational reform to occur (Hargreaves & Fullan, 1991). The processes involved in action research automatically create this type of environment in schools, that is, a collaborative engagement in learning, corrective analysis and change. School Boards and those in leadership positions must involve and support skilled teachers to create better accountability systems through their own action research and then pay attention to those results and options for change. Those who do not know the process of action research must allow others to assist them to learn. Educators and systems will continue to spin wheels and react to opinion instead of factual data until this occurs. If it does not, not only do we as a profession lose but our kids do as well.

DISCUSSION QUESTIONS

1. How is education a microcosm of society?

2. Why haven't past educational reforms led to positive changes in education?

3. What are the components of action research? What are its benefits?

4. What is the usefulness of assessment triangulation?

5. How does action research result in a collaborative engagement in learning, corrective action and change?

6. Do you agree that the No Child Left Behind Act is a nemesis? What are its strengths? What are its weaknesses?

7. Why is ambiguity a part of change? How is action research a partner of change?

8. Using the steps of action research, how would you match the state standards in reading for grades K-3 to the reading standards in a school district?

Chapter 3:
Assessment vs. Evaluation:
A Systems View

OBJECTIVES

After studying this chapter, the reader will be able to define, analyze and apply the tenets of:

1. Reductionism vs. constructivism;

2. Empiricism vs. phenomenology;

3. Sustainable vs. non-sustainable systems;

4. Systems-related principles;

5. Formative assessment vs. summative evaluation;

6. Realms of assessment;
   - Multi-faceted;
   - Multi-dimensional;
   - Inclusive;

7. Types of assessments;
   - Products;
   - Performances;
   - Tasks;
   - Tools;
   - Anecdotal observations;

8. Evaluation;
   - Technical quality;
   - Quantitative methodology;

- High stakes consequences;

9. Systems-related concepts;
   - Construction;
   - Complexity;
   - Feedback loops;
   - Self (re)organization;
   - Sustainability; and

10. Promising practices.

INTRODUCTION

"Given our new understanding of the learning process and the relationship between assessment and both teaching and learning, there is little doubt that reformed assessment practices are long overdue." (Marzano, Pickering & McTighe, 1993)

Assessment and evaluation are terms that are often used interchangeably. However, when the origins of the two are uncovered, and each is then practiced accordingly, it quickly becomes evident that assessment and evaluation and their respective purposes are very different from one another, and that the way in which evaluation is often conducted in schools is, from a systems theory point of view, arguably flawed. To explore this more fully, this chapter first addresses an overview of systems theory, then an overview of classroom assessment and evaluation, and finishes with an exploration of classroom assessment and evaluation as they relate to systems theory.

AN OVERVIEW OF SYSTEMS THEORY

"The whole is within the part." (Goethe {Bortoft, 1996})

There are many dimensions to systems theory, some of which were presented in Chapter 1. This chapter explores additional dimensions of systems theory fundamentally relevant to educational assessment and evaluation.

Beginning in the 1500s, the works of scholars such as Bacon, Newton, Galileo, and Descartes provided the dominant lens through which people viewed their world, a view that would eventually support a scientific revolution that would thrive well into the 1900s (Worster, 1994). The paradigm that evolved from their work is what is now referred to as reductionism or mechanistic science—looking at and thinking about the world in a way that focuses on the parts and assumes that by understanding and mastering the parts, we can logically understand and master the whole. In other words, it is a view that suggests that the whole is simply the sum of its parts. During this time period, positivist thinking (the belief that what "counts" is only that which is directly observable, quantifiable, and irrefutable) and empirical research (quantified experimental research) both attained high standing (Pinar, Reynolds, Slattery, & Taubman, 1996).

Since the mid-1800s, however, there has been much written in opposition to reductionism and positivism. Scholars in a multitude of different fields*, including education, have been converging toward a more constructivist way of looking at the world, a view known as systems thinking. Collectively, what is reflected in their works is a belief and understanding that the whole is not simply the sum of its parts, but instead is actually greater than the sum of its parts (Golley, 1993). Their work reveals systems as being complex, with ever-changing, ever-evolving interdependent parts, able to self-renew and sustain themselves as a result of that very complexity (Capra, 1996).

Along with this theory have emerged systems-related principles such as dynamic equilibrium, feedback loops and self-accountability, self- (re) organization, self-renewal, self-amplification, nested systems, and sustainability (all of which are addressed later in this chapter within the context of education). Systems theorists have come to recognize that there are certain notions, principles, and processes common to all systems, social and natural. One such notion is that linear systems, simple input-output systems in which the resources being used are not being replenished internally, are ultimately non-sustainable, whereas systems that are sustainable are those comprised of self-renewing cycles fueled by continual feedback loops (i.e., internal accountability checks) (Wiener, 1961).

Key principles at work within sustainable systems include diversity, complexity, interdependence and partnership, adaptation and co-evolution, feedback, cycles, disturbance, resiliency, and sustainability (Capra, 1996).

* Some of these scholars include Ernst Haeckel, Eugene Odum, and Arne Naess (ecology), Howard Odum and Friedrich A. Hayek (economics), George Perkins Marsh and Aldo Leopold (conservation), Peter Berg and Edward O. Wilson (biology), Norbert Weiner and Ludwig von Bertalanffy (physics), Wendell Berry and Wes Jackson (agriculture), Alfred North Whitehead and John Dewey (education), and Thoreau, Emerson, Wordsworth, and Dickinson (humanities). Contemporaries include Peter Senge and Paul Hawken (economics), Frijof Capra and James Lovelock (physics), and David Orr, Chet Bowers, Robert DuFour, Mike Schmoker, and Douglas Reeves (education).

An example of a general process involving these principles is shown in Chart 3.1 below, illustrating the overall cyclical nature of a sustainable system, with sustainability (re)amplifying diversity.

CHART 3.1: SELF-RENEWING CYCLE

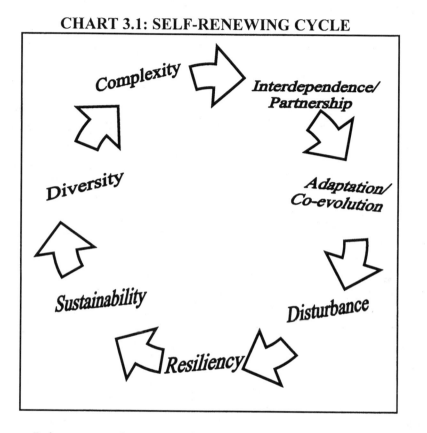

It is commonly accepted that the greater the diversity within a system, the greater the system's ability to sustain itself (Wilson, 1992). A simple example of this can be seen in nature in cases of diverse habitats versus monocultures (e.g., pine plantations, corn fields, turf farms). Nature tends toward greater and greater diversity. This explains why so much energy and effort are needed to maintain monocultures such as those above. Lawns, for example, without constant mowing and use of fertilizers and pesticides, gradually evolve into more diverse meadows. Coincidentally, when a disturbance (e.g., disease) occurs in a monoculture and decimates its primary species, due to a lack of other species to "fall back on," the system as a whole collapses. Both situations demonstrate how systems that lack diversity are less sustainable than those that are diverse.

With greater diversity comes an increase in complexity and connectivity within the system. In other words, the more "parts" there are, the more potential interactions there are between those various parts. With an increase in potential interactions comes a greater likelihood that multiple interdependencies and partnerships (symbioses) will evolve. As these interdependent relationships and partnerships develop, the parts involved are continually adapting and co-evolving with one another. This co-evolution is triggered by feedback loops, circular processes in which the output of one part within a system serves as input for the next, culminating with the last link feeding back into the first link in the cycle. These internal cycles are the system's self-renewing process. Without them, systems cannot sustain themselves (Capra, 1996).

Throughout this process, as with any system, periodic disturbances (perturbations) occur which disrupt the system's internal network, further stimulating adaptation, co-evolution, and diversification among the system's parts, which in turn stimulates reorganization and transformation of the system's cycles. The greater the system's diversity of parts and complexity of internal cycles, the more resilient the system is to disturbance (Capra, 1996).

Resilience (flexibility), therefore, is a measure of a system's sustainability. Since resilience ultimately depends on the degree of diversity within the system, diversity, too, is an indicator of a system's sustainability. Over time, the longer a system is able to sustain itself, the longer it is able to continue renewing its internal diversity, thus perpetuating both the cycle and the system itself (Capra, 1996). These principles and the ways in which they apply to teaching and learning, particularly within the realm of classroom assessment and evaluation, are revisited later in this chapter.

Just as positivist thinking and empirical research rose in prominence alongside reductionism, with the emergence of systems theory has come renewed support for the concept of phenomenology (the view that reality is fluid and context-dependent, "truth" is relative to perspective, and that the results of empirical research neither tells the whole story nor holds all the answers) and ethnographic research (research that honors non-empirical data and factors in qualitative data). As the last section in this chapter reveals, the resurrection of these two constructs have contributed greatly toward improving our understanding of learning and promoting systems-related praxis in teaching (Pinar, Reynolds, Slattery, & Taubman, 1996).

AN OVERVIEW OF CLASSROOM ASSESSMENT AND EVALUATION

Assessment

"Without question, effective, efficient, productive instruction is impossible without sound assessment."(Stiggins, 1997)

The root word of assessment is *assidere*, which means to sit beside and assist (Herman, Aschbacher, & Winters, 1992). The image of a teacher sitting beside her students as they engage in learning is a powerful one. When one pictures classroom assessment in action, one is equally moved because the two images are essentially identical; teachers working alongside their students, monitoring their progress and providing ongoing feedback as their students construct meaning, uncover mysteries, and perpetuate their innate curiosity. This image is strikingly different from the image conjured when one pictures students undergoing evaluation (Skelding, 2002).

Practically speaking, assessment is the ongoing gathering and documentation of information for the sole purpose of monitoring and measuring student learning. From a systems standpoint, two words in this definition that are especially important, and key in distinguishing assessment from evaluation, are the words "ongoing" and "measuring."

Learning is ongoing. It is an ever-evolving, constructive process (Brooks & Brooks, 1993). There is no finality in learning. Therefore, it is vitally important that the process used to monitor a child's learning measures the child's continual construction of knowledge as opposed to her supposed "attainment" of knowledge.

In addition, since learning is constantly evolving, the process used needs to evolve alongside that learning. True assessment, as defined above, is such a process (Skelding, 2002).

There are two general levels of assessment, formative and summative. Formative assessment is assessment that is ongoing. It is the process of continually measuring learning as it emerges and develops ("forms"), while at the same time providing feedback that shapes ("forms") both the learner's and instructor's subsequent learning and teaching. Summative assessment, on the other hand, is what occurs when the teacher and student periodically measure the student's progress based on the collection of evidence that the student and teacher have accumulated at that point in time (Wiggins, 1998). In both cases, evidence is being gathered solely for the purpose of monitoring and measuring (following the growth of) the child's learning.

There are three different realms of assessment that are important to consider any time students are assessed. Those realms include multi-faceted assessment, multi-dimensional assessment, and inclusive assessment (Stiggins, 1997).

Multi-faceted assessment is assessment that utilizes multiple means to gather evidence on student progress. Children in our classrooms possess a diversity of learning styles and employ a variety of different intelligences as they construct knowledge. If children learn differently, it follows that children best express what they know in different ways as well. This is just one reason why it so important to use a variety of different means when instructing and assessing students.

A second realm of assessment important to address is multi-dimensional assessment. This is assessment that checks in on the student on many different levels. Holistic and brain-based learning theory explain that learning is the result of a complex interplay between the cognitive, social, emotional, physical, and moral/spiritual domains. A simple example . . . educators have long known that if a child is not emotionally available for learning, any attempt to measure cognition during that time generally will not yield a true picture of what the child knows and understands. If students are assessed in only one domain (which, in schools, is typically the cognitive domain), those results are an incomplete picture of the child's true knowledge and understanding. A second example of multi-dimensional assessment, although domain-specific, is what occurs when one purposefully assesses students at every level in Bloom's Taxonomy, a scale of higher order thinking skills delineated by Benjamin Bloom that begins with simple recall of facts and ascends to skills such as being able to apply knowledge and synthesize divergent bits of information into new knowledge (Bloom, Englehart, Furst, Hill, & Krathwohl, 1956).

The third realm of assessment is inclusive assessment. Inclusive assessment is assessment that incorporates as many different perspectives from as many different stakeholders as possible. This is an especially critical realm given what phenomenology and ethnographic research say regarding the importance of factoring in perspective. Inclusive assessment at the classroom level can include the teacher, student, peers, and parents. Including community members in the process provides a particularly valuable "outside" reliability check.

Inherent in each of these three realms is a process known as triangulation—having at least three different points of measure as a way to ensure reliability of assessment and evaluation results. Building all three realms into the overall assessment process ensures "triangulated triangulation." The concept of triangulation is especially critical when it comes to a systems approach to assessment and evaluation, an approach that acknowledges the phenomenological nature of learning and, hence, the importance of perspective (Schmoker, 2004).

There are five general types of assessments that can be used to help ensure that all three realms of assessment, particularly multi-faceted assessment, are addressed (Skelding, 2000). These are outlined in Chart 3.2.

Again, in all cases, these assessments are conducted solely for the purpose of monitoring and measuring (following the growth of) a student's progress, while at the same time providing continual opportunities for further learning in the knowledge, skills and criteria in which the student is being assessed. In other words, true assessment is more than just assessment of learning. It is also "assessment for learning." It is an approach that allows for assessment while, at the same time, promoting further learning (Black & Wiliam, 1998).

CHART 3.2: TYPES OF ASSESSMENTS

Products	Concrete, student-generated creations that directly reflect the knowledge, skills, and criteria the student has attained, with documentation of that learning being the products themselves, artifacts of the products, or photographs of the products (e.g., written pieces, models, dioramas, drawings, projects, diagrams)
Performances	Authentic demonstrations of the actual skills and criteria in which students are being assessed, documented through anecdotal records, photographs, or audio/video tapes (e.g., simulations,, role playing, problem solving, research, investigations)
Tasks	Teacher created check-in exercises, which students are asked to complete as a way of providing information regarding their learning (e.g., surveys, journal entries, questionnaires, worksheets, un-graded quizzes and tests, and graphic organizers such as Venn diagrams and concept webs)
Tools	Formal rubrics and checklists with spelled-out criteria against which a student's performance is compared/measured
Anecdotal	Relatively informal (mental notes, jotted notes) or more formal
Observations	(field notes, anecdotal logs) records of observed student progress/performance

In summary, assessment is a deliberate process by which all parties involved continually observe and reflect on how well students are progressing toward desired goals, specific outcomes, and attaining local, state, and national standards. Purposeful assessment is informative (i.e., provides meaningful feedback), influences lesson planning, directs subsequent instruction, prepares students to perform well when it comes time for evaluation, and ultimately assists students in attaining academic standards. Simply put, assessment is a qualitative process of guiding students as they progress.

The most common criticisms of assessment, as defined above, are the subjectivity of qualitative data, the subjectivity of those doing the assessing, and the technical quality (i.e., validity, reliability, fairness) of formative assessments (CCSSO, 2003). These concerns are explored in the next section where common criticisms of evaluation are discussed.

Evaluation

"You don't fatten the cattle by weighing them." (Anonymous)

"American students are the most tested but least examined students in the world." (Resnick & Resnick, 1985)

"Too often, educational tests, grades, and report cards are treated by teachers as autopsies when they should be viewed as physicals." (Reeves, 2000)

The term "evaluation" comes from the root words *valu* (to judge, determine a worth, set a value, or appraise) and *valere*, which means strength. Evaluation is a process used to attempt to capture and define something's worth by quantitatively categorizing it and then assigning it a fixed value. For example, when students are evaluated, an attempt is made to define their degree of competency, then categorizing their competency with a letter grade, number grade, or placement within a percentile group. Regardless of the type of grade used, the intent behind giving a grade is to represent the "strength" of what was evaluated. And so, every time a teacher gives a grade, the teacher is conducting an evaluation (Skelding, 2000).

Traditional means of evaluating students include graded assignments, teacher-made tests and quizzes, commercially produced tests, and nationally used norm-referenced tests such as the Stanford Achievement Tests (SAT), the Iowa Tests of Basic Skills (ITBS), and the Comprehensive Tests of Basic Skills (CTBS). More contemporary innovations include scored portfolios and New Standards Reference Exams (NSRE). Report cards are evaluations meant to reflect a student's overall competency in the classroom.

Although educators often list the above items as components of their comprehensive "assessment" plans, the way in which they are typically used qualifies them more as evaluations than assessments. Often, rather than using the results of these items to direct subsequent instruction, guide changes in practice, and provide immediate, constructive feedback to teachers and students informing them on what to do next in order to progress, these items are instead simply scored, students are given a grade, and instruction marches onward while the recorded grade remains fixed.

Unlike assessment, evaluation is strictly a summative process. It is a periodic attempt to provide a quantitative summation of competency at a given point in time. From a systems standpoint, three words in this definition that are especially noteworthy are the words "periodic," "summation," and "competency."

As was discussed earlier, learning is in a constant state of progression, knowledge is in a continual state of flux, and competency undergoes constant transformation. In addition, knowledge, itself, is complex. A body of knowledge is a dynamic, nested system comprised of a multitude of interacting data, each, in turn, comprised of their own complex network of interacting data. When one attempts to summate a complex body of knowledge in its present state, it is critical that one understands that the validity, and therefore usefulness, of these summations is extremely limited. An evaluation is an inherently limited probe that yields a fixed snapshot of what a student is able to recall and how she happens to be synthesizing that particular knowledge at that precise moment in time. In addition, what the student is able to express during that evaluation and to what degree she is able to express it is framed by the construct of the evaluation itself.

Given this understanding of evaluation, concern over the reliability of tests and test data, and the ways in which those data are used has prompted renewed interest in the proper role of evaluation in education and increased scrutiny over the ways in which evaluations are being conducted (Kohn, 2000). Common criticism of evaluation includes concerns over technical quality (i.e., validity, reliability, fairness), quantitative methodology (e.g., averaging and cut-off scores), and the "high stakes" ways in which evaluation results are used. In addition to these is a more large-scale criticism, that being the mismatch between educational evaluation and what systems theory tells us about teaching and learning. That criticism is discussed in the last section in this chapter.

Technical quality issues such as validity, reliability, and fairness are extremely difficult to perfect within the realm of education because teaching and learning are complex, ever changing, and hard to reduce into isolated components. Empirical constructs are hard to fit into phenomenological contexts such as classrooms.

Validity is a measure of how well an evaluation actually measures what it claims to measure. Put another way, the more valid the results, the more confident one can be with any decisions one makes based on those results. A simple example of an evaluation that would not be valid would be to try to evaluate a student's writing ability based on her answers on a true-false test on grammar. One cannot confidently judge whether or not a student is a good writer based on the results of a grammar test. To make as valid an evaluation as possible in this case, the student would need to be engaged in the actual act of writing (CCSSO, 2003).

Reliability is a measure of how dependable an evaluation tool is across time and space. In theory, a standard ruler is a simple example of a reliable tool. No matter when, and in no matter what context, anything that is three inches long will consistently measure three inches long on a standard ruler (CCSSO, 2003).

Fairness is essentially a measure of equity and non-bias. An evaluation that is fair is one that is devoid of all factors that might put a student at a disadvantage or compromise his chances of success during that evaluation (e.g., cultural differences, language variables, developmental appropriateness, etc.) (CCSSO, 2003).

As seen in the discussion on the dynamic nature of teaching and learning, the complexity of this continuous, co-evolving partnership makes it extremely challenging to devise valid, reliable, and fair evaluations. Validity, reliability, and uniform fairness are applicable and important in controlled and predictable settings such as in a laboratory, but are very difficult to apply toward complex systems such as teaching and learning, which is anything but controlled, predictable, and reducible (Johnston, 1989).

In addition to technical quality issues, common grading strategies such as averaging a student's scores/grades and the use of cut-off scores are coming under question as well (Marzano, 2000). In the case of averaging, for example, when a student's scores/grades are averaged, the result is actually a misrepresentation of how much true learning has occurred. The only way averaging works is if all variables remain fixed from the first score to the last. However, with teaching and learning and child development, fixed variables are virtually impossible because they, their interplay, and their interaction with external influences are never static or predictable.

Cut-off scores are the lines drawn that separate one level of proficiency from another. For example, a traditional cut-off score grading scale commonly used by teachers is 90-100 percent = A, 80-89 percent = B, and so on. Although this approach generally allows for ease and convenience in determining and reporting grades, it can easily be argued that it is of poor technical quality for several reasons. First, the drawing of these lines and designation of grades therein was and is an arbitrary and therefore subjective process. Second, this approach neither accounts for the variability in the number of criteria on which the evaluation is being based nor the degree of difficulty of each item being scored. For example, a two out of three on an essay test equates to the same grade (D) as 66 out of 100 on a multiple-choice test. Although the grades are comparable, the performances are not. Since the number of criteria in the first evaluation is only three, the final quantification of that performance does not reflect its qualitative value. Not only is achieving two out of three commendable in most real-world contexts, in this case it was two out of three tasks that required higher order thinking skills. In addition, as Doran (2003) argued, a third fallacy with cut-off score categories is that they are gross measures that fail to recognize growth students are making within the cut-off score category.

A fourth concern regarding cut-off scores is the fact that use of cut-off scores automatically means use of norms (commonly agreed upon acceptable levels of performance). Norm-based grading, as constructivist (systems) theory has helped expose, is an inherently discriminatory process. This will be discussed later in the chapter.

And finally, the role that evaluation plays in retention and promotion decisions, expanding or limiting educational and professional opportunities, and shaping a student's identity and self-worth, are just a few of the high stakes consequences that critics decry, especially in light of all that was described above. In fact, standardized tests are not the only high stakes evaluations conducted in education. Grading is just as "high stakes," if not more. The short and long-term influences that grades have on individuals, and the ripple effect those influences have on society, are wide ranging, as outlined in Chart 3.3.

In summary, evaluation is the quantitative process of grading (determining the worth of, placing a value on) a student's competency. This is very different from assessment, which is the qualitative process of guiding student learning.

CHART 3.3: EXAMPLES OF THE HIGH STAKES OF GRADING

GRADES	GRADING
<ul><li>Grades positively motivate some students.</li><li>Grades reflect achievement and *imply* how much learning has taken place.</li><li>Grades can be a source of stress and anxiety, which, at a minimum, leaves children less than fully available for learning.</li><li>Grades provide a *premature* appraisal of what a child has learned/will learn/is capable of learning.</li><li>Grades imply that there are acceptable (normal) and unacceptable (below normal) stages of progress and levels of learning, and that there is a level that's best.</li><li>Grades impact a child's self-esteem.</li><li>Grades contribute to a shaping a child's identity.</li><li>Grades categorize and stigmatize.</li><li>Grades promote overt and covert tracking.</li><li>Grades promote divisiveness in schools, families, and communities.</li><li>Grades influence a child's future/future direction.</li><li>Grades regulate a child's degree of opportunity.</li><li>Grades contribute toward creating and sustaining a class system (a "haves-haves not" society).</li></ul>	<ul><li>Grading typically categorizes students based on their ability to meet someone else's expectations rather than their intrinsic ability to learn.</li><li>Grading typically imposes a rigid, one-size-fits-all categorization process that does not accommodate all learning styles equally.</li><li>Grading can promote an externally rather than internally driven approach to learning.</li><li>Grading serves as a negative rather than positive motivator for some students.</li><li>Grading can inhibit/prohibit risk-taking and alternative thinking.</li><li>Grading can inhibit/prohibit the natural process of constructive learning.</li></ul>

A SYSTEMS VIEW OF CLASSROOM ASSESSMENTS VS. EVALUATION

"The universe is so successful, I simply want to learn its principles and apply them." (Fuller, 1963)

"Indeed, most educational measurement specialists are still working from century-old understandings and behaviorist perspectives." (Delandshere, 2002)

Assessment and evaluation are two means of accountability, a process critical to the health and longevity of any system. However, these two processes are distinctly different as are their respective place and purpose, particularly in education. The purpose in this final section is to elaborate on the ecologies of educational assessment and evaluation touched on earlier in this chapter.

This section begins with an exploration of the systemic nature of teaching and learning. It starts with the notion of *construction*, a concept that lies at the heart of both systems and learning theory. Additional systems concepts are introduced as they relate to teaching and learning; concepts such as complexity and nested systems; disturbance and resilience (flexibility); (co)evolution and diversification; feedback loops and self-(re) organization; and self-renewal, cycles, and sustainability. The section concludes with a systems-based proposition regarding classroom assessment and evaluation, followed by a brief introduction to some promising systems-based assessment practices emerging in education.

THE SYSTEMIC NATURE OF TEACHING AND LEARNING

"What does education often do? It makes a straight-cut ditch of a free-meandering brook." (Thoreau in Bickman, 1999)

The term "construction" is perhaps the one word that best grounds this discussion of systems theory as it pertains to teaching and learning and assessment. "Construction" implies process. Indeed, its paraphrased definition from *The American Heritage Dictionary* is "the act or process of building or forming something by assembling or combining parts." To take this emphasis on process one-step further, even in cases of the finest construction the "final" product is never final. Continual effort is needed to sustain the construct. Whether through ongoing maintenance, replacements, improvements, and/or additions, over time the construct changes. And so, what actually exists is a work in progress—an evolving construct, a series of emerging constructs.

From a phenomenological standpoint, think of how often we witness the way in which constructs, although they had a place and purpose at the time they were built, inevitably become "outdated" and no longer "make sense" within the continually changing context that surrounds them. These days, the rise and fall of baseball stadiums serves as an excellent case in point. An example from education that nicely illustrates this is found when one looks at questions such as "Name all the republics of Europe and give the capital of each" and "Give four substitutes for caret 'u'," both of which were facts deemed essential for eighth graders living in Saline County, Kansas in 1895 to know (Sadker & Zittleman, 2004).

Learning occurs in this same way. Learners are continually constructing, deconstructing, and reconstructing knowledge as they assimilate and accommodate new information and apply that knowledge within ever-changing contexts. A body of knowledge is a construct that is in a perpetual state of construction (Caine & Caine, 1994). The way in which one understands something today is very different from the way he/she understood it in earlier and varying contexts. Learning is constructive, meaning is contextual, and knowledge is transformational, both in its evolution as well as its impact (Brooks & Brooks, 1993; Pinar, Reynolds, Slattery, & Taubman, 1996).

The same can be said of teaching and learning. The partnership between teaching and learning is ever evolving. As instructors teach and as students learn, a co-evolutionary process unfolds. A reflective teacher learns from his students as they respond to his teaching. Their questions and replies interact with his existing schema/mental model, serving as feedback loops that either renew his body of knowledge or cause disturbance ("cognitive dissonance") that triggers reorganization of that body of knowledge (Caine & Caine, 1994). As mentioned earlier, these two processes—self-renewal and self-(re)organization—are two processes critical to sustaining any system. And while this is occurring for the teacher, in turn, the same is occurring for students as they process information coming from their teachers.

Teaching and learning is a reciprocal process; teachers become students and students become teachers while both are continually learning. Again, at no time during the process is knowledge static. It is continually being organized and reorganized. The longer this co-evolution of knowledge is allowed to progress, the more connections the learner makes. The more connections that are made, the more diversified the knowledge becomes. Greater diversification of knowledge leads to further connections, thus perpetuating a cycle of sustained learning. This continual connecting, reconnecting, and diversification of knowledge that describes how learning takes place also describes the complex, dynamic interplay among the parts of any flexible, self-amplifying, self-renewing, self-sustaining system.

Teaching and learning is just one of the many systems nested within education, all impacting and being impacted by one another, thus co-evolving with one another. Those interdependent systems range from an individual student's brain to the brain-body network to the various systems that comprise education at the classroom, district, state and national level. The systems dynamic described above for teaching and learning applies to all of these systems, one of which is classroom assessment.

THE ECOLOGY OF ASSESSMENT AND EVALUATION: A PROPOSITION

". . . a collection of (evaluations) does not equal a system any more than a pile of bricks equals a house." (Council of Chief State School Officers, 2003)

True assessment, as defined earlier in this chapter, is an inherent process in the ecology of systems. Anytime systems dynamics such as accountability, self-regulation, feedback loops, and resilience (flexibility) are discussed; in essence what is being talked about is formative assessment. Assessment is an intrinsic, ongoing, cyclical process that involves feedback loops and results in continual self-renewal, self-(re)organization, and self-amplification, both of itself and the various systems with which it is connected. It is an inherent, self-regulatory process that promotes continual internal accountability of the systems in which it naturally operates. Assessment is ongoing gathering of information (feedback); information used to monitor progress and stimulate change necessary to ensure the continuation of that progress.

Since true assessment is an inherent part of systems, and teaching and learning is a system, it follows that true assessment naturally occurs in teaching and learning. In fact, assessment is intrinsic to all levels/systems within education. What currently prevails throughout education, however, is a reliance on evaluation rather than assessment. This is understandable given the perceived convenience of quantitative data and the way in which western culture has historically valued empirical data.

Yet, when one comes to understand learning from a systems perspective, one recognizes that not only does learning coexist in partnership with teaching, it also coexists in partnership with assessment. Learning is the ongoing construction of knowledge. It is an emergent, evolving process for which there is no end. True assessment, as seen from its definition, naturally co-evolves along with that learning. And so what exists is a complex system of interdependent parts that interact in a way that creates internal, self-renewing and self-reorganizing cycles. Assessment directs instruction, which in turn directs learning, which in turn directs assessment, which in turn directs instruction, and so on. Thus, formative assessment is an internal mechanism for promoting improved teaching and sustained learning. It is an internal form of accountability as opposed to an externally imposed form of accountability. Evaluations are typically externally imposed forms of accountability.

Given what is known about the nature of assessment and the organic role it plays in sustaining systems, it makes sense that for teaching and learning to continually improve, educational "assessment" plans ought simply to be a simulation of this natural process.

As was discussed earlier in the chapter, formative assessment simulates this process; evaluation does not. Assessment, like teaching and learning, is a co-evolutionary process fueled by feedback loops. Assessment fuels progress, and in turn progress fuels further assessment. For example, typically a teacher begins the process by engaging her students in a pre-assessment. The results of this pre-assessment not only inform the students as to their current knowledge and ability to express that knowledge, but also inform the teacher as to how to appropriately proceed. In other words, the results of the pre-assessment guide her planning and direct her subsequent instruction. This back-and-forth process continually repeats itself as instruction creates rich assessment opportunities, which in turn creates even richer instruction, and so on. In the process, both teacher and student enter into an upward spiral of mutual learning. At no point is the process static. Learning is continuous and knowledge is in a constant state of construction. As we can see, the role of assessment is natural and simple. It fuels continual learning while at the same time monitors and measures that learning (i.e., assessment of learning as well as assessment for learning).

Evaluation, on the other hand, does not fit naturally into the process of teaching and learning. Although evaluation appears to have found a niche in education, when one looks at the ecological definition of niche (an "organism's" role within its "environment;" the interdependent relationship between an "organism" and the "environment;" an "organism's" contribution to the complexity of the "environment" it inhabits [quotations added]) one can argue that this actually is not the case. Although evaluation is currently a part of the system, the static way in which it is typically used does not contribute to sustaining teaching and learning (Black & Wiliam, 1998). In fact, as noted in Chart 3, one could argue that evaluation largely inhibits sustainable teaching and learning. As opposed to being a constructive process, evaluation is more apt to be deconstructive (Reeves, 2004), directly and indirectly as well as literally and figuratively.

In addition to its deconstructive nature, inherent in evaluation is the notion of finality and rigidity. However, as systems theory has helped reveal, there is no finality in learning, and teaching and learning is a fluid, not rigid, system. Knowledge is continually being constructed, deconstructed, and reconstructed by the learner.

Learning is an evolving, transformational process. Therefore, any attempt to categorize and then place a finite worth on a student's cognition at any point in the learning process, which is what is done every time the student's work is evaluated, is artificial given the temporal nature of knowledge and the constructive nature of learning.

Delving further, constructivist theory also helps expose the discriminatory nature of grading. Children, from before birth on, evolve differently due to a multitude of diverse factors. These variables span from physiological to socio-economic to cultural to psychological/ emotional. The complexity of the interplay between all of these factors varies for each individual child as well. And, perhaps most important to recognize, young children do not have control over any of these variables. Children do not choose to be born "learning disabled," nor do they choose where and in what culture they are born. Likewise, they do not choose to be born into poverty. All of these variables influence a child's access to and interaction with experience. Experience is what ultimately dictates the construction and complexity of a child's schema, thus influencing the child's potential for making connections and constructing further knowledge. Consequently, children are not equally able to learn in the same ways or at the same rate, and the knowledge constructs they possess and are continually building upon are, and always will be, *naturally* diverse. Grading, however, is antithetical to these notions.

Grading automatically involves the use of cut-off scores. Cut-off scores, in turn, establish a norm. How close a child comes to attaining that norm within an arbitrarily determined time frame (e.g., the length of a unit of study, a marking period, etc.) determines what grade the child receives. A 'C' used to be considered the norm. It can be argued that today an 'A' has become what is considered acceptable. In the case of standards-based grading, where the attempt to grade students commonly entails giving them a 1 (not yet meeting the standard), 2 (almost meeting the standard), 3 (meets the standard), or 4 (beyond the standard), the 3 is the norm. Those who are best able to meet the norm are those whose life experience most relates to and has best prepared them for the particular curriculum being imposed on them at that time, and whose learning styles best match the opportunities being presented by their teacher. Everyone else is set apart. Hence, grading students at regular intervals based on attainment of norms is inherently discriminatory.

Sadly, not only is the act of grading a naturally discriminatory process, but grades, themselves, discriminate. Those who meet the norm receive good grades and those who do not meet the norm receive lesser grades. Students with good grades get to select opportunity. Students with lesser grades get selective opportunity.

And finally, systems theory helps reveals two ironic flaws with norm-based grading. Grading based on attainment of norms discounts the diversity of life experience students possess and devalues any construction of knowledge outside of the norm. In other words, use of norms dismisses diversity at both the emergent and evolutionary level. As well, it can be argued that use of norms channels us toward further *reduction*, not construction. Benchmark pieces (examples of performance deemed worthy and which students are encouraged to simulate) serve as an excellent example to illustrate this point. Rewarding students for replicating benchmark pieces promotes homogeneity and constrains divergent thinking. Given that both diversity and construction are critical to the sustainability of any system, this irony is striking, indeed. It is assumed that norms serve as high expectations, and teaching toward those norms leads to learning and construction of knowledge. A question worth asking is whether or not the use of norms promotes *true* learning and unbounded construction of knowledge.

Systems theory exposes the artificial, discriminatory, and nonconstructive nature of norm-based grading and evaluation. Anguish over the hold that grading has on education and the regulatory power it wields over students is both understandable and justifiable.

PROMISING PRACTICES IN ASSESSMENT

"Student-centered accountability is more constructive than traditional accountability because it focuses on improvement of teaching and learning rather than merely ren-

dering an evaluation and the publication of a report."
(Reeves, 2004)

Systems theory is helping to bring about a major shift in how
education is viewed. Teaching and learning is no longer being
thought of as simply a linear system involving teacher input and
student output. Instead, a new view, a complex systems view of
education is beginning to emerge. Three leading systems thinkers
in the forefront of this educational reform effort are Peter Senge,
Michael Fullan, and Donald Schon. All three have been cited numerous times throughout this book. Two others worth noting are
Robert DuFour and Mike Schmoker. DuFour's (2004) work focuses on helping teachers learn how to function as professional
learning communities and helping schools become sustainable
learning organizations actively engaged in continual change and
improvement. Schmoker (1999) focuses on the importance of assessment literacy and the need for schools to be feedback oriented,
systematically capitalizing on both short- and long-term assessment results as a means for sustaining continual change and improvement.

Education practices beginning to take hold as systems principles become part of classroom praxis include holistic accountability (Reeves, 2004), action research (Sagor, 2000), lesson study
(Lewis, Perry, & Hurd, 2004), Collaborative Assessment of Student Learning (CASL) (Langer, Colton, & Goff, 2004), and induction (Wong, 2003). Holistic accountability, as defined by
Reeves, is a student-centered assessment system that focuses on
the "story behind the numbers" (p. 6). It is an assessment system
that begins in the classroom with the individual student. Rather
than simply relying on test scores, this approach triangulates both
quantitative and qualitative data gathered from every system nested
within a student's educational experience. In addition, it encourages a shift towards focusing on students' individual progress,
rather than their attainment of norms.

Action research is an ongoing, feedback driven approach to
sustaining improved teaching and learning. Teachers act as classroom researchers, collaborating with their students (informants)
and colleagues as they continually assess and reassess the effectiveness of their own practice. For a more in-depth discussion on

action research, see Chapter 2, "Action Research and Educational Reform: Partners in a Process.

Lesson study, CASL, and induction are similar in that all three rely on collaboration, multiple perspectives, and triangulation. They involve a systems approach to assessment that ensures that, through use of multiple lenses, teaching and learning is viewed in its entirety rather than as isolated pieces of a process. Lesson study involves teams of teachers collaboratively assessing the effectiveness of a lesson(s) through ongoing data collection and collective analysis. CASL uses the same process for assessing individual student performance. Induction is the practice of including new teachers in the collaborative sessions just mentioned as opposed to simply assigning them a mentor or having them learn in isolation.

In all five cases, the complexity of education as a system is not only acknowledged, but taken advantage of in a way that results in continual change and improvement, thus amplifying that complexity and, in turn, perpetuating improved teaching and learning.

A FINAL REFLECTION

Despite these promising practices and all that systems theory has revealed about learners and the learning process, education in this country is still conducted largely through a reductionist and behaviorist approach. Curriculum is fragmented into subjects (parts) and knowledge and skills are evaluated in isolation from one another (disconnected) using rigid, non-constructivist forms of accountability such as grades. Methodology is primarily linear, with teachers serving as sources and students serving as sinks. And it is the acquisition of static knowledge rather than evolving understanding and alternative thinking for which students are primarily rewarded.

When one stops and reflects on the origins of education one realizes that education today has drifted far from its root. And perhaps nowhere is this more evident than in the relationship that has developed between education and evaluation. The word education comes from the root word *educe*, which means to draw out. Before the dawn of formal education, people learned through ways that stretched them to make connections that drew out and amplified their existing knowledge. Experiential learning, tribal and communal upbringing, storytelling, fables and parables, and Socratic discourse are just a few of those methods. When one considers the meaning of education (to draw out) along with the roots of assessment (to sit beside and assist) and evaluation (to judge, place a value) the natural partnership that exists between education and assessment becomes even more evident. Sitting beside and assisting students, helping them draw out their knowledge and understanding is what teaching and learning. . . and assessment . . . is all about.

How is it, then, that in education evaluation has supplanted assessment? In asking this question, an analogy from nature comes to mind, which is perhaps worth considering. It is commonly accepted that humans are having an overall negative impact on the environment (Hawken, 1993). The environment is simply unable to compensate for the rapid rate at which human impact is altering the environment's natural balance. As a result, this disruption in the dynamic balance of natural ecosystems is allowing for some species to become what are known as invasive species. An invasive species is a species which is able, because no natural checks and balances have had time to develop, to rapidly take over a habitat at the expense of those species that were already there naturally coexisting. When this happens, extreme swings of disequilibrium occur, diversity declines, a non-sustainable monoculture ensues, and gradually what was once a viable, complex system collapses (Tokeshi, 1999).

Cycles of reform in education are nothing new. Reform, although it typically carries with it a negative connotation, is an inherently constructive process governed by feedback. As systems theory reveals, for any system to be sustainable it is essential that it undergo continuous evolution and self-renewal (reform).

What are not inherently constructive, however, are the extreme swings in educational reform and the increasing frequency with which those swings occur. With healthy system reform, orderly internal chaos exists. Dynamic equilibrium is sustained which, in turn, promotes constructive transformation and reformation. Assessment is an intrinsic part of that process. The way in which an invasive species transforms a habitat is an excellent example of quite the opposite of what was just described. What occur in this case are disorder, deconstructive transformation, and deformation.

Is evaluation an "invasive species" inhabiting education? Is the climate of destabilization that is so prevalent in education today a sign or symptom of the "invasiveness" of evaluation? If so, ecologists would advise that reining in the spread of evaluation and reintroducing assessment would help establish a more natural ecology in the field of education.

DISCUSSION QUESTIONS

1. Why are linear systems non-sustainable?

2. How do the key principles of a sustainable system interact?

3. What perturbations exist within the educational system and to what degree have they been overcome?

4. What symbioses exist within the educational system and to what degree have they been successful?

5. Distinguish between assessment and evaluation. Are they compatible? How are the place and purpose of evaluation and assessment different?

6. Describe multi-faceted, multi-dimensional and inclusive assessment and support their usefulness.

7. How do the traditional means of evaluating students compare to the five types of assessments?

8. Why are validity, reliability, fairness, cut-off scores, averaging and high-stakes consequences at issue when discussing evaluation of student performance?

9. If evaluation does not fit naturally into the process of teaching and learning, why do we make decisions about a student's future (college entrance, college placement, employment, etc.) based on test results?

10. Compare and contrast formative assessment and summative evaluation. What are the features of each and which is more beneficial?

11. Which of the five promising assessment practices do you think has the most promise for making schools sustainable learning organizations?

12. Is grading harmful to students? Does it have any value?

Chapter 4:
Cultural Diversity

OBJECTIVES

After studying this chapter, the reader will be able to define, analyze and apply the tenets of:

1. Cultural diversity;

2. Dimensions of multi-cultural education;

3. Inter-disciplinary activities;

4. Multi-cultural education legislation;

5. Lessons for being an informed citizen;

6. Use of technology to teach the principles of multiculturalism and diversity;

7. Use of literature to teach the principles of multiculturalism and diversity; and

8. Twelve essential principles for teaching and learning in a multi-cultural society.

OVERVIEW

We live in rapidly changing times. With each new advancement, in technology, medicine, and the sciences our world becomes smaller and more interconnected. Intercontinental communications happen each minute of the day. Businesses cross time zones, language barriers, and cultural mores to conduct trade. The demographics in our own society are changing and so are the populations in our schools. There are approximately 53 million students in our K-12 schools; 35 percent of these students are from racial or ethnic minority groups (Futrell, Gomez, & Bedden, 2003). School districts, classrooms, and communities are engulfed in the changing demographics across the nation. Schools and communities need to address the effects of these rapid and sustainable changes. As we promote democratic principles in our classrooms and society, our culture within the classrooms needs to prepare students to live and work in the global community.

Schools at every level, from kindergarten through college, must address the issue of diversity. The goal of education is to produce lifelong learners who will take their places in our democratic society. The institutions that promote such high ideals need to channel these lofty and important goals into everyday practice. Schools must mirror the changing population and provide quality education to all of its students.

Much of the education world struggles with how and when to make the classroom environments mirror the actions and philosophies needed to sustain a strong sociopolitical climate for all individuals. Part of this dilemma stems from the lack of global understanding regarding diversity and multicultural education.

Researchers and educators in the field of diversity have supplied us with several varying definitions of multicultural education and diversity that can assist us in gaining understanding of what cultural diversity and multicultural education are and are not.

DEFINITIONS

Marshall (2002) defined cultural diversity as:

> the distinctions in the lived experiences and the related per-
> ceptions of and reactions to those experiences that serve to
> differentiate collective populations from one another. These dis-
> tinctions are affected directly by the complex interactions of ra-
> cial/ethnic classification, social status (as determined by group
> economic resources and political power and influence), historical
> and contemporary circumstances, and worldview . . . multicul-
> tural education as a vision of schooling based on the democratic
> ideals of justice and equality (7).

Ronald Takaki, a pioneer in the field of ethnic studies, defines
multicultural education as a serious scholarship that includes all
American peoples and challenges the traditional master narrative
of American history . . . the intellectual purpose of multiculturalism is a more accurate understanding of who we are as Americans
(Montgomery Halford, 1999).

Gibson (1976) discusses the meaning of multicultural diversity
in this way:

> We may now define multicultural education as the process
> whereby a person develops competencies in multiple systems of
> standards for perceiving, evaluating, believing, and doing.

Bigelow (1999) suggests, that at its core, multicultural teaching
is an ethical, even political enterprise. It recognizes our responsibility to fellow human beings and to the earth it has heart and soul
. . . multiculturalism is a search to discover perspectives that have
been silenced in traditional scholastic narratives.

Although these definitions all vary in prose, their commonalities reflect the relationships between humans and humanity, which
are essential for understanding and survival in the global community.

MYTHS AND MISCONCEPTIONS OF MULTI-CULTURAL EDUCATION

Many people, whether critics or proponents of multicultural education, do not fully understand its meaning and purpose. Grant (1994, p.5) identified the following as the most often proclaimed myths:

1. It is both divisive and so conceptually weak that it does little to eliminate structural inequalities;
2. It is unnecessary because the United States is a melting pot;
3. Multiculturalism—and by extension multicultural education—and political correctness are the same thing;
4. Multicultural education rejects the notion of a common culture;
5. Multicultural education is a "minority" thing; and
6. Multicultural education will impede learning the basic skills.

This chapter provides numerous examples of appropriate teaching and learning opportunities that dispel these myths.

EVOLUTION OF MULTICULTURAL EDUCA-TION

While the emphasis on multicultural education began in the United States in the late 1960s and 1970s its historical foundation began in the late nineteenth century. According to Marshall and Banks (1993), there has been a four phase evolutionary process in the development of multicultural education. The first phase was intended to provide educators the corrected versions of the then current traditional curricula. This phase focused on the production of books, journals, and curricular materials. African American scholars were the primary authors of these materials. Their influence can be seen in the topics and focus of much of the writings. These materials were used primarily in the segregated schools and such resources were ignored by the white educational systems.

The second phase is characterized by the need to bring about "structural and systemic changes to the total school that were designed to increase educational equality" (Banks, 1995, p. 20). The third phase materialized when other marginalized groups wanted their voices and history and culture to be integrated into the curricula.

Currently some components of the education system exist in the fourth phase of evolution, which is characterized by the "development of theory, research, and practices that interrelate variables connected to race, class, and gender" (Banks, 1995, p.20). This phase is where the most beneficial learning experiences can take place. The examples given in this chapter underscore how many classrooms and communities have made this phase a reality.

To understand the changing perspectives on diversity and the role of multicultural education, we only need to look at the impacts of historical events and movements.

The current terminology regarding diversity reflects the era in which we live. The philosophies that drive the diversity issues, though, are basic and sustained throughout history. While significant and devastating events, such as world wars and the tragedies of September 11, 2001, pivotal Supreme Court decisions (i.e., Brown vs. Board of Education in 1954), or the tearing down of the Berlin Wall can swiftly change the political climate regarding the prominence of diversity as an issue, it has yet to disappear or fade away. Instead the forces behind the fundamental issues of human rights in a democratic society ebb and flow with the sociopolitical climate.

A HISTORICAL PERSPECTIVE OF MULTICULTURAL EDUCATION AND DIVERSITY

While the phrase "multicultural education" first emerged in the late 1960s, the impetus for its existence, which focuses on human rights and liberation, can be traced back for centuries. Such underpinnings include the Magna Carta of 1215, The British Bill of Rights (1689), and various revolutions, rights movements, religious leaders and philosophers (Payne & Welsh, 2000).

At the onset of the 20th century, educational theorist John Dewey promoted the need for respect of all of the cultures and backgrounds that make up the student population of the time (Glazer, 1995; Payne & Welsh, 2000). The America that was emerging was a union of varying cultures and religions. The schools needed to promote the merging of the backgrounds. Soon cultural pluralism became an avenue to explore in schools as a way to identify cultural diversity within its population. This concept regarding diversity and education remained prominent for some time. Just as it is today, approaches to diversity and multicultural teachings were controversial. Moore (1996) examines this controversy through history and into modern times. Moore suggested that the following statement is as significant today, nearly a century later. "What people often mean by getting rid of conflict is getting rid of diversity, and that is of the utmost importance that these should not be considered the same" (Follett, circa 1920s).

Moore (1996) asserted that the either/or perspective that often has dominated the educational and sociopolitical approaches has permeated our history. Giving a different mindset that focuses on finding common ground would allow for resolution of such conflict. It is important to note the win/lose concept when viewing diversity from a historical perspective.

The atrocities of World War II exemplify Moore's assertions. Hitler made clear that horrific and unrelenting human tragedies could occur when the dangerous beliefs of one culture and set of beliefs are deemed superior and another as vastly inferior. Hitler's acts showed the world the dangers of even the attempts to institutionalize segregation (Payne & Welsh, 2000).

The sociopolitical climate was also affected strongly by the Hitler's atrocities. This in part led to many governments around the world putting human rights as priority and the creation of the Universal Declaration of Human Rights in 1948. This declaration was considered to demonstrate global agreement for the need for equality and human rights.

The pendulum swung again during the Cold War when the United States and Russia fully embraced the "us versus them" philosophies and ethnocentricity was exalted. While there were complex political and economic reasons for the Cold War, the effects on diversity were inarguably clear. Russia was bad and the United

States was good. Patriotism swelled around these issues and the Star Wars were in full swing. Curricula regarding other cultures were filtered through this perspective.

At the same time the Civil Rights movement was gaining momentum. During this time the thrust for diversity and multiculturalism was subsumed under the movements for the abolition of the Jim Crow Laws, Brown vs. Board of Education, the Women's Rights Movement and more. Just as the United States Constitution exalts justice for all, a democratic society encourages and at times requires its citizens to challenge the applications of these ideals. During the times of the rights movements this political practice became the mainstream. The main goal of the U.S. constitution began as, and remains, to be "the creation of a democracy—a more perfect union." (Payne & Welsh, 2000). Multicultural education is a natural outcome of this process. Preparing students to participate in a diverse society that espouses democratic principles of inclusiveness represents the educational applications of the constitution (Moore, 1996).

Many educators cite the beginnings of multicultural education as occurring during late 1960s and highlighted in the mid 1970s. This was the first time that the National Education Association began to address cultural diversity in schools. During this time President Jimmy Carter's President's Commission on Foreign Language and International Studies issued a report that set in motion four major curriculum shifts in K-12 global education (Smith, 2002):

1. Foreign Language Instruction;
2. Geography;
3. World History; and
4. Public Schools with an International Focus.

Significant changes occurred in these areas. For example, over 1000 foreign language programs exist at the elementary level. These were unheard of in 1979. Still, the United States is woefully behind other nations in this area. Critics such as J. David Edwards, the Executive Director of the Joint National Committee for Languages, described United States progress in foreign languages education as a movement from "scandalous to mediocre."

Geography, which was virtually nonexistent in 1979, now has support from the National Geographic Society which has helped to develop alliance between teachers, students, and college professors who are concerned with improving instruction in this area. Alliances exist in all 50 states. National geography standards have been developed and 48 states have standards in geography. Major organizations, such as the American Geographical Society, the Association of American Geographers, the National Council for Geographic Education, and the National Geographic Society have collaborated to sponsor such developments. The fact that these standards are in place is encouraging. Unfortunately recent test scores show little to no improvement in the K-12 sector. Clearly there is much more to be done.

In the area of Word History, improvements to instruction have been made with the help of the World History Association. There now exists an advanced placement course in World History. At the turn of the millennium 20,000 students took the exam. This was a record high for any AP course (Smith, 2002).

Some public magnet schools, discussed later in this book, have taken an international focus. These schools have strong foreign language requirements (often four years), world history requirements, and extracurricular activities with an international focus.

Curriculum content is critical for diversity in that it drives the planning and formal teachings on the subjects. Curricular materials are powerful tools for multicultural education. For example, when legal segregation existed in our country, the curricula content reflected the school's perspective and omitted or diminished the cultural achievements of other groups. Curricular changes therefore have had a significant impact on the teachings and learning regarding diversity.

Several federal initiatives have been enacted as an attempt to institutionalize multicultural education and its philosophies (Gollnick, 1995). Some of these include:

1. The 1965 Elementary and Secondary Education Act (ESEA) Title I, which authorized as part of President Lyndon Johnson's War on Poverty to encourage schools with large concentrations of low-income students to improve their educational opportunities. Title I was replace with Chapter 1 in 1988;
2. 1968 Title VII of ESEA, The Bilingual Education Act;

3. 1972, Title IX of the Education Amendments which prevented discrimination based on gender;
4. The 1972-1980 Ethnic Heritage Studies Act (Title IX of ESEA);
5. The 1975 Indian Self-Determination and Education Assistance Act (ISDA);
6. The 1980 Refugee Education Act (REA); and
7. The 1988 Indian Education Act (IEA) which provided assistance to meet the special education and culturally related academic needs of Native American students in public schools.

MODERN DAY CHANGES

Often significant events serve as catalyst for change. This phenomenon is true when studying cultural diversity as well. The horrific events of September 11, 2001 have changed our country and our world in inexplicable ways. There have been marked changes in our national security procedures, practices regarding law enforcement, and our overall feelings of safety within our country. The concept of patriotism has been reborn and in some sense changed given these tragic events. In the realm of public schools we have witnessed increased security, but also increased awareness and discussions regarding our place in the world. Questions about other countries and beliefs have escalated, fueled by the need to understand disastrous events and look for ways to regain our security. Questions regarding the teachings of history and culture, in particular multicultural education, have gained momentum. Ravitch (2002) defined seven important lessons for our students in order to be informed citizens "who will preserve and protect democracy":

1. It's OK to be patriotic;
2. Not all cultures share our regard for equality and human rights;
3. We must now recognize the presence of evil in the world;
4. Pluralism and divergence of opinion are valuable;

5. Knowledge of United States history is important;
6. Knowledge of world history and geography is important; and
7. We must teach students to appreciate and defend our democratic institutions (6-9).

Ravitch's argument for these lessons emphasizes that a citizen of a nation such as ours must be informed about one's own country in relation to its place in the world. Educators must prepare students who will safeguard and sustain democracy.

The events of September 11 caused many educators to voice the need for a stronger multicultural curriculum. Why there is a need and how this need should be addressed are questions that have sparked much discussion in the education and political communities. In October of 2001 Lynne Cheney, the Vice President's wife, made this strong assertion that those individuals and groups who were seeking a stronger multicultural curriculum were implying "that the events of September 11 were our fault, that it was our failure to understand Islam that led to so many deaths and so much destruction" (The White House, 2001).

Dunn (2002) understood the advocates of multicultural education were attempting to underscore the notion that students were not able to understanding the horrific and significant events in "broader geographic, historical, and political contexts." Dunn proposed that "a new world history curriculum should replace comparison of different cultures with questions that lead students to understand the complex, large-scale changes that have shaped our world." (13).

The United Nations Educational, Scientific, and Cultural Organization (UNESCO) is a multi-governmental organization that has been working for years to promote education for a culture of peace. Post September 11 has brought the interest of more and more countries into taking an active role. UNESCO allows for people of varying nations to get together in a neutral environment. Sir John Daniel, the Assistant Director-General for UNESCO was asked an interview question about balancing national identity and teaching tolerance and global issues. He responded by emphasizing the need to understand your own culture and having a critical view of it and to knowledge of the rest of the world. He believes that

that the message of UNESCO is "that globalization is a good thing, but for goodness' sake, let's root kids in their own culture... Being rooted where you are helps you to go somewhere else rather than washing that away" (Perkins-Gough, Lindfors & Erns, 2002, p.16). UNESCO has the potential to be a powerful catalyst for change during this post September 11 era.

CULTURAL DIVERSITY APPLIED TO A SYSTEMS VIEW OF EDUCATION: STUDENT AND CLASSROOM LEVEL

Most often the phrase "one person can make a difference" becomes a cliché. It is used to make the point that each person adds to a larger whole that has force and power. Regardless of the definition one chooses to embrace, multicultural education implies learning and or understanding about some one or group other than yourself. There are many exciting examples of how the infusion of multicultural teachings is making pathways toward a better understanding of the global society. Several of these examples are shared in subsequent sections of this chapter. The first example indicates that one person can make a difference without having to sign a contract, donate blood, or walk for a worthy cause. Sometimes we can learn the most important lessons from children. It is when we choose to pay attention to their actions and reactions, that we can gain many valuable insights. The following is a story of a second grade boy, who by acting as himself taught his classmates and his teacher valuable lessons in diversity.

The Story of Juan

Juan came to the second grade classroom in mid-October of the school year. Born in Mexico, Juan was one of four children and the son of migrant workers. He spent part of the year in schools in Mexico, and part of the year in schools in the United States. Short for his age, Juan was old enough to be in third grade, but through limited testing opportunities in the Spanish language and Juan's reluctance to communicate, he was placed in a second grade class. The teacher, a white American woman, was in her second year of teaching elementary school. She had not yet experienced a student who did not speak English. Juan was shy; he did not speak to any students or the teacher. His eyes lowered when anyone addressed him directly and if there was a response, it was barely audible. Clearly, Juan was not comfortable in his new learning environment. He looked and acted different from his white American peers. The other students were both fascinated and detached. The teacher gave Juan two "buddies" to help him interpret what was going on in the classroom. She labeled the classroom in both English and Spanish and attempted to communicate with Juan using her very limited Spanish speaking abilities.

It was clear that Juan understood many math concepts and was good with addition and subtraction. He did not speak during most of the day, and he did not act out. In a busy second grade classroom with many needs, it was easy to forget that Juan was there. Yet, he began to have an impact on his buddies and those in close proximity. Juan was most definitely still a child, and children of every race, ethnicity, religion, and origin, love to play. Juan began to make up nonverbal games and through nods, and gestures, he invited his buddies to play. Soon other children became curious and wanted to join in. During math time Juan would help his buddies figure out problems: this was amazing to watch. He would use his own "manipulatives"—scraps of paper, erasers, books—to demonstrate the problems and answers, and then gesture to his games so that the intent was clear "Finish your math work so that we can play." This loud and boisterous class became quieter and keyed in to what Juan was trying to communicate. The teacher adopted nonverbal cues in efforts to find out what Juan knew or understood. The communication without speech was catching. While all of the students were learning reading, writing, and math, Juan taught this class lessons in humanity.

TRADITIONAL CLASSROOM APPROACHES

Traditionally classrooms have attempted to infuse multicultural education and teaching about diversity through stories, festivals, and food. In a desperate attempt to "cover" all of the curriculum demands, teachers have looked to surface examples as efforts for "adding on" cultural diversity. For example, more and more math word problems include names of varying ethnicities and stories include authors and characters from different nationalities and physical appearances. On the surface, these cannot be deemed as bad or hurtful. But when we look deeper, we begin to ask the questions "How do these words, stories, or problems, serve our students in becoming more globally aware? The dangerous numbers game begins. How many names? How many cultures? Which ones to include or exclude? How can everything be covered appropriately in such a small time frame with pressing demands from all aspects of the curriculum?" With few answers and many questions, teachers often resort to the surface approach with the mindset that a little is better than none. This thought process, while understandable, is potentially dangerous as a tool for developing culturally aware students. The next example highlights the progression of this philosophy.

Elementary schools are filled with holiday festivities throughout the year, and most especially during December. Younger grades may look at December as the "Christmas Around the World" month, or a time to examine family traditions that are steeped in culture, religion, and heritage. The intention behind these plans is noble. Teachers attempt to set the stage for learning about other cultures and countries and their holiday traditions. This often involves parents. Families are welcomed to schools for particular days of sharing and learning. Perhaps a mother will share her family recipe for perogies and explain how her grandmother learned how to make these in the Ukraine. Perhaps a father will share a special way of making ornaments that he learned from his father in Korea. These are fun days in the classrooms and most certainly promote sharing and a sense of community. The limitations of these activities though are multiple in number and have potentially negative effects on learning about diversity. The teachers, parents, and students devote much time and effort to these experiences. Therefore it is essential that we look at the outcomes of such events. These classroom experiences *do* promote a sense of involvements among parents, who shared, and the teacher and students.

The question is, though, what do these experiences, most often done in isolation, teach about a particular culture, religion, or country? If the intent of these learning experiences is larger than bridging school and home involvement—as many multi-culturalists and educators believe it to be—than we must look beyond the "one shot deal" or snapshot approach to teachings about diversity. Educators are often ruled by the calendar: certain times of the year require certain learning activities. In the current testing craze, teachers must take time to prepare students for certain scheduled assessments. Unfortunately educators often become locked into a calendar approach to education. Just as studying apples in September is not a tenet of childhood education theory and strategy, teachers do not need to restrict themselves to certain times of the year to address teachings of diversity. Sandra Feldman (2003), the President of American Federation of Teachers, cautioned educators on this very point. In order to dispel stereotypes it is important "not to confuse past ways of life or ceremonial or holiday life with a group's contemporary or daily identity. There is much more to Native American culture than the first Thanksgiving and opportunities other than Hanukkah to spotlight Jewish culture."

A change in mindset is needed to free educators from this one particular mold. The effects of this rigid approach can be seen at all ages from kindergarten through upper levels in high school, i.e., heritage months and days set aside to honor the diversity within schools. These projects are well intended and are matched with strong effort and diligence from all involved. This is often one of the few experiences that parents may have to participate in the middle and high schools. Inviting parents in to discuss their particular heritage or to share a food that is associated with a particular group of people has served the home school relationship well. Unfortunately, this has done little to promote multicultural education and real understandings of diversity. In fact oftentimes it can reinforce the very stereotypes the teachers and schools are trying to defeat. Debrah Menkart (1999, p.19) illustrates this example through the opportunities to celebrate Heritage Months.

> What do students learn if the Hispanic Heritage Month events consist of a dance performance assembly and tacos for lunch? Try asking students at your school what they have learned from the activities. Don't be surprised if they tell you that "Latinos like to dance and eat." The heritage month events have simply reinforces a stereotype that students have already learned from television.

Menkart is not against the philosophy of heritage months, rather she cautions educators concerning how to use their time and efforts for these projects.

George Walker (2001), the Director General of International Baccalaureate Organization, affirms Menkart's concerns, asserting that international education must be more that the five "Fs"— "food, festivals, famous people, fashion, and flags." These surface ideas often lead to misconceptions and perpetuation of stereotype and false notions. When Skelton, Wigfort, Harper, and Reeves (2002) were given the task of developing a curriculum for a primary elementary audience, they identified with Walker's statements. They also understood how many schools default to these surface areas when attempting to reach consensus on which cultures to address becomes a minefield. Skelton et al realized the need to create a well-defined curriculum that had a "significant international dimension."

Unfortunately most schools have not incorporated multicultural education into an integral part of the curriculum (Gay, 2003). Schools have not yet met the ideals of theorists such as Banks and Banks (2002), who contend multicultural education to be an essential aspect of quality education. Instead many schools remain in Marshall's first or second phase of evolution and multicultural curriculum is an add-on, used most often as a luxury or in time of crisis. This approach only propels discussions about diversity when there is a significant event in the local, national, or global community.

One of the dangers of this process is that the discussions that surround such events are inevitably fueled by human emotions and not on research and models (Payne & Welsh, 2000). Without a system or model in place, discussions about diversity during times of crisis have no foundation to draw upon. There is no context for understanding the immediate and at times personal events in terms of history, beliefs, principles etc.

A POSSIBLE APPROACH

Instead Gay asserts that this curriculum is crucial and cannot lie in the periphery of the educational realm. Multicultural education is not about a few isolated lessons that highlight special events. Researchers in teaching multicultural education assert the need to promote significant learning outcomes, including human development, education equality, academic excellence, and democratic citizenship (Banks & Banks, 2001; Gay, 2003; Nieto, 2000). Gay suggests that multiculturalism is interdisciplinary. She offers practical suggestions that encourage teachers to use systematic decision-making approaches to integrate multicultural education through these steps:

1. Creating learning goals and objectives that incorporate multicultural aspects, such as "Developing students' ability to write persuasively about social justice concerns";
2. Using a frequency matrix to ensure that the teacher includes a wide variety of ethnic groups in a wide variety of ways in curriculum materials and instructional activities;
3. Introducing different ethnic groups and their contributions on a rotating basis;
4. Including several examples from ethnic experiences to explain subject matter concepts, facts, and skills; and
5. Showing how multicultural content, goals, and activities intersect with subject-specific curricular standards

Gay's last point is especially significant given the current testing mania that exists in our national education agendas. As education has become standards driven, the focus of teachers remains to address these standards in a comprehensive approach. The curriculum plate is overflowing; there is no room for add-on activities. Instead educators and school district leaders must examine their approaches to multicultural education as a global and integrated entity.

Schools across the nation are becoming more diverse in population with each decade. Ready or not, diversity is here. Schools MUST begin to move through the phases of perception in order to address diversity wholly, successfully, and through a sustainable pedagogy. Futrell, Gomez, and Bedden (2003) report that of the 53 million elementary and secondary students currently enrolled in schools, 35% are from racial or ethnic minority groups. If the trend continues, the minority population will become the majority population by 2050. As the changing school population presses the issues of diversity, technology has also propelled us forward to a progressively more global society.

POSITIVE EFFECTS OF TECHNOLOGY

Technology can, and in many cases already has, served as a valuable tool for teaching and learning the principles of diversity and multicultural education. The Internet has linked small rural schools with larger urban campuses across the United States. Learning and communicating online has connected students all over the world who share common learning goals and vastly different cultural, ethnic, and religious backgrounds. Online learning offers a unique forum for learning. Increasingly, high schools across the nation are linking with other districts and offering students online courses such as Advanced Placement courses or curriculum that a particular district may not have the faculty to address. While there are arguments from proponents and critics of distance learning, one aspect of this forum is widely accepted. Online learning allows the learner to "appear" strictly as a student without any identifying characteristics in regard to race, age, culture, religion, disabilities and at times gender. Students can decide if and when to share these aspects—often after they have established themselves as a student. In the traditional face-to-face classrooms opinions are often formed during the first class meetings and they are based on stereotypes and misunderstandings. Adolescence is a tumultuous time as individuals form their identities—providing a learning opportunity that allows the individual student to share his/her characteristics with discretion is a powerful forum.

Technology can also serve as a catalyst for sharing cultures and broadening understanding of the interconnectedness of the globe. The Internet, email and instant messaging systems allow individuals to have real time dialogue and communication with others around the world. While many, many countries do not have access to safe water supplies, technology is far down on their list of needs. Students of all ages ARE able to communicate with other students in different states, countries, and regions of the world. These efforts require significant orchestration from the teachers involved, but as many will attest, the learning opportunities and outcomes indicate that the time spent has been well invested.

For example, students at Norcossee Community School in Central Florida have utilized videoconferencing, email, Internet programs and real time chat features to communicate and collaborate with students all over the world (McGoogan, 2002). According to McGoogan, videoconferencing has been an exciting learning tool that has allowed elementary students to communicate and literally see students from a variety of states and countries around the world. McGoogan and her team have utilized technology to bridge the understandings of our complex world. It is often said, "the world is getting smaller everyday." The educators involved in this project have taken that concept and grounded it in meaningful learning opportunities. After participating in this comprehensive program, students have real understanding of global awareness—and these students are in vertical teams from first to fifth grade. Students are learning how interconnected our lives are with those around the globe.

> They [students] may not understand how an uprising in Nepal affects their security. They do understand, however, when students their age who live at the foot of Mt. Everest tell them that the water is terribly polluted and that they rode elephants over the weekend. Students can read about destruction of the world's rainforests—but such knowledge only hits home when their peers in the Philippines tell them that they just returned from a field trip to their rainforest, only 10 percent of which remains.

Students participating in this project work toward the culminating activity—"The Big Night"—which is a full 24 hours of communication with students around the world. A well-planned event allows for students to "talk" with peers from around the globe. Parents are active participants in this event and students, parents, and teachers spend a full 24 hours at school "checking in" with students in different time zones as they arrive at their own schools. This culminating event also includes storytelling, games, plays, weaving, and of course food. In this example though, while students may indulge in the international restaurant set up in their classrooms, they have the holistic understandings of specific students and realities from each country that the food may represent. McGoogan and her team have provided a foundation for global awareness through meaningful and sustained student involvement. The integrated learning activities are purposeful, authentic, and provide real life communication. Names of countries, religions, regions, and ethnic terms have gone from abstract concepts to real life connections. Students participating in these activities have become globally aware and have begun life long intercontinental communications.

Another effective use of technology in the teaching and learning about multiculturalism and diversity can be found as part of the United Nations Website. This link, entitled Cyberschoolbus, was developed in 1996 as an interactive resource for teachers and students. The site is filled with intense learning experiences geared to the K-12 students. Major themes of the lessons and information are essential for multicultural education and include human rights, peace education, hunger, communication, and collaboration. Interactive activities are available through many of the links provided. Some of these include "Ask an Ambassador," videos of projects completed by students in Sarajevo and New York, artwork, geography, world summit events and so much more. The vision of the Cyberschoolbus project is "to provide exceptional educational resources (both online and in print) to students growing up in a world undergoing increased globalization." This resource has both static and changing information that reflects the global climate today. It is geared for teaching and learning experiences and it provides vast amount of quality resources for education and global events and issues. Not all classrooms or even school districts have culturally diverse populations. This Internet resource allows students to learn and interact with individuals from a variety of backgrounds and experiences.

LITERATURE AS A POSITIVE MODEL

Using literature to examine different points of view has been a stronghold in English classes. This approach can be applied when studying diversity and cultural issues without having festivals or food. Educators need to be careful when choosing literature for these purposes.

Brakas and Pittman-Smith (2004) have developed a coding system that assists teachers in choosing multicultural literature. Brakas and Pittman-Smith's definition of multicultural literature is inclusive and broad based. The definition alone can assist educators in understanding issues of diversity and approaching teaching learning about cultures, peoples, and beliefs in comprehensive and sustainable patterns. This change in pedagogy, which reflects the ideals of Banks (1995), has promising outcomes for teachers and students. Brakas and Pittman-Smith state the following:

We define multicultural literature as books focusing on people, their ideas, values or practices that include the following:
1. Ethnic groups living inside and outside the United States other than those typically and historically represented as the American macro culture;
2. Religious groups other than the major Protestant groups and Roman Catholic;
3. Regional cultures, such as mountain cultures (e.g., southeast Appalachian), river cultures (e.g., the Louisiana bayou Cajuns) and, the culture of the rain forest (e.g., the Amazon rain forest);
4. The culture of exceptionality, the gifted and the physically and mentally challenged;
5. The culture of low social economic status;
6. Females who have been underrepresented or misrepresented; and
7. The elderly who have been underrepresented or misrepresented.

Another approach using literature as a significant and sustaining avenue for multicultural education was developed Cerylle

Moffet from the United States Peace Corps. As a curriculum design specialist for Coverdell Worldwise Schools, she is the primary author of *Voices From the Field: Reading and Writing About the World, Ourselves, and Others* (2001). This book relates the personal narratives of Peace Corp Volunteers and offers students firsthand accounts of the everyday realities of individuals and communities all over the world. Moffet and her colleagues collected a variety of stories that represent experiences around the world, and then framed these accounts in curriculum units. These selections allow students to develop their reading and writing skills through the venue rich multicultural experiences. The stories are steeped in historical themes that appear in writing. For example, Mike Tidwill is a former Peace Corp volunteer and published author, whose writings are included in the book. According to Moffet (2002):

> Tidwell's stories deal with issues of generosity, justice, individualism, and community, with the complexity of cultural differences and their impact on human behavior. They also illustrate how the experience of moving from one culture to another caused Tidwell to question not just local culture but also his own." (Moffet, p.27)

Teachers who have used the stories and curriculum note the changes in perceptions and expanding ideas of their students and that reading these personal accounts has helped their students begin to think globally. These stories most certainly identify cultural differences. As students explore meanings and literary structures, it becomes clear that these stories also underscore commonalities in humanity, such as determination, friendship, and dignity. As educators continue to look for ways to address the standards driven curriculum, this resource may be a very powerful one. (For more information readers may visit www.peacecorps.gov/wws. This site has a variety of information and free resources.)

HOW CAN WE MAKE THIS HAPPEN?

Banks (1995) describes five interrelated dimensions of multicultural education:

1. Content integration;
2. Knowledge construction;
3. Prejudice reduction;
4. Equity pedagogy; and
5. Empowering of the school culture and social integration.

These five essential dimensions can be seen in some of the promising examples of this chapter. Think about the Big Night Project. Surely students were integrating content and constructing knowledge on many higher levels of thinking and learning. The reduction of prejudice happens naturally when students communicate one on one with students from different countries and cultures. Teachers demonstrated equity pedagogy (the idea that all students can learn (Marshall, 2002) through engaging all students in the vertical teams in varying aspects of the project. It was an inclusive adventure. This project also did much to empower the culture of the school and the community with the strong staff and parental involvement in the cognitive and social aspects throughout the learning experience. The participants in the Big Night project can serve as an example of the applications of Banks' essential components for successful multicultural education.

A panel of experts (many of whose primary works are cited within this chapter) was convened by the Center for Multicultural Education at the University of Washington and the Common Destiny Alliance at the University of Maryland. This Multicultural Education Consensus Panel worked on a four-year project to review and synthesize the research related to diversity. From their work, the panel produced twelve essential principles for teaching and learning in a multicultural society (Banks et al, 2001). These principles are related here.

Teacher Learning

Principle 1. Professional development programs should help teachers understand the complex characteristics of ethnic groups within US society and the ways in which race, ethnicity, language, and social class interact to influence student behavior.

There is a strong call for higher education institutions to take action regarding the development of new teachers who have the understandings, skills, and experiences to address the challenges of diversity in our schools. This can only be accomplished through coherent programs that reflect the best practices regarding teaching and learning in populations of diverse backgrounds. These theories and strategies need to be imbedded and reflected in the mission statements of the teacher education departments. This cannot be achieved through an added a course of diversity alone.

Professional development schools may serve as a testing ground for the strong integration of theory and practice in a diverse learning environment. The intense think tanks allow for continued collaboration and analysis of application of teaching and learning strategies. Teachers, interns, and teacher educators can work together to integrate multicultural education and analyze and evaluate the best teaching practices for its infusion (Futrell et al, 2003).

Student Learning

Principle 2. Schools should ensure that all students have equitable opportunities to learn and to meet high standards.

Principle 3. The curriculum should help students understand that knowledge is socially constructed and reflects researchers' personal experiences as well as the social, political, and economic contexts in which they live and work.

Engaging classes in the game of Barnga (Steinwachs & Thiagarajan, 1990) allows students to begin to understand other's perspectives. This game, which does not allow verbal communication, provides different rules for different teams. Students must figure out a ways to communicate, compromise, and learn from one another. Debriefing this game allows for rich discussion in how each team (culture) played by the rules according to their own perspective (Bacon & Kischner, 2002). This game requires higher order thinking, collaboration, and reflection.

Inter-group Relations

Principle 5. Schools should create or make salient super ordinate or crosscutting groups in order to improve inter-group relations.

Principle 6. Students should learn about stereotyping and other related biases that have negative effects on racial and ethnic relations.

Principle 7. Students should learn about the values shared by virtually all cultural groups (e.g. justice, equality, freedom, peace, compassion, and charity).

Principle 8. Teachers should help students acquire the social skills needed to interact effectively with students from other racial, ethnic, cultural, and language groups.

Principle 9. Schools should provide opportunities for students from different racial, ethnic, cultural, and language groups to interact socially under conditions designed to reduce fear and anxiety.

Stereotypes and misperceptions perpetuate through fear and ignorance. Teachers can facilitate learning experiences that allow for open dialogue and discussions of these issues. We can learn from the efforts that schools are making in Northern Ireland. An area that has been consumed by hatred and violence is beginning to experience subtle change. While the governments and politicians continue to work toward peace initiatives, parents in Northern Ireland have started an integrated school movement (Tell, C. 1999). The first school began in 1981 and today there are more than 40 integrated schools across this region. Tremendous parental support, led by a group "All Schools Together" has sustained the movement that requires balanced ratios in students, staff, and school boards. Many of these schools are located in battle torn areas; most students have lost family members in the ongoing violence. Yet the schools continue to grow and students are all learning together in an open democratic and tolerant environment. Tell explains that the "greatest challenge for integrated schools is to remain sensitive to cultural differences without encouraging social division." These schools take time to honor those who have suffered and died through the "Troubles." These activities are real for the students and create the delicate balance thorough focus on peace. These schools, of course, are not the only way to address integration and understanding of other cultures and religions, but they are ONE way that appears to be working. Tell makes these final statements:

> And as these schools become increasingly accepted alternatives to separate schooling, they are proving to be more than abstract emblems of reconciliation. Through parental involvement, staff commitment, and high academic standards, integrated

schools create rich, open environments for all students to learn together.

School Governance, Organization, And Equity

Principle 10. A school's organizational strategies should ensure that decision-making is widely shared and that members of the school community learn collaborative skills and dispositions in order to create a caring learning environment.

Principle 11. Leaders should ensure that all public schools, regardless of their locations, are funded equitably.

In Seattle Washington, teachers have been trained in facilitating learning experiences that focus on content, exposure to variety of cultures and experiences, and on authentic applications of their learning (Bacon, N. A., & Kischner, G. A., 2002). In 2002 the state had build a network of over 900 teachers involved in the Global Classroom. These educators are using a global curriculum that allows students to learn and think deeply about the essential themes of globalization, human rights, democracy, nationalism, and imperialism. These themes are studied through the real world events, resources, and people. Students communicate through the perspectives of other cultures, they interact with other schools across the country and the world, they learn from a variety of guest speakers representing international perspectives, and work collaboratively with their surrounding communities to experience real world events that are involve multiple perspectives.

An example of community partnerships occurred in 1999 during the World Trade Organization Meeting in Seattle. Working with Seattle's World Affairs Council, high school students experience WTO simulations discussing real cases. Learning from the variety of people and perspectives in these cases allowed the students to prepare for their presentations of the cases to a set of peer judges who had been trained in WTO protocol. These efforts required strong commitments of school and community leaders. These kinds of experiences cannot occur when diversity and global awareness is viewed as an add-on to the existing curriculum demands. Washington teachers, administrators, and community leaders have provided strong examples of the real-life learning possibilities for all students. According to Bacon and Kischner (2002) "classrooms are greatly enriched when they are defined not by the

four walls that enclose them, but as a nexus of community resources that teachers can draw on to build understandings of the
greater world."

Assessment

Principle 12. Teachers should use multiple culturally sensitive
techniques to assess complex cognitive and social skills.

Strong assessment techniques always include a battery of assessments. The same is true in regard to multicultural education.
Not only do we need to consider the assessment itself in terms of
validity, reliability, and cultural sensitivity, we must also provide a
variety of assessments that meet these strong criteria.

These principles are excellent guides for teachers, school districts, and communities that are attempting to address multicultural
education in effective and sustaining ways. Applying these principles will assist schools in preparing students for the globalization
in which they will live.

Banks also provides an excellent list of strategies that teachers
can apply when addressing multicultural education. His list provides goals for all to attain. These goals would serve as plan books
and school district visions well and can be applied easily to the
standards of a particular state (Banks, 1997):

1. A multicultural curriculum education is to help students view events, concepts, issues, and problems
   from a diverse cultural and ethnic perspectives;
2. A multicultural curriculum will contribute significantly to the developments of a healthy nationalism
   and national identity;
3. The multicultural curriculum should help students
   develop the ability to make reflective decisions on
   issues related to ethnicity and to take personal, social, and civic actions to help solve the racial and
   ethnic problems in our national and world societies;
4. The multicultural curriculum should reduce ethnic
   and cultural encapsulation and enable students to
   understand their own cultures better;
5. The multicultural curriculum should help students
   to expand their conception of what it means to be

human, to accept the fact that ethnic minority cultures are functional and valid; and

6. The multicultural curriculum will help students to master essential reading, writing, and computational skills.

CONCLUSION: A HOPEFUL FUTURE

While reading through the promising cases cited in research, many educators and administrators would agree that the exemplars provide exciting, intense, integrated learning experiences for a range of students. These opportunities help prepare students for the global economy and social system in which they will live. These examples all embrace best practices in teaching and learning. The question becomes though, how can I do this in my classroom? How can we bring these ideals to fruition in our school district? How can we find community members to share their experiences and add to authentic learning tasks? How can we as a school system address these important goals and still meet the ever-challenging standards and achieve the test scores our community and governments require? These are all good questions, and the fact that they are being asked is a significant factor in progress. Certainly this is the time for elements of the system to work together to create change. This can happen on small and grand scales. One teacher working with one class, as in the case of Juan, makes a change. One individual from the community who shares experiences and different perspectives makes a change. Classrooms that embrace the broad outcomes that researchers assert as true measures of multicultural teaching make significant changes, especially when the students move on to other classrooms that extol the same standards.

Gay (2003) offers educators important strategies to apply when attempting to integrate multicultural education. This needs to be a systematic approach to ensure the quality and richness of the learning experiences. Brakas and Pittmnan-Smith (2004) offer groundbreaking-learning opportunities through literature used each day in elementary classrooms. UNESCO and the UN offer teachers sound strategies and resources, most of which are available via the Internet. Technology has great value to educators who are attempting to change their teaching and learning patterns regarding multicultural education and diversity. As our society becomes more interconnected the opportunities to share experiences and knowledge are fueled by the advances in technology. Each element of the systems model can find substantive ways to address the needed change in teaching and learning about cultural diversity. It is clear that there is much to be done. It is also clear, as shown in this chapter, that what is to be done is very possible.

DISCUSSION QUESTIONS

1. Why is multiculturalism important to the society; to the educational process?

2. Dispel each myth of multicultural education.

3. Given the recognition of the importance of multiculturalism since the 13th century, why is it taking so long to be imbedded as a goal of education?

4. Why didn't traditional approaches to multiculturalism work?

5. What are the components of an interdisciplinary multicultural education approach?

6. What are the benefits of using technology to teach about multiculturalism?

7. What are the benefits of using literature to teach about multiculturalism?

8. How would the five dimensions of multicultural education and its twelve principles be utilized in the multicultural classroom?

Chapter 5:
Inclusion, Reform and Learning Organizations

OBJECTIVES

After studying this chapter, the reader will be able to define, analyze and apply the tenets of:

1. Brown v. Board of Education;

2. Public Law 94-142: The Education for All Handicapped Children Act;

3. Section 504 of the Rehabilitation Act;

4. Individuals with Disabilities Act (IDEA);

5. Inclusion;

6. Free Appropriate Public Education (FAPE);

7. Individual Education Plan (IEP);

8. Least Restrictive Environment (LRE);

9. Due Process;

10. Child Identification; and

11. Learning Organizations.

OVERVIEW

The conscious and primary educational goal of local school communities is to help all students achieve their highest potential. To some, this may appear somewhat naïve and optimistic while to others, it is a true vision toward which all in educational communities must continue to work. Although a great deal of work has yet to occur, the changes that have occurred in special education in the past 30 years provide clear evidence that we are making significant progress toward this mission. If we truly believe in the vision that it is our responsibility to *help all students achieve their highest potential*, whether they are students with special needs, differing learning styles, disabilities, cultural and/or economic differences, then the continuing goal of inclusion of all students within evolving learning organizations must be of primary importance.

Although special education has been the principal catalyst for the concept of inclusion, advocacy for the inclusion of others within the mainstream is not new, as we will see.

Historical Foundations

For many, PL 94:142, the *Education for All Handicapped Children Act* in the mid-1970s, the mandate for the integration of handicapped students into the educational mainstream was the impetus for greater inclusionary efforts. In actuality, this is not the case. The historical roots of "special" education for those with disabilities are found primarily in the 1800s in Europe. Many know the story of Victor, the wild boy of Aveyron; he was a young boy of 12 years old who was found naked and wild in the forests of France. Victor had not developed any language and his behavior was described as animal-like when he was found (Hardman, Drew & Egan, 1996). Jean Marc Gaspart Itard improved the wild child's behavior and language through sensory stimulation procedures. Itard's work with Victor provided documentation that learning was possible for those children who many thought could not be taught anything of significance (Hallahan & Kaufman, 1988). In the United States in 1779, Thomas Jefferson was an aggressive advocate to include children from poor families into public schools, since they were not able to attend for economic reasons. He proposed the first state-supported education plan in Virginia to allow all children, not only those from wealthy families, an opportunity to receive educational services (Winzer & Mazurek, 2000). Unfortunately, the plan failed since the wealthy did not want to "fund" the education of poor children through their tax dollars. It was quite commonplace for children from poor families and other ethnic groups (Native American, African-American, etc.) as well as those with disabilities to be totally excluded from school and either attend school in separate facilities, become institutionalized or not go to school at all. Children with disabilities were not the only ones against whom such discrimination and segregation existed.

The Civil Rights movement in the 1950s and 1960s in the United States truly became the groundwork for establishing the right to an education for *all* children. Its mission was to insure basic human rights to all people, including children who may have been deemed "different" previously by color, race or disability. It was during this time that all exclusionary practices in education were made public and examined with great detail. Most well known is Brown vs. Board of Education (Topeka, Kansas), whose ruling by the U.S. Supreme Court in 1954 declared that separate schools for black and white children were inherently unequal.

> In these days, it is doubtful that any child may reasonably be expected to succeed in life if he is denied the opportunity of an education. Such an opportunity, where the state has undertaken to provide it, is the right which must be made available to all on equal terms. . . We conclude that, in the field of public education, the doctrine of "separate but equal" has no place. Separate educational facilities are inherently unequal (U.S. Supreme Court, Brown v. Board of Education, May 17, 1954).

Through this ruling, public education was set on a course that could not be reversed. It declared public education's mission to maximize each child's potential through his/her direct and integrated involvement in public education. If the segregation of African American children was unconstitutional according to the *Brown* case, the segregation of children with disabilities would also be unacceptable (Gilhool, 1976). The timing could not be better for many professionals and experts in the field to advocate for more normalized and less exclusionary educational environments for handicapped children. One of those well-known advocates was Wolf Wolfensberger, a researcher, clinician, teacher and administrator in mental retardation. His work surrounding the term as well as the concept of normalization was extensive. He wrote:

> Programmatically, segregation is particularly self-defeating in any context . . . that includes special education. If we are serious about working for the goal of preparing a person toward independence and normative functioning, then we must prepare him to function in the context of the ordinary societal contacts. (Wolfensburger, 1972)

PUBLIC LAW 94:142 AND SECTION 504 OF THE REHABILITATION ACT

Wolfensburger's professional expertise, as well as the aggressive advocacy of others, created the impetus for the establishment of Section 504 of the Rehabilitation Act in 1973, its implementation being guided by the Office of Civil Rights under the Department of Education. This legislation specifically prohibited the discrimination against all people with disabilities in any federally funded program. Federally funded programs included local education agencies (LEA's) and other related educational systems, such as vocational programs. Subsequently, in 1975 Federal legislation known as Public Law 94:142, the *Education for all Handicapped Children Act*, was enacted, perhaps one of the most pivotal pieces of legislation in education for school systems. It provided federal support for a mandate that all children ages 5-21 with disabilities would be educated in public schools. The differences between discrimination and integration through proactive educational support systems were clarified through these two significant pieces of legislation. Within the context of these laws, each state and locality had to have a plan to insure several key concepts; these concepts remain today.

CHILD IDENTIFICATION

Conscious and broad efforts must be made to screen and identify all children with handicapping conditions, before they enter Kindergarten and throughout their school-age years.

DUE PROCESS

A child's and a parent's rights include informed consent in order for an evaluation to occur as well as before a child is recommended for and placed for services. If they do not agree with the results of the evaluation or a recommendation for any type of specialized support, they have the right to an impartial due process hearing.

FREE AND APPROPRIATE PUBLIC EDUCATION (FAPE)

A free and appropriate public education basically means that individually designed instruction ("special" education) and related aids and services are to be provided to students who are eligible free of charge to parents and guardians and through the public school systems. Those who are identified as eligible for special education services have that individually designed instruction written through an Individual Education Plan (IEP). An "all or nothing" or categorical system of eligibility determination is employed by the federal and state special education laws: a child is—or is not—eligible for special education under one or more of several handicapping conditions or disabilities.

INDIVIDUAL EDUCATION PLAN (IEP)

An Individual Education Plan, or IEP, is the written document that identifies the goals and objectives for any special education student as well as the specialized instruction and related services that will assist that student in achieving those goals and objectives. Technically, the IEP is the foundation for determining the placement of that student or where those specialized services would be provided.

LEAST RESTRICTIVE ENVIRONMENT (LRE)

Children who are eligible for and in receipt of special education services have the right to be educated with his/her non-handicapped peers to the maximum extent appropriate.

In an effort to provide common language regarding "least restrictive environment" options, several models were offered during the initial years of PL 94:142. Perhaps the most commonly known was Deno's Cascade of Special Education Services (1979). Levels of restriction were identified, moving from one extreme for another. For example, Level 1 included placements of students with exceptionalities in regular classes with or without services. Level 7, the other extreme, identified placements as in hospital, residential or total care settings (Deno, 1979). Ideally, even as early as the mid-1970s, educational teams' efforts centered on the development of goals and objectives within an IEP that would meet a student's needs and only then identify the placement option that would best provide the supports to meet those goals. If a more restrictive placement was agreed upon, the annual IEP review would then discuss objectives that would perhaps be met in a lesser restrictive environment. With a full continuum of services and on-going communication, educational teams would base their decisions on student outcomes and then on which setting would help that child succeed and become prepared for productive citizenry (Council for Exceptional Children, 1996). However, moving to more restrictive environments would occur only as far as necessary to meet those objectives. Returning to lesser restrictive placements as rapidly as feasible was always the primary goal (Deno, 1979).

The reading of "maximum extent possible" within the "least restrictive environment" has been a source for much interpretation. In brief, according to the initial legislation in 1975, segregation from normal classmates as well as home and family was to occur minimally; the child's life should be as "normal" as possible. This definition was certainly not as simple as it appeared in writing. Specific versions within local educational agencies then created the foundation for litigation in which specific court decisions further interpreted the federal language of least restrictive environment.

Several major court cases held significant implications for placement of disabled students in the least restrictive environment (Osborne & DeMattia, 1994). *Oberti v. Board of Education of the Borough of Clementon (New Jersey)* was based on the parents of Rafael Oberti, an eight-year-old with Down Syndrome, seeking the least restrictive environment within a regular class with supportive services. The final ruling was for Oberti. Judgment was based on a previous court case in 1989, *Daniel v. State Board of Education.* In this case as well as the Oberti case, several factors were examined: the educational benefits of a regular class to the child, if that child was provided with supplemental aids and services; and the possible detrimental effects on others in that regular class. These and other cases frequently serve as the foundation for determining the least restrictive environment (McLaughlin & Henderson, 2000). Although litigation is thought by many to be a last resort, it has the potential of being of great benefit to the legislative process and continued progress in overall reform efforts. The original rationale and purpose of P.L. 94:142, that is, greater normalization, independence and competence of children with disabilities, was making great strides, but much had yet to be done.

INDIVIDUALS WITH DISABILITIES ACT (IDEA) AND EDCUATIONAL REFORM

Congress amended the *Education for All Handicapped Children Act* or P.L. 94:142 in 1990 and renamed the law the *Individu-*

als with Disabilities in Education Act (IDEA). Much remained the same as P.L. 94:142. However, additional provisions relating to the use of nondiscriminatory testing procedures to prevent racial and/or cultural discrimination were added. Assessment was to be done by a multidisciplinary team to insure valid and adequate information was obtained before any eligibility decisions were made and any recommendation for special education services offered (Hardman, Drew & Egan, 1996). In addition, autism and traumatic brain injury were added to the original list of ten (10) disability conditions for eligibility and greater parental involvement in the development of each child's educational program was demanded. Preschool children ages 3-5 with disabilities were also mandated through IDEA to receive a free and appropriate public education (FAPE). In that same year, the *Americans with Disabilities Act* mandated accessibility of all services, programs and activities of state and local governments to those with a physical or mental impairment (McLaughlin & Henderson, 2000).

The provision of a free and appropriate public education for several decades through these major pieces of legislation was of great significance for the field of special education, providing for educational access and equal opportunities for all children, regardless of disability, race or economics. Interestingly enough, at the same time, public education in the United States was in the midst of significant changes. In 1983, *A Nation at Risk: The Imperative for Education* (National Commission on Excellence in Education) was published as a result of concerns regarding student educational outcomes and levels of achievement for all children at that time. Many were of the opinion that schools across the United States encouraged mediocrity and, as a result, threatened the economic viability of the nation (Toch, 1991). When national and state economies are threatened, others become immediately involved. Such was the case in the 1980s and 1990s when groups such as the National Governors' Association and the Center for Education and Economy became involved in the reform efforts. These efforts were intended to insure that schools graduated young people who would be flexible and deep thinkers, problem solvers and, as a result, could be a part of a competitive and global workforce. In 1994, *Goals 2000: Educate America Act* was enacted. It represented the nation's vision for school reform and has been the foundation for standards-based education. Unlike other reform efforts, however, *Goals 2000* provided a more general concept of reform and carried with it no written regulations: states' participation was voluntary with no current mandate for review by the U.S. Department of Education (McDonnell, McLaughlin and Morison, 1997). The intent of *Goals 2000* was to provide a vision for equitable and high quality education, based on standards that would conceptually "raise the bar" for all students. Two particular statements in the *Goals 2000* were particularly significant when considering its goal of equitable access to a demanding curriculum (McLaughlin & Henderson, 2000):

1. . . . all children can learn and achieve to high standards and must realize their potential if the United States is to prosper (PL 103-227, sec 301[1]); and

2. . . . all students are entitled to participate in a broad and challenging curriculum and to have access to resources sufficient to address other education needs (PL103-227, sec 301 [15]).

Even today, the current general education legislation *No Child Left Behind* includes language regarding the inclusion of all children, no matter what label they may have. With more holistic language being incorporated into general education reform, the 1997 amendments to IDEA provided elements directly referencing the requirements of special education within the context of the regular education curricula. Two very separate systems, that is, regular and special education, were beginning to overlap in several ways. Although the amendments were many, the following key changes in IDEA provide the mandate and subsequently the impetus for greater collaborative systems—and subsequently greater opportunities for inclusion—working on behalf of students attending schools that access federal funds:

1. Federal funds now are permitted to be used for costs of special education and related services for a student with a disability in a regular classroom, even if those funds benefit other students without a disability;

2. States now have limited ability to coordinate special education monies with other federal funds, such as Title

I, to provide greater flexibility in preventative and other general improvement efforts;

3. Schools are supported in creating build-based and problem solving systems in order to troubleshoot and brainstorm alternative ideas for all students to be successful. Such systems subsequently create ownership of all students and programs in any school or district;

4. School personnel can now remove students who risk the safety and health of other students, even if they are disabled;

5. All funding mechanisms are now placement neutral (McLaughlin & Henderson, 2000). This means that a child in a residential program no longer receives more funding than a child in a regular classroom receiving accommodations or supports;

6. Students with disabilities are now included in general state and district-wide assessment programs; and

7. Individual Education Plans (IEP's) must now include:
    - Data on how a designated disability impacts the student's progress in a regular education curriculum;
    - Goals that move a child toward greater success in the general curriculum;
    - Systems to be used for accountability;
    - Rationale behind non-participation in the regular curriculum; and
    - Modifications necessary for the child to succeed in state or district-wide achievement assessments.

Intellectually, pragmatically and politically, these educational reforms in conjunction with the amendments of IDEA provide a stable platform for the inclusion of all students within regular classrooms and the general curriculum. The concept of inclusion is neither new nor revolutionary, as we have seen through special education history (Bunch, 1997); its definition has clearly evolved, however. Inclusive educational environments are truly those in which "everyone belongs, is accepted, supports and is supported by his or her peers and other members of the school community in the course of having his or her educational needs met" (Stainback & Stainback, 1990). Such legislative mandates may subsequently provide the vehicle for more rapid progress toward which the mission can be achieved, if we continue to look at educational systems as cultures of learning and continuous improvement.

Although the legislation dictated by the amendments of IDEA in 1997 clearly state that general education classes should be the starting point for placements of students with disabilities, over 30 years of separate yet parallel systems cannot not be undone immediately. Educational systems need time to understand how these parallel systems evolved and avoid "quick fix" solutions. Effective change takes time, a minimum of 3-5 years, with some initiatives taking 10 years or longer (Patterson, 1993). Despite legislative mandates, journeys such as these are often never-ending. Even though we now have innumerable laws and policies against discrimination based on one's color, race, religion, sexual orientation or disability, prejudice continues. Inclusion as an ideology might occur theoretically in the literature but in true learning organizations, there is an understanding that separate and apparently unrelated forces—in this case, special and regular education—can not exist as separate entities. They are intrinsically interrelated and must be discussed as such if long-term and continuous learning and growth are to occur.

INCLUSION: THE DEBATE IN BRIEF

There are innumerable arguments both in support of the maintenance of dual systems—that is, regular and special education—as well as the need for a total merger of the two. Those who endorse special education as a separate structure discuss the field as innately "special" in many ways, citing much of its history and its subsequent evolution and contributions to schools, local communities and society. For those children who are identified as special education eligible, there is significant diversity in the types of disabilities and much variation in depth of specific needs (Winzer & Mazurek, 2000). These students have needs that other students clearly do not have, if they have been assessed and evaluated reliably. As such, colleges and universities have prepared specialists and highly skilled educators who have very specific training in order to diagnose and deeply understand these students and support them so that they are able to learn, progress and become productive and contributing members of our societies. Specific alternative or specialized teaching strategies, modifications and accommodations have been intrinsic in the many systems developed for these students to become successful in a variety of different environments and have become the foundation for many current pedagogical concepts, such as learning styles, differentiated instruction, and multiple intelligences. The field of special education has also been a magnet for significant technological advances, most of which has occurred to accommodate children and students with significant disabilities. In addition, special education has provided a motivating training ground for concerned parents and educators to work together collaboratively and proactively on behalf of their special needs children and respective students (Havelock and Hamilton, 2004). "Compared to the general practice of education, special education is instruction that is more urgent, more intensive, more relentless, more precisely delivered, more highly structured and direct, and more carefully monitored for procedural fidelity and effects" (Kauffman, 1996). As a result, separate learning environments, such as resource rooms, self-contained classes and special schools were developed and are believed by many to be of necessity to provide these specialized services to students with disabilities (Lipsky & Gartner, 1997b, USDOE, 1998). To many, special classes and resource rooms contribute more to the achievement of learners with certain types of disabilities, specifically those with behavioral and learning disabilities, than do regular classrooms (Fuchs & Fuchs, 1995). If special education is not special, why does it continue to exist?

Depending on one's perspective, one might also use these same factors to argue that special education need not be "special" at all, if we in our respective educational communities truly want what is best for all of our children, whether a disability or different learning style exists or not. Proponents of full inclusion present the concept as a moral imperative (Bricker, 1995). To some, the fact that many students never exit from special education services point to the failure of those special interventions, programs and classes. Demographics regarding student outcomes for participants in special education have not been good and many identified students continue to fall through the cracks of the public education system (USDOE, 1997). Critics of special classes feel that such programs have lacked the academic rigor and have not prepared students for the future. More than half of all students with identified behavior disorders drop out of school and about 75 percent of these students are arrested within five years after leaving school (Wagner et al., 1993). Proponents of full inclusion therefore believe that no meaningful transformation in education can occur unless special education and its continuum of placements are eliminated altogether (Kauffman, 1993).

Those professionals who have worked in educational systems and who have experienced the multiple facets of the debate would likely agree with the following statements, believing that none is exclusively correct:

1. Many students in special education services are there because they have experienced failure in the regular classroom (pro-special education);

2. Teachers in the regular classroom have a very broad range of different backgrounds, training and experiences. With an eye on the positive, removal of students with behavioral needs have allowed some teachers to provide greater support to the other students (pro-special education). On the negative side, special education has been used as a dumping ground when openness to addressing students' differing learning styles is non-existent (pro-inclusion). The interest, attitudes and willingness for some educators to work with students with disabilities varies widely, for just as wide a variety of reasons;

3. Students in some special education programs have not learned the necessary social skills to participate successfully in communities because their models have been other disabled students (pro-inclusion);

4. There are critical developmental periods for children to learn certain skills. If these skills are not learned, they may not have the chance to catch up later (pro-special education for individualized intensive instruction);

5. There are benefits for the peers of a disabled student in a classroom. Gaining knowledge about a disability de-

creases fear about it; as a result, prejudice and stereotypes are limited. Students then have a greater respect
and accept others for who they are, a major contribution
to our society long-term (pro-inclusion);

6. Federal and state monies to support special education
   have not been adequate to fully fund the implementation of the regulations guiding the legislation. Funds
   have therefore been protected in many ways and eligibility guidelines adhered to strictly in many local school
   systems in order to make the dollars go as far as possible. If a child is struggling or failing, the automatic response is typically to get special help in any way possible; time is felt to be of the essence (pro-special education); and

7. Waiting lists for referral to special education load special educators' and diagnosticians' assessment and
   evaluation time, leaving little if any occasion for support of the student or teacher within the classroom.
   Such a domino effect creates a scenario that is neither
   pro-special education nor pro-inclusion. More important to realize, the student is the final loser.

The original intent of special education was to offer supports to
students with disabilities in order to bring their performance closer
to their nondisabled peers. Three decades later, in many instances
there has been a shift away from normalization, independence and
competence and a greater dependency on special programs, accommodations and modifications by those identified as disabled.
"The goal seems to have become the appearance of normalization
without the expectation of competence." (Kaufman, McGee &
Brigham, 2004). Supporting and instructing students in learning
environments means that expectations and standards remain high
for all students. Different ways of teaching for different learners
are the norm rather than the exception. Good curriculum comes
first. In many cases of full inclusion, it is questionable whether the
accommodations for those with disabilities are truly accommodations in a curriculum that is rich and thoughtful with high standards
or the "dumbing down" of curricular expectations. If the latter is
the case, an injustice to the education system as a whole is occur-

ring (Dupre, 1998). The need for education to be attentive to both excellence and equity can never be overstated.

The reality is that this is not an "either-or" debate. These two extremes and interpretations of least restrictive environment—one with specialized levels of support and the other with one placement only in the regular classroom—have served to defeat the primary educational mission of supporting all children to ensure their learning and their achievement to their highest potential.

Inclusion and Learning Organizations: the Theory and the Concept

Each classroom, each school and each community is a system—it is a whole rather than separate entities operating of and by themselves. Educational organizations are complex systems since they are interconnected with agents both within and outside; they are also adaptive, since they have the capacity to change, based on new learning experiences (Burrello, Lashley & Beatty, 2001). According to Senge (1990), systems thinking is the cornerstone of the learning organization and should be considered within its overall framework. Given that premise, "special" and "general" education are systems but so, too, is the school or district as a whole in which they function. Failure to understand the structure of learning systems can lead us into cycles of blaming and self-defense; the enemy is always out there, and problems are always caused by someone else (Bolman & Deal; Senge, 1990). As we have discussed thus far, this is happening within the debate regarding special education placement options and the advocacy for full inclusion. In a true learning organization or system:

> . . . people continually expand their capacity to create the results they truly desire...new and expansive patterns of thinking are nurtured . . . collective aspiration is set free and . . . people are continually learning to see the whole together (Senge, 1990).

The framework that Senge offers regarding the necessary disciplines within innovative learning organizations is most compelling when considering the challenge of special education supports and models for inclusion. The ideal of building and *sharing a vision* about what "could be" as part of a long–term dream for a school or a district is of necessity if there is to be a feeling of inspiration and continuous, on-going improvement and innovation. Such a belief statement needs to be built and developed together, not imposed by others onto an organizational team. A pre-determined vision statement is neither shared nor inspirational and subsequently will simply not work. A shared vision such as—We believe that all educators can and should teach all children, that all alternative teaching strategies should be applied to all learners and that all children, no matter the disability, cultural or racial difference, can and will learn within the general education system— provides a purpose for which to work and a long-term goal to which to strive for all who were involved in its development. It is crucial to understand that its conceptualization and its articulation do not mean that it is reality—it is a dream to which successful proactive schools can strive and continue to progress.

The definition of what the general education system "looks like" can certainly be different from one school to another, based on thoughts, perceptions and values of the people in a particular organization. Past, as well as current experiences of individuals within a school, shape these values and thoughts. Terms such as *mental models* (Senge, 1990) and paradigms (Kuhn, 1970; Peters, 1987) have been used to describe these values and experiences. A paradigm shift or a change in one's mental model might be moving from the original view that disabled students should be educated in separate programs and placements to a revised view of understanding how inclusive delivery systems might enhance the total development of all students (Walter-Thomas, Korinek, McLaughlin & Williams, 2000). Clearly, those paradigm shifts cannot occur without on-going learning or without individuals and organizations believing in the discipline of *personal mastery* (Senge, 1990). We are what we think – and what we think can change. Learning is an on-going never-ending process. Garratt (1987) suggests that the learning of the people within an organization, the organizational learning as a whole and its subsequent change, improves the potential for the organization's longer term survival. For individuals and organizations struggling with the challenges of special education and inclusionary education, professional development in its many forms is of absolute necessity. If one's mental model of a learning disability is that of a student whose intellectual potential is limited, increasing one's knowledge and comprehension—personal mastery—is imperative. That knowledge in isolation is not enough, however. Deeper understanding and belief in its reality by experiencing it directly in one's classroom is of vital importance. This can be accomplished through *team learning* or collaboration, the opportunity and the ability of people to dialogue and act together (Senge, 1990). The special educator has focused and intensive training about different types of disabilities, in this case, a specific learning disability. Others may as well, including family members and specialists from within the district or from other outside agencies. A classroom teacher who has had previous teaching experiences with learning disabled children can also be an invaluable resource. To assume or expect all classroom teachers to have that specificity of information and/or experience with all disabilities is naïve. Through the special educator, classroom teacher and others engaging in collaborative activities (talking, developing common standards for all students, discussing differentiated instruction, creating accommodations, team teaching, assessing and evaluating the results of instruction and activities for on-going effectiveness), the learning disabled student and all others in that classroom will reap the benefits. As a result, such community or interagency support teams become change agents as they work together, share leadership responsibilities and commit themselves to making a difference. These four disciplines, as mentioned in Chapter One—shared vision, mental models, personal mastery and team learning—are dynamic processes which lay the foundation for the fifth discipline, *systems thinking* (Senge, 1990). One discipline cannot be effective without the others since they are interrelated and a part of the whole – the system itself.

Senge's disciplines serve as a strong framework for evolving learning organizations such as schools that are striving for effective inclusionary programs. Comprehensive planning is also necessary within this structure to stay focused and not become sidetracked with new initiatives. Intrinsic to this planning is the development of program goals, student needs, curricular standards and instruction, program structures, community involvement by all stakeholders as well as continuous assessment and evaluation processes (George & George, 1993). Action research provides one teacher-friendly vehicle for the on-going assessment and insurance of progress toward the shared vision. Both short and long-term accountability is of crucial importance in such comprehensive planning.

Adequate resources to provide support for effective inclusion in learning systems are also of very high priority. Assigning students with disabilities in regular classrooms without adequate support is not inclusion; it is inappropriate education (Walter-Thomas, Korinek, McLaughlin & Williams, 2000). To make a decision to maintain a child in a district "in the spirit of inclusion" and to not provide the appropriate and individualized support and intervention of specific needs is both unethical and amoral. Without appropriate fiscal, personnel and systemic supports, responsible and successful inclusion cannot occur. Such resources may be direct through adequate funding at the federal, state and local levels to support specialized personnel for support or consultation, adaptive technology, paraeducator involvement or special materials. Other resources may be more indirect through more flexible regulations and policies, school board, administrative and community support, innovative delivery models and creative team decision-making for teachers and specialists. Inclusion is not an opportunity to cut costs in a budget; in fact, appropriate and successful inclusion oftentimes results in an increase in financial expenditures (McLaughlin & Warren, 1993). The amendments of IDEA in 1997 provide an example of giving permission for the limited overlap of funds with other government programs and the use of special education monies for other students in inclusionary environments. A commitment to inclusive and progressive learning systems in schools must parallel views regarding ethical practice to insure that the necessary processes are in place. This will ensure the creation and maintenance of high standards for all students and professionals if successful change is to occur.

Inclusion and Learning Organizations: the Practice and the Reality

A competent system serves the end of enhanced achievement for all students. Meaningful growth can come only by focusing on change from the "inside out". (Zmuda, Kuklis & Kline, 2004)

Inclusion that is responsible must put students first and make decisions that are based on the individual needs of all students. Students' success is achieved when the goals of the individual as well as the group are met. If a student is unsuccessful in an inclusionary setting, systems of support must be discussed, implemented and assessed before alternative placements are considered. Assurances that systems thinking and all of its components are in place must be a moral imperative for those on educational teams if such progressive change is to occur. As stated earlier, a shared vision provides a marker, a "star in the sky" to which to reach: the system evolves, moves ahead, assesses and evaluates, changes, learns more and subsequently makes even greater progress. The student, however, must always remain at the center if such evolution and sustainability of that learning system is to occur. If the system is not ready to successfully include a child, alternative resources may be necessary short-term. However, transitioning that student to his/her own community and age appropriate peers must be of highest priority.

The theoretical premises of inclusion and learning systems demand very high standards and a great deal of work. Some might say that the practice can never match the theory. The reality is that there are practices that are occurring in many progressive school systems that are providing holistic, heterogeneous and flexible learning opportunities, with continuing efforts to assure high standards, differentiated instruction consistently throughout all classes and even more alternatives and unique programs for all students at all levels. The sampling below simply scratches the surface.

Case Study A

The Hillsdale County Schools have a student population of 11, 200 students with 47 percent of the students qualifying for free and reduced lunch. The special education department supported the training of all school personnel (regular and special education) in nonviolent crisis intervention and conflict resolution. Inclusion training has been an integral part of the professional development for special educators for at least seven years (Havelock & Hamilton, 2004). Special educators have also participated in content area training to support team-teaching efforts at the high school level.

As a result, a common language and a common set of high standards, understood by all educators, no matter what their title, were used. That, in addition to a common vision to maximize all opportunities for all students in the district, has provided the foundation for progressive change in the Hilldale County Schools.

Case Study B

In 1988, a suburban school district outside of Burlington, Vermont ventured into the process of assessing its special services programs. This was not due to any mandate or reform requirement, but the district's shared vision of ensuring that all children will learn to their individual potential, ensuring that the resources and supports were fiscally responsible and developing a comprehensive plan for the short-term future. Stakeholders of a Task Force included parents, classroom teachers, special educators, consultants and administrators. There was representation from each school in the district to insure broad-based communication through biweekly feedback and input sessions as a part of building-based staff meetings throughout its work. Major challenges identified included:

1. High numbers of referrals to special services personnel;
2. Ineligibility of referred students for special education, but in need of alternative instruction and supports to succeed;
3. Classroom teachers feeling ill-prepared to support students with differing needs; and
4. Special service personnel feeling that they did not have enough time to assist classroom teachers, since much of their time as being spent evaluating referred students.

Assessment information, including demographic and special services' data collections, surveys to all classroom teachers and special services' personnel, as well as a percentage of parents, confirmed these trends throughout the district. The Task Force took a year and a half to complete its work, discussing, researching, collecting data and communicating with others its work and its relevant to the district's mission. Stakeholders were continually involved and informed. The final development of a comprehensive plan by this group included the objective that all children—whether identified as special education or not—would receive the support that they needed. That support, however, could and would occur in any number of creative ways:

1. Special services personnel might team teach with the classroom teacher and paraeducators to model a different way of teaching phonological awareness, for example. The student, the classroom teacher, support personnel and the specialists are learning together;

2. A substitute teacher could relieve a classroom teacher so that she would be able to observe a brief session with one of her students and a speech-language pathologist working on an alternative communication device that is then introduced to the entire class; and

3. A special services' teacher would work with the majority of the students in a class while the classroom teacher provides small group specialized instruction to a few students after receiving training at a special clinic.

These changes, as well as others, took time and required creative budgeting of local, state and federal funds by district administrators to insure the resources were available for supporting the implementation of this new comprehensive plan and creative delivery options. This was also seven years before the amendments of IDEA in 1997 were enacted, allowing districts to use special education funds for disabled students in alternative ways; this district was clearly taking risks because of their deep belief in their mission. Learning by all together was key and creative professional development took shape in many different ways. Within three years, referrals to special services as well as formal eligibility evaluations had decreased significantly. Upon entering most classrooms, many adults were present; it was, however, difficult to determine who was who and which students had needs. Although it was far from perfect, inclusion was progressing. Most important, however, was the convincing evidence that the best interests of the students were continually placed at the center of all decisions by these educational teams.

Case Study C

The Meadowlark High School's goal was to reduce the dropout rate of youth with special needs. Although an initial school wide needs assessment was completed, it tapped only teachers' opinions regarding the dropout problems and true solutions to the challenge were still difficult to determine. After realizing the superficiality and unreliability of their first endeavor, staff completed a more thorough needs assessment where the students and their parents were also surveyed and a full range of demographic information was collected. It was discovered, much to their dismay, that the students and dropouts needed and wanted help in understanding their learning difficulties and setting goals for their future. After receiving this assistance, they could then determine the most appropriate academic and career development program for these special needs students and plan accordingly. Administrators and teachers quickly realized that complete and reliable assessment and evaluation processes were crucial to the appropriate comprehensive planning for inclusion for their system (see chapter on Assessment and Evaluation). The mere fact that their vision continually centered on making all students successful—which would then quite naturally reduce the dropout rate - provided the impetus and the community the collaborative support needed to identify and correct the gaps in their thinking and processes to begin a true proactive progression. This is simply one more example of a true learning organization.

These are just a few instances of learning systems that persist in making progress to foster excellence as well as equity among all students, no matter how diverse their skills and backgrounds might be. There are many more. If we truly believe that it is our collective responsibility to provide high standards to all children, our systems will continue to evolve, very simply because the people within those systems—children, educators, parents and community members within those organizations—evolve. The more we ask about students' strengths instead of their weaknesses or about their interests and needs instead of labels, the more we will truly progress toward including all students in our schools and community programs.

DISCUSSION QUESTIONS

1. Trace the historical roots of educating students with special needs.

2. What are the basis tenets of, and the benefit to students with special needs, for the following legislation: P.L.94-142 and Section 504 of the Rehabilitation Act?

3. What additional provisions did IDEA mandate?

4. What are the strengths and weaknesses of maintaining dual systems of special and regular education versus the merger of the two?

5. Describe the school as a learning organization. Do these characteristics meet the needs of both special and regular education students? If yes, how?

6. How does the reality of providing an inclusive education differ from the theory? Is it practical or prohibitive?

7. Describe innovative practices with which you are familiar and their impact on special needs' students.

Chapter 6:
Parent Communication

OBJECTIVES

After studying this chapter, the reader will be able to define, analyze and apply the following concepts and strategies:

1. Importance of parental involvement;

2. Obstacles to effective parental involvement;

3. Characteristics of inclusive environments;
    - Promising practices;
    - An evening club;
    - Classroom visits;
    - Parent/teacher conferences;
    - Literacy nights;
    - Parents as volunteers;
    - Classroom/school websites;
    - First response hotline;
    - Drama and theater club;
    - Job shadowing;
    - Transition preparation;
    - After-school programs;
    - College field trips;
    - How-To-Study workshops;

4. Principles of effective collaboration in the special education setting;

5. Principles of effective collaboration in the bilingual setting; and

6. Federal mandates.

OVERVIEW

The role of educators has been changing rapidly over the last quarter of a century. Many roles, formerly associated with the family alone, have transitioned to a minimum of a shared responsibility between the home and school. According to Stein and Thorkildsen (1999) in Turner (2000, p.37), the expectation in the roles of schools is vast: "Not only are schools expected to provide academic instruction to America's children, they also feed, socialize, counsel, supervise, and even baby-sit them. Schools are often called upon to provide public entertainment, information, and other services to the community."

This chapter examines the issues behind parent communication and involvement in K-12 schools. While countless research describes parental involvement as having a positive impact on academic achievement, increased self-esteem, and improved behavior (see, for example, Mapp, 1997; USDE, 1996), the actual involvement is quite low. The obstacles to effective parental communication and involvement are explored, and research-based guidelines for positive communication are identified. This chapter includes real life accounts of difficulties and applications of effective programs that are occurring all over the nation at every grade level. In this chapter, it is shown how all elements of the system combine to bridge the gap in parent and family involvement in schools.

OBSTACLES: THE ACTIONS OF ONE AFFECT MANY

Teachers can relate stories about intrusive and horrific incidents with parents. Parents recall their own negative memories that involve unresponsive or hurtful actions by teachers. In these situations the teacher will recall a parent who was particularly inappropriate, demanding, or out of control. The parent will relate the stories of one teacher who was neglectful, enforced unbearable rules, or was completely unfair. For example, one teacher recalled a difficult parent situation that involved a parent accusing her of inequity in the classroom and wanted more attention focused solely on her child. Her child was bright and the teacher was spending too much time working with the kids who were slow. The teacher listened to the parent's complaints, took notes, and verbally identified areas where the curriculum was individualized. She also explained that her course of action would be to assess the student again and plan for more individualized assignments. The teacher evaluated the student again and designed further individual assignments that addressed the student's strengths and interests. Individualized assignments, opportunities for inquiry learning, and performance assessments did not satisfy the parent's need for her daughter to have the spotlight. This came to a head when the parent burst into the classroom and berated the teacher in front of the entire class. When the ordeal, which included meetings with the principal, was over, the teacher proclaimed emphatically, "I do not want parents in my room any more."

Parents also have scars from teacher confrontations. The parent of a student with a learning disability related the following:

> From now on I keep my mouth shut at parent teacher conferences. I cannot jeopardize my child's learning by asking questions or pursuing his goals on the IEP (Individualized Education Plan). Two years ago my son needed classroom accommodations in order to succeed. One of the things he needed was to be seated near the chalkboard. At Open House I noticed that his desk was toward the back and faced away from the board. In private I politely asked the teacher for his seat to be moved so that he had better access to the board. Her reply was that all children need access to the board and he will get there when she rotates the seating chart. As the year progressed it was obvious that none of his accommodations were being provided. I approached on three more occasions, twice in a very quiet and polite manner. I also explained that I expected him to give his best effort every day and to be respectful and well behaved. She agreed that he was a hard worker and didn't give her any "trouble" but when I asked about meeting the accommodations, both times I was met with curt replies that did not address my son's needs. When he brought home a failing grade on a math quiz because he copied the problems wrong from the board, I had had enough. I explained that the IEP needed to be followed so that my son could learn and that this was an unfair grade. The teacher exploded, accusing me of trying to give my son an unfair advantage and

questioning her professional judgment. After that my son started to receive progress reports for bad behavior, his effort grades dropped, and he began to hate school. I pressed hard on him at first for not being respectful—I was shocked at this behavior. His answer was "She hates me now. Don't talk to her anymore." At the spring conference I expressed my concern about this radical change in behavior. The teacher again was curt: she informed me that my child was disrespectful, unwilling to try anything, and lazy. She wondered what we were doing at home to support such unacceptable behavior. I crawled out of that conference in tears. It wasn't until I started asking for progress reports from his scout leader, religion teacher, and coaches that I realized that my child hadn't become this awful boy the teacher insinuated. Without exception my son was described as extremely hard working, respectful, and kind. Driving home from baseball practice one afternoon I was listening to my son and his friend and classmate talk. The friend was saying "Just don't talk at all, she always gets mad at you if you ask any questions. She hates you, so keep your mouth shut." I counted the days until that year was over. Since then I have found my son tutors, learned how to apply accommodations at home and prayed everyday that his teachers won't ridicule him. I also take the advice of my son's friend. I keep my mouth shut. (Barbara)

These stories are not uncommon. They also play on emotions so strongly that it is almost makes sense to stop the interactions between parents and teachers. Yet in both of these scenarios we can realize several important points: First, it was just one parent, or one teacher. Neither of these individuals represents the entire parent or teacher population. Second, there were other alternatives that could have been explored. Questions arise in the first scenario, such as, why was the parent allowed to barge into the room? Were the unrealistic expectations shared with the principal or other staff that could have assisted the teacher? What is actually happening with the child? In the second scenario questions include – what role is the special educator playing? Does the general education teacher realize her role in the IEP? Has the parent expressed concerns to the special educator or principal?

Most importantly, it is critical to realize that these are two *individual* cases. If policy regarding parental involvement in the school or with the IEP process is decided based on one case, then the system is broken. The questions asked in probing for reasons and alternative outcomes all involve other elements of the system, as well as the role that the parents and teachers have within the system. These are two very powerful groups in the education of the future. It would be negligent to dismiss the potential power in collaboration. Yet the impetus for miscommunication is prevalent.

DISHEARTENING RESEARCH RESULTS

Research indicates that parents, students, and teachers all agree that parental involvement is vital, yet the actual participation level is low (Turner, 2000). While teachers perceived that parents are not involved due to apathy or lack of interest, research has identified that factors such as school bureaucracy, time, cultural misunderstandings, and health are preventing parents from being involved (Leitch & Tangri, 1988).

Involvement in schools also is affected by the age of the students. According to the U.S. Department of Education, 33 percent of parents of first grade children serve as volunteers in the schools. By the time students reach the middle school, only 8 percent of parents volunteer (Shinn, 2002). This is correlated with the level of positive school interactions. In the eighth grade the percent of positive interactions drops to 36 percent. In the first grade the percentage was 52 percent. Shinn notes a caveat to these statistics, stating that that likelihood of parental involvement increased when parents were given consistent and effective communication. That is a profound caveat given the significant drop in participation and positive interactions.

While the obstacles to successful parent involvement are clear, so is the necessity for this interaction. Parents are their children's first teachers and have a very powerful role in how the student views school, prepares for school, and achieves. While there will always be parents like the one noted in the example above, the vast majority of parents want to work with their children and the school to promote success. This is true not just in the middle and upper class school districts. When parents are asked to be involved AND are given explanations as to how to be involved, the response can be overwhelming.

AN ENCOURAGING APPLICATION

Guastello (2004) has had such an experience. Concerned with the focus of the No Child Left Behind Act (NCLB) on classroom reform, Guastello and her colleagues set out to promote "No Parent Left Behind" to ensure that parents were included significantly in the reform process. The NCLB indicates parental involvement as a stronghold for success. Overcoming the misperceptions regarding universal parental involvement must be part of this process. Traditionally, parents in urban, low socioeconomic school districts were perceived to be apathetic in regard to school involvement (Pong, 1997). Guastello and a colleague decided to address this issue through joining the local community in efforts to address the goals of NCLB. Targeting ten small K-8 New York City Public Schools with low income, multiethnic populations, the Training Innovative Educators (TIE) program, set out to improve math and literacy instruction and achievement. This effort was funded through the NCLB and involved parents as an integral part of the reform process.

The literacy improvement plan began to involve parents by sending personalized invitations to attend an evening orientation. An impressive 85 percent of parents attended. Parents responded to a questionnaire that asked about student attitude toward writing, parent understanding of the writing process, and state standards. The media has covered the intense focus on standards-based assessments and the political weight of the state standardized tests very well. Parents read and hear about the importance of and judgments made from such testing. There has been less information for parents regarding exactly what the standards are and how they relate to their child's learning and everyday assignments. From the survey, Guastello and her group learned that 95 percent of parents wanted more information about how writing was taught, what the standards were, how work was assessed, and most importantly how they could assist their child to develop as writers. This information was shared with teachers and administrators. The involvement of parents continued throughout the year, with four workshops that described the standards and school expectations, the writing process, writing assessment, and the use of computer programs to motivate children to write. When the survey was administered again at the end of the school year, these districts saw promising results. Students were beginning to generate ideas for writing at home and follow through with revisions of writing through a guiding question format. Ninety percent of parents indicated that they were more confident in interacting with their children concerning writing (Guastello, 2004, p. 82). Guastello concludes with this profound statement:

> To actively participate in their child's literacy learning, parents need to understand how the school's literacy program works. Response to the parent survey and the high rate of attendance at the parent workshops dispel the myth that parents in urban districts do not want to get involved with their child's learning experiences. The village clearly wants to know how it can help its children in the learning process. If schools and students invite parents, they will come (p. 83).

Guastello (2004) provided encouraging results in traditionally non-participative environments. The literacy project described is just one avenue for parental involvement. Holding sessions at night, sending personalized invitations, listening to parental concerns and questions, and then following up with information and learning opportunities allowed for this project to be successful.

This case study exemplifies the analysis conducted by Stein and Thorkildsen (1999). These authors reviewed an abundance of research concerning parental involvement and success. Their conclusions indicate a "moderate positive relationship" between parental involvement and student achievement.

Possibly most important, parents' expectations of their children's academic achievement have the strongest positive relationship with children's actual level of achievements, a finding that is pervasive. Expectations should be set high early in a child's schooling. Furthermore, communication systems between schools and parents need to be clear, structured, and consistent. Parents tend to participate more if they are involved in planning parent involvement programs, and parents can be more helpful if they know details about instructional programs in which are engaged at school (p. 34)

CREATING A SCHOOL COMMUNITY

Schools need to create an inclusive environment that invites parents to be involved in specific and consistent ways. Community building is essential to fostering a sense of trust. When students enter a school building, they need to realize their bonds to the people within the school. They also need to realize that the school is connected to their home. It is the fundamental needs of physical and emotional safety, as well as a sense of belongingness and autonomy that shapes human motivation (Schaps, 2003). The strength of this sense of community has academic, as well as social effects.

> When a school meets students' basic psychological needs, students become increasingly committed to the school's norms, values, and goals. And by enlisting students in maintaining that sense of community, the school provides opportunities for students to learn skills and develop habits that will benefit them throughout their whole lives (Schaps, p. 34).

Few schools are well equipped to provide a strong sense of community. Schools that may exhibit the strongest needs, such as low-income schools and those with large minority populations, have a lower sense of community compared to affluent schools with majority populations (Battistich, Solomon, Kim, Watson, & Schaps, 1995). While this is discouraging, the solutions for strengthening a sense of community are practical. Schaps (2003) identifies four coherent strategies to do so. The integral connection to parents is visible and interwoven:

1. Actively cultivate respectful, supportive relationships among students, teachers, and parents;
2. Emphasize common purposes and ideals (for example, fairness and personal responsibility);
3. Provide regular opportunities for service and cooperation; and
4. Provide developmentally appropriate opportunities for autonomy and influence.

Some practical applications of these ideals include class meetings run at least in part by the students, a buddies programs to connect older and younger students within a building, or "homeside activities [which] are short conversational activities for students and parents or other caregivers to do at home once or twice a month . . . mostly interviews conducted by students with their parents, link school learning with home experiences and perspectives" (Schaps, p. 33).

Trust in school communities has been identified as a critical component for school reform, effective communication, and increased achievement. Meier (1995), in her book *The Power of Their Ideas: Lessons for America From a Small School in Harlem,* argued that building trust among teachers, school leaders, students and parents was a key component of the success of the middle school [that was created in Harlem] (Bryk and Schneider, 2003 p. 41). Bryk and Schneider, who conducted almost a decade of research and analysis on social trust, documented the influence that trust has in school reform. These authors noted the need for all role relationships, between teachers, students, parents, and administrators, to be agreed upon in terms of expectations and personal obligations. They collected data from over 400 Chicago schools and spent over four years in 12 school communities. From their longitudinal analysis and case study approach, these researchers identified four considerations that emerge when individuals are trying to discern the intentions of others (parents of teachers, teachers of principals, etc.) to establish and maintain relational trust in the school community. These included respect, personal regard, competence in core role responsibilities, and personal integrity. According to Byrk and Schneider, respect includes genuine listening and valuing others' opinions, even through disagreements. Personal regard refers to the individuals' abilities to go the extra mile, perhaps beyond literal interpretations of job descriptions. Competence in core responsibilities indicates the desire for the interactions between school community members to have the desired results. This can only happen when each individual has aptitude and confidence in his or her role. Personal integrity asks the question, "Will individuals keep their word and will they keep a moral-ethical perspective?" When school communities exhibit strong relational trust, then reform processes are more likely to have buy-in and individual responsibility to do the work required to make the changes. While this type of effective relationship promotes pride in schools, and a strong sense of a connected community, it also relates to academic improvement. Byrk and Schneider reported that schools with a high relational trust score demonstrate an average of eight percent improvement in reading and 20 percent increase in math. Those schools with a low relational trust score demonstrated declines in reading and virtually no change in math. A significant concern was demonstrated in the analysis of data, which indicated that schools with chronically low relational trust scores had nearly no chance for improvement in reading or math. The academic scores in these schools remained low throughout the course of this longitudinal study. These researchers' findings underscore the critical need for schools to build trusting communities. This cannot happen with one parent conference day or a single parent orientation night. Rather trust is developed over time through continued interactions. The leaders of the school have a strong and vital role in promoting cooperative opportunities and in supporting teachers in developing relational trust with parents. The academic improvements and the positive social emotional effects of a strong school community make the need for relational trust a critical factor in school reform.

WORKING TOGETHER ON COMMON GROUND

Often controversial issues may impede the building of trust and community commitment among stakeholders. Difficult topics have included the extent of religion in schools, AID/HIV curriculum, and sex education. Controversial topics are often fueled by extreme right and left wing agencies that tend to intensify the conflict rather than search for peaceful and community wide acceptable solutions. Jacobsen (2000) offers an alternative approach that has the potential to encourage cooperative thinking and working, while acknowledging personal differences.

Common ground thinking serves to provide a framework for people on different sides of an issue to work together. Whether the differences lie between parents and teachers, parents and parents, school officials and the community, this process does not seek a resolution to the issue. Jacobsen (2000) identified five things that common ground thinking accomplishes:

1. Common ground thinking removes educators from arbitrating social conflicts;
2. Common ground thinking helps people appreciate and apply religious neutrality;
3. Common ground thinking switches the dialogue from what I want for my child to what is fair for all children, including mine;
4. Common ground thinking eliminates confusion, suspicion, and anger generated by advocacy groups; and
5. Common ground thinking recognizes the priority of the family in faith and values (p.78).

Modesto City Schools in central California employed common ground thinking when this vast school district ran into difficulties as it attempted to create new policies regarding discrimination and harassment free environments. The inclusion of sexual orientation as a descriptor for tolerance erupted in parental outcries that accused the district of promoting homosexuality in the schools. There was bitter fighting on all sides. The district committee, composed of teachers, administrators, parents, and community members, was all but defunct. Then Modesto Schools received training in common ground thinking and applied its principles successfully. The superintendent of the schools reported the success in the project when he explained the following:

> Everyone agreed that no student should be harassed or discriminated against in a public school—whatever his or her race, religion, gender or sexual orientation. And just as important, everyone acknowledged that such agreement doesn't require "acceptance" of the religion, philosophy or lifestyle of others (Jacobsen, 1999, p.77).

The Modesto Schools followed these steps to completion:

1. Face issues head on;
2. Invite all stakeholders;
3. Get training;
4. Formulate and approve policy; and

5. Train staff and the community to understand the process.

This school district faced head on what other districts have been trying to circumvent for some time. Ironically, the success of their approach was NOT trying to solve the controversy. Finding common ground on controversial issues is practically an oxymoron. The district created a safe environment for discussion and found success not through unanimous agreement, but rather through learning how to live and learn among one another despite differences. Parents played significant roles throughout the process and were able to have a stronghold in crafting the final documents for the new policies.

These exciting examples demonstrate the possibilities that strong and consistent communication allows. They indicate the roles that different members of a school community can have and most significantly the roles that parents can embrace. Jacobsen (1999) concluded his argument for common ground thinking by commenting "If public education is to survive into the next millennium, we will have to take seriously the role of parents" (p. 80). Parents can connect with schools through taking substantial roles in the pursuit of these lofty goals.

THE POWER OF THE ONE TO ONE CONNECTION: SAMANTHA'S STORY

Parents may also develop connections with schools beginning with one to one relationships. Students, who have opportunities to witness the connection between their parents and teachers, benefit from the understanding that this is a working relationship. This is helpful when students are struggling. No longer is the "My teacher said I don't have to," or "My Mom said just to do it this way" a viable argument. Teachers and parents who communicate regularly are aware of processes for home and schoolwork. Behavior becomes more accountable and the red flags that may get raised are examined carefully and thoroughly. Such was the case with Samantha.

Samantha was young for first grade. With a November birthday and short stature, she often looked more like a kindergarten child than a first grader. Yet, as soon as she spoke it was clear that Samantha had a vibrant personality and much to say on any given topic. Samantha was polite, helpful, and never afraid to ask questions. Samantha asked a lot of questions, often the same ones over and over. As the fall progressed and first grade students became accustomed to the workload and routine, Samantha continued to struggle to complete assignments and understand the components of language. She was often exhausted at the end of the day, and complained of a headache. Samantha's mother was a regular volunteer in the classroom and witnessed her daughter's struggles both in and out of school. The classroom teacher and mother spoke often about Samantha, both in her determination and her lack of progress. Samantha began a Title One Reading Program, in hopes that small group and remediation would assist her. Her progress was inconsistent. The classroom teacher employed many individualized techniques and the parents worked diligently at home to reinforce basic skills. Samantha never gave up. In January, the parents and teacher met again formally to discuss Samantha's continued difficulties. At this time Samantha was also suffering from acute and chronic asthma. The winter was difficult on her physically and the parents thought any kind of change in program would be too much at this point. The teacher agreed. In early March Samantha, though feeling better physically, began to run out of steam. The work was too difficult in all subjects. She would know something one day and not the next. Her short-term memory difficulties were becoming more prominent as the reading process continued to be very slow and labored. Samantha's teacher suggested that now was the time for formal testing and the mother agreed. The mother had great concerns that Samantha was losing ground. She wasn't sleeping well and appeared to have a continual feeling of being overwhelmed. She was also concerned that Samantha would think that she did something wrong if they told her she would be tested. The teacher and mother decided to approach Samantha together, and explain the process. A "lunch date" was set and Samantha and her mother ate lunch in the classroom with the teacher (a huge honor in this class of young students). The teacher explained how she and Samantha's mother had important jobs of teaching Samantha and trying to find the best ways for Samantha to learn. The teacher identified

some of the class and home activities they used. She then told
Samantha that some of these ways weren't working because
school was too hard and learning was too difficult. Samantha's
mother agreed reminding Sam of the long nights of homework
and frustrations in trying to read. The teacher explained how as
the teacher and mother, they needed to work together with other
important people to find the ways that Samantha learned best.
She then explained the testing process. Samantha's mother supported the teacher and reinforced the critical idea that they were
all working together to help Samantha. Samantha was asked
throughout this meeting if she had questions or if she wanted to
say anything. She only nodded or shook her head. When the
teacher was done explaining, Samantha put her head in her
mother's lap. She said nothing for a long time. Both the mother
and teacher filled with tears, but quickly tried to continue.
Samantha then took her mother's hand and looked into her
teacher's eyes and said slowly and clearly "thank you." She
hugged her teacher and began to cry. This six-year-old girl fully
understood the power of parents and teachers working together
and was grateful that her struggles would be in the hands of
adults who loved her and wanted her to succeed.

Today Samantha, who is classified with a language processing
disorder, is entering high school. She has succeeded with the assistance of competent special education teachers, general education
teachers, tutors, and most significantly her parents and her own
determination. While each of these relationships was not equally
strong, Samantha learned a valuable lesson early in her learning
career: parents and teachers are a powerful force when working
together.

The parents and teacher in this situation did not set out to
change policy or begin a new program. While those things are important, so is the student who is in front of the teacher and parent
today. Instead these adults communicated consistently and sought
to find solutions for the common goal—educating Samantha.
Teachers and parents are working together in this kind of format
every day. Often these stories go untold, and instead we hear about
what is wrong with the school or what is wrong with the parents.
When we choose to nurture the parent teacher relationship and
when this is genuinely supported and commended by school lead-

ers, the potential of this critical connection can be realized and students can reap the benefits.

HOW CAN TEACHERS INVOLVE PARENTS AND REMAIN SANE?

Many teachers want the support and assistance of parents but are not sure how to achieve this without giving up control or inviting onlookers with the potential to gossip about and or criticize the activities and interactions in the classroom. Teachers of young students often fear the overbearing parent or the one who wants to "check up on" his or her child. Yet, at the same time, early childhood education is exhausting and requires the help of several hands. Teachers would be able to work much more one on one and in small groups if parent volunteers were teaching and supervising educational games or assisting with art aspects of the projects. How can an elementary teacher strike the right balance for parental involvement without creating more work?

At the other end of the spectrum are high school teachers who rarely see parents at all, and then the contact is often through rushed parent conferences. At some schools the policy is for the parents to follow their student's schedule, which allows about four minutes per teacher. Clearly this policy does not acknowledge the need to build relational trust. Schools put forth the image of assembly line connections that do little to foster true communication. At the same time, research on parental involvement indicates that parents of adolescence back away too soon as they attempt to allow their children to assert independence (Shinn, 2002).

PROMISING EXAMPLES FOR PARENTAL COMMUNICATION AND INVOLVEMENT

The following models are highlighted in an effort to demonstrate the myriad of ways that school districts and teachers can begin to invite parents into the learning process and view parents as a vital force within the educational system. These are not lofty goals, rather the real life applications of some encouraging initiatives. Many teachers, parents, and administrators have found creative uses of time and methods of communication.

An Evening Club

One such example occurred at an elementary school that was concerned with test scores on the latest state exams. As these scores are published in the newspaper and were used to make judgments on both student and teacher performance, the data was viewed by the whole community and interpreted in a variety of negative and finger pointing ways. Instead of entering into a defensive battle about test results, one teacher devised a plan that would begin to look at solutions and involve parents and students in interactive learning activities. This teacher created an evening club that centered on math and science. The club was open to all students in upper elementary grades AND their parents. The club was run in the evening so that parents had a better opportunity to attend. In addition, this allowed the teacher, who was also a mother, to take her own children to after school activities and return for the club in the evening hours. It became a family event. The club ran for two months and met once a week. The activities were hands on and cooperative, with a friendly competition built into the culminating activities. The teacher demonstrated a commitment to learning and parental involvement. She did not claim the ability to raise test scores and transform the school district. Rather she found one way where she could apply her talents and strongest skills and make a difference in an issue facing her school and community. Parents witnessed a dedicated professional and were given opportunities to participate in their children's education. While the club ran for a short amount of time, the premise of the club had a big impact.

Classroom Visits

High school teachers have a difficult task of recruiting parents into their schools. There are many dynamics in this scenario, including the research cited previously that parents are encouraging adolescents to act independently at an early age. What kinds of interactions are appropriate for high school parents and teachers? How can this relationship be built so that all can benefit? Shinn, who has conducted much research on parental involvement, explained her own classroom approach, entitled "Visit Physics" (Shinn, 2002). As a high school physics teacher, Shinn had her students send personal invitations to their parents on the first day of school. She asked parents to choose a few tentative dates to come into the classroom. A monthly calendar assisted parents in choosing dates; most arrived for activity days. Parents took part in data collection, lab exercises, and calculations. Some chose to observe and ask questions of their own children. Parents came at different times and stayed for different intervals.

While some parents may not be able to stay at school for long periods, many are able to find an hour when the dates can be flexible. Providing an ongoing element of parental involvement allowed for accommodations to several schedules and meaningful interchanges between students, parents, and the teacher. Many teachers hold special events that invite parents for a night to culminate the event. These are also ways to bridge communication. The unique and hopeful aspect of Shinn's approach is in the way that parental involvement became an integral and seamless component of the student's education—and in an unlikely place—a high school physics class.

Action Team Model

The following list of family interactions with schools stems from the work done by the National Network of Partnership Schools at Johns Hopkins University (Epstein & Salinas, 2004). Through this network, over 1,000 schools in the last eight years have developed and implemented partnership programs involving the school, family, and community. This has all been accomplished while working with researchers from Johns Hopkins University. The framework for successful practice in building a school learning community begins with an action team, comprised of teachers, parents, administrators, and community partners. The action team joins the school improvement team (or school council) and "writes annual plans for family and community involvement, implements and evaluates activities, and integrates the activities conducted by other groups and individual teachers into a comprehensive partnership program for the school" (p.12).

This model allows for a variety of sustained relationships with all of the stakeholders. The team applies a research-based framework that addresses six types of involvement. These include parenting, communicating, volunteering, learning at home, decision making, and collaborating with the community (see Table 1 for explanation). When schools devise and implement activities for all six categories they are able to address a variety of family needs and schedules and allow for participation in a myriad of ways.

The following examples are occurring in schools across the nation in urban, suburban and rural school districts (Epstein & Salinas, 2004):

- Madison Junior High in Naperville, Illinois incorporated all six types of family involvements that are connected to goals in the student improvement plan. Some of these activities include family literacy nights, honor role breakfasts, evening discussions on adolescence and effective parenting strategies, building connections with business partners, creating databases for volunteers, and publishing newsletters for weekly information;
- The Second Cup of Coffee program was established in Roosevelt Elementary School in St. Paul Minnesota. This monthly event invited parents to meet with teachers and administrators;
- Many schools within the National Network of Partnership schools involve the parents and community in focusing on achievement. Reading, writing, and math programs that integrate parents into the plan are common among these schools. Some of these programs are geared toward the state exams, such as the math workshop series in Thurmont, Maryland. Monthly evening meetings were held with parents, teachers, and students to assess math achievement and provide lessons and materials to address the state exams;
- Homework is addressed through creative uses of involvement in many of the National Network of Partnership Schools. Teachers Involve Parents (TIPS) changes the view of homework into an interactive activity that extends the learning outside of school. It allows elementary and middle school students to share what

they are learning with an adult and understand the process to be connected to school, family, and community (Epstein, J, Salinas, & Van Voorhis, 2001);

- Transitions to college and the workforce are addressed by assisting students in formulating their goals and then understanding the academic needs to achieve those goals. For example, school districts in Los Angeles have developed the Go On To College (GOT) program. The GOT program explains aspects of postsecondary education starting in the middle school years. GOT guides students and families in visiting colleges and planning for the academic and financial requirements.

These schools also work with many partners within the community to expand student learning. For example, the program, "Try it At Lunch" that was developed in the Good Shepherd School in Peace River, Alberta, asked community fitness instructors to volunteer during lunch hour and teach students new types of fitness. Classes have included tai chi, tae kwon do, and hip-hop dance. Another example of community relationships occurred in Canton, Ohio, where medical center volunteers provided health care information, presentations, healthy snacks, and medical testing to the elementary students and families. The students provided community service by creating art displays and giving performances at local hospital events.

These highlights demonstrate the possibilities of effective collaboration and indicate the positive effects that the connections have on student learning. While many schools demonstrate aspects of these activities, the schools involved in the National Network of Partnership Schools have certain advantages. They are: organized; linked to school specific goals; and have sustainable partnerships (Epstein & Salinas, 2004). For more information about this network, see the World Wide Web at partnershipschools.org.

Table 1 outlines six types of parental involvement (Epstein et al., 2002).

TABLE 6.1: Six Types of Involvement

Parenting	Assist families with parenting skills, family support, understanding child and adolescent development, and setting home conditions to support learning at each grade level. Assist schools in understanding families' backgrounds, cultures, and goals for children.
Communi-cating	Communicate with families about school programs and student progress. Create two-way communication channels between school and home.
Volunteering	Improve recruitment, training, activities, and schedules to involve families as volunteers and as audiences at the school or in other locations. Enable educators to work with volunteers who support students and the school.
Learning at home	Involve families with their children in academic learning at home, including homework, goal setting, and other curriculum-related activities. Encourage teachers to design homework that enables students to share and discuss interesting tasks.
Decision Making	Include families as participants in school decisions, governance, and advocacy activities through school councils or improvement teams, committees, and parent organizations.

Parent/Teacher Conferences

Of course, one of the most intimate connections between parents and teachers can occur during the traditional parent/teacher conferences. These meetings have the potential for forming and solidifying bonds or for destroying the possibilities of connection. Such a powerful face-to-face experience must be met with preparation and commitment to a collaborative atmosphere. This is a critical time for teachers to take steps to invite the parents into the learning collaboration in a formal and directed manner. Many parents arrive at these conferences with one burning question "Is my child okay?" This is true whether the child is six or sixteen. Teachers must communicate an enormous amount of information in a very short time (usually 15-20 minutes) while attempting to answer this ambiguous question the parents pose. This task is often overwhelming for the educator. At times much information is given to parents who are anxious and unsure. It is difficult for them to absorb the teacher comments. The meeting is rushed, and though polite, it often remains in a purely information giving mode. Implementation of the following suggestions for teachers can serve to open communication and assure that all the information is disseminated:

- Begin with a positive (and truthful) statement about the student. Parents need to be assured that the teacher really knows their child and sees positive qualities. It is much easier to discuss difficulties *after* the positive statements have been made. This simple rule also allows for parents to relax and attend to the information that will follow;
  a. Be over prepared
  b. Have a written plan
  c. Show student work
  d. Highlight aspects of the work to demonstrate student strengths and weaknesses
- Speak with confidence about the specifics of each student's progress—address content areas in elementary grades and topic areas in adolescence education;
- Highlight specific work to illustrate student progress/growth/accomplishments;
- Identify areas of need and point to specific work as evidence;
- Clearly explain how these needs will be addressed within the classroom and school (review sessions, more practice time, alternative approach, after school help etc.). Identify how strengths will be used to address areas of weakness or how enrichment opportunities can build on student strengths;
- Give the parents specific tasks to coordinate with this plan (reading at home and asking a set of questions, playing educational games, reading college prep books,

providing quiet space in the home, encouraging attendance at review sessions);

- Provide a copy of notes and plans from this conference.
This allows parents to listen attentively without the
worry they may forget an aspect. It also identifies the
teacher's and parents' next steps for addressing the student's needs;

- Ask parents if they have questions. If the response is
no, acknowledge ways to answer questions that may
arise after the conclusion of the meeting;

- Thank parents for attending. Some parents may have
had negative school experiences that impact their view
of school; others may not know how to be involved, etc.
The teacher can provide a strong positive message that
values the collaborative efforts between teachers and
parents;

- Identify how the communication will proceed after the
parent teacher conference and adhere to these guidelines; and

- Follow up. If plans included collaboration with other
members of the school and larger systems, be sure to
follow these promptly. Keep parents informed as to the
changes and progress that has been made.

LOGISTICS OF PARENT PARTNERSHIPS

The research base for the effectiveness of parent involvement
from both the academic and social emotional perspectives has been
described. It is clear that families who feel connected to their
school view education and day-to-day learning activities in a positive light. Promising exemplars of schools and communities that
have found ways to partner and share resources, all for the benefit
of the students, have been explained. The question now is, how
does one teacher, or one school, or one district, get started in the
change process toward more positive family and school communication and involvement? There are many answers to this question.
Consistent with the systems approach, schools must look at their

goals and visions and either refine them to include family in- volvement or enhance their practices to align with the family in- volvement goals. Districts need to incorporate broad based plans that are sustained throughout the year and that support the school administrators and faculty at every level. It makes sense that the parent involvement programs at the high school level would func- tion very differently than the programs at the elementary level. Each set of plans needs to address the particular population while simultaneously being connected to the master district plans for family involvement.

Table 2 reflects best practice in family involvement. It includes both the "big ideas" and routine activities that focus on communi- cation. These are partial lists, intended to facilitate the brainstorm- ing process in an individual school or district. It is critical to real- ize that each of these ideas will require support from many levels of the system. Some of these activities require the classroom teacher to be and encouraged to initiate and sustain family com- munication. Other of these ideas will require support from staff and administrators. For example, weekly homework nights can be handled logistically in a variety of ways. Some teachers may want to rotate, others may wish to be in charge, and principals, assistant principals, and district coordinators can also be part of the rotation. This list often requires evening events. This is a model that many teachers have avoided since they give so much during the day. It is critical though, that districts look at a

TABLE 6.2: Examples of Best Practice for Parental Involvement

Elementary School	Middle School	High School
Literacy Nights— students sharing their own work and ask for parent feedback. Parents begin to take part in the writing process	A Time To Talk—a night where students share what they really want to say regarding school- work and home- work. Facilitated	Transition Prepara- tion—a four year program where par- ents and teens attend workshops together as teens make deci- sions regarding fu- ture

	small group discussions followed by reports to the whole group and dessert	
Parents as—once a week, once a year, in their child's classroom, art room, playground, other grades etc. Parents fill out a questionnaire describing their abilities, talents and time available—a master parent involvement calendar is made that allows parent involvement to be maximized	School Newspaper with a parent communication section—parents can contribute and adolescents can address family topics	School and Grade level Website—containing both static and interactive elements—parents can find relevant information and ask questions pertaining to the events of the particular year
Bring Your Work to your Child—invite parents to explain their careers to class or small group (allows parents to demonstrate involvement through a one time activity)	Bring Your Work to Your Child—similar concept as elementary. At this level the parent can be placed in the area that best aligns with the career (computer lab, English class etc.)	Job Shadowing: Ask parents to allow interested teens to shadow them at their workplace—this can be the parent's own child and/or other interested students
Classroom Websites—contains reminders of important dates, book reviews, home-	Drama and Theater Club: Invite parents to be a part of this experience by work-	Drama and Theater Club: Invite parents to be a part of this experience by working on scenery, help-

work tips and an area for parent questions. Teacher indicates turn around time for questions	ing on scenery, helping students learn lines and songs, or assisting with homework during down times, or adding a helping hand in final event	ing students learn lines and songs, or assisting with homework during down times, or adding a helping hand in final event
First Response Hotline: in both telephone and internet form: Give parents access to immediate feedback regarding questions they have. Encourage parents to address their thoughts here and question what they "heard" about the district, testing, homework or any school rumors. Publish district responses in monthly newsletter and on website	First Response Hotline: in both telephone and internet form: Give parents access to immediate feedback regarding questions they have. Encourage parents to address their thoughts here and question what they "heard" about the district, testing, homework or any school rumors. Publish district responses in monthly newsletter and on website	First Response Hotline: in both telephone and internet form: Give parents access to immediate feedback regarding questions they have. Encourage parents to address their thoughts here and question what they "heard" about the district, testing, homework or any school rumors. Publish district responses in monthly newsletter and on website
Invite parents who cannot come to school, to participate from home by helping make educational games, typing children's stories, making	How to study Workshops: Invite parents and students to evening workshops that teach study skills and address the family dy-	College Field Trips: Hold workshops about how to look for the right college for your child. Conduct family field trips to local colleges and highlight

costumes etc.	namics regarding homework and study habits. (Provide food)	the aspects to look for and compare with others.
How Do I Help My Child Learn to Read/ Write/Do Math? Hold Workshops that address these areas. Add this information to the online Website Resources	Homework Help: Provide Weekly homework Help Nights and invite parents and students to attend together.	All Night Graduation Parties/Prom Night/Senior or Sports Banquets: Provide roles for parents in terms of coordination and planning, chaperoning, and photography. Ask students for input regarding how parents can be involved
Homework Help: Provide Weekly homework Help Nights and invite parents and students to attend together.	After-school Programs: Invite parents to participate as co-advisors with faculty. Encourage parents to share their skills and talents in the afternoon or evening hours	After-school Programs: Invite parents to participate as co-advisors with faculty. Encourage parents to share their skills and talents in the afternoon or evening hours

master plan that addresses parent and family needs. This of course will require many late afternoon, evening, or weekend events. Administrators need to be proactive in their planning and actions when asking teachers to extend their time. Will there be monetary compensation? Can there be flexibility in other parts of the day? There can be creative solutions to issues of equity and commitment. As districts formulate and refine their parent involvement plans, these issues will need to be addressed.

INVOLVING PARENTS OF STUDENTS WITH SPECIAL NEEDS

While districts plan to involve parents in consistent and meaningful ways, certain populations will need different things in forms of communication and practices. Just as parents of kindergarten students will have very different communication needs as those of high school seniors, so too will parents of students with special needs. Currently federal law, the Individuals with Disabilities Education Act (IDEA), dictates parental involvement as an intricate part of the student's education and accommodations. For example, parents must sign consent forms for their child to be tested, parents must be part of the IEP (Individual Education Plan) team, and must sign the IEP before it is put into practice. Everyday practice varies across special education settings in terms of parental communication both on the part of teachers and parents. Blue-Banning, Summers, Frankland, Nelson, and Beegle (2004) conducted intensive research in order to understand what makes for successful collaboration between parents and professionals in the special education settings. Their findings can also be applied to general education settings. Blue-Banning et al. (2004, p.174) found six themes that need to be addressed to guide effective collaboration:

- Communication: The quality of communication is positive, understandable, and respectful among all members at all levels of the partnership. The quantity of communication is also at a level to enable efficient and effective coordination and understanding among all members *(for example, sharing resources, being honest and clear, listening, and communicating frequently;*

- Commitments: The members of the partnership share a sense of assurance about (a) each other's devotion and loyalty to the child and family, and (b) each other's belief in the importance of the goals being pursued on behalf of the child and family *(for example, demonstrating commitment, encouraging the family and child, being consistent, being sensitive to emotions);*

- Equality: The members of the partnership feel a sense of equity in decisions making and service implementation, and actively work to ensure that all other members of the partnership feel equally powerful in their ability to influence outcomes for children and families (*for example, avoiding the use of "clout," empowering partners, advocating for child or family with other professionals, coming to the table/avoiding "turfism"*);

- Skills: Members of the partnership perceive that others on the team demonstrate competence, including service providers' ability to fulfill their roles and to demonstrate "recommended practice" approaches to working with children and families (*for example, taking action, meeting individual special needs, considering whole child or family, being willing to learn*);

- Trust: The members of the partnership share a sense of assurance about the reliability or dependability of the character, ability, strength, or truth of the other members of the partnership (*for example, being reliable, keeping the child safe, being discreet*); and

- Respect: The members of the partnership regard each other with esteem and demonstrate that esteem through actions and communication (*for example, valuing the child, being nonjudgmental, exercising nondiscrimination, and avoiding intrusion*).

This list can be used as a template for all parent communications. Blue-Banning et al. (2004) have identified these themes as the essential framework for effective collaboration. Through analysis of focus groups and extensive interviews, these researchers were able to identify the above traits, and also came to realize an underlying theme of humanity. According to Blue-Banning et al. (2004), "The results of this study underscore the point that common sense and ordinary human decency are at the heart of positive partnerships between families and professionals serving children with disabilities" (p. 181). These sentiments are true of all parental communication, regardless of the age or abilities of the child.

INVOLVING PARENTS WITH CULUTRAL AND LANGUAGE DIFFERENCES

Parents of students who are English language learners (ELL) and/or who come from homes where the primary spoken language is not English, will have particular needs for parent communication and involvement. This is also true for parents who come from culturally different backgrounds. These parents may not understand the nuances in the United States school systems and will need explanations as well as need to feel welcomed and valued (Manning & Lee, 2001). The language and differences between home and school are a challenge for all elements of the system. Parents may not be able to read information sent home in English, or may not be able to understand its meaning. Olsen (1998) highlighted this point by sharing the example of the Chinese father, who having understood the grading system began with an "A", punished his child for receiving an "S" for satisfactory. Teachers may not understand the reason the parent has not been attending school functions and conferences is that he/she cannot read the notices that are sent home in English.

Other differences include listening behaviors, concepts of time, perceptions regarding group work, sharing versus ownership, and competition versus collaboration. These differences reflect the subscription to a different values system, for example collectivist value systems instead of competitive and individualistic value system that are part of the United States (Rothstein-Fisch, Greenfield, and Trumbull, 1999). Manning and Lee (2001) devised a short list of practical applications for involving parents with diverse cultural and linguistic backgrounds:

1. Write personalize rather than general letters to parents;
2. Provide a language translator for parents who have difficulties with English; or, when sending communication, attach a translated version;
3. Ask parents to loan materials (signs, pictures, and artifacts), that reflect the unique cultural heritages and customs, to the classroom;

4. Express a genuine interest in learning about and respecting parents' different backgrounds;
5. Provide parent education programs conducted in parents' native languages, and focus on culturally relevant
   issues;
6. Invite parents to serve on school advisory councils to
   represent cultural perspectives; and
7. Consider language proficiency when hiring school office staff in an attempt to have as many languages as
   possible available when parents contact the school (p.
   163).

Advances in technology allow teachers to translate letters into
a variety of languages with just a few clicks on the Internet or
through translation software programs. These suggestions are not a
"to do" list for teachers. This list incorporates many elements of
the system and underscores trust, honor, and respect. If implemented properly these steps would lead in part to the building of
relational trust. Information is key in communication. Many parents of diverse cultures are not plugged into the traditional parent
networks, such as the Parent Teacher Association (PTA) or even
carpooling and after school activities. Faculty and administration
need to look for alternative pathways to infuse academic information and remember that if parents are not visible at meetings and
school functions it does not mean that they are not involved. Many
barriers limit the parent contact with the school, but do not limit
their ability to stress the importance of education in the home (Yonezawa and Oakes, 1999). School districts need to identify the factors that hinder the information and communication flow with
families of diverse backgrounds. These impediments may include
immigrant status, language barriers, skepticism regarding school
officials, realization of inequity in the educational system, permit
status, and single parenthood (Yonezawa and Oakes). Once the
barriers are identified, then the first steps can be taken to address
the communication gaps.

THE ROLE OF GOVERNMENT

In the past two decades federal government has underscored the importance of parental communication through passing legislation that mandates improved practices. For example, in the Goals 2000: Educate America Act signed by President Clinton, one of the national education goals was for parental and family participation (Riley, 1994). The No Child Left Behind Act (NCLB) signed into law by President George W. Bush in 2002 includes over 40 provisions that demand school-parent communication (Blaschke, 2003). Regardless of the political party, parent communication has risen to the forefront in priority for educational reform. The impetus for improved communication is coming from the highest level in the system. Therefore, there is more likelihood for the actions by school faculty toward parental involvement to be supported and creative solutions to be welcomed and honored. The interest in parent communication at the federal level provides many interesting opportunities for communities, school districts, principals, and faculty. While the latest legislation includes a plethora of mandates, it, along with the previous legislation, has potential for support in new and refined parent programs. Educators and administrators will need to address the complexities of a variety of standards and testing driven provisions. It makes sense that schools take advantage of the potential latitude in this legislation as they explore options for improvement in communication. Federal grants may also support exploration, development, and refinement of parent communication programs and procedures.

SIMPLE STEPS FORWARD

This chapter has identified many different examples of innovative ways to communicate with and involve parents in the education process. Many of these exemplars require a district wide commitment and community resources. As more elements of the system are involved in meaningful and consistent ways, the change process for improved parent communication can be sustained. This does not, however, diminish the powerful effects that teachers can have when working one on one with parents. The rules of the game are simple: be positive, be consistent, be honest, and follow through. The power of a positive message is often forgotten when we are driven by test scores and judgments. A parent of a high school junior recently related the effects of positive messages.

> When my daughter was in the second grade her teacher sent me a note the first week of school. It came home in a sealed envelope in her folder. I was so nervous to open it! My daughter had never been in trouble in school and I could not imagine what had happened during the first week. My daughter had no idea either and we were both anxious as I opened the envelope. The teacher had written me a letter relating the positive experiences of the first week. My daughter was very shy, so it meant a lot to read that the teacher recognized this and was proud of my daughter for contributing to class discussions during the first week of school. This letter meant so much to my family, especially my daughter and me. We saved it and I still read it from time to time—and she is sixteen now!

When teachers begin interactions with positive and personal messages, it paves the way toward effective communication. A foundation that accentuates positive communication assists the teacher in future dealings with parents. Parents can listen to teacher concerns and support interactions when they understand that the teacher knows their child and has his or her best interests in mind. As Blue-Banning et al. (2004) remind us, common sense and human decency are the backbone for effective collaboration between teachers and parents.

DISCUSSION QUESTIONS

1. What positive impact does parental involvement have on student achievement?

2. How can a teacher overcome the obstacles to effective parent involvement?

3. Was the parent component of Guastello's Training Innovative Educators project successful? How would you generalize the principles of what was learned in this study to other situations?

4. Using Schapps' strategies, Meier's principles and Epstein's model for strengthening a sense of community within a school, how would you outline a parent involvement protocol of activities to be implemented throughout the school year?

5. How would you apply the tenets of common ground thinking to a problem that exists in your school?

6. How would you use the Blue-Banning et al. "six themes" approach when conducting a parent/teacher conference?

7. In what ways do federal laws, such as NCLB and IDEA, protect and involve parents of children with disabilities, English language learners and other special populations?

8. Do you agree that parents should be partners in the educational process? If so, why? If not, why not?

Chapter 7:
Technology:
The World of Wonder

OBJECTIVES

After studying this chapter, the reader will be able to define, analyze and apply the following concepts and strategies:

1. Basic technology definitions;

2. Obstacles to using technology;
   - Ubiquity;
   - Amplification and leveraging;
   - Ephemerally;
   - Sovereignty;
   - Dehumanization;

3. Staff development tenets;

4. Basic technology skills for students;

5. Best practices for teaching and learning using technology;

6. Digital Divide;

7. Parent/teacher web communication;

8. Assistive technology; and

9. Funding.

OVERVIEW

Web casts, real time, chat rooms, java applets, video streaming, hyperlinks, e-learning, e-conferencing, e-motes, HTML, ISP, IM, VLE, PC, WWW, MLE . . . w, x, y, and z!   The language of technology is fast becoming its own, filled with jargon and colloquies that would scare off the most determined educators. While current students are the information generation, many teachers struggle in a continual catch up pattern trying to understand the latest technology and its applications to education, before the latest becomes the old and out of date. In this fast paced and changing technological world, this catch up game is no easy task. The demands of addressing national and state standards, more diverse students' needs in the general classrooms, and several other agendas vie for the number one spot in an educator's attention, technology and the catch up game often take second or third seat. This is not hard to understand. Teachers with limited time and resources will concentrate on accomplishing those goals that *are* possible. Understanding and applying all of the latest and greatest technologies to the classroom is not often viewed as an attainable goal in a short period of time.

Research indicates the need for intense as well as ongoing training for the proper and appropriate uses of technology (see for example, Tubin and Chen, 2002). Research also tells us that teachers are given the least amount of training for the effective implementation of technology than any other professional field. Computers in the classroom are geared almost exclusively for the students. Teachers have restricted access to almost all technology, including the telephone (Vojtek & Vojtek, 1997). How can this be so, when the focus of our society continues to swell around technologies? Employers demand computer skills and applications more than ever before. Colleges and universities expect students to arrive fully prepared for the applications of technology. Communication is increasingly revolving around computers and the Internet as we try to prepare students for a global society. And yet, the training that is offered to educators is often too little, too late. Teachers are given one shot in-service courses, or half-day workshops with little or no follow up for individual needs and applications. While there are promising examples of how this ineffective model is changing, elements of the system must work together to create effective and systemic change in education and support of teachers and students in technology and its applications. Teachers need to understand the basics. Teachers need to see how technology can be an effective teaching tool, although it is not the teaching itself. Technology has tremendous power; teachers can guide the use of that power through purposeful integration and applications.

In this chapter readers are given the fundamentals of technology and are presented with promising examples of its applications in a variety of educational settings. Technology is here to stay, although its composition is evolving continually. Educators addressing the Internet generation must become competent and comfortable with the teaching tools of technology in order to guide students with the educational experiences associated. Jane M. Healy, who has been involved with educational technology from its inception, has become a cautious critic and urges that "teachers take charge of technology use in their classroom practice . . . to teach children to understand technology and to reflect on its consequence and its relationship to human development" (Tell, 2003, p.12).

THE ABC'S AND HTML'S OF TECHNOLOGY

Understanding the essential components of technology is an important first step to internalizing its uses. This step is often glossed over in order to move on to the important information regarding the uses of technology. Effective educators know the importance of the basics—we teach them. Therefore it is important that we fully understand the foundations of technology in order to teach this to our students and to guide their applications. Internalizing the intricacies of an educational tool allows educators to make reflective decisions regarding when and how to use such tools appropriately. Additional resources for navigating the Internet and definitions can be found on the worldwide web at learnthenet.com/english/glossary/search.html. The following describes some of the basic components and definitions of technology today:

1. Applet: a small software application, typically in the Java programming language.
2. Chat: the way people communicate online in real time. The term "chat" is actually a misnomer. Typically, people in online chat sessions type messages to each other using their keyboards. The message then appears on the screens of all the participants. Chats can involve two or more people.
3. Chat Room: an electronic space, typically a Website or a section of an online service, where people can go to communicate online in real time. Chat rooms are often organized around specific interests, such as small business owners, gardening, etc.
4. Cyberspace: a term coined by science fiction author William Gibson to describe the whole range of information resources available through computer networks.
5. E-mail: short for electronic mail, e-mail consists of messages, often just text, sent from one user to another via a network. E-mail can also be sent automatically to a number of addresses.
6. HTML: an acronym for Hypertext Markup Language, HTML is the computer language used to create hypertext documents. HTML uses a finite list of tags that describe the general structure of various kinds of documents linked together on the World Wide Web.
7. Hypertext: usually refers to any text available on the World Wide Web that contains links to other documents. The use of hypertext is a way of presenting information in which text, sounds, images, and actions are linked together in a way that allows you to jump around between them in whatever order you choose.
8. Internet: sometimes simply called "the Net," is a worldwide system of computer networks (a network of networks) in which users at any one computer can, if they have permission, get information from any other com-

puter and sometimes talk directly to users at other computers.

9. Intranet: basically an internal Internet designed to be used within the confines of a school district, company, university, or organization. What distinguishes an intranet from the freely accessible Internet is that an intranet is private. Until recently most corporations relied on proprietary hardware and software systems to network its computers, a costly and time-consuming process made more difficult when offices are scattered around the world. Even under the best of conditions, sharing information among different hardware platforms, file formats and software is not an easy task. By using off-the-shelf Internet technology, intranets solve this problem, making internal communication and collaboration much simpler.

10. Java: an object-oriented programming language developed by Sun Microsystems, Inc. to create executable content (i.e., self-running applications) that can be easily distributed through networks like the Internet. Developers use Java to create special programs called applets that can be incorporated in web pages to make them interactive. A Java-enabled web browser is required to interpret and run the Java applets.

11. Multimedia: the simultaneous use of more than one type of media such as text with sound, moving or still images with music, and so on.

12. Network: two or more computers connected to each other so they can share resources. The Internet is a "network of networks", whereby anyone—from an individual at a home with a PC to a large corporate multi-department system—can freely and easily exchange information.

13. PDF: an acronym for Portable Document Format, PDF is a file type created by Adobe Systems, Inc. that allows fully formatted, high-resolution, PostScript documents to be easily transmitted across the Internet and viewed on any computer that has Adobe Acrobat Reader soft-

ware (a proprietary viewer is available for free at the Adobe site).

14. Search Engine: a type of software that creates indexes of databases or Internet sites based on the titles of files, keywords, or the full text of files. The search engine has an interface that allows you to type what you're looking for into a blank field. It then gives you a list of the results of the search. When you use a search engine on the Web, the results are presented to you in hypertext, which means you can click on any item in the list to get the actual file.

15. URL: an acronym for Uniform Resource Locator, a URL is the address for a resource or site (usually a directory or file) on the World Wide Web and the convention that web browsers use for locating files and other remote services.

OBSTACLES TO USING TECHNOLOGY IN SCHOOLS

Before describing the potential for technological opportunities for teachers, it is useful to consider what prevents teachers from using these technologies.

Despite tight school budgets and difficult financial decisions, districts have been acquiring computer hardware over the past 20 years. It is estimated that by 1994 18.1 million computers had been installed in schools and universities in the United States (O'Donnell-Dooling, 2000). Yet in 1995 The Congressional Office of Technology and Assessment reported that few teachers are utilizing computers in their teaching. Another teacher survey indicates that 84 percent of educators believed that Internet access for students can improve education quality, yet only 33 percent indicated that the use of online resources is well integrated into learning and teaching in their classrooms (Harris, 2002; Netday, 2001). Educators often view the Internet solely as a technological library and do not examine the web for its potential in communicating with other colleagues and sharing ideas. This disparity is concerning, yet it often does not slow the continued stream of new technologies in schools. District technology budgets break down as 55 percent on hardware, 30 percent on software, and 15 percent on repairs and training (OTA, 1995). This leaves very little room and money for staff development. When teacher training does occur it often focuses on how to use the equipment, rather than the integration of technology. Oftentimes funding from bonds that may have paid for the acquisition of new computers and software cannot be applied to staff training on the computers or with the software (Hall, 1999).

Countless reports and research findings concur. Teachers are not using the hardware and software that districts purchased. Why? It is clear the concentration of funds has been on supplying students with computers and software. Staff development is an expensive commodity both financially and politically. School districts can demonstrate to the public in a visual and tangible sense how the tax dollars have been spent regarding technology through showing the numbers of computers and the additions of smart classrooms. Demonstrating the positive effects of staff development is much more difficult. To the public, monies for staff in-service days are seen as a frill and therefore, are often cut during tough budget times. Vojtek and Vojtek (1997) assert that technology and staff development must occur simultaneously. Time and explanation of software are significant needs, but are not the only needs educators face. Assisting teachers in the application of technology tools is essential. Vojtek and Vojtek discuss the barriers that staff developers face when addressing teachers:

1. Varying levels of competence and confidence;
2. Fear of technology;
3. Outdated equipment;
4. Lack of technical support;
5. Lack of models to demonstrate the value of integrating technology; and
6. Dispelling the myth that computers, especially the Internet are a fad.

These obstacles cannot be addressed in a two-hour after school in-service course. Comprehensive and ongoing staff development and support is necessary for appropriate and consistent integration of technology as a viable learning tool. Educators also cite lack of time as one of the main reasons for not using the Internet more in their classrooms (Harris, 2002).

Ohler (2000) describes six barriers that affect educators who are trying to reconcile the role of technology in teaching and learning:

1. Ubiquity: technology goes on forever in a stream of peripherals and it is a challenge to stay current;

2. Stealth: much of technology goes unnoticed as we do not suspect its actions and/or are too busy to investigate them;

3. Amplification and leveraging: technology provides us with tremendous power to affect many—both close and at very far distances. When that power used to promote an incorrect data or poor examples, the then serves a negative purpose;

4. Ephemerality: changes are continual and strong so that we have difficulty getting our footing "emotionally, intellectually, politically, ethically";

5. Sovereignty: as we interact with technological tools we become more like them and the social forces behind them. When we come in contact with something we become like it whether it be "mineral, vegetable, animal, or digital"; and

6. Dehumanization: we believe that the world of technology is overwhelming; although many of us would crave an orderly machinated lifestyle, we feel that the technology is dehumanizing. (16)

Barriers and obstacles to the effective integration of technology abound. At the same time there are promising examples of how a thoughtful and reflective change process has assisted students, teachers, school districts, and communities in making important and effective decisions regarding technology.

ESSENTIAL STEPS TO EFFECTIVE INTEGRATION

Wires and hardware won't make all the technological connections. The human connections must be in place as well. (Vojtek and Vojtek, 1997, p. 42)

As noted previously in this chapter, effective technology integration requires much more than lots of computers. Vojtek and Vojtek assert that there are five kinds of educators that staff developers must address when attempting to institute change, especially a technological one (1997). These educators include:

1. The trailblazers: most often computer coordinators and other technological experts, these staff members have strong computer skills and have usually been part of the process of acquiring and wiring;

2. The pioneers: these classroom teachers and support staff are quick to sign up and are eager to get started and make their own mark;

3. The settlers and the stay-at-homes: these are the staff members who will need strong and sustained support in integrating technology. They will proceed, but will require many examples and evidence of higher-level applications to ensure the efficacy of this teaching tool; and

4. The saboteurs: while they may eventually join the telecommunications environment, it will not happen without a fight. Vojtek and Vojtek (1997) believe that in the presence of technology integration, these educators will need to choose between entering the superhighway and abandoning the ship.

Building the learning community that will need to embrace technology integration in some format, takes time, effort, and planning. Each level of expertise including novice must be honored. Just as a teacher's role is to move each child forward from wherever he or she is at, staff development for effective integration of technology must hold the same holistic view. Again, as Vojtek and Vojtek (1997) discuss building the human infrastructure, they identify essential tenets for staff development, as outlined in Table 7.1.

TABLE 7.1: TENETS FOR STAFF DEVELOPMENT IN TECHNOLOGY

Staff development is not just for teachers; the entire school community must be involved in the learning process. This includes parents. A school's culture must support the changes. Staff development must be included as an intricate part of the school improvement plans and performance standards. This type of change cannot occur with the "add-on" ideology. Staff development efforts must be results driven. Teachers must learn how to make decisions regarding technology so that they can use it and demonstrate their reasoning for doing so. Making choices regarding the when and how of technology are key skills for teachers to internalize and then teach to their students.
Technology training must be embedded in content specific staff development. Staff development must focus on how to embed technology in the content areas, so that it becomes another valuable teaching and learning tool that is interconnected with the process and the product. No longer should training focus on how to use the computer. Instead we must focus on how to integrate technology effectively into day-to-day learning activities.
Staff development must include collegial sharing and ongoing follow-up and support. The Internet has great potential to remove some of the isolation barriers that teachers face. Through connecting online with e-mail and chat, staff development can provide a catalyst for this kind of communication. Penuel, Means, and Simkins (2000) explain how the success of multimedia technological projects for students relies heavily on the support and networking between teachers. This informal professional development allows sharing of inspiring ideas and modeling innovative methods. Penuel, Means, and Simkins (2000).

Once strong staff development is in place and represents the systems model through involving all of the elements, much can happen in regard to effective teaching and learning through the integration of technology. The following section highlights examples of real classrooms and communities who have applied best practices in order to make substantive changes in their approaches to technology.

STUDENTS AND TECHNOLOGY

The current student population is technologically savvy. Ask any veteran teacher who is using technology how he or she learned about a program or weblink, and the answer will often be "my students showed me." While many teachers and parents remain hesitant about pressing certain buttons or working through programs, the current generation of students has no fear in this regard. They press, cut, paste, delete, refresh, move text, find lost text, and navigate the web as fast as their cable modems will allow. Instant messaging has reached a level of nuance, and there is nothing that today's students won't try in navigating the world of technology. These students have many critics, as any new generation does. Many adults—parents, teachers, and administrators, are uncomfortable with the potential secrecy of the Internet. Certainly there are dangers—access to inappropriate websites is a significant issue. Technology is very powerful. The current generation uses the Internet as a major form of communication. Kids are e-mailing and using chat rooms to keep in contact with family and friends, and to meet new people. Teen cyber culture provides outlets for students to express themselves and keep their identities private. There are few options for adolescents to be able to express their beliefs without being judged or at times even ridiculed. During a tumultuous time in their lives, the Internet provides young people with the freedom to convey their ideas and opinions while keeping their physical selves anonymous. Jon Katz, a media critic, defends the role of technology with teens (Tell, 1999). Katz explains that technology is part of teen ideology. He claims that many parents and educators are hesitant to learn more about the intricacies of the computer world. While many adults push for strong censorship, few teach students how to safely use these vast and powerful resources.

The reluctance among adults to fully understand technology has applications across the cognitive realm as well as the social domain. Ohler (2000) explains how:

> In an era where students design web sites for projects and integrate video, graphics, and animation into their presentations, art is fast becoming the new literacy of our times . . . the multimedia environment of the Web, as well as much of what we experience through our computers, requires students to think and communicate as designers and artists. The age of art has arrived (16).

Ohler explains his experience of observing a tenth grader attempting to create a multimedia presentation.

> He wasn't struggling with the technology—like any infoage kid he could click around the screen with considerable ease. It was the aesthetics that seemed insurmountable. As I watched him clumsily cramming together scads of video clips, graphics, sounds, buttons, and a few words, it suddenly hit me like a ton of bits: He was trying to create art, and no one had shown him how. In the process of fumbling with the medium, he was losing his sense of what he wanted to communicate in the first place (16)

Students need to be taught how to make decisions regarding the use of technology and then how to use its features to communicate ideas and processes. Students grow up playing computer games and exploring interesting websites. The skills needed to integrate technology, as a profound form of communication, cannot be absorbed through Yahooligans and Sim City experiences. Students need to learn how to make the critical decisions regarding this learning and communication tool. Just as teachers discuss the essential points of a persuasive essay, educators must also address the intricacies of effective power point and video streaming.

The workforce in which this generation will enter will require technological literacy. Schools musts find ways to address these skills in an integrated format. The Montrose County School District in Colorado has begun to address these needs in a systematic format. A technology committee set forth to determine what students needed to know and be able to do regarding the integration of technology. The committee identified basic skills for K-12 students. Some of these include:

1. Students identity and use hardware components;
2. Students learn basic keyboarding skills, as well as basic trouble-shooting, care and safe use of hardware;
3. Students learn to enter and exit software applications using onscreen cues;
4. Students write research documents and reports using word processing software and create graphics, tables, charts, and graphs;
5. Students create multimedia projects integrating graphics and text;
6. Students use databases to search for information; and
7. Students incorporate global information with electronic online communication tools (Kriss, 1996).

This district made powerful decisions to involve both students and staff in the learning process. Teachers needed to increase their own knowledge of technology and its applications to teaching in order to be able to serve the students in this realm. The district offered 25-30 technology in-service courses each semester. The teachers will be provided with utility software that can assist in assessment and record keeping. A district infrastructure is being developed that will allow teachers and administrative offices to communicate both individually and through electronic mass messages. Certainly much hardware is going into each classroom; equally important though, is that all staff is undergoing training and support that will enable them to utilize the hardware and infrastructure to improve teaching and learning.

Students themselves have indicated many of their needs regarding technology integration. According to O'Donnell Dooling (2002), "The effectiveness of computer technology experiences at school depends on the student's prior knowledge, the teacher, access to hardware and software, and scheduling" (22). Teachers who express enthusiasm, demonstrate expertise, and provide ongoing support, are more likely to engage students in effective integration of technology. Just as students have varying degrees of competency in English and math, technological competence will be demonstrated with different levels of success. Teachers need to apply effective teaching methods of individualization and flexible grouping to meet the different needs of their students. Peer tutoring, even in the most informal sense, is effective for technology. Students will naturally share tips and ideas about using certain software or search engines. Teachers need to encourage this and perhaps build in a debriefing time when all students can share and benefit from one another's tips.

PROMISING EXEMPLARS

Bickford (2002) described his experiences as a member of the evaluation team for the eMINTS (enhancing Missouri's Instructional Networked Teaching Strategies) program. Through this program teachers were asked to combine what they know about effective teaching strategies with unlimited technological resources. Through applying comprehensive assessment procedures this team focused on the definition of an effective eMINTS classroom: "[the classroom] is characterized by observable attributes that result in improved students' performance, increased parent involvement, and enriched instructional effectiveness." (21). The eMINTS rubric for evaluation was developmental in approach, indicating the teacher's road to mastery. The rubric for teacher evaluation included the following categories: teacher facilitated learning, student centered learning, unique teaching pedagogy and learning strategies, community of learners, technology richness, curriculum, assessment of student performance, and professional collaboration. The evaluation design underscores a strong message regarding technology. Effective integration of technological resources is one of several valuable teaching strategies. The language for the master eMINTS teacher in regard to technology richness reads as follows: "Full complement of multimedia technologies (including video-conferencing or Internet 2 projects) used fluently and seamlessly by students and teacher in the learning process on a daily basis where appropriate in interdisciplinary instruction." (21). The ideals expressed in this definition reflect best practices for teaching and learning with technology. It is a fully integrated method that asks the teacher to make decisions regarding the use of technology as a vital teaching tool. While the technology itself is "high tech," it is facilitated by a master teacher, who makes effective decisions about the learning process.

Bickford and his team described the student-centered, teacher facilitated lessons as the best format for integration of technology. These environments provided detailed and intellectually stimulating plans that allow for seamless integration of technology. Technological methods and equipment were used to serve and facilitate the teaching and learning process. Students became masters of technological applications through the effective facilitation and setting of the learning environment that their teachers provided. Master eMINTS teachers demonstrated the use of several research based practices. The integration of technology has become a significant tool among many used to promote the learning process.

WHAT DOES IT TAKE TO BE EFFECTIVE?

The Ohana Foundation, a nonprofit organization with a mission of bringing technology to all children, set out to answer this question. This foundation commissioned the Center for Information and Communication Sciences at Ball University. This commission conducted five years of research regarding the "impact of technology on educational excellence" (Bossert, 2001, p. 62). Through extensive interviews and study, the research team identified twelve school districts as finalists. There were certain criteria that each district needed to meet in order to reach this level. The list, which follows, can serve any district well as it plans and refines plans for effective technology use and integration:

1. Demonstrate a variety of technological tools (video, audio, digital, distance learning;
2. Embrace the philosophy that networking is an important part of innovation—connectivity leverages the power of technology;
3. Demonstrate of leadership qualities such as the willingness to take risks;

4. Understand fully the importance of integration of technology into the curriculum; and
5. Commit that teacher training must play an important role in technology integration.

From among the twelve finalists, four school districts were given Technology in Education Leadership Awards. One of these districts was the Wilson County School District in Wilson, North Carolina (Bossert, 2001). This rural district developed a widespread implementation plan that included acquiring 4,000 PCs and 73 servers for its 12,000 students in 23 schools. All classrooms were given at least 2 PCs and 81 percent of the district is Internet connected. Extensive staff training included summer technology integration projects, a free, credit bearing, weeklong Summer Technology Conference, and many forms of ongoing training. During a five-year implementation, the district provided more than 100,000 staff development hours to ensure that educators were comfortable and proficient in using technology and integrating its resources effectively. Teachers were given free Internet access from home in cooperation with East Carolina University. The district also implemented project T.E.S.T. (technology empowering teachers and students) that focuses on reading and writing through the integration of technology. This model addresses the state and national technology goals and involves student mentors who receive technology training and assist both students and teachers in technology-related projects. The evidence collected is very encouraging for Wilson School District. In five years, the on grade level percentages for students in grades 3-8 went from 60 to 80 percent in math and reading. These numbers indicate a significant and effective change.

This district was able to integrate technology effectively through intense concentration on learning for both staff and students. The district looked to other members of the system to assist in this endeavor, including higher education institutions and county government and grants to address the high financial costs of such a comprehensive project. Wilson School District built a strong infrastructure for this kind of change through involving all school staff and allowing various mechanisms for involvement.

Some of the other award winners also demonstrated innovation and long range thinking with their approaches to the integration of technology. These districts focused on both getting the best equipment into the hands of the students and teachers, and providing the learning opportunities for the integration of such technology simultaneously. Certainly these were not easy tasks. Through securing county, state and federal grants, forming partnerships with higher educational institutions and businesses, or forming nonprofit organizations, these forward thinking school districts found the ways and the means to accomplish the extraordinary goals for technology integration. In one encouraging example, the Beaufort County School District in South Carolina formed the nonprofit organization entitled "The Schoolbook Foundation" (Bossert, 2001). The purpose of the group was to address the Digital Divide that existed in the county. The school sponsored a "Learning through Laptops" program that provided laptops to all interested students in the middle school. The Schoolbook Foundation subsidized the costs of the computers for any needy student. Research results from an independent study indicated improvement in academic achievement in those students who receive reduced lunch and had a laptop compared to those students who just received reduced lunch. This school district identified its needs on many levels and then set out to form a comprehensive implementation plan to address those needs and integrate technology successfully. There were many, many obstacles for effective integration in all of the award winning school districts. The forward thinking and execution of the systems view of solutions to those obstacles allowed for success.

THE DIGITAL DIVIDE

As more and more classrooms and school districts move toward technology integration for lessons, homework and communication, districts must be cognizant of their student and family socioeconomic status. The availability of computers and access to the Internet is related to such factors. The Digital Divide refers to the trend that threatens to separate different income, ethnic, and racial groups into technology "haves" and "have-nots" (Rose, 2001, p.

10). There is a disparity between the access to and equity of technology according to race, gender, education, and location (Swain & Pearson, 2001). Equity in education has been a problem without a solution for many decades. The era of technology adds another layer to this dilemma. This concept was discussed when the age of technology was in its infancy stages. Now, when computers can be seen everywhere from schools and businesses to sidewalk cafes, we sometimes minimize this important issue.

By the turn of the century two thirds of all American households have computers and 46 percent of these are Internet connected (Revenaugh, 2000). These statistics indicate a significant growth in a ten-year period. Still, there are disturbing gaps in who has access to technology at home. While half of the households earning $75,000 or more have Internet connections at home, if the income drops to $40,000, then the Internet percentage drops to 12 (Grunwald Associates, 2000). In a two-parent household that earns less than $35,000, white households are apt to have a computer three times more than African American households, and four times more than Hispanic households (National Telecommunication and Information Administration, 1999). The ongoing needs for safe and proactive learning environments as well as for funding sources are issues that are easily identified. Determining the needs happens readily. Finding and implementing solutions is more problematic.

Some school districts, such as the one in Beaufort County, South Carolina, applied for and received grants to fund the bridging of the Digital Divide. (Bossert, 2001). The Beaufort County district also created a nonprofit organization to assist in getting the technology into the hands of every student, regardless of ability to pay. Other school districts have teamed with businesses and higher institutions to gain equal and sustained access to technology. An example of this is can be seen in the cooperative relationship formed between the Poughkeepsie School District, Marist College, and IBM all located in Poughkeepsie, NY. This collaboration is highlighted in the distance learning chapter of this text.

Utilizing community and grant resources is a creative and powerful approach to securing funding. Conversations at every level must address this topic. There are public and private businesses that may be resources to tap for such monies, as well as Boxtops for Education programs and other PTA (Parent Teacher Association) initiatives. Federal grants are also a strong area for financial resources to address the integration of technology in all schools. It is essential to highlight though, that placing computers in classrooms is only the beginning of the solution. Acquisition of hardware and software, and training for staff and students must occur simultaneously. Districts that are faced with Digital Divide issues are often faced with many obstacles for quality and equity in education. Policies regarding teaching and technology clearly underscore the importance of effective teaching as a hallmark for change in the Digital Divide issue: "teachers' knowledge and skills influence student achievement at least as much as student characteristics such as income, race, language background, and parent education" (Darling-Hammond, 1999, p.3).

Swain and Pearson (2001) believe that teachers have the strongest influence on bridging the Digital Divide. They suggest several logical strategies that teachers can utilize to address this issue. Simple aspects such as where the computer (s) is located in the classroom can set the tone for how technology is perceived and used. These authors caution that keeping computers solely in a lab instills the notion that technology is separate from the learning process and then is viewed as an extra. Computer labs do serve important roles for both teachers and students; keeping these labs open and available throughout the school day and before and after school can serve the integration of technology well. Students and staff can then see computers as an accessible tool for teaching and learning. Perhaps family computer nights can be established. Introductory courses in computer applications and "How your child uses the computer at school" in-services also may be beneficial.

Monies are in short supply, especially in districts attempting to address the Digital Divide, and careful decisions must be made as to how to spend such limited funds. According to Jane M. Healy as described in an interview with Carol Tell (2002), funds used for technology need to be very carefully spent. If the objective of using the computer is for word processing, then the district should invest in much more cost-effective electronic typewriters. Healy asserts that technology in schools should be both innovative and cost efficient. Teachers need to be actively involved in researching software and making decisions based on best educational practice. Too often the programs geared for students are more entertaining than educational. Teachers are the ones who need to be in charge of students, not the computer game.

Brown, Higgins, and Hartley (2001) describe several strategies that can serve to bridge the Digital Divide:

1. Collect information to determine which students and families have access to and use technology, and which do not;
2. Identify and share with others the barriers to the use of and access to technology;
3. Teach all students and families the skills they need to access information via technology, and offer technology courses, workshops, and camps at times that are convenient for students and their families;
4. Establish partnerships with businesses and community-based organizations such as libraries, colleges, and community centers to make technology available to students and their families after school;
5. Provide students and their families with a list of free or low-cost resources that can help them get online (e.g., the local library);
6. Create a technology lending library so that students and their families can borrow laptop computers and other technological devices; and
7. Print hard copies of products available for those students and families who cannot access the materials online.

Brown, Higgins, and Hartley (2001) describe many factors that require elements of the system to work together. While one district or one classroom cannot surmount the barriers of the Digital Divide alone, community groups and businesses working in tandem with schools and families can accomplish lofty goals in addressing the disparity in education. The suggestions provided by Brown et al. would serve all systems well when the goal is to provide equal access to quality education.

PARENTS AND TECHNOLOGY

The technology explosion has captured the attention of most schools and classroom teachers. This is also true for many parents. This era of technology has many people turning to the Internet as their first resource for information. Many school districts are responding to this by developing websites that contain district and school information regarding policies, calendars of events, and special news bulletins (Revenaugh, 2000). While this information is helpful, parents and students who connect to the Internet regularly are seeking a more interactive online environment. Grunwald Associates (2000) reported that 60 percent of Internet connected families sought to communicate with the classroom teacher online and 50 percent wanted similar communication access with the school board. More than half of the families requested the ability to view homework online.

Changes toward this form of communication are happening slowly. In order for web communication to be effective, the teachers must be comfortable and competent with this form of facilitated dialogue. The creation of a classroom web page with interactive features is an opportune time for education staff to collaborate. Instructional technology specialists can play a key role in guiding this work. It is important that teachers start small and proceed gradually in this endeavor (Salend, Duhaney, Anderson, & Gottschalk, 2004). Besides staff collaboration, there are many companies that are refining tools to assist teachers in this kind of communication. Examples of these companies are Powerschool, bigchalk.com, Blackboard or Lightspan.com. Some of these programs allow for schools to share grades and attendance information with parents online; other programs provide tools for posting homework assignments, while most encourage the use of e-mail. These technologies help to facilitate the online experience for the teacher, parent, and student. Salend and colleagues provide guidelines for teachers to review as they work through the process. Some of these include:

1. Welcome and introduce users to the web site. It is help-
    ful to have a frequently asked questions (FAQ) section
    and identify contact information clearly;
2. Share homework policies, practices, and assignments.
    This can be updated throughout the year. Suggestions
    for assisting children during homework time can also be
    included;
3. Individualize homework assignments and communica-
    tion. Teachers can adapt and modify assignments for
    students with special needs. Whether the teacher is
    varying the content, length, or response mode, this can
    all be accomplished via the computer; students and par-
    ents can even have online access to modified assign-
    ments through a password protected system;
4. Create authentic and innovative homework assign-
    ments. These can be made available through the Inter-
    net to allow for more motivating and meaningful learn-
    ing experiences. Examples of this include web quests
    and cyber guides;
5. Allow for homework to be submitted online. This can
    minimize the difficulties when a student forgets an as-
    signment or it gets "lost" on the way to school;
6. Set guidelines for how families should assist students in
    the homework process;
7. Establish online homework groups;
8. Provide immediate feedback; and
9. Evaluate homework practices and web-based home-
    work systems.

These kinds of computer interactions demonstrate the human
connections that can be developed via the Internet. Companies
such as America Online have tapped into this phenomenon and
have cultivated several avenues for communication. For example,
there is a Kids Only area of AOL. During scheduled time periods,
teachers are available in real time to field questions; there are also
kids only chat rooms (Revenaugh, 2000). Online tutoring services
also exist for all subjects as well as for test preparation such as the
SAT. Online tutoring services appeal to many families and the interest in such programs is gaining momentum. The parent commu-

nication chapter of this book explores other additional online activities for parents and teachers.

ASSISTIVE TECHNOLOGY

Another golden benefit from the technological advancements has been the development and refinement of assistive technologies. These tools are designed to assist students with disabilities to perform their educational and communication tasks. The official definition for assistive technology is described in The Assistive Technology Act of 1998 (29U.S.C. 3002) and reads as follows:

> Any item, piece of equipment, or product system, whether acquired commercially, modified, or customized, that is used to increase, maintain, or improve functional capabilities of individuals with disabilities (see World Wide Web 4. law.cornell.edu/uscode/29/3002html).

This definition is broad and it requires that the device be tied to the individual's functional capabilities. When first hearing about assistive technology, some may react by thinking that these sorts of tools are for those students with severe disabilities. Others may think that these tools must be purchased immediately. Often these purchased items are not used, or not utilized to their potential when there has been little investigation before buying. There are many misconceptions and concerns about assistive technology. Richard Wanderman, (2003) has been a technology consultant, trainer, presenter, and teacher for over 20 years. He also has dyslexia and dysgraphia. Wanderman has identified some of the issues about assistive technology, and explained some of the reasons for the barriers that keep technology from being used to its capacity, as follows:

1. The tool is poorly designed and too difficult to use;
2. The user doesn't know where the hard work to learn the tool ends, and the problems associated with dyslexia begin;

3. Power and control issues: "you *said* to use it, therefore I won't" or "I just bought you this expensive gizmo so your grades *better* go up";
4. The tool comes with a stigma: being seen using the tool "labels" you as "learning disabled";
5. There is a poor fit between learning style or maturity of user and tool: the tool should not overwhelm the user, no matter how profound its effect;
6. Attitudes about disability get in the way: "you're broken and the use of this tool will fix you"; and
7. Confusion about getting the job done vs. underlying understanding: electronic cash registers help you make change but they don't give you the underlying understanding of why a shopper just gave you $1.01 for a $.66 bill (p.6).

Wanderman identified many areas that hinder the use of assistive technology. Educators need more information as to the types and appropriateness of assistive technology. Teachers also need to apply common sense. As Wanderman (2003) asserts, all technology assists us when used properly. Computers assist all students, yet when a student who has a disability uses a computer, it is labeled as assistive technology. This has implications for funding as well. When a tool is deemed as assistive technology, the funding for such a device comes from a special education source. This can muddy the waters in terms of use and ownership.

Educators know that when beginning something new, students need time to explore, time to learn, and time for much practice. Assistive technology needs to be explored, learned, and practiced, by the student *and* all of the individuals involved in the student's learning—the teachers and the parents. Involving several elements of the system in assessing the technology applications will allow for best results in learning and participating opportunities for the student and will address many of Wanderman's concerns.

Follansbee (2003) provides suggestions on how to involve elements of the system through a formal and consistent approach. While Follansbee was concentrating on specific applications of speech recognition software, his strategies can be generalized to good practice for all of assistive technology. Follansbee notes that it is essential for schools to be committed to providing the necessary fundamentals. Staff and students must be ready to work together with the technology in order to improve both competency with the technology and most significantly improve learning. Table 7.2 describes the needs and roles that Folansbee identified for such elements within the system (p 10-13).

TABLE 7. 2:
ASSISTIVE TECHNOLOGY STRATEGIES

SCHOOLS	STAFF	STUDENTS AND PARENTS
Employ a staff member to provide training and support	Be willing to learn how to use technology	Acknowledge that one technology is not the correct solution for all
Provide collaborative opportunities for trainer and teachers to work together	Provide a gradual "ramping up" of work requirements for student using the technology	Acknowledge that mastery of the technology requires effort and some flexibility in ways of working
Provide training in implementation for appropriate staff members, including workshop and supported practice time	Be committed to providing some kind of "make up" instruction	Acknowledge that mastery of the technology will entail an increase (hopefully gradual) in workload to reflect the level of work expected for the grade level (or depending on other identified disabilities) and express a willingness to participate on that basis

Provide consulting support for staff And students as needed during implementation	Be willing to try technology with some students who may not be able to use it completely independently	
Provide adequate hardware and technical support for hardware problems, software installation, etc.		
Provide adequate space for technology and users		
Provide time for staff to work with student during initial stages of technology use		
Provide academic (substitute) credit for students who learn to use technology (rather than adding an extra requirement for the already over-burdened student with LD)		

There are many ways to connect the school, staff, students, and parents in the integration of assistive technology. The more that these groups work together, the easier and more sustaining the integration of technology tools can be.

TECHNOLOGY AND THE COMMUNITY

There are also exciting ways to involve the local and global communities in technology that allow for a more connected atmosphere. The examples of school and classroom websites and homework helpers online demonstrate only a small amount of the Internet's potential. According to Revenaugh (2000) connected learning communities are the future for technology and education.

> For many technology-focused educators, the holy grail of connected school community [is] they'd like to see the Net bring to their students the kind of group synergies that technology makes possible in the "real world," where work teams conduct projects across great distances and communities form around common interest (27).

These kinds of activities are happening in pockets across the country (see for example the cyberschoolbus project, or the work with the WTO in Seattle that was explained in the chapter on Diversity). These projects and others (such as ThinkQuest and other web quest models) allow students to collaborate with other students, educators, researchers and other professionals, politicians and government figures, through the use of e-mails, chatrooms, message boards, and digital media. As businesses begin to require more technology competencies from their prospective employers it serves business' best interests to begin this collaboration early. Collaboration among the elements of the system has potential to be symbiotic. The examples listed above provide concrete evidence to support these relationships.

FUNDING

Transitioning from the current status of technology to the potential technology opportunities, requires the cooperation, commitment, and collaboration of many elements of the system, it also requires money. This is often a major stumbling block for education. Finding funds requires creativity and forward thinking. Some of the exemplary schools that have integrated technology were able to do so because of creative funding measures including local, federal, and private grants, the creation of non-profit organizations, and collaboration with existing non-profit organizations such at the PTO. The chapter on change provides us with avenues to pursue regarding grant opportunities. This is a growing source for funding during constrained budgetary times.

Blaschke (2003) offers another source of funding through the prominent federal legislative act, the No Child Left Behind Act (NCLB). Blaschke has examined several aspects of NCLB and has provided the following areas of NCLB to suggest for funding within this piece of legislation:

1. Improving student achievement in math and /or reading: Blaschke explained that Integrated Learning Systems (ILS) have been studied thoroughly and have been indicated as effective in increasing student achievement in math. Therefore the purchasing of these comprehensive instructional systems should be supported by NCLB;

2. Aligning to state assessments and standards: Opportunities for technology-based alignment and teacher-monitoring tools are significant, and cannot be done on paper;

3. Diagnosis, prescription, and intervention: Federal funds may be spent on the instructional systems as well as on teacher training. This would also include online instruction and distance learning opportunities;

4. Accommodating special needs assessments: The use of computer-based testing will increase due to the fact that it can be designed to handle all of the requirements for data reporting, and it can facilitate "reasonable accommodation" in assessments for certain groups of special education students and English language learners;

5. Administrative tracking, reporting, and data warehousing: Under NCLB much of the funds allocated to technology during the initial stages of implementation will likely be for administrative tracking, reporting, and data warehousing activities;

6. Mitigating against unintended AYP (adequate yearly progress) consequences: Districts can defend themselves against charges of a lack of progress by using a

student data-information system that keeps two sets of books, one for what the current interpretation of the law allows and reportable and once that reflects the actual achievement of students in their subgroups;

7. School-parent communication: The demand for school-parent communications systems is being generated by more than 40 provisions in NCLB . . . technology certainly is a necessary component of any such system;

8. Paraprofessional training and state teacher certification: Technology will play a critical role in training and certification of newly hired aides and the roughly 400,000 existing paraprofessionals who do not meet NCLB "highly qualified" requirements and in providing online staff development for individuals who are in the process of achieving state teacher certification through alternative routes;

9. Leveraging, tracking and reporting "flexible" transfer of funds: Under NCLB, up to 50 percent of funds in any title (with the exception of Title 1 and 21st century Community Learning Centers) may be transferred into other programs. A technology-based system would be able to provide the tracking information necessary; and

10. Leveraging IDEA: IDEA funds . . . can be used to purchase certain types of technology applications that also can serve non-special education students under certain conditions (Blaschke, 2003, p. 22-24).

CONCLUSION

Technology has tremendous potential to serve as a significant educational tool. Much of technology is transforming the ways in which we interact with each other on an everyday basis. This kind of paradigm shift has a significant impact on education. Teachers and administrators need to make decisions regarding the use and applications of technology. The power that technology brings can often be misconstrued. Teachers, administrators, parents and community members need to have an understanding and appreciation for what technology can and cannot do. Technology offers a means to an end, but is not the end itself. The most powerful and productive examples of technology applications involve several elements of the systems model, with the human infrastructure guiding the implementations, and reflecting and evaluating on the process. Vojtek and Vojtek (1997) underscore this important concept: "Most of all we must remember that it isn't the technology that will impact how students learn, but how educators transfer their technological knowledge and skills transparently into the curriculum and instruction of the classroom" (p. 43).

The system elements need to consider what are the essential technological competencies needed for students and why those selected skills are crucial to the learning process. The use and applications of technology need to be decided upon very carefully. The computer industry is savvy and aggressive. Technological bells and whistles are used to draw the consumer and student into the programs and through a maze of websites. Educators need to evaluate the "latest and greatest" in technology with a critical lens and keep the educational decisions in the hands of the appropriate professionals. Healy asserts this concept by stating "Educators have to get their wits about them and take charge of technology, take this potential back from the industry and put it firmly where it belongs—in the world of educationally, and humanly sound practice." (Tell, 2000, p.13). When the power of technology is tempered by best practices in teaching and learning then the positive outcomes of an interconnected learning environment can abound. This critical and thoughtful view of technology is an essential concept to instill in today's learners. Our society has become accustomed to the flashy and visually and auditorally intense images of technology. Evaluating the effectiveness and appropriateness of the immense technological options is key to effective learning. Ohler (2000) provides an intriguing definition of technology literacy "the technology literate student [is] one who knows when to use technology and when not to, and who understands that the technologies which connect us to new opportunities disconnect us from others." Ohler's definition implies the need for careful decision-making and a broad understanding of the consequences of such decisions. It is when elements of the system can work collaboratively from this definition that students and society can gain the real benefits of technology.

DISCUSSION QUESTIONS

1. What impact does knowing the fundamental components of technology have on teaching and learning?

2. What prevents teachers from using technology as a tool for learning?

3. How would you implement a professional development protocol for teachers on the integration of technology into the curriculum? Describe the course content, participants, follow-up and support.

4. In what ways are computers advantageous to students? To parents? To the community?

5. As a school board member, what steps would you take to ensure that students have effective technology experiences? Comment on teachers' attitudes and competency level, the classroom, scheduling, building an infrastructure, bridging the Digital Divide, parent communication, and involving the business community.

6. How will the Digital Divide ultimately impact the workforce and the economy?

7. How would you implement professional development for parents on communicating with the school and providing at home follow-up using technology? Describe the course content, and follow-up and support activities.

8. How would you overcome the barriers to using assistive technology?

9. What funding sources are available to sustain district-wide technology use?

Chapter 8:
Distance Learning:
Flexibility in Education

OBJECTIVES

After studying this chapter, the reader will be able to define, analyze and apply the following concepts and strategies:

1. The definition of distance learning;

2. The benefits of distance learning;

3. Obstacles to implementing distance learning;

4. History of distance learning; and

5. Distance learning as a system.

OVERVIEW

The age of technology has had the most influential impact on all levels of the systems model than anything else in the second half of the twentieth century. That is a profound statement. For an era that is noted for its revolutionary changes, the one entity that signifies the most change is technology. Through the use of technology, nations share information, or sell and buy information, to gain the vital knowledge for remaining or gaining a superpower status. Federal and state governments utilize technology to research, communicate, and form legislation that impacts all levels within the systems model and allows for communication between countries, states, counties, towns, communities and families. In essence technology is everywhere and it, and we as a society, are evolving with the onslaught of information "en mass." More and more politicians, corporate businesses, small business owners, community organizations, religious groups, schools, families, and friends are communicating and learning through technology. When surfing the net, for example, the individual gains knowledge from several elements of the systems model with the simple click of the mouse. Many of us have become entranced with the search for information via the Internet. Some have called this the "internet addiction" (Scileppi, Teed & Torres, 2000). Often this quest is both efficient and in-depth. For example, a fifth grade student assignment calls for a rudimentary research report on one of the nine planets. When the fifth graders use the Internet as its main resource, they will discover a plethora of information in a very short period of time. This information appears almost immediately and contains far more information than is necessary for the assignment. The entire interaction may take place at one setting, whether it is the classroom, library, or home. The information can be saved and stored electronically, and the student and teacher can avoid the frustrations of lost papers and books. Technology provides a vast amount of resources and tools for teaching and learning. Its purpose is not to replace teaching, but rather to enhance the learning process for both the student and the teacher.

Simonson, Smaldino, Albright, and Zvacek (2002) define distance education as institution-based, formal education where the learning group is separated, and where interactive telecommunications systems are used to connect learners, resources, and instructors. Distance education has potential to reach into every corner of our world and invites the student to interact with varying levels of the system while in his or her own proverbial living room. While there are many hybrid versions of distance learning that calculate a face-to-face and Internet learning formula, distance learning virtually creates alternative pathways for the systems model. Often one presupposes direct communication across the elements of the system in order to meet goals, achieve an agenda, or change a course of action. Currently distance learning addresses the communication goals via technology and most often the Internet services. While collaborative learning remains an intact and effective teaching mode, those who are collaborating may in fact be doing so asynchronously. The traditionalist and education expert may question this form of learning, and rightfully so. There are many obstacles in distance learning and several different kinds of experiences that are relatively new to this format of education. There are many questions to be asked and issues to be examined. This chapter will provide a brief history of distance learning, and examine the potential of distance education across the systems model, identify and explain the characteristics and needs of each element of the system, including students, teachers, learning institutions, community, and state and federal agencies. Each section will highlight encouraging examples of real-life distance learning experiences.

THE MAZE OF DISTANCE EDUCATION: WHY SHOULD WE ENTER?

An important distinction for educators and those who will interact with distance education is that this is a vehicle that allows for the production of educational practice. It is not, in itself, education. We are not as far as the mythical Star Trek Enterprise where we can order the computer to teach us, give us, and save us from the evils. While aspects of that voyage can sound enticing, learning requires the student and teacher to interact. This is, and remains, essential to the learning process. The relationship between teacher and student continues to be the epicenter of education

(Manathunga 2002; Walker, 1997). Educators and learning institutions are merely looking at different forms of communication for that relationship to evolve. There are numerous issues to deliberate to ensure quality and effective education. Educators appreciate the truth in that statement when examining *any* vehicle for learning. What are the needs of the learner? What are the essential concepts and ideas to be developed? Which learning and teaching tools will suit the learner and teacher in the best match? How will the interaction between learner and learner, teacher and learner, be most productive? Facilitators of any learning process must ponder these questions. Those who choose to use technology as the form of delivery must also consider a unique set of questions and overcome some practical obstacles to allow for the learning situations to proceed. Also unique to this learning environment are benefits that enhance the learning and eliminate obstacles seen in other learning environments.

Barriers to distance learning exist in a variety of categories and span the elements of the systems model. It is essential to identify these barriers ahead of time so that they can be addressed before one enters into the distance learning environment. Obviously some of these will affect all learners, or some learners, or one particular group or person. As we examine these barriers, it is helpful to keep in mind while learners rely on the human interaction to process knowledge and ideas; the need to do so through distance education is becoming increasingly essential. Distance education is not meant to replace face-to-face instruction, but rather to complement it. Increasingly, postsecondary institutions are moving toward a flexible model for instruction due to several factors including new technology, reductions in funding, and an understanding of a globalized university (Mamathunga, 2002, Symes, 1996). Many individuals in the workforce live a great distance from colleges and universities, and this prohibits the continued education that is often required in one's field (Broady-Ortmann, 2002).

A BRIEF HISTORY

Distance education began over one hundred sixty years ago with the beginnings of correspondence courses. When Isaac Pitman was allowed to offer shorthand instruction through correspondence in 1840, distance education had commenced (Simonson et. al., 2002). Pitman had the foresight to realize that flexibility was critical for the expansion of education and the sharing of such interactions need not be limited to those in his local environment. Many students have benefited from correspondence courses before the wake of technology in today's world. Students of correspondence schools needed to demonstrate considerable patience as they waited for feedback from their instructors.

While in today's world we consider a student with a dial-up modem connection and no instant messaging capabilities as one who possesses infinite patience, students of correspondence schools functioned virtually in isolation and waited weeks or months for feedback.

Distance programs grew slowly over the years until the age of the Internet. The Department of Defense and a variety of research universities were the forefathers of the Internet. Their original interest in this form of communication was to develop a means for scientists to share information that was of scientific and technical nature. In 2001 there were 1,680 institutions offering over 54,000 online courses (Smaldino et al., 2002). In 2000, eleven states had created virtual high schools, and the numbers continue to rise (Carr, 2000). Most of these schools began with offering the Advanced Placement courses in a distance format.

Distance learning comes in many formats. Today distance learning includes interacting via a continuum of technological resources. The spectrum of options ranges from "pure" distance learning in which course material, assessment, and support is all delivered online, with no face-to-face contact between students and teachers (McKimm, Jolie & Cantillon, 2003, p.871). At the other end, teachers of traditional face-to-face courses utilize an intranet to house course materials and resources to support materials. Many web-based courses contain some face-to-face teaching and learning time and use the technology for both stationary support materials and interactive learning opportunities. Distance learning includes a multitude of possibilities, limited only by the curriculum designers and their resources. This chapter highlights several real-life examples of distance learning programs for the K-12 and postsecondary levels. Many of these programs incorporate the technological vocabulary that appears in district and school plans.

One example of a hybrid use of distance learning can be seen in one of the elementary school projects developed through Inter-ACTS (Advancement of Classrooms through use of Technology Systems) (Campbell & Guisinger, 2003). InterACTS is a virtual school model that was created and is used in Bloomfield Hills, Michigan. Through this collaborative model, students learn in face-to-face classrooms and share new knowledge, questions, and experiences across three elementary schools in the Bloomfield Hills School District. Students post messages using an online bulletin board and request students to respond to the findings indicated. Teacher collaboration facilitates this process and ensures meaningful messages and target audiences.

DISTANCE LEARNING AND THE ELEMENTS OF THE SYSTEMS MODEL

The Student

Distance learning offers the student a range of educational opportunities that can serve as supplements and/or alternatives to the traditional classroom settings. Sometimes distance education can offer students learning experiences that are otherwise not available. School districts are facing tighter budgets each year. In small or rural public schools the need for specialized courses (such as the AP courses) demand does not warrant supply. Distance learning offers students in these environments opportunities to take such courses via distance learning avenues including online course models, videoconferencing, or video/phone line based Real Time. School districts believe these opportunities will expand to include students who are home-schooled, students who need to work during traditional school hours, and those who dropout before completing high school (Woods, 2001). Evidence of the exponential growth in this distance model is apparent in the state of Kentucky where the student enrollment in a virtual high school increased from 47 to 300 in one year (Woods). Many of these distance education experiences exist due to the collaboration of several elements in the systems model. School districts team with universities and businesses (such as AT&T or IBM) to multiply resources, solicit funding and necessary technologies, and build collaborative learning environments. When several elements of the systems model commit to sustained collaboration, the potentials of distance learning opportunities become long lasting realities for the student. Later in this chapter an example of such collaborative efforts is examined in detail.

The Learner

The long distance learner needs to have capabilities, both perceived and real, to function within the technology and not despite it. Many higher education learning institutions that are accepting students for Internet based coursework require minimal technological competencies as part of the application requirements (see, for example, Nova Southeastern University). Students and teachers in the K-12 settings need initial and ongoing training in the technology and in strategies for learning in a distance setting.

These requirements will allow the student occasions to enter and learn in distance environments.

In order to achieve a successful learning experience the student must possess or internalize certain characteristics. Successful students of distance learning need to be self-reliant, motivated, flexible, demonstrate initiative, possess competent writing skills, and be comfortable with technology as a learning tool (Hiltz, 1994; Simpson et al., 2002; Shaw, 1999). Shaw reported an interesting dynamic among type-A and type-B students participating in a virtual high school (VHS) music class where 90 percent of instruction and interaction occurred via the VHS Website. Students with a type-A personality demonstrated frustration with the lack of immediate feedback and the mistakes made. Students with type-B personalities who typically progressed slowly but surely in non-web based courses did not demonstrate frustration as quickly.

Students who are successful with distance learning experiences range in cognitive abilities. The effectiveness of the instructors and the support environments are key components of successful programs. One example of this is the Learning Across Time and Distance (LH-LT) program that allowed for third and fourth grade students from urban schools to be tutored in English Language arts by college students enrolled in a reading methods course for teacher education (Gutknect & Gutknect, 2001). The at-risk elementary students received one-to-one tutoring via videoconferencing and electronic interactive journaling through the Internet. The tutors were trained in formal settings to address teaching methods, deficit areas in Language Arts, lesson and assessment designs, and communicating with young students through technology. The college and school district developed collaborative protocols to guide the process. An offshoot of this project was a list of characteristics and participation criteria developed by the teacher participants and leadership members. The following outlines learner characteristics; they:

- Are active participants in the learning process;
- Learn through experiencing, questioning, sharing, construction, own learning;
- Identify and solve problems;
- Practice divergent and convergent thinking;
- Engage in critical/creative thinking and problem solving;
- Are process-oriented;
- Have input into decisions;
- Exhibit intrinsic motivation; and
- Work cooperatively in flexible groups (p.103).

Higher education institutions that are searching for alternatives to traditional classroom settings have fueled much of the progress in web-based distance learning. We can learn much from the experiences of undergraduate and graduate students who participate in distance learning environments. While some of the issues in this setting are specific to postsecondary learning, the process, obstacles, and benefits are often the same for all learners.

Consider for a moment Clarissa, a graduate student who enrolled in a hybrid online and face-to-face class. This was the first course in a series to complete a masters program in Sociology. Clarissa had attended a traditional undergraduate institution and had earned her bachelor's degree in four years. Now that she was working full-time in a rural area and living in suburbia, Clarissa needed a master's degree to further her career and increase the depth and breadth of her knowledge. The nearest college or university to offer sociology was an hour from her home. This commute after work would put a huge strain on her time and finances. When she heard about a distance-learning program that would only require her to commute once a month, she thought this might be ideal to complete her goals. Clarissa used technology in college to write papers and had begun to explore Internet sites that were career and entertainment related. When reading further about the requirements for distance learning, Clarissa became apprehensive about such a decision. Would she know enough to navigate the technology? Was her personal computer system adequate for the classroom demands? Would she stay motivated to complete assignments, readings without reporting regularly to a traditional classroom? It would take the intervention from other elements within the systems model to allay Clarissa's fears, assess her capabilities and encourage her to pursue this form of learning.

Clarissa decided to begin with one distance course and enlisted the assistance of the help desk features offered by the university information technology and support divisions. Through utilizing resources at this level in order to achieve her personal goal of a successful class, Clarissa was able to complete the first course and enrolled for two more the following semester. Certainly there were difficulties along the way. For example, during the first online chat, Clarissa kept getting bumped out of the chat room and was unable to contribute in a meaningful way. While her instructor was able to note her attendance, none of Clarissa's comments appeared in the chat room text. Clarissa was frustrated but sought the help of others within the distance model. This included emailing other classmates to see if anyone else had this difficulty, contacting the help desk for advice in how to stay in a chat room, and emailing the professor with an explanation and summary of what Clarissa would have entered in the chat.

This course presented a completely new set of circumstances for Clarissa. She realized, though, that every semester in her undergraduate career had brought new circumstances and this experience had those elements just in a different medium. While there were obstacles in the distance-learning model, there were also many rewards such as the sheer feasibility of taking a graduate course as well as the depth of learning she gained from the total experience. Most often distance learners choose to be in the distance setting and display a high degree of motivation (Simpson et al; Hiltz, 1994). Also, studies have indicated that once students completed one distance-learning course, they were inclined to take additional classes. Certainly, as in the case with Clarissa, students must adapt to their new environment and in this case, assume more responsibility for their own learning (Simpson et al.).

Instruction

One of the reasons that Clarissa was able to be successful was the depth of interactions she had with her instructor. While this is almost inconceivable as the two did not meet for the first seven weeks of class, the online communication was structured, accurate, and individualized, as needed. These characteristics become essential elements for effective communication in this format. Distance education and online learning should not look to replace face-to-face communication. Humans are social beings and can derive great satisfaction and complex learning experiences when interacting in the same room. Yet in today's educational and economic systems, one must look for a variety of ways to meet the same needs and then, when facing the path of distance education, be prepared to address the unique aspects of this learning environment. Clarissa was lucky that her instructor understood the role clearly and had both the passion for teaching and the technological savvy to assist this student. Educational research indicates that effective teaching highlights the "infectious nature of a teacher's passion for their subject" (Manathunga, 2002; see also Ramsden, 1992; McFadden & Perlman, 1989). Distance learning may be a tricky medium to convey this passion. It is essential for the instructor to infuse informal language and appropriate personal information to ensure the human qualities across the modem lines. This includes accepting a teaching paradigm that views the teacher as facilitating and managing the learning rather than dispensing the information (Hiltz, 1994).

Clarissa's instructor had a clear understanding of her role as a facilitator of the learning process. There are several essential elements for the teacher to address when using a distance format for instructional delivery. Gutknect and Gutknect (2001) reported the following list of teacher characteristics and participation criteria:

The beliefs and instructional practices of teachers in LH-LT (a distance learning model for Language Arts instruction) reflect the following characteristics.

The classroom:
- Provides an open and supportive atmosphere;
- Is child-centered; and
- Involves the community in meaningful ways.

The instruction:
- Includes integration/application of skills across subject areas;
- Acknowledges differences among perspectives;
- Is adaptable;
- Acknowledges various forms of intelligence;
- Includes reading/writing instruction using whole, natural language;
- Involves technology and print materials which included children's literature, original personal writing, and published literacy programs;
- Emphasizes meaning and understanding;
- Is evaluated on internalization of learning, via teacher judgment, portfolio and/or other authentic measures;
- Accommodates self-selection and learning alternatives; and
- Is more facilitative than direct (p. 103).

The Teacher

Incorporating distance learning methods into traditional classroom teaching often requires a paradigm shift for instructors. An effective approach to online teaching and learning was developed by Jamie McKenzie, author of the book *Beyond Technology: Questioning, Research, and the Information Literate School (2000)*. Mckenzie emphasizes the importance that teachers pose the essential questions for the theme or big idea. Then the teacher acts as facilitator assisting students in asking questions and investigating answers through online resources.

In order for teachers to be successful at incorporating distance learning components, extensive initial and ongoing staff development is essential (Campbell & Guisinger, 2003; Farley, 1999; Shaw, 1999). Many school districts seek the assistance of colleges and universities who have had more experience in utilizing the technology. Higher education institutions can provide initial training and ongoing support through classes or consultant models.

This symbiotic relationship had positive outcomes for the Cyberspace Rationalization consortium in New Jersey, that linked an award winning suburban high school, an at-risk urban high school, and a local university (Farley, 1999). The start-up costs of this project were filled through a three-year grant from the AT&T Foundation and the AT&T Learning Network. Compaq Computers also donated a substantial number of computers to the urban school. The critical first steps of this program began with intensive training for the teachers of the urban schools. The training was varied with the focus on learning both the technology and teaching methods for high-tech instruction. This allowed for participating teachers to gain the same knowledge level as those teachers at the suburban school district who had already been afforded these opportunities. Once the teachers were trained and ongoing staff development and support were in place, the teachers were ready to invite their classes into the virtual interactions. Students from both high schools communicated at a distance using videoconferencing and sharing of electronic manuscripts. The professors from the university served as online mentors and often critiqued the students' work via the Internet. In the beginning the students from the suburban high school served as trainers of electronic publishing for the urban students. Later the two schools collaborated on several interdisciplinary projects such as creating an online chemistry magazine. Students from both schools collaborate routinely, sharing, reviewing, and analyzing one another's data. They also videoconference routinely with a professor from the university for elucidation of content. Farley underscores two essential elements for utilizing the potential of distance learning: "Teachers in both districts interact with students from both schools to broaden opportunities for all. None of this would have been possible without careful training and appropriate implementation of instruction to integrate technology in a cyberspace environment" (41).

The format of web-based delivery involves contemplation and analysis as well. Educators in distance learning settings communicate with students in a synchronous and/or asynchronous format. Branon and Essex (2001) reported results from an international survey of distance educators. These teachers were asked to explain their reasons for selecting the types of communication. Respondents cited synchronous communication as most effective for "holding virtual office hours, team decision-making, brainstorming, community building, and dealing with technical issues" (36). Asynchronous communication was best suited for "encouraging in-depth, more thoughtful discussion, communicating with temporally diverse students, holding ongoing discussions where archiving is required; and allowing students to respond to a topic" (36).

Think back to the Michigan school district that utilized distance education within its own district. Teachers facilitated synchronous communications through live videoconferences, while students who posted messages on the online bulletin board worked asynchronously in order to create a reader response format of communication. Both types of online communication are effective for different learning tasks.

Whether the communication occurs in real time or not, the study conducted by Branon and Essex (2001) outlined guidelines for instructors (36), as detailed in Table 8.1.

TABLE 8.1: COMMUNICATION GUIDELINES

Using Synchronous Tools	Using Asynchronous Tools
Meet with smaller groups of students online	Have students work in teams
Provide frequent and multiple chat times	Provide feedback in summary form, rather than trying to respond to each individual posting
Allow a limited amount of "lurking" by students	Have students provide peer feedback
Choose tools and procedures that facilitate moderation of online chats	Choose tools that provide posting notification
Provide a specific protocol for online chats	Provide clear requirements for posting and reading discussion entries

Encouraging studies (Simonson, 2000) that analyzed the workings and effectiveness of distance education indicated that once a student completes one distance education course, she/he is likely to continue in this mode of learning. Studies also indicate that there are no significant differences in student success between on campus and online learning formats of the same material (Caywood & Duckett, 2003; Sun, Bender, & Fore, 2003). The barriers then would appear to be at the initial stages and affect all elements within the systems model. There will be (and have been) students and instructors who show interest in distance learning models. These will only be able to be actualized when critical levels of the systems model are involved in the conceptualization and application of the particular distance model. School districts and higher education institutions that wish to offer courses online and through a variety of distance models will need to recruit instructors with a passion for teaching and an appreciation of these flexible modes of delivery. Educators will be able to identify the benefits of teaching through distance models, as opportunities to teach a class that has low enrollment in the face-to-face model, addressing individual student needs, communicating consistently, effectively and succinctly with students, parents, and colleagues across the district, state, country, and around the world. Many educators struggle with the need to be in two places at once. Distance learning can allow for a teacher to be face to face with several students and simultaneously teach distance students through videoconferencing and webcams.

As distance education is not for every student, the same is true in regard to instructors. Many educators hold the need to see and interact with their students in a real life classroom forum. The idea of not seeing students' faces and expressions and letting go of the spontaneous discussion options is unacceptable to them. Every instructor and every student should not necessarily participate in this mode of learning. It is essential to remember that distance learning should not serve to replace face-to-face learning. Instead it has become a necessary option to continue (and in some cases initiate) learning in a variety of areas throughout our country and the world. The instructors in distance learning models need not be technological experts; rather they must have a strong appreciation for this mode of instruction. Research indicates that faculty who pursue this mode of teaching successfully have access to instruction support for the faculty member including software support and training for web-based platforms such as Blackboard, WebCT, or Ucompass Educator (Sun, Bender, & Fore, 2003; Cutwright & Griffith, 2000).

Teaching is sharing knowledge and ideas, and the format for this interaction does not define the interaction. The correspondence instructors of the 1860s must have seen a need for learning to be available in a variety of formats. Now with the current technology instructors can bring rich learning experiences to the online environment. The essential concepts of correspondence education are the underpinnings of online instruction. The technological advancements allow this instruction to be more sustained, consistent, and far reaching, with some interesting bells and whistles along the way. Instructors in these models must continue to be experts in their particular fields and skilled at teaching and interacting, as well as learn the nuances of online communication. How will an instructor get a feel for his or her students without meeting them face-to-face? How can one transpose the vibrant interactions of the traditional classroom into cyberspace? With the assistance of critical technological tools such as discussion threads and chat rooms, instructors begin to view the vital interactions as occurring through different modes. The need for structure and planning, two icons for traditional classrooms, remain a fundamental strategy for effective communication and learning. Small group interactions via discussion threads allow for students from all over the region, the country, and the world to interact with learning material and have meaningful discourse around essential topics. As with any effective teaching model, it remains the role of the instructor to facilitate and monitor the discussions, provide scaffolding, correct any miscommunications and wrong assumptions, and stretch the students to higher thinking levels and in-depth knowledge. While this many not always be possible in synchronous time, students and instructors then have the ability to reread the essential learnings and discussion items, as well as time to reflect on the learning therefore increasing both knowledge level and certainly application of such experiences. Through the nature of its format, online learning captures and saves the text of the lesson content and the discussions. Students are encouraged to review these fundamental learnings and reflect on the process. Instructors have the luxury of analyzing the salient features for each experience and preparing changes through simple cut and paste procedures.

THE LEARNING INSTITUTION

Turn to the Week in Review section of the New York Sunday Times, school district website, professional development center, Teacher Union Bulletin, or any current issue of The Chronicle for Higher Learning and you will find more and more educational institutions listing distance learning or online courses as one of their many options. Technological advances have made possible, and in some cases required, learning environments to accommodate the distance learner. In order for a college or university to remain a viable option for new and continuing students, online learning resources must be an option. From the very first steps of the college search, perspective high school juniors and seniors are utilizing web resources as the initial filter. While the traditional mailings or visitations continue to be useful, they are secondary in the search process. This is a radical change in the manner in which students engage in the selection process. If the institutional Website is not current, appealing, and diverse for the prospective student, that college or university may lose out early in the competition for new students. Even the most selective colleges advertise their product—an excellent education—via the Internet.

School districts are witnessing the impact of tremendous growth of virtual high schools (see for example, Carr, 2000). While many scholars will continue to debate the quality, efficacy, and sustainability of such programs, these learning environments are growing tremendously and graduating more and more students from across the country. The admissions staff at colleges and universities is aware that potential students are given an array of options to degree completion and internships. In order to compete within and beyond their normal perimeters, postsecondary institutions must begin to offer a variety of educational options. School districts, while under different sets of financial pressures, may begin to view virtual high schools as viable alternatives for students who have difficulties in the traditional school settings. These issues may be as complex as learning, behavioral, and emotional issues, or as rudimentary as addressing homebound students and those who must work during the day. This will create a tremendous impact of the public school teachers. Extensive training and an ongoing support network will be critical in the success of the distance learning option. School districts will need to set aside funding for this growing field.

College presidents and trustees, as well as those in the marketing areas, are aware of the strength of these trends and are working diligently to accommodate prospective students. Therefore, at the institutional level, though it may be fueled by financial reasons, the larger institution is looking to support the teacher and learner in this endeavor. Training for instructors and advertising for the students has become an integral part of the college package of the millennium. While the vast majority of postsecondary institutions are not looking to completely transform the traditional teaching and learning experience, universities such as the University of Phoenix, a completely distance learning institution are gaining recognition.

Critics of this mode of learning caution educational institutions not to lose their academic and scholarly integrity, in order to meet the current trend (see for example, Luke, 2000). Russo (2001) also identifies significant limitations to include "[ongoing] upgrade costs . . . learner isolation, technical glitches, lower-than-average completion rates, lack of evaluative data, and objections from teachers unions" (9).

A hallmark of many older institutions is the tradition of face-to-face learning and the immersion in the complete on campus college experience. Certainly the need and the population for this experience has been the sustainable force in colleges and universities to date presently. Though, there are several factors that threaten that sustainability. College tuition has increased exponentially and continues to rise steadily while state aid appropriations are decreasing (Harranek & Brodwin, 1998; Seline, 1996). This financial impact on individual students and their families had begun to adversely affect the student's ability to commit to a particular institution. More and more students are applying for financial aid and yet the rate of increase that colleges can lend or grant to students as not been able to match the demand. Podmolik (2000) highlights these issues with the following statement: "Liberal Arts schools' competition for students had become increasingly difficult in recent years with technology promising to transform higher education, more students looking for hi-tech careers, and more older students combining school with work" (4).

Aspects of this obstacle involve the state and federal levels as both lending institutions to the students and as financial aid for the colleges and universities. The current formula of increasing demand for education plus enormous rises in college costs and the restriction of funds from state and federal government equal the need for alternative approaches to delivering education. As institutions grapple with financial planning and meeting prospective (as well as current) students' needs, they also look to alternatives in order to circumvent the depth of this problem. In many ways, online learning can reduce overhead costs, required classroom space, and even parking issues. Rosenberg (2001) underscores the financial benefits of distance learning through examining the e-learning models. Rosenberg explains that courses offered through e-learning environments reduce costs for the individual student and teacher by decreasing travel expenses. Most significantly though are the drastic institutional savings that allow for colleges and universities to defer construction of new classrooms and buildings (Hall, 2001; Rosenberg). A larger question is do the colleges and universities have the technology available in order to offer a quality and sustainable distance-learning program? Is there a viable information technology division to support the technological needs of faculty and students in this mode of learning? Where can funding come from for such vast startup costs? This is when the learning institution may turn to the community for assistance.

THE COMMUNITY

Schools and communities strive to have productive and symbiotic relationships. When there is effective communication and willingness to work together by the leaders and constituents of these entities, then much can occur to serve the needs of both groups. While this is ideal, many communities do realize this collaboration in varying degrees. In the best of circumstances, the community utilizes the schools and the schools utilize the communities to share resources in both tangible and human varieties.

The community connections in Palm Beach County Florida are enhanced significantly through the use of distance learning options. In 1991 Southern Bell formed a business partnership with the five high schools in the Palm Beach County (Meyer & Crawford, 1994). A significant technological base was installed in the schools. This allowed for a plethora of communication opportunities. The high schools collaborated with Palm Beach County Community College and offered an array of Advanced Placement courses. These sites are also utilized by the faculty to attend in-service workshops, and state and national teleconferences. Community members enjoy the distance features for assemblies and communications. The potentials of distance learning are being actualized by a variety of groups and individuals in this large community.

A common goal of businesses in communities is to establish and maintain a positive relationship with the larger community. Bridge programs that link the schools, communities, and business endeavors together are viewed in positive light by all of the elements involved as well as state and federal agencies. In order to encourage and support these links, state and federal bureaus award business incentives and grant funds for the school and community levels when these links are structured and productive. The business industry goal is to demonstrate philanthropic contributions in ways that sustain and even increase the quality of life for the larger community. When companies can demonstrate how they can assist in the sharing of ideas and resources, they have begun to fulfill a major industry goal. School districts that link with businesses for learning purposes provide a tangible connection between education and the real world. Colleges and universities that join in these projects assist the community and local school districts; they also benefit from the expertise of the business world, and allow their students to partake in a variety of community commitments. Students of all ages can learn first hand from the business industry and begin to assess these future possibilities. The state and federal grants programs look highly upon these kinds of endeavors are often willing to offer support through financial contributions and recognition.

The Cyberspace Regionalization consortium of New Jersey (Farley, 1999) exemplifies this type of collaboration in an interdisciplinary social studies project. High school students traveled through cyberspace to email issue positions to delegates across the country, witness online Congress, gain access to the US Holocaust Museum, and prepare multimedia presentations of their findings through the Internet. An AT&T grant funded this project, school districts worked collaboratively with one another, and university faculty served as mentors and content experts.

One example of a strong symbiotic relationship that is built on the premise of distance learning is The Greystone project. This project is based in the northeast and involves IBM, Marist College, and a local school district that had been identified as a high needs district. Marist College formed a partnership with IBM and received grant monies to join the school district, college, and business in a distance learning venture to improve learning and communication for students and faculty. The IBM Corporation installed advanced technology in the school buildings and connected this to the mainframe computer at the college. Online courses for high school students and for faculty pursuing graduate degrees have been developed and are taught currently. Representatives from IBM and Marist IT department systematically conducted needs assessments, developed technology training sessions, and created Internet portals to address the specific needs of the school district. School district administrators, faculty, and students engage with technology for teaching, learning, and communication purposes. Faculty at the college serves as instructors, mentors, and consultants to the district and business liaisons. IBM provides the hard and software and the group and individual training to ensure that the new technology is understood and used in purposeful ways to support district needs. This is an important example of how the elements of a system can work together in order to produce better results.

The students will benefit from this project in several ways. High school students will have more access to college level courses and begin their college career as they finish high school. This has several implications to assist in the financial dilemmas many of these students will face. It also allows a new group of prospective college students to learn through technology in a distance format. High school students enrolled in college courses have access to the higher institution's electronic library and are expected to utilize this resource in order to complete assignments. Students in certain high school courses benefit from technology support offered by "hi-tech" corporations such as IBM and other business groups, and students of those teachers involved in support modules and online continued learning benefit from more informed and better-prepared teachers. The teachers in the school district benefit from the ability to take graduate courses online. As teachers in New York State the current requirements for professional certification include the completion of a Master's Degree within five years of the start of teaching. This is an extremely difficult task to accomplish as one begins a teaching career. Partaking in an online program that allows for flexibility in time is essential in meeting this educational and career goal. This project allows each element of the system to benefit and demonstrates the potential for symbiotic relationships within the community systems. Of course there have been, and will be obstacles along the way to see this program as a success. The potential, though, is awesome. The elements are in place. The roles are defined. The needs have been long established. The connections between the elements of the system are growing through communication, learning, and sharing of information and processes at each level. This group has tremendous power to make a systemic change.

STATE AND FEDERAL AGENCIES

In education, this level within the systems model often appears the most detached. This element is often perceived as the bureaucratic hole that sucks away all of the well-intentioned good ideas for change in the educational processes and chokes those brave enough to serve as change agents with the infamous red tape. Often, it is difficult to visualize the links between the student in need of instruction, the resources in a school that is overcrowded and understaffed, the community in need of services and support, and the state and federal agencies that complete this system. How do these agencies play a vital role in the educational system? Are they more than a gatekeeper to financial resources and permission for change? How can the link be viewed as symbiotic in nature even under the most utopian of circumstances?

Part of the difficulty with this element of the system is that the other elements do not physically see these agencies in progress unless there is a specific need or want. While the student may drive by the businesses in town on the way to school and the community members may enjoy a cultural event hosted at the local college or university, state and federal agencies are not obvious within the routine of everyday life. These agencies administer the laws and regulations that the other elements within the system must follow. They dictate what the teacher or instructor may or may not do when approaching a course outline. At the K-12 level, these agencies set the standards and plan curricular change to ensure for quality education. They govern the content, approach, and assessment of the content and applications. Yet, teachers and students do not connect with state officials and lawmakers. A mutual working relationship between these entities becomes virtually impossible in the eyes of many. Yet, it is often the grant money behind a particular program, or the state guidelines that hope to promote consistency that is the real link at this level. When new microscopes arrive in a classroom or white boards are added to an elementary school, there is often state or federal grant money behind them.

Little is known about the details of what happens at the state and federal levels. The perception is that these agencies are entities and not human resources functioning from a different perspective. There is a communication break down at this level and it seems to be the most difficult to repair. There may be a small connection to be enhanced via distance learning.

There have been profound examples of the effectiveness of governing bodies collaborating for progress in technology. One such experience was in 1998 when Bruce Babbit, the (then) US Secretary for Interior, announced the Access Native America program (Shaw, 1999). The goal of this program was to connect all of the schools affiliated with the Bureau of Indian Affairs (BIA) to the Internet. U.S. West and other phone companies formed partnerships with the BIA to help fulfill this goal. The strong initiative was fueled by effective technology and allowed for schools to invite students to collaborate on curricular projects with students from remote areas.

As students, instructors, and educational institutions move toward the option of distance learning and begin to offer services and courses to the community at large, the federal and state agencies can do much to support each element. The promotion of grant monies for these endeavors can assist in alleviating the financial start up burden that both individuals and institutions will face. Collaboration among the elements of the system has potential to build (or repair) connections with this systems level. Co-creating and refining guidelines for web based research and communications including the copyright issues will allow for these agencies to interact on a collegial level. Obviously it would not be appropriate for each level to interact with all of the information and decision-making, but the need for a collaborative model is crucial to the connection of the state and federal levels with the other elements within the system.

Recognition and honors can serve as another avenue for linking within the system. For example, when a student completed a grant-funded program, the Greystone project, the supporting agency could issue an award or certification of completion to the individual. This exercise could also work in reverse. The students and instructors who operate within the classroom filled with new technological resources could write thank you notes to the financial and educational supporters of such projects and publish the vital work in the local newspapers and online sources. One of the major benefits of technology is its enhanced communication. All of the individuals utilizing the technology decide how and when to communicate. Appreciating each level within the system—even those that appear to be the most distant, will only enhance the experience for all involved and for future endeavors.

THE BARRIERS

Transitions often require overcoming obstacles. This is true for the transition to distance education as a form of delivery for instruction. Members at all levels of the system will need to address perceived barriers for this format of learning. Many of these potential difficulties have been identified. Berge and Muilenburg (2000) conducted a survey of managers and administrators regarding problems associated with distance education. The following list is a rank order of their results:

- Increased time commitment;
- Lack of money to implement distance education programs;
- Organizational resistance to change;
- Lack of shared vision for distance education in the organization;
- Lack of support staff to help course development;
- Lack of strategic planning for distance education;
- Slow pace of implementation;
- Faculty compensation/incentives;
- Difficulty keeping up with technological changes; and
- Lack of technology-enhanced classrooms, labs, or infrastructure.

Teachers also share concerns regarding the efficacy of implementation for distance education. In a series of focus groups conducted by Simonson and Simonson (2001) teachers identified the following reasons why they were reluctant to engage in the distance learning process:

- Fear;
- Training;
- Time; and
- Changes needed.

This school population also identified the following areas as impediments to achievement of distance learning in schools:

- Need for training;
- Need for and lack of support;
- Time needed;
- Fear of the process;
- Scheduling problems; and
- Technical problem.

The list of possible limitations also includes access difficulties, congestion on the internet, delays in feedback by hours or days, the essential need for students to be motivated, self-reliant, and possess self-discipline (Hiltz, 1994), the labor intense efforts to design and implement online courses, and possible lack of structural and instructional support. Every face-to-face learning experience should not be put online. McKimm et al., (2003) offer educators a list of guiding questions to help determine the efficacy of an Internet project:

- What is the educational purpose of the web based learning project?
- What added value will online learning bring to the course or to the students?
- What resources and expertise on web-based learning exist in the institution?
- Are colleagues and the institution aware of the planned course? (Your need to avoid duplication of effort and be sure that the institution's computer system can support the course)
- Has the project taken account of existing teaching resources and ongoing maintenance costs after initial development?
- Have you allowed enough time to develop or redevelop materials?
- Have the particular design and student support requirements of web based learning courses been taken into account? (871).

The current forms of technology support certain areas of learning and certain types of learners more than others. For example, if a student is a strong visual learner, he or she may have difficulty not seeing the instructor. There are social and economic implications, as well. While technology provides the potential for instructional delivery all over the world, the entire world is not ready for such implementation. This form of education presupposes that all students will have access to a computer. Even as schools continue to gain desktops in classrooms and computer labs, the instruction is not guaranteed and most significantly, there is no assurance that students have access to computers and the Internet once they leave school grounds. Distance learning through technology has not yet accounted for the potential of the digital divide and the ramifications on education for the haves and have-nots (Berge & Collin, 1995).

Many of these factors that may affect distance education can be overcome with the support, instruction, and diligence from the instructor and the learner. The need for distance education is evident. Therefore, overcoming these obstacles will involve all elements of the system. Luckily, there are numerous benefits to this mode of instruction.

THE BENEFITS

The growth of distance education has stemmed from the growth of a need for coursework to be offered through alternative settings. For all of the reasons mentioned previously, distance education has become a necessity for colleges and universities to survive and thrive in the new millennium. Currently there are economic, pragmatic, and psychological reasons for the effectiveness of distance learning. Distance learning overcomes obstacles faced by traditional instruction by its sheer design. Access is now available to any qualified student who has the proper technology and Internet access (Simonson et al., 2002). When presented in asynchronous form, students can access the course materials and assignments twenty-four hours a day and seven days a week. This form of instruction is not constrained by time schedules or time zones. The interaction occurs when the learner is ready and allows for the essential process of reflection on the part of the learner as well as the instructor. An overwhelming benefit to distance education is access. Students who were once unable to take courses due to location now have a plethora of educational opportunities at the click of a mouse. This is beneficial not only for the undergraduate and graduate students, but for continuing education in the form of in-services, certificate programs, conferences, and the dissemination and assimilation of new materials and products for various aspects of the business world.

Distance education offers unique benefits from the psychological and social domains. In the absence of face-to-face instruction, the instructor and the students are unaware of the ethnicity, physical appearances, or possible disabilities within the class (Simonson et al., 2002). Every student enters on equal ground and the possible social and psychological barriers are removed. An interesting dynamic emerges in a distance learning course: the students are free from the traditional social barriers, and yet there is no opportunity to "sit in the back of the class." If a student does not log on and enter his or her thoughts, assignments, or comments, he or she is essentially absent. In this case the lack of real time face-to-face interactions can raise the bar in discussions and input as one student reads the comments of another and then has time to process and reflect before entering his or her own response. Many of the essential elements of wait time can be used effectively in this setting.

DISTANCE EDUCATION IN THIS MILLENNIUM: THE TRANSITION CONTINUES

The world of distance education has transformed several times over since Isaac Pittman's correspondence course in 1860. New ground in the area of merging technology with teaching and learning through this vehicle are emerging daily. It is the essential role of each element of the systems model to examine, analyze, and find the best fit for this area of education. The need has been identified and the resources are among us. The careful and purposeful application of those resources critical to continued quality and flexible education.

DISCUSSION QUESTIONS

1. What are the advantages of distance learning?

2. How can a school district overcome the barriers to distance learning?

3. How can the teacher of a diverse student body enable all students to use distant learning?

4. What is the impact of distance learning on higher education institutions, the business community, the family, and the student?

5. How does distance learning reflect the key elements in the systems model of education?

Chapter 9:
The School and the Mental Health System

OBJECTIVES

After studying this chapter, the reader will be able to define, analyze and apply the following concepts and strategies:

1. Three types of mental health institutions;

2. Collaborative mental health model process and its benefits;

3. Caplan's model of psychiatric prevention: primary, secondary, tertiary;

4. Institute of Medicine model of prevention: universal, selective, indicated;

5. Forms of primary prevention;

6. Prevention criteria;

7. Prevention programs: Head Start and Perry Preschool, Primary Mental Health Program, Seattle Social Development project, Linking the Interests of Families and Teachers;

8. Multi-systemic therapy;

9. Universal substance abuse prevention programs;

10. Federal role in prevention policy development and

funding; and

11. Ethical concerns regarding prevention programs.

Those who have a higher conception of education will prize most the method of cultivating a (mind) so that it fulfills to perfection its own natural conditions of growth. -Carl G. Jung

OVERVIEW

The major theme of this book has concerned the role of the school as central to the educational system and the process of educational change. Teachers, administrators, board members and parents have the potential power not only to create in-school innovations, but also to encourage change at other levels of the educational system. They can, for example, institute parent education programs, or support policies for enhancing cultural diversity or support the use of technology in the curriculum or encourage community participation in school decision-making. The services rendered by the school need not be limited only to the educational system. The school has been an integral component of many social systems in the community. For example, county public health officials have viewed the school as an important structure for preventing, diagnosing and treating health problems. The fact that nearly all children attend school enables these officials to maintain health records on the younger population and to administer mass inoculations to prevent major epidemics of childhood illness. Throughout the nation, parents must provide evidence of vaccinations before their children can be allowed to enter school. In addition, each school has incorporated health topics in its curriculum and these offerings have resulted in a better-informed and healthier society. Thus, the school can serve many functions in the community.

The focus of this section is to discuss how the school can become an integral arm of the community mental health system. Specifically, the rationale for using schools to enhance the psychological well being of students and the value of intervening early in the development of children to prevent mental illness are presented. Ways of developing a collaborative relationship between school staff and mental health professionals are discussed and the chapter concludes with examples of mental health programs that have been implemented in the schools. While this represents a digression from the major theme of how schools affect academic learning, it does serve to demonstrate another channel through which the school is linked to the community and that, by serving society in a diverse manner, the significance and credibility of the school can be improved. In addition, mental health programs in the school, which increase the students' ability to deal with personal problems and which reduce acting-out and disruptive behavior in the classroom, provide an atmosphere more conducive to student learning. Thus, programs that focus on mental health education can also enhance academic learning in the schools.

THEORETICAL RATIONALE: THE SCHOOL AS A KEY INTEGRATED SOCIAL SYSTEM

The rationale for locating mental health programs in the schools is that many forms of mental illness are at least partially developmental in nature and that, by providing psychological supports early in life, later severe mental problems can be prevented. Thus, children who are taught successful strategies for adjusting to life stressors and of relating to others are more likely to lead normal healthy adult lives than those without this training. Since the vast majority of children attend school, providing this training as part of the educational curriculum is an excellent method of reaching a large segment of the community. In addition, utilizing the schools in this manner helps to make the concern for mental health an integral component of students' lives, and the stigma associated with receiving psychological services is greatly reduced.

Bower (1972) discussed the need for a fully integrated mental health system in the community. He noted that the system is composed of three types of institutions:

1. Key Integrated Social Systems (KISS): KISS includes schools, families and church groups. These agencies provide a sense of belonging, a spirit of community and a source of meaning for their members. Most individuals participate in these social institutions and they

are central to the everyday life of the local neighborhood;
2. **Ailing-in Difficulty Institutions (AID):** AID includes mental health centers and social service
agencies that treat those who are not functioning
well in the community. Since those who utilize the
services of AID agencies are branded as being ab-
normal in some way, there is often a social stigma
attached to receiving these services. Also, the fact
that those who are treated by these agencies must
temporarily disrupt their routine and receive the
service away from their KISS institution reduces
the effectiveness of the treatment provided; and
3. **Illness Correctional Endeavors (ICE):** ICE institutions
are places, such as mental hospitals and jails, where
those who no longer function well in society are sent on
a long-term, and often permanent, basis.

Bower argued that if KISS institutions were more effective in
maintaining the mental health of their members, fewer individuals
would need to utilize AID or ICE structures. Also, if the KISS and
AID agencies were more closely linked, AID professionals could
help KISS staff to bolster the psychological well-being of the
community, thus preventing illness. If this occurred, the AID agencies would be able to focus on the fewer individuals referred by
KISS and they could offer more effective individualized service,
reducing the need for ICE. "To paraphrase Bower, prevention is
geared toward providing children with a personally enhancing
KISS so that they will require less AID and fewer will ultimately
have to be put on ICE" (Allen, Chinsky, Larcen, Lockman, & Selinger, 1976, pp.7-8). Thus, instituting mental health programs in
the schools will enhance the psychological well being of the community and reduce mental illness.

Establishing A Cooperative Relationship

In order for any potential mental health program intervention to
be effective, it must first be accepted within the school. The interventions are usually a joint effort of school staff and mental health
professionals. Typically the school psychologists, social workers

and counselors serve as the link between the school community and the mental health professionals in the community or university.

One group of community psychologists from the University of Connecticut (Allen et al., 1976) collaborated with the teachers and administrators in a nearby school district to develop a mental health program for the students and discussed in detail the process of designing and implementing the program. The collaborative relationship took 18 months to develop, due to the complexity of the program and because of the number of people involved. By the time the intervention began, some 80 university teachers and students and 20 school staff were involved in implementing the intervention.

The consultants utilized three strategies to insure the acceptance of the program and its correct implementation. These methods included:

1. Obtaining support from the school administration;
2. Developing a collaborative working relationship with the school staff; and
3. Providing extensive in-service training.

In gaining access to the school, the consultants entered slowly, developed a mutual trust and respected the different competences of all the participants. The administrators and school board accepted the program because it was innovative, capable of producing many benefits to the students, and was very cost efficient. (College student volunteers who received credit for their participation performed much of the work of the program free). In addition, the university had a positive reputation in the community and the school administration was eager to utilize the personnel resources of the university. In their interaction with the school staff, the consultants carefully identified the rights and responsibilities of both the school-teachers and the university staff. Also, the benefits to the teachers, in terms of greater interpersonal involvement with their elementary school children, less need to discipline students in class and free college credit for participating in the intervention, were stressed.

The consultants established a collaborative relationship with the teachers, acknowledging the expertise of the latter group. In the workshops, for example, a consultant identified a program objective. Then the teachers and the consultant worked cooperatively to design feasible educational materials and procedures that enabled the objective to be implemented. In this way, the teachers perceived themselves as collaborators in the program and the consultants related to the teachers as equal partners in the intervention.

In developing the program jointly, the consultants established effective communication channels to accomplish their collaborative objectives: to allow for mutual feedback between the teachers and consultants regarding program progress; to allow for the free and open expression of complaints; and to build rapport among the consultants, school teachers and college students. To develop a smooth running program and to create mutual trust, the university staff listened actively to any criticisms expressed and changed the program accordingly. To avoid any personality conflict, the consultants stressed the need to keep everyone task-oriented.

Most of the in-service training consisted of workshop-type experiences for the schoolteachers and for the college students. The consultants planned the workshops in a manner that insured that the trainees developed a positive attitude toward the learning, highlighting the significance of the program and the interpersonal rewards in the classroom to be gained through the program. The curriculum was described in small sequential steps with well-defined objectives and meaningful opportunities for involving the participants.

The college volunteers were selected on the basis of their interpersonal skills, verbal fluency and social tact. In addition, as the college students were gradually made more aware of the program through the workshops, some decided not to participate further. This self-selection process helped to insure that those who remained would be well-motivated and competent volunteers.

Taking the time to plan all aspects of the collaborative relationship is well worth the effort in that the resulting prevention program is more likely to be effective as a result. A working collaboration should function smoothly, and the knowledge, skills and energies of all involved should be fully utilized. Consultants should adopt an attitude of "one downsmanship" (Caplan, 1964) and be respectful of the professionalism and expertise of the host staff.

PREVENTION MODELS

The Caplan Model

In 1964, Gerald Caplan presented a three level model of psychiatric prevention, which has served as the basis for much of the research in the field for 30 years, until it was replaced in 1994 with a newer categorization system which spans both prevention and treatment methods. Caplan argued that the mental health system has over-emphasized the treatment of those already ill; this is a practice typically used by medicine (until recently) and carried over into the mental health field. Caplan believed that fewer individuals would become mentally ill if programs were initiated that helped those who were likely to become ill to adjust better to their environment. This approach led to the beginning of community mental health centers in the United States. These centers treated individuals who were still able to function in their work and interpersonal roles, thus preventing them from needing to become institutionalized. Caplan further argued that, if all individuals were provided psychological support for dealing with normal life-crises, fewer people would require the services of community-based facilities. Based on a developmental model of mental illness, the preventive approach that emphasizes early intervention should be more effective, more humane and less expensive than traditional treatment methods.

In addition, such prevention models are becoming increasingly necessary as society becomes more complex and the ability to cope with life stresses becomes more crucial. In the original system, Caplan identified the three levels of prevention, as follows:

- Primary prevention is aimed at keeping healthy persons healthy. Interventions at this level target children who have no symptoms of emotional or mental disorders.
- These programs either supply additional environmental resources or bolster personal competencies to decrease the likelihood that the target individuals will succumb to difficulties in living. An example of supplying an environmental resource might include encouraging and training older students to serve as buddies for children in a lower grade. Alternatively, teaching social skills to students could be an example of bolstering a personal competence;

- Secondary prevention programs attempt to help those individuals who are at high risk of developing psychological disorders. Typically the targeted students already show some initial symptoms of distress. These programs attempt to "nip the problem in the bud," and as a result reduce the severity and duration of the illness. Programs designed to help students who have lost a classmate deal with the grieving process are examples of secondary prevention; and
- Tertiary prevention is aimed at alleviating the harmful consequences of emotional or mental disorders. Those already suffering from chronic disorders are targeted in these programs. While similar to clinical treatment, the objective of tertiary programs is to help individuals return to as normal a lifestyle as possible. The goal of clinical treatment is often to reduce illness. Tertiary prevention programs rarely attempt to cure disorders, and psychiatric diagnoses are not usually changed. Instead, the goals of such programs include placing children with emotional disturbances back in regular school as soon as possible. Tertiary programs focus on teaching children to live with their condition and to improve the quality of life in spite of the disorder.

TABLE 9.1: THE CAPLAN MODEL

LEVELS	GOAL	TARGET	SAMPLE INTERVENTION	SAMPLE PROGRAM
Primary	Stay healthy	Persons without symptoms	Provide additional environmental resources Bolster personal competencies	Head Start
Secondary	Help the high risk person	Persons with initial symp-	Deal with the problem at onset	Primary Mental Health Program

		toms		
Tertiary	Alleviate the negative consequences of the disorder and reduce illness	Persons suffering from chronic disorders	Provide life and coping skills	Programs integrating those with emotional disturbance into schools

Caplan's three-level model has been used in the research literature to describe prevention programs since 1964. Many psychologists, however, have found it challenging and often arbitrary to identify specific programs as primary, secondary or tertiary. In practice, most interventions cross over these boundaries. The Caplan model, outlined in Table 9.1, is still useful. It enables interventionists to conceive of and develop many program alternatives to prevent mental disorder.

The Institute of Medicine Model (IOM)

Since precise definitions and boundaries are ideals that social scientists strive to realize, a new system for categorizing types of prevention has been developed (Mrazek & Haggerty, 1994; Munoz, Mrazek, & Haggerty, 1996). As this new system was presented in a major report of the federal government's Institute of Medicine, it has "established rigorous standards for prevention research, highlighted the scientific credibility the field has achieved, and prompted constructive debate regarding priorities for future research, practice and training" (Weissberg, Kumpfer, & Seligman, 2003, pp. 425-6). In this new category system, the spectrum of mental health interventions includes prevention, treatment and maintenance. Preventive programs aim to reduce the likelihood of mental disorder. They are presented to individuals or groups before the onset of the disorder. Treatment programs, on the other hand, are applied to those already displaying the criteria and symptoms of a diagnosable mental illness. Finally, maintenance programs are implemented after the acute episode of the disorder has subsided. Maintenance programs aim to reduce relapses and re-occurrences and to provide rehabilitative services in the school or community. Since treatment and maintenance programs are intended for individuals seriously affected by mental illness, and are not typically provided in the school setting, these modalities are not discussed in this chapter.

Prevention programs are further divided into universal, selective and indicated interventions focusing on the population to be targeted. These categories and sub-categories are described, as follows:

- Universal Prevention:

     Universal preventive interventions target general populations who have not been identified as being at increased risk. Generally, a good universal preventive program should have little risk of negative side effects, be acceptable to the public and have a low cost per individual targeted. Stress management workshops or problem solving skills training programs administered to all students in a class or school are examples of universal prevention. Universal prevention is similar to Caplan's primary prevention concept, and its forms and criteria are discussed in the next sections of the chapter;

- Selective Prevention

     Selective preventive interventions target those whose risk of disorder is greater than average due to some biological, psychological or social risk factor. The individuals chosen to participate in such programs have not yet displayed any symptoms of the disorder. For example, a school psychologist might develop a selective prevention "banana split" group designed for students whose parents are in the process of divorce or separation. In such a program, selected student are encouraged to share their feelings and experiences, receive the support of others and learn from each other strategies for dealing with the problems created by this change in family life. These students are not displaying any symptoms, but it is likely that without adequate peer social support, they might later exhibit such behavior. Selective prevention is similar to Caplan's secondary prevention concept in that the participants are high-risk candidates but are symptom free; and

- Indicated Prevention Programs

The indicated preventive interventions target high-risk individuals who have minimal and detectable symptoms, but not all the diagnostic criteria of a mental disorder. School children who already display some conduct disorder behaviors might be singled out for a conflict resolution-training program. Such programs are still worthwhile if they only delay rather than prevent the onset of the disorder. Generally, the public accepts these programs even if the cost per targeted individual is high and there are some risks associated with the intervention. This type of strategy is not a separate category in the Caplan Model. Most of the programs at this level would have been "forced to fit" into the secondary prevention concept. Caplan's tertiary prevention is more similar to the IOM treatment and maintenance strategies.

The IOM model, outlined in Table 9.2, has provided a framework for reviewing the full range of programs present in the mental health system. It has also encouraged rigorous empirical evaluations of preventive and treatment-oriented programs. However, no model is perfect. It is likely that specific programs will still straddle two or more categories. A participant may be chosen for a selective preventive program and then display initial symptoms of the disorder. At that point, the intervention will include both selective and indicated individuals. It is unlikely that the indicated students will be required to leave the program to maintain the research boundaries. The real value of the system is not to differentiate types of prevention. Instead, the major benefit is to encourage creative thinking on the part of intervention planners to devise alternative programs to meet the needs of all segments of the population.

TABLE 9.2: THE INSTITUTE OF MEDICINE MODEL

LEVELS	GOAL	TARGET	SAMPLE INTER- VENTION	SAMPLE PRO- GRAM

Prevention				
Universal	Reduce the like-lihood of men-tal dis-order	General popula-tion not identified as at risk	Stress man-agement workshops Problem solving skills training	Head Start Seattle Social Develop-ment Pro-ject
Selective	Prevent symp-toms	Persons whose risk of disorder is greater than av-erage due to psy-cho-logical, social or biologi-cal at-risk factors	"Banana split" groups for children of parents in the process of divorce	Primary Mental Health Project Seattle Social Develop-ment Pro-ject
Indicated	Delay the on-set of the dis-order	Persons who are high risk with minimal detect-able symp-toms	Conflict-resolution Training for violent prone students	Multi-systemic Therapy
Treatment	Treat the mental illness	Persons display-ing crite-ria and	Psychothera-peutic ser-vices in a group home	

		symp- toms of diag- nosable mental illness		
Mainte- nance	Reduce relapses and provide re- habili- tation after an acute episode has sub- sided	Persons display- ing crite- ria and symp- toms of diag- nosable mental illness	Rehabilita- tion	

TWO FORMS OF PRIMARY PREVENTION

Cowen (1996) differentiated between two forms of primary prevention. The first type attempts to reduce the likelihood that healthy individuals will experience psychological dysfunctions. Risk factors are targeted and these programs are aimed at reducing the incidence of mental illness. Cowen, however, favored the second form, which seeks to promote psychological health and wellness. Such programs that target protective factors benefit everyone and enhance positive mental health in the community.

While this distinction is one of degree, promoting health has the added value of aiming for a higher objective, and successful programs designed to enhance health will also achieve the slightly lesser goal of preventing illness. By analogy, many of those who participate in various aerobic exercise programs in health clubs are hoping to be more fit, to look and feel better. Others who "work out" to reduce the likelihood of cardio-vascular disease have different motivation and perception of these activities. Similarly, most students attend school not to reduce their ignorance, but rather to improve themselves and to obtain more meaningful employment. It is likely more will want to become involved in programs which are described as wellness-enhancing than in those presented as illness-preventing, and there is no stigma involved in such activities.

The Prevention Task Panel recommended both forms of primary prevention in 1978 in its report to the President's Commission on Mental Health. This report noted the dual objectives of lowering the incidence of mental disorders and promoting conditions that reinforce positive mental health. Unfortunately, more recent government-sponsored commissions have de-emphasized the wellness enhancement approach. Albee (1996) noted that reports published by the National Institute of Mental Health (1994) and the IOM concluded that since mental health promotion does not target specific disorders, it is not as important as risk reduction. While the two reports did not call for a halt to such research, these conclusions reduce the likelihood that interventions based on wellness enhancement will receive increased funding by governmental agencies. Also, wellness promotion activities are excluded from the category of universal prevention.

CRITERIA FOR GOOD UNIVERSAL OR PRIMARY PREVENTION PROGRAMS

Nation, Crusto, Wandersman, Kumpfer, Seybolt, Morrissey-Kane, and Davino (2003) identified nine characteristics that have been associated consistently with effective prevention interventions. "Programs were comprehensive, included varied teaching methods, provided sufficient dosage, were theory driven, provided opportunities for positive relationships, were appropriately timed, were socio-culturally relevant, included outcome evaluation, and involved well-trained staff" (p. 449). Thus, a good prevention program in the schools has more than one component, provides opportunities for student participation as well as teacher controlled activities, involves many sessions over a long period of time, is based on empirically derived principles, encourages positive modeling and social interaction, is presented at a time when the children are ready to learn the skill and in a manner consistent with the children's age and culture. When planning a prevention program, these criteria provide a good checklist of attributes to include.

Examples of Prevention Programs

The programs presented are typical examples of what has been done in various school systems to enhance the psychological and social well-being of students and to prevent specific disorders or problem behaviors. Hopefully they will serve to "pique" the reader's imagination regarding potential interventions to implement. In addition, some researchers have conducted meta-analyses of many similar studies. These researchers sought to find factors that consistently resulted in significant beneficial effects. These meta-analyses are presented as well. The program that has generated the greatest interest and controversy over the past 40 years is the Head Start Program. This intervention is presented first, and then programs are arranged chronologically according to the age of the targeted individuals.

The Head Start Program

Perhaps the most significant large scale example of universal prevention, Head Start was initiated in 1965 as a preschool program designed to overcome the effects of "cultural deprivation." The program had a number of lofty goals: to improve the physical health and social and emotional development of young children; to improve the level of their mental processes; to raise their expectations for success; to instill responsible attitudes toward family and society; and to increase dignity and self-worth (Zigler & Valentine, 1979). Over one half million children participated in 3000 local projects in the first Head Start summer program, and Head Start swiftly expanded to a 12-month program affecting millions of preschool students.

The program needs to be viewed from a systems approach. Both the development of the program and its near early demise were affected greatly by politics at the national level. The Head Start concept originated as part of President Kennedy's "New Frontier" and was implemented through the Johnson Administration's

"War on Poverty" and the Office of Economic Opportunity, during a period when liberal politics dominated. Medicare, Medicaid, community mental health and civil rights legislation were either initiated or strongly supported at this time (Moynahan, 1969). By 1969, a more conservative administration had been elected and support for the above initiatives waned. Early evaluations of Head Start yielded disappointing results. This, coupled with the publication of Arthur Jensen's (1969) Harvard Educational Review article defending the position that innate racial differences in IQ cannot be changed, supported President Nixon's attempt to dismantle Head Start. As was mentioned earlier, political and economic ideologies affect social scientific theory and research, and as the nation's mood changes so does the nature of studies conducted and published (Riegal, 1972; Rappaport, 1977).

In it early days Head Start, like other federally-funded programs of its time, was mandated to include some degree of parental involvement, which enhanced the community's sense of empowerment and ownership of the program. Parental involvement, however, had an unintended consequence that affected evaluation. Local control converted Head Start into a large number of separate projects, each with its own unique curriculum and other characteristics. There was not one, national, uniform program, and evaluation studies either summed the results of many diverse projects or focused on only one small-scale local intervention. The former alternative increases error variance, which makes it harder to detect real effects of the program, while the latter choice reduces the ability to generalize the findings.

Early research utilized the former approach, and the results were disappointing. In a controversial evaluation called the Westinghouse Study, Cicirelli (1969) found no lasting IQ effect due to participation in Head Start. When measured just after completing the program, the IQ scores of the Head Start children were significantly higher than that of the controls, but after three years of attending public school, the initial IQ gains disappeared.

Some social scientists have criticized this study. Given the multi-faceted goals of Head Start, perhaps IQ was not the correct outcome to measure. Even if an educator believed that improving mental processes was the most significant objective, among measures of mental processes, intelligence is too stable to be affected by a short-term program such as Head Start. Over time, any temporary IQ changes disappear. Haggard (1954), for example, found that "prepping" a naïve child on how to take an intelligence test can result in a temporary gain, but this gain disappears as the control group children gradually gain more experience in test taking. Achievement test scores and even school grades are measures of mental processes that are more sensitive to interventions than are IQ scores.

Other critics of the Westinghouse study believed that its findings demonstrated the faults of the public school system and not those of Head Start (Zigler & Valentine, 1979). The participating children gained from the program, but their initial enthusiasm for learning was dulled by the public school experience. Consider that Head Start is highly responsive to the needs of the targeted minority children, whereas public schools follow a state-mandated curriculum. Parental involvement and local control guaranteed that Head Start met local needs of participating families. While public schools have school boards, the members of the board might be more concerned about school taxes and administrative issues than about the quality of education. Also, boards rarely represent minority cultures, and typically there are fewer cultural amplifiers in public schools than in Head Start programs.

Stanley Murrell (1973) viewed the problems that minority children encounter when they enter public school as caused by the lack of social system synergy. As mentioned in the first chapter, a child belongs to three systems: the family; peer group; and school. When members of all three systems are encouraging the same goals and values, synergy exists and a child is likely to behave in a manner consistent with these forces. When the systems conflict, the child is less certain about goals and feels confused. Behavior appears more erratic and less focused. In Head Start, the three systems are more synergistic, but in public school, the minority child confronts an alien culture and the school system is no longer in step with peers and family.

Perry Preschool Project

Other researchers have found permanent gains due to Head Start when they focused on evaluating individual well-run programs rather than summing over the outcomes of many different projects. The Head Start program that has been researched most extensively using the best experimental design is the Perry Pre-school Project in Ypsilanti, Michigan. This program targeted Afri-can-American children from low socioeconomic backgrounds whose initial IQ's ranged from 60 to 90. The program consisted of a child development curriculum geared toward intellectual, physi-cal and social development, and weekly home visits. Children at-tended half-day classes during a 30-week period (Schweinhart & Weikart, 1989). The research participants were assigned randomly to either the program or to a no preschool control (Levine & Per-kins, 1987). Various researchers followed these children over a 23-year period, and observed them to age 27 years.

Based on the empirical evidence from a variety of studies, the Perry Preschool Project has been a huge success. Darlington, Royce, Snipper, Murray, and Lazar (1980) found that children who participated in a preschool program were far less likely to be la-beled as mentally retarded (35 percent of the controls vs. 15 per-cent of the preschool children) and less likely to need special edu-cation classes. Berreuta-Clement, Schweinhart, Barnett, Epstein, and Weikart (1984) and Schweinhart, Barnes, and Weikart (1993) listed the continuing statistically significant benefits of participa-tion in the Perry Preschool Project as including fewer teenage pregnancies, lower arrest rates, higher school grades, higher rate of graduation from high school and overall level of educational at-tainment, higher income, lower welfare and unemployment and greater social responsibility. The researchers estimated that seven dollars were saved for each dollar spent in this one-year preschool program. While the empirical data is striking and the economic cost/benefit analysis impressive, the total gains in promoting well-ness and preventing pain and misery is incalculable.

Statistical significance in research is often not sufficient to sway policy makers and the general public. For example, the U.S. General Accounting Office (GAO, 1997) reviewed 22 Head Start evaluation studies and concluded that there was insufficient evi-dence of long-term effects. The GAO noted that large-scale studies demonstrating significant benefits had not been performed. As a result, a consortium of researchers has begun to conduct a national study to evaluate Head Start. (Ripple & Zigler, 2003). A parallel program, Early Head Start, designed to assist preschoolers and their parents, has been evaluated on a large scale. Love, Kisker, Ross, Schochet, Brooks-Gunn, Paulsell, Boller, Constantine, Vogel, Fuligni, and Brady-Smith (2002) performed a national random assignment study of 3001 families who participated in 17 Head Start programs. They found that the toddlers in the program developed more swiftly in cognitive, socio-emotional and language areas, and that families' home environment, parenting and economic condition improved. While the empirical debate continues, political interests are more likely to sway policy. President George W. Bush expressed the position that Head Start should focus more exclusively on literacy learning, and that it should be transferred from the Department of Health and Human Services to the Department of Education. This change would transform Head Start from a national to a state-directed program, and the comprehensive scope and national orientation of the program might be lost (Ripple & Zigler, 2003).

While Head Start and Early Head Start are classified as examples of universal prevention, there are other large-scale programs that deal with students who have been identified as being at-risk. One of the largest of these programs is the program that is described below.

The Primary Mental Health Project

Perhaps the most famous selective or secondary prevention program, which has been in operation for the longest time, is the Primary Mental Health Project (PMHP). This program, begun by Emory Cowen in 1957 in the Rochester, New York School District, has grown to be present in 2000 schools in over 700 school districts throughout this country (Cowen, 1996). It is a good example of the selective prevention model. The PMHP was aimed at the early detection and prevention of school adjustment problems. Cowen initiated this program as he discovered that individuals currently presenting themselves for treatment have histories of psychological maladjustment dating back to their early years in school. Cowen reasoned that, by assessing children psychologically in the primary grades, mental health professionals might identify at-risk children, and together with teachers and parents, design programs to help these students. Also, paraprofessional volunteers, such as college students, could be recruited and trained, and then provide inexpensive direct care to children in the program.

Typically, primary grade teachers, and sometimes parents, would observe the young students as they performed their routine activities. If the adults noticed unusual or inappropriate behavior, they would identify the child as being at-risk and the child would then receive various services. These services might include additional testing, counseling, tutoring or social skills training. Sometimes the child would be referred to professionals outside the school for more intensive treatment.

Satcher (2000) noted that the PMHP produced significant improvement in the students' grades, achievement test scores and behavioral ratings. The program was relatively expensive, however. as the screening instruments were unable to differentiate which students were truly at risk. Levine and Perkins (1987) listed problems common to both the PMHP and most other selective or secondary prevention programs that tend to limit effectiveness. Early detection of problems led to many false positives. Many children were identified as being at high risk that in reality were not. Consider that children's behavior in the first grade is affected by many transient factors, and a teacher, parent or even psychologist observing a student on a "bad day" might interpret a temporary behavior as an early warning sign of illness. In the original version of the PMHP, fully one-third of all first graders were classified as needing services offered in the program. Yet, by one estimate (Levine & Perkins, 1987) over 80 percent of those identified children did not really need treatment, and if left alone would develop into healthy adults.

Treating many false positives is very costly, as only a small percentage of the consumed resources are helping those who truly need the service. A more significant concern arising out of identifying so many false positives involves labeling. As was discussed previously, labeling affects how a child is viewed. It is likely that parents, learning that their child is at-risk for developing a psychiatric condition, might lower their expectations concerning the child's future. Teachers and classmates might isolate the child. Even the identified child might begin to act in a way consistent with the label—a type of self-fulfilling prophecy. This leads to a great deal of emotional turmoil and ironically, the faulty diagnosis itself may cause the problem the program was designed to prevent.

Unfortunately, the percentage of false positives increases the earlier the diagnosis is made. If problems are allowed to continue for a longer time prior to the diagnosis, the observed behavior becomes more apparent and consistent, and confidence in the accuracy of the assessment increases. However, the behavior becomes more resistant to change. On balance, although some selective prevention programs are effective, whenever possible, universal preventive strategies applied to groups of individuals who have not yet displayed any symptoms are the methods of choice. Universal prevention does not require labeling and the services offered are not stigmatizing.

Elementary School-Based Primary Prevention Programs

There are many benefits of locating prevention programs in schools. Elementary school "is the first point in the lifespan when the majority of children enter a service system that includes a broad cross section of the population" (Eddy, Reid, & Fetrow, 2000, p.167). Cowen, Hightower, Pedro-Carroll, and Work (1989) noted that the audience is captive and available and these programs can reach populations that may not actively seek out therapeutic help in the community. Also, school-based programs allow the interventionists some options regarding how to deliver the program. They can choose either to train regular teachers to present the program, or to present the program themselves to the children. There are great benefits to training teachers. Typically students know and like their teacher and rapport building is an easier process. Also, if the teachers believe the program is effective, they are inclined to offer it repeatedly in future years, and the preventive program becomes more accepted by and integrated into the school. Finally, a secondary effect of many prevention programs is to enhance the student's ability and motivation to learn, a benefit consistent with the goals of the school. Educators, after viewing the data demonstrating such programs improve academic achievement and reduce classroom management problems, are eager to embrace the program. Prevention need not take time away from traditional learning. Psychologists, working with teachers, can integrate the program's objectives into regular academic lessons. For example, a problem-solving curriculum can be built into the typical selection of short stories read during literature class. Having the students brainstorm alternatives available to the hero at a critical moment in the story adds to the students' motivation to read, as well as their understanding of how to solve social problems and cope with crises. Thus, there are many benefits to school-based prevention programs. Examples of specific preventive programs in the school are described below, arranged by the type of behavior targeted by the intervention. The first two programs address some of the antecedents of delinquent behavior.

The Seattle Social Development Project

The Seattle Social Development Project is an elementary school-based program designed to promote academic achievement and pro-social bonding, and to prevent crime, teen pregnancy, drug abuse and school dropout (Hawkins, Catalano, Kosterman, Abbott, & Hill, 1999). The program is both selected and universal as it targeted all students in Grades 1–6 in schools located in high crime, high poverty neighborhoods. The program consists of teacher training in classroom management, parent training and social competence workshops for the youth. The behavior of students was assessed at age 18, six years after they completed the program. The treatment group differed significantly from the controls. They had stronger attachments to the school, less involvement in school misbehavior and higher scholastic achievement. In addition, the treatment group committed fewer violent acts, drank alcohol less heavily, engaged in sexual intercourse less frequently or had multiple sex partners less frequently.

Linking the Interests of Families and Teachers (LIFT) Program

Another elementary school-based program that targeted antecedents of delinquency is the LIFT Program. LIFT, designed and evaluated by Eddy, Reid, and Fetrow (2000) targeted child oppositional, defiant and socially inept behavior and the parents' style of disciplining and monitoring their children. The program participants were chosen from the general population of students in elementary schools in the Eugene-Springfield, Oregon metropolitan area. The three month long program consisted of three components: classroom based training sessions in social and problem solving skills for the children; playground based behavior modification; and group-delivered parent training sessions. The classroom modules for the children and parents utilized lecture, discussion, role-play and practice methods. The playground component consisted of teachers and other adults rewarding students for using pro-social and positive relationship behavior while playing a game. In a three-year follow-up evaluation, compared to controls, program participants delayed the time they first became involved with anti-social peers, their first alcohol and marijuana use and their first police arrest. Also, behaviors such as inattentiveness, impulsivity and hyperactivity, empirically predictive of later delinquent and conduct problem behavior, were decreased in severity at the three year assessment compared to the behavior of the controls.

Curwin and Mendler (2002) added a system-level factor to enhance the effectiveness of programs aimed at preventing violence. These authors argue that the school should include, as core to its mission statement, the values of finding nonviolent expressions of resolving conflict and of challenging hostile and disrespectful acts on others throughout the school community. Curwin and Mendler believe programs will be more effective if they are embedded in a value based school system.

In reviewing the results of 84 studies which teach children social skills to prevent antisocial behavior, Losel and Beelmann (2003) found that while many treatment modalities were effective, cognitive behavioral programs had the strongest impact on students' behavior. Consistent with other researchers, these authors found that targeting at-risk groups had a greater likelihood of achieving significant differences than programs that included all students. This is probably due to an artifact in the assessment process, as there is a much lower frequency of serious antisocial behavior in the general, as opposed to the high-risk populations. They concluded that more research using well-controlled studies, larger samples and long follow-up periods is needed.

CHILD SEXUAL ABUSE PREVENTION PROGRAMS

In addition to those elementary school programs that teach students to behave more socially, other programs are designed to prevent children from becoming victims of child sexual abuse. Davis and Gidycz (2000) reviewed 27 programs focusing on this issue and found most programs to be effective. "The average effect size for all programs was 1.07, indicating that the children who participated in prevention programs perform 1.07 SD [standard deviations] higher than control group children on the outcome measures used in the studies" (p. 257). For example, on a measure in which 50 percent of the control group members scored favorably, 69 percent of the treated children would have met this criterion. These researchers also found that the best programs were those in which the children participated actively, and attended at least four sessions. In other studies, it has been found that students attending abuse prevention sessions become more knowledgeable about abuse, but do not always learn how to respond appropriately in potential abuse situations. Ko and Cosden (2001) surveyed high school students about an abuse program they attended in elementary school. Those who participated in the earlier program were more knowledgeable about abuse and reported fewer incidents than controls, but their responses to abuse were not significantly better.

PREVENTION PROGRAM FOR STUDENTS WITH EMOTIONAL DISTURBANCE

Among the types of elementary school-based prevention programs, those dealing with assisting special needs children with emotional disturbance (ED) are important, as success with these children now may reduce the incidence of adults with a parallel diagnosis later in life. A number of prevention programs have focused on this population. Kamps, Kravitz, Rauch, Kamps, and Chung (2000) reported on a program for students at-risk or with ED that was conducted in the Kansas City, Kansas Public Schools. The intervention spanned 1½ school years, and included weekly social skills training, peer tutoring and classroom behavioral management using token economies and student contracts. The students in the program ranged from 5–10 years old when the intervention started. They were assessed over a four-year period. Compared to a delayed control group, participants' inappropriate behavior such as aggression, out-of-seat and negative verbal acts (teasing, threatening peers) decreased and appropriate behaviors such as academic engagement and behavioral compliance increased. The effect improved over time, and the greatest effectiveness occurred in classrooms with high structure and in those students who attended more sessions.

Similar findings were reported by McConaughy, Kay, and Fitzgerald (2000). These researchers evaluated a prevention program for first and second graders at risk for ED. The program utilized collaborative teams of parents, teachers and a mental health professional for each child, and classroom-wide social skills training. These teams met monthly on average and assessed each child' strengths and problems, set goals, and designed and monitored the intervention. Children were assessed at the end of the first and second year of the program. Compared to matched controls that only received the social skill training, the participants' problem behaviors decreased somewhat after the first year and the benefits were more pronounced after the second year. Consistent with other researchers, McConaughy et al. found that the longer the program is maintained, the greater the effect.

Prior to leaving the topic of prevention programs for children at risk for ED, it should be noted that McArdle, Moseley, Quibell, Johnson, Allen, Hammal, and leCouteur (2002) reported on a program that used an innovative treatment method—drama-group therapy. Their research compared the drama group that consisted of 12 one-hour sessions against a curriculum studies approach and a waiting list control group. At risk students were randomly assigned to the various groups. The behavior of the drama group therapy treatment participants improved significantly greater than that of either of the other two groups, and this effect continued over a one-year follow-up assessment.

SCHOOL AND COMMUNITY-BASED PREVEN-TION FOR HIGH SCHOOL AND COLLEGE STU-DENTS

As students get older, many of the patterns of behavior—good and bad—have been established and become more resistant to change. While it becomes more challenging, it is still possible to design effective primary prevention programs to meet the needs of high school students. If one considers the effect of a program on the future generation, these programs have multiple benefits. For example, effective programs targeting drug abuse among adolescents will reduce in relatively few years the likelihood of fetal alcohol syndrome or the birth of cocaine-addicted babies. Similarly, programs addressing impulsive violent behaviors of teenagers about to become parents will reduce the likelihood of later child abuse. From the perspective of the babies and young children, these programs are definitely preventive in nature and very useful to society. Below are some examples of prevention programs that focus on high school students. Issues such as antisocial and violent behavior, adolescent suicide and drug abuse behavior are discussed.

JUVENILE VIOLENCE AND SUICIDE PREVEN-TION PROGRAMS

Consistent with other areas of prevention, effective interventions in programs for adolescents should be multifaceted and multi-level. For example, Speaker and Peterson (2000) recommend that programs to prevent juvenile violence and suicide should include family participation and involve school staff as well as the adolescents themselves. The school staff should be trained in values education and the youth should be encouraged to develop success-oriented self-identity and to utilize non-violent conflict resolution skills. Finally, programs should advocate for the use of media in both the schools and the community that stress appropriate respectful social interaction. Huey and Henggeler (2001) have echoed the same theme of targeting multiple components of the youths' life space to prevent antisocial behavior and juvenile delinquency. These authors cite a number of programs that have been found to be cost effective on a long-term basis. Among the most beneficial is multi-systemic therapy (MST). MST is an alternative to incarcerating youthful offenders, and involves problem-solving activities at the peer, family, school and neighborhood levels. In terms of the IOM categories, this intervention can be viewed as both indicated prevention and maintenance, in that it reduces the risk that juvenile delinquents will become career criminals, and it enables the youth to remain in the community without committing additional offenses. The MST program involves individualized on-going care and supervision both in the home and school settings.

SUBSTANCE ABUSE PREVENTION PROGRAMS

Perhaps substance abuse prevention programs are the most common interventions in the schools. Nancy Tobler and Susan Ennett and their colleagues have performed a series of meta-analyses over the past ten years (Ennett, Tobler, Ringwalt, & Flewelling, 1994; Tobler & Stratton, 1997; Tobler, Roona, Ochshorn, Marshall, Streke, & Stackpole, 2000; Tobler, 2000; Tobler, Lessard, Marshall, Ochshorn, & Roona, 1999; and Ennett, Ringwalt, Thorne, Rohrbach, Vincus, Simons-Rudolph, & Jones, 2003). Summing up their empirical findings are the following points about the effectiveness of universal substance (tobacco, alcohol, marijuana, other street drugs) abuse prevention programs:

1. Drug Abuse Resistance Education (DARE) is almost completely ineffective;
2. Teaching the content of interpersonal social skills such as assertiveness is far more effective than teaching knowledge about drugs in reducing drug abuse;
3. Interactive programs are more effective than lecture-oriented sessions. Tobler (2000) cited a 21 percent reduction in the prevalence of drug abuse among adolescents in the schools when presented with an interactive approach;
4. Small-scale programs are more effective than large-scale interventions, perhaps because the program proto-

col is more closely followed in the smaller programs; and

5. Teachers in the substance abuse programs have not been utilizing the research findings. In a study of 1800 teachers of middle school prevention programs, Ennett et al. (2003) found that while the majority of teachers used effective content, few (17 percent) used an effective delivery system, and even fewer (14 percent) utilized both effective content and delivery. This last finding is particularly important as educators and mental health providers are urged to utilize evidence based treatment methods as part of best practice guidelines.

Other researchers generally agree with Ennett's and Tobler's findings. In a separate meta-analysis, Wilson, Gottfredson, and Najaka (2001) found that self control and social competency instruction utilizing cognitive behavioral and behavioral training methods were more effective in preventing substance abuse than interventions based on other therapeutic techniques. Also, Cuipers (2002) found that among interactive programs, peer-led interventions were somewhat more effective than adult-led sessions. Peer-led programs are probably more interactive than adult led classes, and may be better received by the adolescents.

The studies presented here are representative of the literally hundreds of researched and effective prevention programs. It is beyond the scope of this book to provide an exhaustive review of interventions in each area of interest. Additional resources for those wanting in-depth descriptions of a greater range of case studies in prevention include a two-volume review of programs for children by Weissberg, Gullotta, Adams, Hampton, and Ryan (1997a, 1997b) and a more recent overview of prevention across the lifespan by Gullotta and Bloom (2003).

THE FUTURE OF PREVENTION: THE FEDERAL GOVERNMENT'S ROLE IN FUNDING PREVENTION AND SETTING NATIONAL POLICY

The federal government is a great resource in funding prevention programs, but ambivalence and politics tends to dilute its effect. For example, the federal government has spent over $55 billion on Head Start since 1965, but still only half the eligible children are enrolled (Ripple & Zigler, 2003). Even beyond the funding, the policies set by the government establish the national agenda, but as presidential administrations change, so do the national thrusts. Ripple and Zigler identified three aspects of the current sociopolitical context that affect federal policies regarding prevention:

1. Partly due to a desire to support states' rights and partly due to the government's ambivalence about its role in affecting family life and parenting style, pressure is being exerted to move prevention programs from federal to state control. The benefit of this is that the programs can be "tailor fit" to the needs of each state. The drawbacks to this devolution process are that the program loses its national integrity and that the funding for many programs is bundled together into block grants and the funds are used for other purposes;

2. Politically, it is easier to fund programs in which there is a severe problem. This results in the program tending to target high-risk students. While this policy seems to be a common sense approach, it results in marginalizing and stigmatizing the targeted group. After a short time the targeted "have nots" are separated from the policy-maker "haves". When the initial period of funding expires, the policy makers are able to politically sidetrack the program and its funding either stops or is sharply decreased; and

3. Similarly, it is easier to gain federal funding support for specific problems, such as school violence. Yet high risk factors tend to cluster, and targeting one concern without addressing related ones results in non-synergistic piecemeal programs with limited effect.

Ripple and Zigler (2003) recommend directions for the federal government to take to remedy some of these concerns. First, adopt a universal prevention approach. All children can gain from Head Start. This reduces the likelihood that low income or ethnic minority children will be marginalized. The energies and expenses consumed by checking eligibility requirements more productively. Voters everywhere can experience the benefits of the program and the program is easier to defend politically.

Second, target communities in which the school is located, rather than targeting individual problems or specific groups of students, and develop multiple component programs to deal with the cluster of problems present in that community. Poverty is associated with poor nutrition, substandard education, inadequate housing (where there is a higher likelihood of peeling lead paint causing poisoning), high unemployment, etc. Joining the programs to address all the needs in the community allows for the possibility of spillover effects, in that the solution for one concern could also remedy a related one. In conclusion, Ripple and Zigler recommend that the government sponsor comprehensive programs with universal access.

Throughout the twentieth century, prevention in physical and mental health areas has demonstrated its effectiveness in reducing both the incidence and prevalence of illness and in promoting health. It is expected that preventive interventions will continue to flourish in the current century.

THE ETHICS OF PREVENTION

Before concluding this chapter, it is useful to reflect on the ethical issues surrounding primary or universal prevention programs. Some primary prevention programs are conducted on a large scale, and it is not always possible to inform all students that they will be subject to an intervention. Neither students nor parents are told that a social problem-solving workshop is to be integrated into a lesson on literature. Similarly, it is difficult to pinpoint which community leader has the authority to give the informed consent of the population when a radio station decides to air a drug abuse prevention program. Finally, some programs have unplanned unhealthy consequences. For example, the federal government mandated that all automobiles built after 1996 have dual front seat air bags as a measure to reduce auto fatalities. From 1990 to 1998, air bags have saved over 2600 lives. However, 87 individuals have been killed due to their sitting too close to the air bag when it was deployed (National Highway Traffic Safety Administration, 1998).

Pope (1990) presented eight areas of ethical concerns regarding primary prevention programs:

1. Make certain that the program harms no one. While harm is not intended, there may be aversive secondary effects of the program. Participants who do not achieve the desired goal might perceive themselves as failures. The individual providing the treatment is responsible to assess and then to remedy such potential harmful effects;

2. "Practice with competence." Before a preventive program is implemented on a large scale, it should be tested on a smaller sample and the consequences examined. The interventionist needs to ensure that all components of the program are implemented as planned. Of course, one is never certain that even a well-researched program will work with a new population or in a new setting, yet it is important to reduce any risks of failure or harmful effects beforehand;

3. Do not exploit the participants for the interventionist's self-gain. The program should be designed to benefit the targeted students and not the educator or mental health professional. The primary purpose is not to advance one's career or social status, but to provide an opportunity for students to change their lives for the better;

4. Treat participating students with respect and dignity. Interact with them as human beings and do not attempt to restrict unnecessarily their freedom or right to decide their future;

5. Maintain confidentiality. Both in implementing the program and in any evaluation of it, the anonymity of participating students is to be preserved. Interventionists have a social responsibility to evaluate programs and to disseminate effective primary prevention programs, but they should do so without divulging personal characteristics that could identify specific individuals;

6. Act only with informed consent. This is a challenging requirement, as was mentioned previously. Whenever possible, inform potential students and their parents in advance and fully disclose both what is expected of them and what they can expect the potential consequences to be. Ask for voluntary involvement. The right of the student or parent to refuse treatment and opt out of the program at any time must be maintained. Students should not be coerced, by threatening to withhold some needed service, if they refuse to participate. In community-wide interventions, consult in advance as many civic leaders, public officials and clergy members as is possible, and revise the program based on their advice. In a school-based program, the administrator and, ultimately, the school board are the legitimate authorities and their permission is needed prior to implementing a program—even if a classroom teacher approves the plan;

7. Design the program to promote equity and justice. Primary prevention should enhance access to resources for those unable to obtain them. In addition, educators should be sensitive to cultural differences and respect the values and traditions of the targeted population. The program should not be seen as a method of imposing the values of the dominant culture on minority groups; and

8. Be ethically accountable for all effects of the program. Unanswered questions must be investigated fully and remedies found for any undesirable consequences that may have occurred.

Prevention is a highly effective strategy for enhancing the well-being of students. Educators, in collaboration with mental health professionals, should attempt to design and implement such programs in their work. Prevention is a hallmark of the community health movement and it is useful to apply this principle whenever possible.

DISCUSSION QUESTIONS

1. Should improving the psychological well being of students be a goal of a school?

2. How can a school become an integral arm of the community mental health system?

3. What is the value of early intervention in a child's development?

4. What are the distinguishing characteristics of KISS, AID and ICE agencies? In what instances would each be beneficial to students?

5. How would you establish a new mental health program within a school?

6. How does the Caplan model differ from the Institute of Medicine model? Do you think the IOM model would be effective in a school setting? What types of universal, selective and indicated interventions would be appropriate to establish?

7. Which of the two forms of primary prevention do you favor and why?

8. What other programs would you add to Tables 1 and 2 to serve as examples of specific types of prevention programs for each model?

9. What impact has the federal government had on prevention programs? What should its role be?

10. Select a prevention program with which you are familiar. Does it satisfy Pope's eight areas of ethical concerns? If not, how would you modify the program to do so?

Chapter 10:
Strategies for Educational Change

OBJECTIVES

After studying this chapter, the reader will be able to describe, analyze and apply the following concepts and strategies:

1. Theoretical basis for change;

2. Values of the change agent;
   - Cultural diversity;
   - Empowerment;
   - Mental health;

3. Organizational change;
   - Diagnostic/prescriptive model;
   - Alternative participatory model;

4. Techniques to encourage organizational change;
   - Decree from a higher authority;
   - Replacement of personnel;
   - Presentation of information;
   - Social reinforcement;
   - Perceptual bonding process;
   - Cognitive consistency approach;
   - Presentation of information, using persuasion techniques such as;
     a. Social reinforcement;
     b. Perpetual bonding process;
     c. Cognitive consistency approach;
   - Skill training;
   - Individual counseling and therapy;

- Sensitivity group training/team building;
- Survey feedback;
- Clinical experimental method;
- Demonstration projects;

5. Institutional change;
   - Sarason's Alternate Settings model;
   - Alinsky's Community Organizing Method;

6. Components to consider when planning change;
   - Energy;
   - Power;
   - Culture and beliefs;
   - Competence;
   - Legal and administrative factors;
   - Information and communication;
   - Relationships; and

7. Funding innovative programs: grant writing;
   - Researching the funding source; and
   - Writing the proposal.

Some men see things as they are and ask "why?" I dream things that never were and ask, "why not?" Robert F. Kennedy

OVERVIEW

Thus far in the book, a systematic perspective toward education was introduced, and contemporary issues in education were described from this perspective. It is expected that readers would utilize action research to investigate perceived needs in their school districts or determine whether a particular innovation enhances student learning. Similarly, as one reads the chapters on cultural diversity, technology in the classroom, distance learning, parent-teacher communication or student psychological well-being, ideas for worthwhile interventions would come to mind. Paraphrasing Karl Marx, "The role of the scholar is not to interpret the world but to change it." The purpose of this chapter is to provide the educator with the necessary conceptualizations and techniques to institute meaningful change in the school system. Hopefully, by utilizing a systems approach, the change agent will be aware of the complexities and interrelatedness of education. The interventions proposed would not result in piecemeal change, but instead will produce substantial, effective and long-lasting educational reform that will become embedded within the total system. All too often, programs based on quality research that should have been successful have failed or were quickly terminated because the change agent had not developed a strategy to persuade others of the program's benefits.

In this chapter, the theoretical basis for change is presented first. The differences between organizational and institutional change are described, along with the values needed by educational reformers. Methods of assessing the quality of functioning of a school or school district to find opportunities for improvement are also discussed. The tactics of organizational change and the methods of institutional change are presented next. The chapter concludes with some practical information on funding innovative programs by writing grants.

THE POLITICS OF PROBLEM DEFINITION

Everyone does not view educational problems in the same way, and the way in which an issue is defined affects the type of solution chosen. Levine and Perkins (1987) presented a strong case for conceiving of social and educational problems not as absolute truths but as relative interpretations of reality. Diverse publics have opposing vested interests in how a problem is approached and these constituencies advocate for opposing solutions.

For example, suppose students in a poor inner city school are not achieving at grade level. According to the provisions of the No Child Left Behind Act, the school must remedy this problem within a set time interval or the school may lose federal funding. The citizens who believe in this approach are likely to view the problem as indicative of the school staff not providing sufficient effort. Another group might see the problem as students in this inner city school not having the capacity to learn. A third group may see the problem as one aspect of the effect of poverty and discrimination. These three interpretations of the same achievement score data are only a few of the possible, perhaps plausible, explanations.

The way the problem is "interpreted" affects the types of solutions suggested. The solution for the first group of citizens is to remove resources from the ineffective school after a trial period ends. Their solution is seen as increasing the problem from the third group's perspective. The second group has no problem with removing resources from the inner city schools, as they believe no amount of resource will benefit students unable to learn. The third group advocates for large-scale intervention in the community. They call for crime prevention to make the neighborhood safe for the children to get to school, for an increase in local jobs and job training programs to give students some "light at the end of the tunnel", for better housing and the removal of lead paint to prevent neurological damage resulting from lead poisoning, and for more effective laws preventing discrimination. Of course, there are many other groups of concerned citizens, each seeing the problem differently, and each advocating for his or her own pet solution.

Deciding who can "frame" the problem is an important first step in determining what approach is taken to solve it. Unfortunately, educators frequently interpret their role narrowly to deal with only issues that fit in a classroom. In some instances, this position has merit, but on a larger level, it is perhaps more useful for teachers to advocate for new programs and to persuade the public to understand educational issues from the perspective of the larger system.

SHOULD EDUCATIONAL REFORMERS BE VALUE FREE?

If educators do not participate in the process of defining problems, others in society will fill that leadership vacuum, and the way in which the problem is understood might not be in the best interest of the students. Issues such as cost, preservation of the status quo, fear of change, and prejudice could take precedence over the value of serving the children and facilitating their development. Some believe that teachers, in their role as educators of youth, must be value free. These individuals hold to the myth that to be objective, educators and researchers must be completely neutral investigators of the issues they study.

In actuality, all who advocate for quality education hold values and incorporate their beliefs in their work. In some cases, the values are commonly accepted, and at other times the values reflect vested interest. To be objective, educational researchers must hold certain universally-accepted values. Researchers should design their studies in a manner that reduces the likelihood that the data obtained can be interpreted as supporting rival plausible hypotheses (Campbell & Stanley, 1963). To be credible, researchers must use appropriate scientific methodology and carry out the study as it was designed. They must value the accurate collecting and recording of data, careful analysis using appropriate statistical instruments and fair reporting of the study findings.

Educational research also involves vested interest. Most applied research projects require extensive funding, and researchers who agree with the values of the funding agency are more likely to receive the resources needed to conduct the research. Consider the following example. A major controversy that has been debated for over 30 years involves the issue of whether television violence causes youth to become more aggressive (Hughes & Hasbrouck, 1997). If so, should the government restrict such broadcasts? Parents and other concerned citizen groups believe violence and sexual exploitation on TV contribute to increased aggression in the school and community. Media network executives believe that such "action packed" shows increase the number of viewers and advertisers pay more to present their products on shows that have higher "Nielson ratings." The issue pits the values of free speech and the right to make a profit against the responsibility of legislators to preserve the common good.

Educational research could provide a means to resolve the issue, and legislators might cite studies that support their views. Will studies be conducted which fairly represent the effect of TV violence on aggression in schools? Each side has vested interest. Citizen groups hire researchers to demonstrate TV violence does increase aggression and media networks fund those who attempt to show the opposite. Large-scale research in the community is costly and the ability of each side to fund studies affects the proportion of empirical projects that are conducted. If one side has access to more funds, the number of research studies supporting their position will increase, and relatively few studies opposing that viewpoint will be conducted.

In many ways, society "stacks the deck" regarding which research is to be conducted, what data collected and which findings disseminated. This is true in the biological as well as the social sciences. The federal government, through the National Institutes of Health, differentially supports research projects investigating genetic versus environmental causes of cancer depending on the prevailing beliefs of the time. Similarly, the National Institute of Justice funds either more crime prevention or more law enforcement projects depending on the political views of the party in power. In addition, scientific journal editors, mass media gatekeepers, university faculty, school administrators, boards and the public itself restrict the types of studies funded, conducted and published.

Given the above argument, educational change agents need to become involved in the political process to support certain values. Remaining "above the fray" and apolitical allows those with opposing values a greater opportunity to present their case unchecked and without the needed balance.

THE VALUES OF THE EDUCATIONAL RE-FORMER

Educators who consider themselves to be reformers adhere to a set of values, which permeate their research and interventions. The values of the field include:

- Respect for cultural diversity and individual differences;
- Increased access to resources empowering the disenfranchised; and
- Improved psychological well-being or mental health of the students.

Cultural Diversity

Educators and psychologists prefer programs that promote respect for ethnic and racial values and traditions over those which attempt to eliminate such differences. Rappaport (1977) considered that programs that discount cultural differences are attempts at culturocide (i.e. killing a culture) and oppression. Similarly, educational psychologists oppose the implicit thrust of those who interpret individual differences as deficits. In earlier times, practitioners judged students according to "one standard" and any deviations from this "good student" profile were considered symptoms of poor learning. Gardner and many others note that there are various forms of intelligence and each type has a preferred learning style (Gardner, 1983). A good educator does not judge students on the basis of one's own culture but attempts to support as appropriate the values of the students' culture. In addition, at the end of the intervention, students need not behave like the teacher, but rather progress toward their own goals and objectives. While all educators agree that behaviors that pose a threat either to the student or to others must be confronted, they believe other behaviors that represent different approaches to life or personal preference need not be changed unless they are truly counter-productive to learning.

Empowerment

Educational change agents realize that students and their families need greater access to resources and that problems develop when this accessibility is denied. For example, many studies show that unemployment, crime rate and poor student achievement are correlated. Community and educational psychologists interpret this correlation as follows. The lack of access to jobs and suitable job training limits the range of behaviors an individual can perform to earn a living, and this increases the likelihood the person will resort to crime. Students perceiving the lack of legitimate jobs in the community have few role models and see little or no connection between doing well in school and success as an adult. Individualistically-oriented educators might interpret the correlation differently. They might assume the student had a character defect or learning disability that caused the unemployment, criminal activity and low achievement. Educational psychologists view the concept of empowerment as one mechanism for increasing the availability of resources to those in need.

Like "personality," the term "empowerment" is extraordinarily difficult to define; yet, most individuals draw on their own internal, universal understanding of this concept. Perkins and Zimmerman (1995) began an issue of the American Journal of Community Psychology devoted to this construct, by noting that definitions of empowerment abound, and that community psychology, as a scientific discipline, needs to focus attention on more clearly defining the concept and consequences of empowerment theory. Within this idea of a universal understanding of the term, Perkins (1995) noted that the concept of empowerment has infiltrated popular culture. Widespread usage (and frequent misusage) of this term can be seen in areas, such as: organizational management and development; public programs such as Head Start; and other areas such as community development and national and foreign policy. He notes as an example, that a search of the root "empower" turned up hundreds and sometimes thousands of entries in: White House press releases, speeches and policy statements; U.S. House and Senate bills; and state house bills.

Many agree that the widespread usage coupled with the general ambiguity of this critical concept can result in its misuse (Zimmerman, 1995; Rappaport, 1995) and that a current goal in the field is to operationalize the term, enough to allow for the most appropriate applications and outcomes assessments. That being said, Perkins and Zimmerman (1995) offer a multi-theorist definition of empowerment as:

> An intentional ongoing process centered in the local community, involving mutual respect, critical reflection, caring, and group participation, through which people lacking an equal share of valued resources gain greater access to and control over these resources (Cornell Empowerment Group, 1989) or simply a process by which people gain control over their lives, democratic participation in the life of their community (Rappaport, 1987), and a critical understanding of the environment (Zimmerman, Israel, Schultz & Checkoway, 1992, p.570)

The incorporation of empowerment, a fundamental and evolving principle in the fields of community psychology and education, into the conceptualization of educational issues and subsequent change plans, has many positive implications for those in need.

Mental Health

The final value held by educational reformers is the desire to enhance the psychological well-being of the students. As was mentioned earlier in the book, students who are prepared for transitions from one level of schooling to the next and for upcoming developmental stages are more likely to cope successfully with these typical changes. Effective coping reduces stress and the students are less distracted in class. As they attend and participate more fully in worthwhile classroom learning activities, there is less disruptive behavior and learning is enhanced. Also, psychologically and emotionally healthy students become better citizens in society and will contribute more to the quality of life in the community. Teaching interpersonal communication, assertiveness, conflict resolution skills and providing character-building opportunities ultimately increases student achievement and improves society.

ORGANIZATIONAL VERSUS INSTITUTIONAL CHANGE

Rappaport (1977) differentiated between individual and organizational change on the one hand and institutional or societal change on the other. While the former are effective in modifying an individual student's behavior or helping a school become more efficient in meeting its goals, the latter alter the goals of the social system and re-arrange the status relationships among groups in the community.

Institutional and societal change tactics are primarily political in nature. These methods help to alleviate problems caused when one group within a community is alienated, powerless, or unable to gain access to institutional resources. The change agent works for the group in an advocacy role, helping group members organize together to reduce the power inequity. It is important for the change agent to consider at what level the problem exists so as to plan an appropriate change strategy at the same level of complexity.

For example, if one student is performing poorly, a teacher might analyze the problem as occurring at the level of the individual and have the child referred for a battery of tests to determine the nature of the learning disability. As a result of the testing, appropriate counseling or instructional supports could be given to enable the child to fit better within the system.

If a number of children are performing poorly the problem might be more correctly understood as being at the interpersonal or group level of complexity. Perhaps the problem is that the teachers are not sufficiently flexible in their response to the needs of these students. An appropriate intervention might address the teaching methodology of the school or its ability to adapt to individual differences.

If the students are not learning well because the values of the school conflict with those of the community, the change agent might design an institutional level intervention which will target the school's value system. The change agent might perceive that a particular group of students is not doing well academically because these children are members of an under-represented group, which is discriminated against in the community. These students might have lowered self-confidence, little expectation for academic success and no hope that working hard in school will have any effect on their lives because of the social discrimination. In this case, the interventionist might analyze the problem as existing at the societal level of complexity and realize that the values of the community itself need to be modified. The change agent would then seek a more equitable set of power and status relationships in the community and a more equal distribution of resources. The change program would consist of social action, community organizing and the development of new alternative institutional structures. Each type of change is considered below.

Organizational Level Change Strategies

Most of the principles for instituting educational innovation have come from organizational psychologists working in business settings and from community psychologists and other social scientists consulting with human services agencies and grass roots groups. Organizational psychologists have concentrated on attempting to alter the organization's structure and day-to-day procedures to enhance the system's efficiency in attaining its stated goals, while others such as community psychologists have attempted to alter the system's values in meeting the needs of minority groups in the community. Authors Argyris (1964), Bennis (1966) and Katz and Kahn (1966), as well as other authors, devised the devised the basic principles of planned organizational change in large industrial establishments, and Miles (1964) and Johnson (1970) applied these methods to education. Much of the contribution of these industrial and social psychologists presented in this chapter was taken from Johnson's review. The work of Barker (1964), Sarason (1972) and Alinsky (1972) in promoting institutional change in society and the human service field is presented later in this chapter.

The Diagnostic-Prescriptive Model

The industrial or organizational psychologists as a group believe that any comprehensive change program in a business, school or social system should be conducted within a diagnostic-prescriptive model. That is, the consultant or change agent should first determine what type of problem or deficiency is inhibiting the organization from growing or becoming more effective in achieving its goals. After the diagnosis is complete, a prescription or remedy for the deficits is proposed. The diagnostic stage should include an assessment of the overall organizational health of the system and an evaluation of the degree to which the institution is effective in meeting specific objectives relevant to the proposed intervention.

The Diagnosis

Johnson (1970) listed three areas to consider when determining an organization's well being. These areas include: a) task accomplishment; b) internal integration and; c) growth and change. In the task accomplishment area, a consultant should determine whether the goals of the institution are clear, appropriate, achievable and accepted by all the members. In a school, it is useful to survey the teachers and administrative staff, the students and the parents regarding how they see the goals of the school now and what they would like the school's priorities to be. The change agent can, then, observe the effectiveness of the school administrators in communicating school policy to all involved. Also, the synergy of the school, that is, the degree to which the energies of all school personnel are directed towards the same objective, can be assessed. When considering the task accomplishment aspect of the diagnosis, the consultant should observe the process by which the school measures its success in achieving goals. Such measures should include both objective assessments, which can be used as baselines for evaluation of proposed innovations, and subjective opinion-oriented feedback devices.

The internal integration area consists of the degree to which human resources are fully utilized and the degree to which all members feel they are part of an attractive organization (Kelly, Ryan, Altman & Stelzman, 2000). When applied to schools, the consultant should consider the degree of bureaucratization of the school and its effect on staff and students. Moeller's (1964) bureaucratization scale is a useful instrument for measuring this factor. The goodness of fit between the person's personality and his or her position in the role structure should be assessed. It is particularly important in the school to study the principal's fit. One means of evaluating the person-position fit is to apply Fiedler's (1967) contingency model of leadership. Fiedler found that the relative effectiveness of leadership style depends on the group situation. In those groups in which the leader's power, group morale and the degree to which tasks are objective are either very high or very low, an authoritarian style of leadership is more effective. In groups that are moderate in these characteristics, a socio-emotional leader who is concerned about the members' feelings and interpersonal relationships is able to achieve greater productivity with the group. If the person-position fit is not good, it is possible to either adjust the role demands of the office, or to alter the style the person uses in performing the role. Either change will result in an increased utilization of the human resources within the school.

The third diagnostic area concerns the ability of the organization to grow and to change. Every open system must interact with the social environment and as the cultural context changes, so must the organization. A healthy institution adapts in a manner consistent with the society. Diagnostically, it is important to assess how well the organization monitors external changes, its planning process and its willingness to innovate. It is also useful to determine which structures, policies, or staff members in the bureaucracy inhibit planned change. In the schools, a change agent might interview staff regarding their perceptions of how society has changed and how the school addressed the change. Also, as change frequently requires decisions to be made and problems to be solved, the school's abilities and strategies in these areas need to be studied. In addition to the diagnosis of general organizational health, the change agent might want to focus on some specific facet of the school's task accomplishment area, internal integration or its ability to change that might be specifically relevant to a potential intervention. For example, the innovator might want to develop a baseline, charting attendance rates, hours spent in reading instruction or changes in achievement test scores over a set period of time in the task accomplishment area. These measures, when compared to some standardized norm, might indicate the need for a new program to improve student performance, or serve as the basis for evaluating the success of the possible intervention.

The Prescription

After the diagnostic stage is completed, the change agent or consultant is now in a position to prescribe a new policy or program to enhance the school organization.

Often, the change agent already has a program in mind, or at least a general idea of the factors that should be modified to remedy some deficiency. It is important to review the research literature to find if such a program has been attempted before, and if so, whether it was successful. Frequently, the specific program has not been established elsewhere, but research might indicate that certain variables which could be operationalized in a program have affected student achievement. This literature review serves two purposes: to develop the program more fully, and to provide persuasive evidence for school administrators to accept the innovation. An excellent reference source for the research review is the Educational Resources Information Center (ERIC), a Federal depository of both published articles and unpublished evaluation studies concerning education. The ERIC system, present in many university libraries and on line, contains both abstracts and entire articles indexed by topic.

After the relevant literature has been reviewed, it is necessary to state the general goals and specific objectives of the intervention. It is also useful to describe a scenario or a conceptualization of the program. Often the scenario will assist the innovator to conceptualize the intervention and help others to understand the type of innovation being suggested. This scenario has only one possibility: the change agent must be willing to modify this picture while keeping the basic goals and objectives fairly fixed.

ENCOURAGING THE ADOPTION OF THE PROGRAM: ORGANIZATIONAL METHODS OF CHANG

This scenario, along with its supporting research, however, does not "sell itself." The change agent must develop a strategy for encouraging a school to accept the innovation. The more the staff "buy into" the new program, the more invested they will be in its success. Johnson (1970) listed the following nine methods or strategies to encourage change.

Decree from a High Authority

One means of having a new program accepted by a system is by presenting it to the superintendent, principal or the board and securing their support. The head administrator has endorsed nearly all successful programs, but the method is more effective if used in conjunction with additional strategies, which convince others in the system of the value of the innovation. Used alone, a decree from a high authority increases resistance by the staff, who are less likely to participate in and become committed to the innovation. The teachers may also be less willing to provide support services for the new program, thus isolating it from the rest of the school. After a short time the isolated program, which is not synchronized with the rest of the system, is likely to fail. A decree from higher authority is more successful in a highly bureaucratized organization in which the principal has the power and willingness to offer incentives to those staff that help the program succeed.

Replacement of Personnel

Another strategy to insure that an organization will accept a new program is to replace those members who oppose the change with those who support it. This method is based on the belief that as the program changes, the role requirements also change and the staff occupying those roles cannot adapt. While this belief is true in some cases, it is contrary to the most central premise of educational institutions: that people - including staff as well as students - can adjust to new environmental demands if they are motivated and provided with necessary information, training, rewards and encouragement.

Replacement of personnel can cause tension and lower morale among other staff who feel their own positions are no longer secure. This method can be successful, though, in large school districts in which teachers who oppose a new program can be transferred to other schools within the district without penalty. Then, new educators whose attitudes and training are more consistent with the philosophy of the intervention can be found to fill the vacancies.

Presentation of Information

Providing information and empirical research evidence supporting an innovation will give advocates a credible rationale for the new program but, if used alone, this strategy will rarely motivate persons opposed to the program to change their position. Often, change agents believe that appealing solely to reason will cause staff or administrators to "see the truth" and change their approach. This is unlikely to occur, as individuals hold their beliefs for many non-rational reasons, such as a fear of the unknown, a fear that the innovation might disrupt other useful activities, or even a concern that their status or other vested interest might be threatened. In addition, the information presented will be processed through the target person's attitude filter, or frame of reference, and the message received will not be identical to the message sent. Finally, information alone is not motivating, and the person's affect, or emotion, must be addressed.

One strategy for presenting information in a manner that will motivate others to change is to use a persuasion technique. Such attitude change methods are particularly useful for persuading personnel to accept a new program.

The first process involves social reinforcement theory (Hovland et al., 1953). In this approach, the new program is associated with a pleasant or favorable image. The change agent stresses how the program will result in some reward or incentive for the staff person, or is endorsed by a respected public figure.

A somewhat similar approach is the perceptual value bonding process (Sherif, Sherif & Nebergall, 1965). In this persuasion method, the change agent attempts to connect the new program to some value prized highly by the target individual or group. For example, since teachers generally are person-oriented and like to interact closely with students, a change agent should emphasize how the innovation will free teachers from mundane tasks and allow more time for interacting with students. Nearly every school innovation can be tied to this value. Skinner (1958) used this argument to sell the concept of teaching machines. For this approach to work, the innovator must learn the values of the target group and creatively tie the new program to these values.

A third attitude change approach is called the cognitive consistency approach of Festinger (1957), Rokeach (1968) and others. In this approach, the consultant skillfully encourages the target group to become more aware of the inconsistencies between their ideals and their actions. The staff develops a greater consciousness that a problem exists and they are motivated to resolve the problem. The change agent then presents the new program as the solution to the difficulty, thus reducing the perceived inconsistency.

In conclusion, the presenting of information might work with staff that is already seeking a new approach, but combining the information with an attitude change method will be more effective in a wider range of circumstances.

Skill Training

In-service training programs for teachers are effective means of insuring that a new innovation will be implemented properly; and this method can also help in motivating them to accept the new program. Moynahan (1981), for example, investigated the effect of staff development on implementing magnet school and other desegregation programs. In her review of 39 studies, Moynahan found that four programs failed due to the lack of in-service staff preparation. In the majority of studies in which the new programs were successful, this researcher found that in-service training helped to sensitize school staff to the interpersonal and attitudinal problems associated with desegregation. Moynahan suggested that staff preparation should be comprehensive and include not only a presentation of the technical details of the program but also training in human relations, multi-cultural issues, and community participation. Thus, staff training is critical in determining whether a new program will be successful.

In-service training is a necessary but insufficient method for inducing an agency to accept a new program. Similar to the method of presentation, this technique is most effective with staff motivated to accept the program and with staff who are at least neutral. Teachers and administrators who are resistant to change usually require some additional incentive to attend the training sessions and to accept the new program.

Individual Counseling and Therapy

Occasionally, a key administrator blocks change due to personal problems. These problems might cause the individual to feel insecure and threatened by an aggressive change agent who recommends sweeping innovation. As a result, the administrator or teacher becomes defensive and chooses to remain with an ineffective policy as a means of finding security in the old routine. Therapy can unblock this obstacle to change, help develop a greater sense of self-confidence and reduce the fear of attempting some new program.

Unfortunately, in such cases, the context of the situation is often unfavorable to the development of a warm, trusting relationship. The administrator may not be open to the idea of forced counseling, particularly with an associate of the change agent who is seen as having a vested interest. This technique can work if the supervisor of the targeted individual suggests it and if the counseling is performed informally.

In actual practice, the interaction between the consultant and the defensive staff member is rarely seen as a counseling relationship. Instead, the consultant searches for opportunities to talk with the individual casually in a teachers' lounge or office. As the staff member gets to know the consultant, he or she becomes more open and trusting. In addition, the individual is more able to voice fears about the program in a one-to-one situation and as these fears are confronted and resolved, the employee feels a greater involvement in, and acceptance of, the innovation. Thus, individual counseling can work as long as a suitable context for developing such a relationship is obtained.

Sensitivity Group Training and Team Building

Another technique for encouraging the members of a school to accept change is sensitivity training through T-groups. Although less in vogue, these T-groups were used extensively in the 1970s. Sensitivity training consists of groups of approximately 15 to 20 members of the staff who meet for an extended period of time, such as over a weekend. Groups can include either horizontal or vertical slices of the organization or a combination of the two. Thus, all administrators or all teachers might compose a group, or the participants might be made up of the principal, a few teachers and a few parents. The group's only agenda is to study itself and the relationships among the participants. A facilitator encourages each participant to clarify and to express feelings, thoughts and experiences. The goal of sensitivity training is to provide a setting in which free, direct and role-free communication can occur. Each member becomes aware of the other participants' perceptions, and status differences are eliminated during the group sessions. As a result, the typical roles and norms of the organization are temporarily set aside, allowing for new communication patterns and decision-making processes to emerge.

This method is very useful if the desired intervention involves a reduction in the rigid bureaucratic style of the organization. In addition, since the top administrators become aware of the perspectives of teachers and parents, it is possible that innovations described by these latter groups might be understood and accepted more by the top decision makers as a result of these sessions. Finally, if the change agent communicates his or her diagnosis of the state of health of the school's internal integration area prior to the sensitivity training meetings, the participants might discuss the problems mentioned in the diagnostic report and find creative solutions for them.

Organizations have resorted to sensitivity training groups less often recently than in the past for a number of reasons. This training is usually very expensive and the results are largely unpredictable. Frequently, participants change their style of interaction during the group session but return to the usual routine patterns upon returning to work. For other participants, role demands at work become ambiguous and concerns regarding feelings and interpersonal relationships reduce staff productivity. In at least some cases, group members disclose too much of their feelings and personal experiences during the sessions and they feel embarrassed and personally disoriented. The group facilitator needs to be available for some time after the group meetings to help individuals through these difficulties. Finally, this method of encouraging change is time-consuming, as nearly all the staff of the organization must participate in the training sessions before any significant effect is possible. Thus, while this technique can be useful, many schools and organizations have not chosen sensitivity training groups due to potential difficulties that can result.

A technique similar in some respects to sensitivity training has been gaining prominence in organizational development and change. This technique, called team building (Dyer, 1977; Boss, 1983), seeks to develop a spirit of cooperation and interdependence among staff members. One aspect of team building consists of group problem solving sessions. In these sessions, group members are free to identify problems and to brainstorm creative solutions in a role-free, non-critical group atmosphere. These group problem-solving sessions are also known as "quality circles" (Marks, 1986). Team building can be a useful tool for change, particularly if the interventionist is able to provide input regarding policies or proce-dures that might interfere with client improvement. This strategy is more effective and less threatening than sensitivity training as the group remains focused on program concerns rather than personal-ity conflicts. Also, the new styles of interaction begun through team building can be maintained for a much longer period of time through follow-up sessions and regular interviews between the program director and each staff member.

Survey Feedback Method
        Instead of using team building and sensitivity training groups, many schools have found other methods of encouraging teachers and parents to participate in the change process. One such tech-nique is called the survey feedback method and it is similar to the action research model discussed in Chapter Two. In this interven-tion, a consultant asks the staff, and in some cases students and members of the community, to indicate their concerns regarding the school's internal functioning and task performance. These con-cerns are then converted into questions for surveys. The surveys either can be specific to one part of the organization, or global as-sessments. The questionnaires are then distributed to the staff, stu-dents and community members. The consultant tabulates the re-sults (broken down by respondent group), without performing any extensive analysis or interpretation of the data. The results are then presented at an open meeting. Each participant is able to see the extent of agreement among survey respondents as to which prob-lems are the most significant, and then each person is encouraged to draw conclusions and implications from the data. In order to maximize free and open discussion, a consultant who does not

have any particular bias relevant to the school usually facilitates these group meetings. Typically, at the end of the meeting, a representative group of the participants is formed to make specific recommendations for change based on the survey data. The interventions are then developed and implemented by the staff, sometimes with the assistance of the consultant, and the same survey is re-administered at regular time intervals to assess the success of a new program in reducing the perceived problems.

Clinical Experimental Method

Another method of assisting a school to adopt an innovation is the clinical experimental approach. This approach is similar to the survey feedback method in that a collaborative relationship is formed, but it differs in that the consultant assumes a more active role when interfacing with the client system. In this approach, the consultant's work is divided into two parts: conducting diagnostic research, and assisting in the implementation of the prescription. In the diagnostic stage, the consultant gathers data regarding the school's organizational health. These data include both objective statistics, such as client outcome measures, as well as subjective perceptions of student/parent/teacher satisfaction and survey results. The consultant analyzes the data and presents his or her conclusions or diagnosis to the administrators and teachers of the school at a faculty meeting. Together, the school personnel and change agent develop a prescription and recommendations for change. The change agent can also review the literature on innovative programs attempted elsewhere (sometimes called a best practices evaluation) that might be relevant to enhancing this program's performance. For example, the consultant might provide interpersonal communication skills workshops if the staff perceives difficulties in this area, or possibly the change agent might design a new intervention to enhance student functioning more directly. Using the diagnostic research as a baseline, the consultant can also evaluate the success of the intervention once implemented, and fine-tune the prescription accordingly.

This method has a number of advantages. As in the survey feedback approach, the clinical experimental technique insures that teachers participate in the development and implementation of a new program. In addition, the expertise of the consultant is utilized more directly. Finally, excessive staff time is not consumed as the consultant organizes the change process, researches possible interventions and locates resources to implement this intervention.

Demonstration Project

Among the most successful methods for decreasing resistance to change is to have the teachers of the targeted school visit a successful innovative program in operation. They can then observe that the new idea can be implemented effectively and can consult with the staff of the demonstration program regarding the new methods to resolve any concerns they might have with the new program.

This approach is most effective in producing support for the new innovation if the teachers perceive much similarity between the conditions present in the demonstration project and those in their own classroom. Thus, it is good to choose a demonstration project in which the type of student, size of the school and financial and human resources available are nearly identical to the target organization.

If it can be done, establishing a demonstration project in the target school itself is often effective, as the conditions present in the project are then identical to those of the rest of the program. In the mental health field, Fairweather and Davidson (1986) found that psychiatric hospitals that accepted a small-scale demonstration project were more likely to adopt the full innovation later than those institutions that wanted only to review literature or talk with a consultant about the new program. The drawback in establishing a demonstration project is that there is a great likelihood of initial "start up" problems that might produce some staff resistance to the program. This resistance might cause the demonstration project to become isolated within the school, and the prevailing social structure of the rest of the system might force the project to be terminated prematurely. Assuming the initial problems are not great, an effective demonstration project is likely to produce greater acceptance.

Once the innovation is accepted, it is important to provide teachers with on-going in-service training and other technical assistance to insure that the new program is running smoothly and is operating according to the intended guidelines. Also, the target school can later be used as the demonstration for other agencies experiencing similar difficulties.

The above nine techniques of encouraging organizational change are not mutually exclusive, and the change agent should consider combining as many methods as is feasible to increase the likelihood that the change program will be accepted and that it will be implemented effectively. For example, suppose a consultant was asked by a school principal to investigate why a large number of minority students were dropping out of school, and to offer recommendations to reduce the problem. The consultant might begin by diagnosing the organization's well-being, perhaps using a survey feedback approach. If the original problems surface in the responses of a large number of students, parents and teachers, the school staff might decide to address the issue. The consultant might become more active, and use the clinical experimental method. He or she might review the literature and find that a new program, in which teachers adopt a student—rather than curriculum-centered instructional style for a portion of the school day, would be effective in reducing the minority student dropout rate. The consultant might then convince the school board or superintendent to support the program by presenting information in a persuasive manner that linked the new program to the district's desire to preserve the racial balance and retain its minority students. Then, to familiarize the school staff with concerns of the minority group's culture, sensitivity training groups composed of teachers, students and parents might be attempted. The consultant might also provide in-service skills training for the staff to learn the new teaching method. Those staff strongly opposed to the philosophy of the new program, even after lengthy discussions with the consultant might be transferred to other schools in the district. Finally, a demonstration project in one school might be initiated. After an appropriate time period, the initial survey might be re-administered and other data gathered to detect whether the new program had the desired effect. In this manner, the change agent would have utilized all the methods for implementing the intervention, thus enhancing the probability that the change program will succeed.

ALTERNATIVE PARTICIPATORY MODEL

The techniques outlined above represent traditional strategies for change. The diagnostic-prescriptive model examines organizational functioning in the here and now to determine and correct deficits in order to help groups advance to the next level of functioning. Subsequent change strategies are suggested to help implement the prescription in the most productive manner. While it is important for change agents to be familiar with these seminal concepts, there has been a great deal of literature written over the past few decades dealing with alternative, participatory methods for organizational change.

Education and business-oriented change agents such as Stephen Covey (1991, 1989), Peter Senge (1994) and Maira and Scott-Morgan (1997) advocate future-focused strategies that require all members of an organization to examine not where they are, but where they ultimately wish to be in an on-going process. This proactive model involves creating the philosophy, vision and action plans.

Determining a school's philosophy

Maira and Scott-Morgan (1997) note the importance of developing an organization's philosophy to serve as a secure and comfortable constant for all members of the organization. Reinforcing these common, guiding principles is particularly useful during times of organizational change when many are feeling disenfranchised. In developing a school's philosophy, it is important to address three key elements, described below:

      a. Mission: Much like the U.S. Constitution, the mission is simply the answer to the question, "why do we exist?" (Senge, 1994). It is, as Covey (1989) points out, the focal point from which all activities derive their meaning. The mission addresses issues such as who makes up the school, which students are served and which services are offered. The manner in which the mission is executed depends largely on an organization's values and principles;

b. Values: A key element in an organization's ability to change is the underlying understanding of "what we are and what we want and value" (Covey, 1989). Given this, all members of an organization should participate in the development of its philosophy, and the process of developing these ideals is nearly as important as the product. Participation breeds a familial buy-in that helps each member of the organization to feel a shared sense of responsibility and commitment; and

c. Principles: These are a set of declarative, all or nothing statements that do not change under any circumstances. For example, one principle in a school might be to respect students as individuals. This principle is a constant regardless of funding pressures, leadership changes or advances in teaching techniques. Values, on the other hand, are ideas we prize more highly than others, and they can exist in varying degrees and are frequently adjusted by organizational circumstances. For example, a school district's value might be to promote from within when a vacancy arises before hiring outside staff. A district might have a very loyal secretary who appears deserving of advancement to a managerial position. However, if funding pressures are such that the school needs to hire an individual with experience administering government grants, they may well suspend the value of promoting from within in this particular instance. The organization may also change the degree to which this value is employed by offering inside candidates a raise for loyalty or additional responsibilities that might enhance their application in the future.

Developing a group vision reflective of this philosophy

Feeling as though one is a member of an organization with a meaningful philosophy is not enough. Most innovations begin with a "dream," and a change agent needs to help the group begin to develop a platform for innovation by way of a shared vision. Hamel and Prahalad (1994) define vision, or "strategic intent," as the animating dream that provides the emotional and intellectual energy for the journey, implying a sense of direction, discovery and destiny. Direction comes from determining where an organization, as an entity, is trying to go. Discovery offers employees the enticing journey to a new destination, and destiny, which commands the respect and leadership of every employee, must be both distinctive and worthwhile.

In simpler terms, Senge (1994) defines vision as the answer to the single question: "what do we want to create?" To Senge, group vision is similar to individual vision. Instead of carrying around individual images in one's own head, organizational vision involves the development of shared images that create a commonality, which gives coherence to diverse activities. A good vision statement should take into account the needs of all of the organization's stakeholders to avoid fostering a state of compliance rather than commitment. Therefore, a change agent should work carefully to insure that there is true bottom-up participation in the development of an organization's vision.

Senge (1994) recognized that developing a vision statement leaves a gap between an organization's current situation and it's desired one. This gap is perceived as a creative tension that is frustrating and inspiring and motivates all stakeholders to move to the next level of functioning.

Operationalizing these shared concepts into strategy and action plans

The best way for an organization to channel this tension is to utilize its philosophy and vision to develop concrete plans that will bring reality into line with the vision of where the group wishes to be in the near future. According to Maira and Scott Morgan (1997, p. 12), "To be truly effective, strategy must be a lot more than a neat construct. It must reflect the vision of the external world, the internal world, and the journey to realize the goal, and it must inspire the entire organization to take that journey." They note that five elements must be present within the organization to establish change readiness: a) an understanding that change is necessary; b) agreement that the proposed innovations are appropriate; c) the feeling that members have been acknowledged as individuals; d) the understanding that members have the skills to achieve the goals and; e) the organization supports the required changes.

Once this change-ready atmosphere is established, the following concrete steps can be taken to develop measurable plans. Maister (1993) suggests that the organization be divided into teams and each team provided with a sheet of paper labeled with one of the following objectives of the school: raise student achievement scores; increase skill building and application of skills; improve respect for cultural diversity; and improve parent – teacher communication. The following columns should be listed beneath each objective: a) actions proposed to achieve the objective; b) person responsible for each action; c) time required; d) due date and; e) completion indicator.

The change agent has an opportunity to meet with each team to help facilitate the development of these plans, while infusing some reality regarding the feasibility of the proposed strategies. At the end of this discussion, the final plan becomes a contract between the change agent and the school. The change agent should return after approximately three months to assess progress against the plans of action and to help the teams refine their ideas and develop new strategies to reach goals over the next few months. In this way, there is a continuous cycle of creativity, productivity and evaluation.

In many respects, these newer methods of organizational change implicitly incorporate many of Johnson's strategies for facilitating change. The primary difference in this approach is the issue of labeling. In working together to develop shared philosophy, vision, and goals, an organization has an opportunity to focus on competencies. There is a proactive attempt to look at where the group can go rather than the reactive position of trying to address what is currently wrong. In this sense, individuals have an opportunity to think outside of the box and create true innovation. This proactive approach empowers members of an organization through a collective sense of membership and power to effect creative and meaningful change, and continuous quality improvement.

INSTITUTIONAL AND SOCIETAL LEVEL CHANGE STRATEGIES

The above techniques are effective in promoting changes within a school that are consistent with the organization's values. Often however, innovation requires modification of not only the program's goals, but also the community's values and social structure. For example, in the situation described earlier, if the school's administration was not interested in reducing the dropout rate among minority children, a program designed to achieve this result would not be accepted.

As was mentioned previously, institutional change attempts to alter the goals of the system, and societal change methods target the status relationships among groups in the community. Institutional and societal change tactics are presumably political in nature. These methods help to alleviate problems caused when one group within the community is alienated, powerless, or unable to gain access to institutional resources. The change agent works for the group in an advocacy role, helping the group members organize together to reduce the power inequity.

The failure to design an intervention at the level appropriate to the problem can lead to ineffective or counterproductive programs. For example, if the above problem resulted from social discrimination, an intervention consisting of placing a minority child in a special education class will only increase the child's lack of self-esteem and reinforce the notion that the child's cultural background is deficient. As William Ryan (1971) noted, those in power tend to "blame the victim" of discrimination for his or her own plight, and viewing the problem from the wrong perspective or level of complexity will increase this tendency. Using the above example, not only will the individual level intervention not work, but also worse problems can result. The educational system might interpret the failure of the intervention as proof that such children cannot learn and that they are truly hopeless academically. The school then absolves itself of all responsibility in searching for the solution (or even the real problem) and, with their prejudice validated, the staff might criticize the child's family and cultural background as being responsible for the learning failure. The problem was defined at the wrong level and the resulting solutions will always miss the mark in a "game without end" (Watzlawick et al., 1974).

Instead of blaming the victim and the victim's sub-culture, Ryan suggested that both the school and the community realize that the problem resulted from social discrimination. To do this, the change agent must persuade the public that reformulating the problem is required before any effective solution can be designed or implemented. In this above example, the appropriate solution would include adding cultural amplifiers that highlight the accomplishments of members of the sub-culture to the curriculum. Instead of discounting the victim's culture, the effective intervention builds on cultural and personal strengths, not weaknesses.

Sarason's Creation of Alternative Settings

Sarason (1972) described one approach to institutional change and Alinsky (1972) discussed strategies useful in achieving societal change. As with other distinctions in this field, there is considerable overlap between these two types of change, and attempting to create institutional change may also result in societal change, and vice versa. The distinction is useful if it stimulates the change agent to generate more options. Sarason's approach to institutional change involved the development of alternative settings. He argued that when an institution is not adequately meeting the needs of a group of people, attempting to change the institution is often ineffective. Instead of initiating a "piecemeal" innovation within the organization, Sarason recommended that a new structure or setting be created which could allow its members to strive for a somewhat different goal. He believed that small "band-aid" changes within an existing program are ineffective and will soon be forced to comply with the goals, bureaucratic structure, and regulations of the rest of the institution. Alternative settings could be either sub-units of existing institutions or new independent organizations but, in either case, the innovation must be autonomous. Using this method, the change agents, along with the group that they serve, develop their own "rules of the game," their own social structure and role relationships.

The new settings will not only be more effective in meeting the groups' needs, but will also provide a mutually rewarding network of cooperative relationships, a greater psychological sense of community and, most significantly, a means of overcoming learned helplessness. For example, people who would normally be viewed as recipients of treatment might form their own organizations to assist each other. Such self-help groups as Alcoholics Anonymous or day care centers staffed by single parents would be alternative settings with goals and status relationships greatly different from those in traditional institutions. In education, this change structure could include either the establishment of an innovative school within a large public school system or it could involve a group of community residents creating a new school outside the school system.

An example of the former is the magnet school concept. In magnet schools, the curriculum is organized around a desired theme such as science, drama, or art. While all the usual subjects (reading, writing, mathematics, etc.) are still covered, extra class periods are dedicated to the specific theme of the magnet school. Students interested in the theme are drawn to these schools because of their unique emphases, as a magnet pulls in iron filings. These sub-units must still conform to all the regulations and policies of the school district, and unfortunately, over time the unique elements of the magnet schools are sometimes lost as the state and district mandated curricula consumes greater chunks of the school day. A more in-depth discussion of the magnet school is presented in the next chapter.

The other manner of using Sarason's tactic occurs when a neighborhood group decides that change within the public school system is impossible and it chooses to establish an alternative school. Over the past 40 years, thousands of alternative and charter schools have been started across the United States. Often, these schools are small and operate on minimal budgets in storefronts, churches, or private homes. These alternatives vary greatly in their structure, educational philosophy and teaching methodologies. In all cases, these schools are designed by groups within the community to meet the unique needs of the students who attend. As such, they have the advantage of being free of all rules and regulations imposed by the system's bureaucracy. Alternative schools that are not officially designated as charter schools, however, must be self-sufficient and independent of all support from the public school system. Finding financial resources for such schools is challenging and time consuming, and most of the autonomous schools close within 18 months of their opening due to a lack of funding (Scileppi, 1988). Thus, the change agent and the community groups need to consider the relative benefits and drawbacks of either developing a program within the system or establishing an entirely new structure outside the system.

Sarason's method of creating alternative settings is basically an institutional level change process, as it involves the altering of system goals to make them more consistent with the values of a subculture within the community. The next strategy to be considered is aimed at changing societal values themselves.

Alinsky's Community Organizing Societal Change Method

Perhaps the most radical of the non-violent methods of promoting change is Alinsky's (1972) description of community organizing for true social change. Alinsky emphasized the need to develop a process of change in the community rather than the adoption of a particular program. Through community organizing, a new politically active core group emerges which shifts the power base away from the status quo group. Specific policy changes are only by-products of the more significant modifications in the social structure.

The community organizer works for one or a number of disenfranchised groups within a community and uses the group's "people power" to overcome those whose status is based on "money power." Instantaneous change is not expected as the organizer assists the group in realizing that they must struggle to gain power and community resources rather than be given them. In this manner, Alinsky's approach represents true second order change, as the structure of society itself is altered and the status relationships between the dominant and minority groups become more equitable.

The goals of the community organizer are to gather a group together, to assist the group in attaining power and to use the power for the benefit of the community. For example, an Alinsky-trained organizer might assist a group of parents who have children with special educational needs, or even a group of teachers who are advocating for a specific reform. In order to achieve these ends, the organizer should possess the following attitude: the organizer should have a curious and questioning approach to the values of society, taking the irreverent stance that nothing is sacred. The organizer must not feel inhibited about attacking any institution, corporation or bureaucrat. Also, the change agent should have a good imagination, both to use creative means of organizing the group and to identify with the sufferings of people.

Alinsky believed that an organizer should have a blurred, non-dogmatic view of a better society and should never become a "true believer" of any political cause. This allows the change agent to compromise with the system after the client group has attained equal status with the formerly dominant group. Similarly, Alinsky believed that the non-dogmatic organizer has more leeway in assisting the group to attain its goals. He reasoned that a group that has no power should fight for total control and then, flexibly compromise to attain half of its demands. After successfully completing this process, the group exists as a significant force in the community and its members feel less helpless, as they now possess political power. In addition, the empowered group and its grass roots leaders can continue the process of change through negotiation with the heads of institutions long after their organizer leaves. A change agent who is too dogmatic or idealistic is not able to compromise later on and the group might not realize any of its goals.

In addition, the change agent should have personal characteristics such as an open mind, a good sense of humor, and a high tolerance for ambiguity. The change agent must not desire to lead but must strive to be a catalyst, organizing the group to use its own "people power" to obtain social change.

In order to describe his method more fully, Alinsky (1972) provided the organizers with a large number of principles and tactics to use when achieving change. Some of these "rules for radicals" and successful tactics for applying these principles are presented below:

1. Never go outside the experience of your friendly audience, but baffle your opponents by devising tactics outside of their experience. For example, in order to obtain some employment concessions from the mayor of Chicago, Alinsky threatened to mobilize people power to occupy all the rest room facilities at O'Hare International Airport using jobless members of his group. The city swiftly conceded, as they realized that Chicago

would lose greatly. Business leaders might be less inclined to hold conventions in the city and airlines would
choose other airports to schedule connecting flights and
layovers. In addition, Chicago police could not arrest
the protesters, since no laws specify the length of time a
person can spend using the public facilities;

2. Never tell another what to do, but rather ask loaded
    questions and follow up any questions about tactics
    with a second question, "What do you think?" Alinsky
    used this modified "Socratic method" frequently to
    generate creativity and a sense of self-competence and
    power in the local leaders;

3. Create the belief that change is both possible and prob-
    able. Consider that this is not an easy process, as op-
    pressed people recall many instances in which they
    were powerless and they perceive that any activity to
    create change is futile. Generally in such a situation,
    oppressed persons experience learned helplessness (Pe-
    terson, Maier, & Seligman, 1993) and refrain from get-
    ting involved to improve their condition. Alinsky engi-
    neered situations in which the group could win an easy
    battle initially to foster faith in the power of community
    organizing. For example, he scheduled a large group
    meeting in a public park and arranged for the necessary
    public permit. After securing the bureaucrat's permis-
    sion, and after being told that such permits require 24
    hours to process, Alinsky went back to the group indi-
    cating that the city was stalling regarding issuing the
    permit. The group, then, decided to picket city hall on
    the following day, demanding that they be allowed their
    right to gather. The officials, confused about the sup-
    posed communication mix-up and seeking to avoid a
    confrontation, presented the group leaders with a per-
    mit. The group members believed that the city con-
    ceded due to their efforts and they felt that ultimate vic-
    tory was very likely, if the group organized itself fully.
    It goes without saying that change plans should be free
    of duplicity for ethical and practical reasons. If

Alinsky's scheme were uncovered, the group would have unified in their mistrust of the change agent;

4. Organize diverse community groups by appealing to super-ordinate values and cultural truisms. Alinsky assisted in gathering over 100 local social and religious groups in Rochester (NY) under a coordination group called FIGHT, which stood for Freedom, Integrity, God, Honor, Today. Nearly every minority organization in that city found some common positive cause with a group so named, and this group quickly gained thousands of supporters. Its leaders harnessed this "people power" to gain important job concessions for minorities from the Eastman Kodak Company, the largest industrial employer in the area;

5. Make the best use of "people power," particularly if the other side has "money power." In the Rochester effort, Alinsky capitalized on the free classical concerts that Kodak offered in the community. Typically, the company's executives and their spouses attended these concerts. The FIGHT organizers obtained a large number of tickets for the concert and distributed these tickets at a pre-concert "baked beans party" attended by the FIGHT members. Later on, the atmosphere at the concert was definitely affected by those who attended the earlier cookout. The company executives quickly found that "people power" was a force with which to be recognized and negotiated; and

6. Seize the moment; invent new creative tactics as presented by current events. In a Midwestern city, Alinsky and his group were attempting to persuade the city council to pass rat control laws to encourage landlords to improve the living conditions in the poorer neighborhoods. The city administration was unsympathetic about the problem until the group leaders collected a large number of rats from the slum buildings and freed them in City Hall. The action of course was not illegal, as the city had no rat control laws. Alinsky's group made it's point, and the legislature swiftly passed the necessary bill.

With all these community organizing tactics, Alinsky demonstrated that true social change is possible and that minority groups can gain their fair share of institutional resources. However, as Alinsky found, the dominant society does not relinquish its power readily and those who choose to organize minority groups in the community must be prepared for a long and difficult struggle.

In looking at Alinsky's many contributions to the field of community organizing, Speer and Hughey (1995) noted that Alinsky's greatest legacy is the notion that empowerment, in its true sense of the word, must be more closely aligned with a power-facilitating process, whereby individuals develop new competencies in their pursuit of community change. This represents another example of the benefits of looking at problems at the highest level, in that individuals, through their membership and integration in a community change plan, have an opportunity not only to effect change, but to grow personally as a result of this action.

As can be seen, Sarason's method of creating alternative settings and Alinsky's strategy of organizing minority groups to gain power and resources in the community are very powerful methods of altering the values and status relationships of the social system to create true change. These techniques emphasize the fact that, at times, the interventionist must revamp the entire social system to produce real change, as innovations at lower levels might be ineffective and counterproductive. Change attempted at these high levels will initiate a positive spiraling process, resulting in positive community changes and individual growth, belonging and a sense of empowerment for those who participate. The change agent must be aware of possible intervention strategies at all levels of the system to choose the appropriate type of innovation and to avoid being confined to a single approach.

Table 10.1 summarizes the principles of individual/organizational and institutional/societal change strategies.

TABLE 10.1: ORGANIZATIONAL AND INSTITU-TIONAL CHANGE STRATEGIES

	PURPOSE	STRATE-GIES	PROCESS COMPO-NENTS
Indi-vidual/ Organiza-tional	To modify behavior To create an efficient school, while ad-hering to current goals	Diagnostic Prescriptive Model	Diagnosis -Task accom-plishment -Internal inte-gration -Growth and change Prescription -Review re-search -State goals and objectives -Conceptualize the program -Modify, as necessary

		Alternative Participatory model	Philosophy
			  -Mission
			  -Values
			    -Principles
			Vision
			Strategy action plan

Institu-tional Societal		Creation of Alternate Set-tings Method	New structure or setting with new goals for a sub-culture within the com-munity Participants de-velop rules, so-cial structure,

			role relation-ships
	To alter the goals of the social sys-tem To rear-range the status quo relation-ships among groups in the commu-nity	Community Organizing Method	Politically ac-tive core group shifts power from status quo group People power over money-power

COMPONENTS TO CONSIDER WHEN PLAN-NING CHANGE

When planning change, it is essential that the interventionist consider the effects of the new program on all components of the system. Levine and Perkins (1987) have provided a checklist of the sets of interest that must be taken into account when planning an innovation. Failure to do so could readily turn a very noble inter-vention with potentially significant outcomes into a worthless fail-ure. Levine and Perkins' seven sets of interest are as follows.

Energy
Implementing a new program frequently requires staff to work harder and longer, at least initially. During the transition, personnel are needed to staff both the old and the new programs. These staff members are probably required to complete research forms moni-toring the new program and documenting its outcome. If the pro-gram is operating at a new site, there are many "start-up" costs as-sociated with setting up the new location. All of these new expenditures of energy require money or other forms of compen-

sation. The program planner needs to secure funds to pay for the extra time and effort.

Power

Beneficial innovations affect the power and status relationships among staff at different levels or between staff and clients. The change agent must obtain the explicit support from the highest authorities in the agency to motivate those who might lose power to accept the new program or at least allow it to operate.

Culture and Beliefs

Some staff may block change because the new program challenges their beliefs and values. If many staff members believe that all students should conform to the cultural norms of the dominant society, attempts at increasing respect and tolerance for diversity are doomed to failure. The change agent must confront commonly held beliefs and educate all involved to a more conducive ideology.

Competence

Changing staff duties can create self-doubts about one's ability to perform the new activities. Also, others in the system may question whether certain staff effectively can carry out tasks previously reserved for those with other job titles. Attempting to incorporate teachers into the mental health programs will fail if program staff does not trust a teacher's ability to provide this service. Again the change agent needs to anticipate these doubts and provide the needed staff training to address concerns.

Legal and Administrative Factors

Innovative programs are not exempt from local and state laws, relevant agency regulations, and union contract stipulations. A change agent must be aware of all these rules when planning an intervention. Requirements for teacher certification and laws governing schools differ from state to state. Contracts with teachers' unions mandate specific conditions affecting length of the school day and the number of students assigned to a classroom. In other cases, a new program might require a worker to assume a duty previously assigned to a staff with a different job title. This might violate a union contract. Similarly, such contracts might require that staff be paid overtime if they are required to attend training sessions outside their normal work shifts. It is beneficial to involve union leaders in program planning to encourage cooperation in resolving these work issues.

Information and Communication

In organizations, information is power and erroneous rumors can jeopardize the successful implementation of a new program. The change agent must employ good judgment in deciding how much information to provide to staff and at what time. Too much information can be overwhelming and procedural details should be left to agency personnel to discuss and resolve. Insufficient communication from the interventionist can create a climate of mistrust, fear and misinformation throughout the school. Typically, the program should be discussed first with senior level administrators, senior teachers and union leaders, as other staff relies on these individuals for accurate information and guidance. When agreements on major issues have been reached, open meetings with all affected staff should be scheduled. To enhance staff "ownership" of the innovation and to insure the new program is implemented smoothly within the system, the change agent should encourage much teacher input in program implementation. To preserve program intent however, such input should be limited to procedural matters and not to modifications of the program's goals.

Relationships

Frequently, change agents develop new programs without considering day-to-day issues of great importance to staff. Teachers over time develop pleasant and productive relationships with peers, and innovations that alter the composition of the work team can produce a great deal of staff resistance. These changes affect morale, productivity and job satisfaction, and interventionists must respond to these concerns when developing new programs. Strategies to deal with staff relationship issues include maintaining current work teams, allowing for staff input in any work unit changes and conducting team-building exercises with members of new work units.

Quality, well-researched innovations with solid theoretical bases have either not been accepted or have been prematurely discontinued because change agents have not adequately considered these seven concerns. They represent practical, process-oriented issues that must be "tailor-fit" to the ecology of each agency in which they are applied.

Funding Innovative Change: Grant Proposal Preparation

A discussion of practical strategies for implementing meaningful change would be incomplete without considering the issue of how to fund innovative programs. After deciding on the nature of the innovative program, change agents need to explore which funding sources are dedicated to assisting the development of their type of program and then consider what needs to be included in the grant proposal.

Researching Funding Sources

Private foundations and government agencies have mission statements that describe their areas of concern and form the basis for Requests for Proposals (RFP's). Such RFP's may target a particular educational problem, a special population or a type of program activity. Some focus on issues such as reducing dropout rate, facilitating the transition to employment or enhancing mental health, while others fund programs which service the needs of groups of people such as troubled teens, students living in inner city neighborhoods or those with developmental disabilities. Finally, some funding sources support research and program evaluation studies, while others consider only those proposals that establish demonstration projects capable of being disseminated to other parallel school districts throughout the state or nation.

There are local, state and national funding sources. At the local level, the school district hosting the new program might provide support. Such a school board has a strong "innovativeness tendency" (Johnson, 1970), as the members realize that their school's mission statement requires resources be set aside to develop new programs which meet more fully the changing needs of their student population. In other cases, a local government agency is empowered either to channel state and federal "block grant" money or to utilize local tax receipts to encourage and support innovations proposed by community groups collaborating with the local school district. For example, a county youth bureau might fund programs designed to reduce problems related to juvenile delinquency or violence in the schools. Also school boards, neighborhood business organizations (such as the Rotary or Chamber of Commerce), local merchants and religious groups fund new programs, and a change agent may wish to explore these sources first, particularly for small innovations.

Either major private foundations or state and federal agencies usually fund larger scale projects. An interventionist can find information about these possible grants from print and electronic databases at college, university, or large public libraries.

Most grant writers now search for funding sources by using electronic resources on the Internet (D. Berger, 1997, personal communication). Government agencies and private foundations have homepages on the World Wide Web. Also, there are on-line clearinghouses of grant information such as the Federal Information Exchange (FIE) and the Federal Register. FIE (http://web.fie.com) has information on grants available from many agencies and offers free e-mail alerts available upon request. The Federal Register (http://www.access.gpo.gov/su_doc/aces/aces140.html) has a searchable database including funding opportunities for many government programs.

Finally, other electronic resources are available on compact disks (CDs). They include the Sponsored Program Information Network (SPIN), which contains over 7000 public and private sources for educational funding, and the Foundation Center that lists some 40,000 foundations and gives workshops for grant seekers. The Foundation can also be contacted on the Internet as http://fdncenter.org (D. Berger, 1997, personal communication).

Writing Grant Proposals

Each funding agent includes in the RFP specific guidelines for the content of proposals, and those should be followed precisely. Reviewers often assign scores to each aspect of the proposal, and thus not following the guidelines could result in a section being omitted, causing a proposal to be non-competitive. In general, most grant proposals are comprised of seven components: executive summary; need statement; project description; evaluation; budget;

information about the recipient organization; and conclusion. Berger (1996) described these sections as follows:

- The executive summary, also called abstract though presented first, should be written last. It includes a statement of the problem and how the project will solve it. This one page section should also summarize the funding requirements and the expertise of the change agent and/or the groups who will implement the project;

- The statement of need includes statistics demonstrating that a need exists and information about the individuals who will benefit from the project. Typically, this section is about two pages in length and should present a compelling and accurate argument that a significant problem needs to be remedied;

- The project description, typically three pages long, should include the goals and objectives, activities to be performed; timeline, benchmarks and staffing issues. The more abstract goals should be followed by logically connected specific and measurable objectives. The project activities should be discussed in detail and their rationales linked to the objectives. Frequency of tasks to be performed and the qualifications of the providers should be described (ex: fifteen 45-minute presentation workshops will be presented by teachers possessing Master's degrees). A timeline for the completion of each task should also be stated, with benchmarks that outline target milestones. Finally, information regarding the staff should be presented. Identify the project director and the number, qualifications and duties of the staff to be supported by the proposed grant. If key personnel have already been chosen, summarize their relevant credentials in the section and attach resumes in the appendix of the proposal. The project description is significant in that grants fund activities, not ideas. Even if the idea is very good and in line with the funding source's mission statement, the proposal will not be funded until a plan of action which is logically connected to goals, objectives and outcomes, is articulated;

- The evaluation section should be closely related to the goals, objectives and project activities, and should include both process- and outcome-oriented measures. The criteria for determining success should also be stated. Whenever possible, present details such as who will conduct the program evaluation, what assessment instruments will be used for data gathering and how the results will be analyzed and disseminated;

- The budget component has a narrative section as well as an actual budget form and should describe both direct and indirect costs. Direct costs include staff salaries and benefits, consultant fees and other expenses such as equipment, supplies and travel. Indirect administrative costs refer to the proportion of general school expenses for utilities, overhead, maintenance, office rent, bookkeeping, etc. that will be consumed by the new program. Some RFP's encourage recipients to provide part of the resources to support the proposed project and the budget section of these matching grant proposals should include the types of cash or "in-kind" contributions which will be supplied by the agency, school or group. If appropriate, include the value of the service contributed by college students and community member volunteers recruited to assist in the program. It is also useful to describe the nature and degree of school district support for the new program;

- Organizational information should include a description of the recipient institution and how the proposed project conforms to its mission and goals. The ability of the school district to implement the new project should be highlighted in this section; and

- The conclusion section should identify relevant plans for the future after the project is completed and what continuing activities (if any) will occur after the grant funding ends. In addition, plans for disseminating the results of successful projects should be described, as this increases the potential benefits realized by the grant.

Given the number of proposals submitted for each RFP, it is very possible that initial attempts at grant writing may not be successful. If a proposal is not funded, it is useful to request feedback from the reviewers. Since funding agencies send out similar RFP's on a regular (often annual) basis, a well-crafted proposal that incorporates the reviewers' earlier criticisms has a higher probability of being funded. The first draft of a proposal is more difficult to compose than later revisions and even if the initial attempt is rejected, it is still of value if it becomes the basis of a later successful application.

Armed with the strategies for change and the guidelines for implementing new programs, the educational change agent should be better able to plan and establish innovations that enhance the quality of learning in contemporary schools. While each proposed project must be uniquely fit to the social setting in which it will be implemented, utilizing these tactics will increase the likelihood that a new program will be successful.

DISCUSSION QUESTIONS

1. What is the theoretical basis for change in an educational setting?

2. From the perspective of the student, parent, teacher, administrator and the business community, what are the most pressing problems in education? What values does each group espouse and how does this impact its definition of the problem?

3. Distinguish between organizational and institutional change. What are the defining characteristics and do they effectively modify student/school/district goals and behaviors?

4. Of the organizational change strategies discussed in this chapter, which do you think are the most effective and why?

5. Of the institutional and societal change strategies discussed in this chapter, which do you think are the most effective and why?

6. How would you convince your school board to implement Sarason's alternate setting method to solve a particular educational problem?

7. How would you convince your community to implement Alinsky's community organizing method to solve a particular educational problem?

8. Reflect on a recent unsuccessful innovation in your district. Which sets of interests were violated and how did that negate the sustainability of the change?

9. Using the strategies discussed in this chapter, describe an educational problem and create an outline of a mini-grant proposal to fund an innovative change.

Chapter 11:
The Magnet School
as a Model System for
Educational Reform

OBJECTIVES

After studying this chapter, the reader will be able to define, analyze and apply the following concepts and strategies:

1. Magnet schools as a social system;

2. Origin of magnet schools;

3. Definition of magnet schools;

4. Characteristics of magnet schools;

5. Prevalence of magnet schools;

6. Educational benefits of magnet schools;

7. System components of magnet schools;
   - Inputs;
   - Outputs; and
   - Throughputs;

8. Curricular approaches in magnet schools;

9. Contemporary reform strategies in magnet schools;
   - Action research;
   - Assessment;
   - Diversity;

- Inclusion;
- Parent communication;
- Technology;
- Distance learning;
- Mental health; and
- Change

Begin with the premise that there should be only one reason to restructure a school system—the students. A vision of what a community wants for its students establishes the basis on which all subsequent restructuring decisions should be made. -Robert Blum, Program Director, North West Regional Educational Laboratory

OVERVIEW

While the magnet school concept unites the best of educational practices in a creative and stimulating way, perhaps its most compelling feature is the premise upon which it is built—that a quality education may be provided in a setting other than the neighborhood school, where children of different cultures can learn and thrive together. It is for this reason that the prospective teacher should study the lessons learned from the magnet school experiment and infuse the relevant instructional methods, specialized curriculum and diversity strategies into daily practice.

This chapter defines the magnet school, explores its goals, delineates its characteristics, describes the educational benefits derived by the students and the community at large, and provides data on the prevalence of magnet schools across the nation, all as an example of a social system—the educational system—and its implementation as a model for school reform and change.

Characteristics Of Education As A Social System And Their Relevance To Magnet Schools

As described in Chapter 1, "Introduction to a Systems Approach to Education", a system is a set of elements that link together to form a complex whole. The elements are ordered, interconnected, functional and supportive of each other, yet each maintains its independence as a sub-system of the whole. The hierarchical layering of these elements creates a mechanism for communication and control. An inherent feedback loop monitors the achievement of the system's goals, thereby ensuring that it adapts to environmental changes.

The viewpoint of each stakeholder for whom the system has meaning is considered, as are its relevance and benefit. This chapter validates the magnet school as an example of successful utilization of a systems approach to education. The inputs (student and other stakeholder attributes and needs), the throughputs (mission, goals, curriculum, funding, marketing/admission, transportation, instructional practices, assessment, technology and facility) and the outputs (student achievement, reduction of racial isolation, school climate, program quality, systemic reform, college entrance, employment, improved graduation rates, enrollment in college preparatory courses, and participation in the Scholastic Aptitude Test (SAT)) form the elements of the system. Each element is interconnected and interdependent, each functioning as a sub-system with contributing parts, each communicating and controlling the other, and each participating in an evaluation of its effectiveness.

Summary Of Characteristics Of Educational Reform

As described in Chapter 1, it is imperative to define the problems preventing the meaningful functioning of an educational system (i.e., achieving its goals and meeting adequately the needs of its stakeholders), before changing it. The problem must be framed according to the values of the stakeholders and with supporting research and data. Using the diagnostic-prescriptive model, the change agent defines the deficiency in terms of the overall health of the system, evaluates the degree to which the system meets its objectives, and outlines a prescription and strategies for change. This chapter will validate the magnet school model as an example of educational change using the diagnostic-prescriptive method. A description of the problems leading to the development of the magnet school remedy, based on supportive data, research and the values of the stakeholders, as well as its success as a solution, is discussed.

THE MAGNET SCHOOL CONCEPT

History Of Magnet School Development

The historic *Brown v. Board of Education of Topeka* decision of 1954, in which Chief Justice Warren delivered the opinion of the United States Supreme Court, provided the impetus for desegregating public schools. The unanimous decision stated that separating children in public schools solely on the basis of race violated the Fourteenth Amendment of the Constitution and that the principle of "separate, but equal" no longer held validity. The decision denied states with segregated schools the legal basis for continuing this practice. In the 1960s, as schools began to deseg-regate and children were bused to schools outside their neighbor-hood, public school options became available to children (Waldrip, N.D.). Street academies emphasized the basics, but also included African-American history and civil rights. The "open classroom," a popular British model that gave students and teachers schools without walls and certain instructional freedoms, was implemented in many communities. In 1968, McCarver Elementary School in Tacoma, Washington was designed to reduce racial isolation by offering a choice to parents; in 1969, Trotter Elementary School in Boston, Massachusetts was opened for the same reason. A system of public vouchers was initiated as early as the seventies. In the ensuing years, the Federal and State courts accelerated the progress of desegregation efforts by ordering mandatory desegregation plans. Desegregation plans were also ordered by State education agencies (based upon a determination that State law was violated) and the Office for Civil Rights (OCR) (under Title VI). In addition, many local education agencies wrote and implemented voluntary plans to be approved by the U.S. Department of Education (USDE) (Federal Register, 2004). The establishment of magnet schools was a natural outcome of these actions and served as a viable solution to the problem of segregation. Magnet schools attract both minor-ity and non-minority students by design, by promising an interest-ing and motivational education that is oftentimes unavailable in a regular public school setting. The use of magnet schools to achieve voluntary desegregation has increased dramatically since its incep-tion, with over two million students (of whom over sixty-five per-cent are non-white) in attendance nationwide.

Definitions

There are several definitions of magnet schools, each con-taining similar elements. The U.S. Department of Education, rep-resenting the national educational perspective of Congress and the President, defines the magnet school as "a public elementary school, public secondary school, public elementary education center, or public secondary education center that offers a special curriculum capable of attracting substantial numbers of students of different racial backgrounds" (USDE, 2004). The Association for Supervision and Curriculum Development, representing the entire profession of educators, defines magnet schools as alternative public schools that usually focus on a particular area of student interest, for example, performing arts or science and technology, while also offering more traditional school subjects. Students from any part of the school district may enroll and the schools often maintain waiting lists (ASCD, 2004). The Education Commission of the States, representing governors, state legislators and state education agencies, defines magnet schools as public schools that provide specialized curriculums and instructional approaches to attract students from a variety of neighborhoods in a metropolitan area. Enrollment for magnet schools is often regulated, to ensure that they remain racially balanced. Enrollment is controlled in a variety of ways, such as through admissions criteria, first-come, first-served applications, lotteries and/or percentage set-asides for neighborhood residents (Education Commission of the States, 2004). The Mid-Atlantic Equity Consortium, representing school systems and educational organizations, defines a magnet school as a school or education center that offers a special curriculum capable of attracting substantial numbers of students of different racial backgrounds. Magnet schools were conceptualized as a response to remedy racial segregation in school enrollment, and as a desegregation strategy, allow for the reassignment of children in order to reduce, eliminate or prevent minority group isolation in one or more K-12 schools of a local education agency (LEA). Magnet schools are usually part of a broader desegregation plan stemming from litigation. A key feature of magnet schools is the special curriculum designed to embrace a subject matter or teaching methodology that is not generally offered to students of the same age or grade level in the same local education agency, such as a science-technology center or center for the performing arts (Mid-Atlantic Equity Consortium, 2004). Dr. Donald R. Waldrip, founder of Magnet Schools of America, an organization that represents individual member schools and school districts, states that magnet schools are based on the premise that all students do not learn in the same way, and that if a unifying theme is found or a different organizational structure for students of similar interest is provided, those students will learn more in all areas (Waldrip, N.D.). From a State perspective, Connecticut education law defines an inter-district magnet program as one that supports racial, ethnic and economic diversity, offers a special and high quality curriculum, and requires students to attend at least half-time (Connecticut General Statutes, Section 10-264l).

Characteristics

Magnet schools are distinguished from traditional public school settings in several ways. They promote diversity as an explicit goal and mandate a racial balance of students through enrollment regulation. They provide an educational program based on a unique and distinctive thematic curriculum. They employ innovative and accommodating instructional approaches. They provide a choice for parents in selecting a school that fits the needs, aptitudes and abilities of their children. They accept students from various attendance zones, both within and outside the district. They promote a positive school climate and provide a professional community among teachers. They enroll students by lottery, by application, or by achievement in the area of the school's area of concentration, not strictly by the neighborhood attendance area. They are often governed by a regional board, comprised of participating districts. They often have more autonomy in hiring, recruiting and assigning teachers on a voluntary basis, not strictly by seniority. They often have state-of-the-art facilities, equipment and supplies related to the theme, highly qualified teachers and instructional leaders, support services, and the ability to infuse technology. They have parents who are actively involved and invested in their child's program (Connecticut State Board of Education Report, March 2003). They have a mission, upon which goals are determined and curriculum integrated. They have instructional leaders who are highly regarded and teachers who are highly motivated. They are created as whole school models (those that make the magnet available to all students in the district who are in the grade level in which the program operates) and as programs-within-a-school (those that offer the specialized curriculum to some, but not all, students in a school). And most importantly, magnet schools have been found to increase student achievement, improve the school climate, increase student motivation, improve teacher satisfaction and sense of professional community, and improve parent involvement and satisfaction (Flaxman, Guerrero, and Gretchen, 1999).

National Prevalence and Trends

The demands of a rapidly changing society and increasing pressure for desegregation (coupled with a rise in absenteeism, dropout rates and academic failure in traditional schools) have led to the creation of over 1,000 magnet schools in urban school districts across the country. In order to facilitate the transition to a multiracial community and meet the prevailing desire for academic excellence, magnet schools have adopted innovative educational practices as an enticement for voluntary integration. Magnet schools meet racial quotas through voluntary enrollment and open access beyond established attendance zones. They emphasize a special curriculum or educational structure. And they attract students and parents by creating supportive, personal environments while placing high expectations on student progress and potential (Klauke, 2000).

The number of magnet schools has nearly doubled since between the early 1980s and the year 2000. The percentage of students enrolled in public chosen schools (magnet, charter, inter and intra-district) increased from 11 percent in 1993 to 14 percent in 1999. Students living in large districts with more schools have more opportunity for public school choice within the district. Students in an area with few schools may only be able to choose a school in another district. In 1993, one third of districts with 10,000 or more students had intra-district choice compared to 9 percent of districts with less than 1000 students. Students from families with low incomes and racial/ethnic minorities use public, chosen schools at a higher rate than do other students. The variation in state legislation also creates regional variation in the availability of school choice. During the 1999–2000 school year, 71 percent of school districts in the West, 63 percent in the Midwest, 44 percent in the South and 19 percent in the Northeast allowed for intra-district or inter-district school choice options. Data from the 1993 and 1999 October supplement to the Current Population Survey (CPS) show that students who attend publicly controlled schools are more racially and ethnically diverse than students who attend privately controlled schools (U.S.D.E. National Center for Education Statistics, 1993-1999).

Table 11.1 reflects the number of magnet schools reported to the United States Department of Education in the 2001-2002 school year (U.S.D.E. National Center for Education Statistics, 2001-2002, Table 9). There were 1,736 magnet schools in 30 states (reporting states' totals exclude states for which data were missing for 20 percent or more of the schools or districts). The percentage of students in these schools ranged from .1 percent to 14.8 percent. The number of schools ranged from 456 in California to one each in Maine and New Mexico. Since the 2001-02 school year, a significant number of magnet schools has been opened, but audited data is not yet available on the number of these schools.

TABLE 11.1: Number of Magnet Schools and Percentage of Students: 2001-2002

STATE	NUMBER OF MAGNET SCHOOLS	PERCENTAGE OF STUDENTS
Alabama	41	3.0
Alaska	17	3.2
Arkansas	7	1.0
California	456	9.4
Colorado	2	0.1
Connecticut	17	1.1
Delaware	2	0.9
District of Columbia	2	1.1
Georgia	62	3.6
Illinois	420	14.8
Indiana	23	1.3
Kansas	33	3.1
Kentucky	35	4.3
Louisiana	74	6.3
Maine	1	-
Massachusetts	7	0.4
Minnesota	66	3.4

Mississippi	5	0.5
Missouri	49	2.4
Nevada	9	1.3
New Jersey	2	0.1
New Mexico	1	Rounds to zero
North Carolina	165	8.3
Rhode Island	17	7.3
South Carolina	25	2.3
Tennessee	18	1.2
Virginia	166	11.4
Washington	14	0.8
Puerto Rico	151	10.8
Virgin Islands	1	7.2
TOTAL	1736	

Table 11.2 reflects the number and percent of magnet schools, as well as the percentage of students in magnet schools, in the 100 largest public elementary and secondary districts in the United States in 2001-2002 (National Center for Education Statistics, 2001-2002, Table 6). Twenty-one of these districts in thirteen states report having 279 magnet schools, ranging from one to fifty-one per district (2.1–23.9 percent of schools in the district), and 0.4 to 36.1 percent of students in the magnet schools.

TABLE 11.2: Number/Percentage of Magnet Schools and Percentage of Students in the 100 Largest Elementary and Secondary Public Schools: 2001-2002

STATE	REPORT-ING DISTRICT	NUMBER OF MAGNET SCHOOLS	PER-CENTAGE OF MAGNET SCHOOLS	PER-CENT-AGE OF STU-DENTS
Alaska	Anchorage	10	10.2	7.4
Alabama	Mobile County	9	8.8	8.0
California	San Francisco Uni-	5	4.4	8.9

	fied			
	San Bernardino City Unified	25	38.5	36.1
	Oakland Unified	11	11	22.4
	Sacramento City Unified	6	7.6	17.5
	San Juan Unified	5	5.8	8.0
	Elk Grove Unified	1	1.9	3.1
Georgia	Atlanta City	6	6.2	14.7
Kansas	Wichita	27	29.3	23.0
Louisiana	East Baton Rouge Parish	27	25.5	27.4
	Caddo Parish School Board	20	27.0	34.0
Minnesota	Minneapolis	20	13.9	19.2
North Carolina	Guilford County	13	12.9	8.6
	Forsyth County	51	75	69.6
Nevada	Washoe County	2	2.1	0.4
South Carolina	Greenville County	12	12.8	14.8
Tennessee	Knox County	4	4.5	5.0
Virginia	Prince William County	21	28.4	39.8

	Chester-field County	1	1.7	3.1
Wash-ington	Seattle	3	2.3	4.3
Total: 13	21	279		

Educational Benefits

The benefits of magnet schools to the student body and the community at large are significant. Their ability to foster desegregation, ensure equity, foster cultural understanding and decrease isolation has had a positive social impact. The specialized theme and innovative methodology and pedagogy motivate students to stay in school, achieve at high levels, graduate, seek further educational opportunities and be gainfully employed. The opportunity for students from low performing schools to have the choice to attend a higher performing magnet school makes parents feel involved in their child's education and creates a sense of hopefulness; they are no longer forced to settle for a school that does not meet their child's needs. Students who attend a racially diverse school improve their performance on standardized tests, are less likely to drop out of school, are more likely to attend college, benefit from better employment opportunities, and live as adults in integrated communities (Banks and McGee, 1995).

Parents recognize the educational benefits of sending their child to a magnet school and report their reasons for doing so as follows: the school's theme; the academic program; the quality of teaching staff; the quality of the administrative staff; the location of the school; the academic support services; the diverse student population; the use of advanced technology; the dissatisfaction with the neighborhood school and the lack of student progress (Connecticut State Board of Education Report, March 2003).

SYSTEMS COMPONENTS

As was noted in Chapter 1, a system is comprised of a series of inputs, throughputs and outputs, all of which are interrelated; and so it is in the design of the magnet school. Table 11.3 provides a summary of the system components of a magnet school; it describes the orderliness of the magnet system as a whole, the interrelatedness of its parts, and the hierarchical structure of its layers. It validates Smith's (1995) definition of a system; organized, integrated, orderly, predictable and functional. It mirrors Capra's principles of a sustained system, as noted in chapter 3; it is diverse, complex, interdependent, adaptive, resilient and sustainable (Capra, 1996). A more detailed explanation of each component follows the table.

TABLE 11.3: SYSTEM COMPONENTS OF THE MAGNET SCHOOL

INPUTS	THROUGH PUTS	OUTPUTS
Student attributes -Birth order -Family size -Parental education and practices -Minority status [1] -Mental health -Physical health -Genetic disorders -Ethnicity and ethnic values -Social status -Economic status -Intellectual ability -Achievement level -Self-attitudes -Developmental stage -Achievement motivation	Mission	Improved student achievement in academic and vocational areas

Student needs	Goals	Reduction in racial isolation
-Organization of day -Organization of the classroom (heterogeneous/ homogeneous ability grouping) -Mechanisms for support (counseling, remediation) -Special education (mainstreaming, inclusion) -English as a second language -Migrant education -Focused learning -Match of teacher/student teaching/learning styles (person-environment fit) -Quality of the classroom -Forces at national and state levels -Size, type and age of the school -Interface of school and community -Student-teacher ratio -Relevant and interesting curriculum -Social, racial and ethnic diversity -Value climate emphasizing academics and high expectations		

Teacher attributes -Experience -Education level beyond bachelor's degree -Race -Expectations -Preferred method of teaching (didactic/authoritarian/participatory) -Knowledge of the special curriculum -Classroom management style -Certification -Recruitment (seniority, application, interview, lottery)	Assessment	Improved school climate
Teacher needs -On-going professional development -Professional community -Safety -Job satisfaction -Diversity	School climate	Improved program quality
Administrator attributes -Race -Roles and responsibilities -Leadership style -Management style -Education level beyond master's degree -Experience level	Funding	Systemically reformed education and provision of mechanisms for change
Administrator needs -On-going professional	Marketing/ Admission	Participation in further education

development -Motivated teachers -Professional commu- nity -Safety -Sound governance structure		
Parent attributes -Education level -Socioeconomic status -Values	Transporta- tion	Full employment of students
Parent needs -Communication -Involvement -Support services (counseling, referral)	Instructional practices	Decreased dropout rate
Community-at-large attributes -Economic and ethnic composition -Age and education demographics -Attitudes of police, business leaders, civic groups, faith-based groups, mass media -School board values	Specialized curriculum and theme aligned with state stan- dards	Improved gradua- tion rates
Community-at-large needs -Employability of stu- dents -Adequacy of finances -Compliance with state and federal mandates	Technology	Increased enroll- ment in college preparatory courses
	Facility -Size of school -Quality of	Participation in and improved perform- ance on SAT

	laboratories -Quality and quantity of technology equipment -Adequacy to accommodate theme	

Inputs

The inputs are the raw materials and resources available to the system. They represent the perceived educational needs and attributes or characteristics of the school stakeholders, the most important being the student. At the very inception of the magnet school design, consideration is given to the attributes and needs of students, teachers, the administration, the parents and the community-at-large, through a series of planning events, open discussion meetings, and information-gathering sessions. Focus groups are conducted and data about each of the stakeholders' needs and values is reviewed and analyzed. These inputs provide the underpinnings for developing the goals and philosophy of the school, the group vision reflective of this philosophy, its program design, the selection of curriculum, and implementation of diverse instructional methods. As a model of a well-performing social system, the stakeholders who are brought together to determine the organizational purpose of the magnet school achieve consensus on the through-puts.

Teacher characteristics are an important consideration when hiring staff or determining teacher assignments in a magnet school. Summers and Wolfe (1975) found that high achievers performed best with experienced teachers, yet low achievers performed best with less experienced teachers. Mayer, Mullins and Moore (2001) found that students learn more from teachers with strong academic backgrounds and more than three years experience in the classroom. Students in middle and high school performed better under teachers with a degree relevant to their subject area. Since learning is enhanced when there is an emphasis on high academic expectations (Mayer, Mullins and Moore, 2001), teachers in magnet schools are often assigned based on this research.

Parental involvement is an especially critical input that contributes to student success and has an indirect attribution to achievement (Vassalo, 2000). The No Child Left Behind Act (NCLBA) of 2001, in fact, devotes a considerable number of requirements to: implementing effective, research-based parental involvement practices; providing information and notifications to parents in their native language, promoting informed parental choice, and establishing parent information and resource centers. Magnet schools ensure that parents are involved from the onset – planning and design of the school, participating at school functions and events (open house, parent-teacher conferences, subject area special events, parent-child learning activities), sitting on governance councils, and providing input about instruction, budgets, curriculum, etc. Parents are active partners in the learning process as well, assisting their children with homework, ensuring school attendance, visiting the classroom and volunteering their services.

Throughputs

Throughputs are the combination of the basic processes within the system. They are the factors within the school itself; the energies needed to meet the needs of the stakeholders and to realize the final outputs. They include the school mission, goals, curriculum, school climate, funding, enrollment, marketing, admission, transportation, instructional practices, assessment, technology and facility. These are the gears that make the system functional.

Mission: The mission is an encapsulation of the school's philosophy about education and the teaching and learning processes. It contains the shared beliefs of the stakeholders about expectations for student achievement, as well as the relevance of the specialized curriculum, theme or pedagogy, and provides a basis upon which the other throughputs are determined. As an example, the content of the curriculum and the choice of textbooks are aligned with the mission of the school. The following are examples of magnet school missions:

      a. To prepare students for lifelong learning and purposeful participation in their community and global society;

b. To educate the whole child in conjunction with promoting multicultural understanding and interaction;

c. To serve as a resource for and meet the needs of families, since children require strong family supports to be successful learners;

d. To develop a responsive community of learners working to help students develop academically and socially in a nurturing environment; and

e. To celebrate diversity, find common themes and value the traditions of many cultures, which broaden the perspectives of all.

Goals: In Chapter 1, the importance of goal setting is highlighted. When the goals of the public school system are modified, as in the case of a magnet school, all the elements of the system are readjusted and as a result, a second order social change alters the purpose and underpinnings of the system. The goals are monitored through assessment, which provides intermittent feedback on the quality of functioning of the throughputs. These, in turn, are modified and the cycle begins anew.

Prior to determining student goals, the stakeholders have clarified their values around the issues of respecting diversity, empowering parents and determining what constitutes an education that results in future employment and the ultimate well being of students.

Magnet schools have as their primary goals to improve student achievement and reduce racial isolation. Secondary goals include improving school climate, improving program quality, implementing systemic reforms and mechanisms for change, participating in further education, decreasing the dropout rate and improving the graduation rate. Each state has specific laws governing magnet schools, and these are considered when determining school goals. Consideration is also given to aligning the goals with the following goals required under the No Child Left Behind Act of 2001:

a. By 2013-14, all students will reach high standards, at a minimum attaining proficiency or better in reading/language arts and math;

b. All limited English proficient students will become proficient in English and reach high academic standards, at a minimum attaining proficiency or better, in reading/language arts and math;

c. By 2005-06, all students will be taught by highly qualified teachers;

d. All students will be educated in learning environments that are safe, drug free and conducive to learning; and

e. All students will graduate from high school.

Theme/ specialized curriculum: The theme provides the unifying structure for all curriculum integration; it is the foundation upon which all lessons and activities are built. The theme may be a specialized area of instruction, a specific teaching methodology, or a formal program.

The special curriculum focuses on a distinct theme with challenging content. It lies at the heart of the uniqueness of the magnet school concept. It is defined as a course of study embracing subject matter or a teaching methodology that is not generally offered to students of the same age or grade level in the same LEA or consortium of LEAs, as the students to whom the special curriculum is offered in the magnet schools. The term does not include a course of study or part of a course of study:

a. that is designed solely to provide basic educational services to students with disabilities or to students of limited English-speaking ability;

b. in which any student is unable to participate because of his or her limited English-speaking ability;

c. in which any student is unable to participate because of his or her limited financial resources;

d. or that fails to allow for a participating student to meet the requirements of elementary and secondary education in the same period as other students enrolled in the LEA's schools (USDE, 2004).

The curriculum needs to be aligned with state and district standards and assessments, in order to demonstrate that students in the magnet schools are learning on a par with their non-magnet school counterparts. Federal law requires the curriculum to: include challenging content standards in academic subjects that specify what children are expected to know and be able to do; contain coherent and rigorous content; and encourage the teaching of advanced skills (Section 1111(b)(1)(D) of the No Child Left Behind Act).

The following offers a sample of magnet school specialized curriculums, categorized as those that focus on unique subject matter or unique instructional methods.

a. Unique subject matter

- Among the unique subject matter that magnet schools offer are those that focus on business/finance, communication, foreign language, health and physical development, social justice and the law, public affairs, basic skills, gifted and talented, language arts, and technology. While all other disciplines are integrated to form part of the course content, the unique subject matter prevails, focusing on the acquisition of in-depth knowledge and its application in the specific area. Enrichment activities in concert with real-world experiences augment the curriculum. For example; the mathematics and science model immerses students in an integrated curriculum rich with math and science activities. Real-world mathematical and scientific problem solving is used to reinforce basic concepts. Enrichment activities include trips to science museums, environmental agencies, Science Centers, and related businesses and participation in research symposia, math leagues, etc. Math and science labs provide the forum for an inquiry-based learning mode, which is applied across all disciplines.

- The International Baccalaureate *(IB)* model (Peterson, 2003) focuses on developing students who are inquiring, knowledgeable, caring and able to create a peaceful world culture through intercultural understanding and respect. The curriculum focuses on international education within three programs; the Primary Years Program (ages 3 –12), the Middle Years Program (ages 11-16); and the Diploma Program (ages 16-19). In each program, a specific curriculum is provided for each subject area, with related external required assessments. Students have online access to international resources, subject area experts, and discussion sessions. The Primary Years Program focuses on the academic, social, physical, emotional and cultural needs of the student, and includes learning in the classroom as well as in other environments. The curriculum is based on six organizing themes and uses inquiry-based learning to promote concept understanding and socially responsible behavior. The Middle Years Program is a five-year curriculum that focuses on the interrelatedness of traditional academic disciplines through a trans-disciplinary approach and concept-driven inquiry. The Diploma Years Program is a comprehensive two-year curriculum for students in grades eleven through twelve. A pre-university course of study, it consists of six subject areas: English, a second language, Individuals and Society, Experimental Sciences, Mathematics and the Arts and Electives. It also includes the additional components of: Extended Essay (investigation of a topic of special interest), Theory of Knowledge (an interdisciplinary requirement that stimulates critical reflection, develops the ability to analyze evidence that is expressed in a rational argument, and fosters an awareness of subjective and ideological biases), and Creativity, Action and Service (community service). The curriculum is enhanced through interdisciplinary and project-based learning, cooperative learning, authentic assessment, and the use of technology. The culminating activity is the IB examination, which gives the diploma holder access to the world's leading universities. Further information is provided on the worldwide web at ibo.org.

- The Early or Middle College Program, first developed at LaGuardia Community College in New York, consists of a partnership between a high school and a community college. The curriculum, developed jointly by high school and college faculty, articulates both high school graduation and associate degree requirements (Jobs for the Future, 2001). A dual advisory board comprised of staff from both learning environments traditionally governs the project. In these small schools that offer individualization and interest exploration, students earn a high school diploma and two years of credit toward a college degree by taking both high school and community college courses. A modified school calendar with an extended school day and year enables accelerated learning and optimizes time on task. Individual learning plans are developed and mentors are assigned to each student. The model meets the needs of the non-traditional student who has had difficulty succeeding in a standard high school setting but wishes to pursue an alternative educational program. Further information is provided on the worldwide web at mlva.net/Middle College.

- The Edison Schools model, developed in 1992, focuses on student achievement through its unique prescriptive curriculum based on academic standards that outline what students must know and be able to do, an aligned assessment protocol, and the integration of technology across the curriculum (Edison Schools, 2004). The school's fundamental features include a rich and challenging curriculum, better use of time, motivating teaching methods, a professional environment for teachers, use of technology, partnership with families, an organizational structure that ensures success for each student, schools tailored to the community, and the advantages of a system and scale. There are four academies in the Edison model; Primary and Elementary Academy (grades K-5), Junior Academy (grades 6-8), Senior Academy (grades 9-10), and the Collegiate Academy (grades 11-12). The Primary Academy curriculum includes reading, science, world language, writing and language arts, mathematics, history and social science, fine arts, and physical fitness and health. Additional supports include cooperative learning and one-to-one tutoring. The Chicago Math program and the "Success for All" reading programs are required, and curriculum specialists are on staff to support teachers in the instructional process. An emphasis on reading includes the study of phonics, word attack, comprehension and study skills, each of which is embedded in a literature-based approach. The Junior Academy curriculum includes reading and language arts, history and social science, mathematics, world language, fine arts, physical fitness and health, science and a home base advisory, in which students meet in a group for fifteen minutes daily with an advisor who monitors their progress. The Senior Academy curriculum includes math, science, history and citizenship, literature and language arts, world language, fine arts, physical fitness and health, tutorials and a 30-minute daily meeting with an advisor to monitor progress. The Collegiate Academy curriculum includes history, literature and language arts, science, math, and electives (advanced placement U.S. History, U.S Government and Politics, Economics and European History, Government/Civics and Economics). This academy provides a university-like environment; tutorials and advisor meetings provide additional supports. Further information is provided on the worldwide web at edisonschools.com/home and edisonproject.com.

- The Success For All/Roots and Wings model developed by Robert Slavin and Nancy Madden from Johns Hopkins University, is a preK-grade 6 program that is designed to improve basic academic skills, in concert with developing problem solving, critical thinking and creativity skills (Slavin, Madden et al, 2000). The prescribed, research-based curriculum, matched to state standards and assessments, includes 90 minute reading periods using Success for All materials, 75 minute primary math and 60 minute intermediate math periods using MathWings materials, and social studies and science classes using WorldLab materials. These classes are enhanced through physical education, music and visual arts. Family support teams, one-to-one tutoring, and cooperative learning augment the academic aspects of the model, which may be funded through use of federal comprehensive school reform grant funds. There has been a strong correlation of participation in this program and improved achievement outcomes (Slavin

& Madden, 2003). Further information is provided on the worldwide web at nwrel.org/scpd/catalog and at successforall.net.

b. Unique instructional methods:
- The Montessori model includes the educational theories and practices of its founder, Maria Montessori, who started the first school in Rome, Italy in 1907. Montessori classrooms are characterized by multi-age grouping, spontaneous and purposeful activities, the use of didactic materials, a sense of community, and independent learning at the student's own pace and rhythm. Instruction is focused on problem solving through inquiry, working in teams to engage in complex and challenging tasks, uninterrupted work cycles, integrated subject matter based on developmental psychology, the use of prepared kinesthetic materials and specially developed reference materials, and a unified, internationally developed curriculum (Montessori, 2002). The model addresses development of the whole child, including psychosocial, physical and academic needs. It fosters the development of initiative and persistence, decision-making, self-discipline, responsibility and a positive attitude about school. A series of prepared environments, around which content material is taught, is the cornerstone of this model. The "Mathematics Area" provides a base for understanding mathematical concepts by working with concrete materials to progress to the abstract; to move from the simple to the complex and from the quantity to the symbol. The "Practical Life Area" includes self-care, developing good work habits and functioning in the environment. The "Sensorial Area" provides opportunities for the student to explore the physical properties of the environment and to use materials that teach refining, classifying, matching and grading sensory experiences. The "Cultural Extensions Area" includes geography, history, biology, botany, zoology, movement, art, music, and exploration of culture. The "Science/Botany Area" provides opportunities

to create the foundation for scientific knowledge. The "Language Area" provides experiences in development of the spoken and written language. Independent activity comprises eighty percent and teacher-directed activities twenty percent of the day. How students arrive at what they know is as important as what they know (Lillard, 1996). Further information is provided on the worldwide web at montessori-ami.org.

- The Schools of the 21st Century model, implemented in 1988, was based on the philosophy of Professor Edward F. Ziegler of Yale University's Bush Center for Child Development. It is a community-school model that combines childcare and support services provided in schools (U.S.D.E, 1999). Also known as Family Resource Centers, these programs focus on whole-child development; the school is seen as a responsive community of learners whose goal is to assist students to develop socially and cognitively in a nurturing environment (Finn-Stevenson & Zigler, 1999). There are six guiding principles which form the foundation for this model: strong parental support and involvement of parents in program planning; creating an inviting school environment and offering services that meet their needs; universal access to affordable child care based on a sliding-scale parental fee; overall physical, social, emotional and cognitive development of the child; high quality programming that meets state and national standards; and professional training and advancement opportunities for child care providers. These program components are non-compulsory, with participation by the family in any or all of the components being on a voluntary basis. Each Family Resource Center offers six core components: guidance and support for parents including home visits, playgroups, parent workshops, support groups, early care and education programs for preschool children; before and after school and vacation programs; health education and services including dental assessments, mental health services, health, fitness and nutrition education, etc;. network and training for child care providers, including workshops, newsletters, etc.; and information and referral services including providing information about childcare options, health care, financial assistance, social services, and family support services available in the community. Further information is provided on the worldwide web at yale.edu.bushcenter/21C.

- The Multiple Intelligence Theory model, developed by Howard Gardner, a psychologist and professor from Harvard University, bases its instructional methods on nine specific types of intelligences that impact learning. Dr. Gardner first identified seven of these types in his book *Frames of Mind* (1993), and then added two additional types in his book, *Intelligence Reframed* (1999). Each of the following intelligences needs to be nurtured and developed in each student through a variety of instructional methodologies: verbal-linguistic intelligence (verbal skills and sensitivity to sounds, meanings and the rhythm of words); mathematical-logical intelligence (conceptual and abstract thinking, including discerning logical and numerical patterns); musical/rhythmic intelligence (production and appreciation of rhythm, pitch and timber); visual-spatial intelligence (thinking in images and pictures and visualizing abstractly and with accuracy); bodily-kinesthetic intelligence (controlling one's body movements and handling objects with skill); interpersonal intelligence (detecting and responding to the moods, motivation and desires of others); intrapersonal intelligence (self-awareness that is sensitive to inner feelings, values, beliefs and thinking processes); naturalistic intelligence (recognizing and categorizing plants, animals and objects in nature); and existential intelligence (sensing and investigating questions about human existence). In this model, the curriculum is not centered on teaching and learning core skills, but rather on an in-depth examination of fundamental questions of existence. The instructional methodology relies on the use of a variety of engaging activities and projects. Opportunities are provided to develop skills in learning stations (reading/writing center, illustration/visual expression center, science/experiment center, music center, math center, build-it/paint-it center and performance center, for example), and to demonstrate/assess learning through simulation activities (role playing, debating) and the use of student presentations. Stefanikis (2002) provides an application of this theory to classroom practice. She combines the understanding of what students bring to the learning environment from their culture, language and environment, and creates a student profile for learning. Further information is provided at the worldwide web at thirteen.org/edonline and Idpride.net/learning styles.MI.

- The Micro-Society Program is an innovative school design for grades K-8, in which students collaborate with parents, teachers and community members to create a micro-society reflecting the real world (Richmond, Richmond, Schweber & Kharfen, 1996). Developed by George H. Richmond in 1992, the curriculum focuses on six strands; technology, economy, academy, citizenship and government, humanities and arts, and volunteerism/ethical aspects of society (Richmond, 1973). The elements that form the foundation of the model are an internal currency, a retail labor market, private property, public property, agencies and nonprofit organizations, agreement on a common purpose, personal goals, contact with parents, contact with community partners, technology, and teacher preparation and planning time. Each student plays a critical role as an entrepreneur, producing goods and services, making laws, electing officials, running businesses, and paying taxes, tuition and rent, etc. Traditional academic subjects are taught in the morning sessions and applied on the job during a one hour afternoon session. This model may be funded through use of federal comprehensive school reform grant funds. Further information is provided on the worldwide web at microsociety.org.

- The Junior Great Books model, developed by Great Books Foundation in Chicago, Illinois in 1962, is an inquiry and literature-based program that teaches students in grades K-12 to read for meaning and to develop critical and creative thinking abilities (Criscuola, 1994). Interpretive discussion, analysis of character development, creative writing assignments and oral presentations are used to teach students to read with comprehension, and to think and communicate as literate and responsible citizens. Three forty-five minute sessions per week form the basis of the program. A pilot study found that 3rd graders participating in this model scored higher on the Iowa Test of Basic Skills and made greater gains in the areas of supporting opinions about a reading selection (Great Books Foundation, 1993).This model may be funded through use of federal comprehensive school reform grant funds. Further information is provided on the worldwide web at nwrel.org.scpd/catalog and greatbooks.org.

- The Learning Network model, developed by Richard C. Owen Publishers, Inc. in 1992, seeks to change the attitudes, understanding and behavior of teachers and to reorganize the school into a learning community, with the goal of improved student outcomes (Herzog, 1997). The Literacy Learning model, which is the foundation of the Learning Network, is comprised of assessment, evaluation, planning and teaching. Its implementation instills in teachers an understanding of the reading and writing processes and the conditions that are favorable for learning these skills. Continuous professional development ensures that the Literacy Learning model is appropriately applied and reinforced. Classroom observation, action plans and instructional dialogue serve as the means of change. This model may be funded through use of federal comprehensive school reform grant funds. Further information is provided on the worldwide web at nwrel.org/scpd/catalog.

- The Direct Instruction model was developed by Siegfried Engelmann and colleagues at the University of Oregon. This theory of instruction purports that learning can be accelerated if instructional presentations are clear, facilitate generalizations, and avoid misinterpretation. Using prescribed curricula and classroom procedures, teachers define tasks clearly, pre-teach sub-concepts and skills, use interactive lessons, elicit frequent oral responses, incorporate a high rate of praise for responses, monitor responses and provide immediate feedback, and review already learned skills and concepts. Mastery tests track student performance on a periodic basis. Students are grouped by performance level and are re-grouped periodically. Instruction is fast-paced and includes frequent student-teacher interactions (Englemann, Becker, Carnine and Gersten, 1998). This model may be funded through use of federal comprehensive school reform grant funds. Further information is provided on the worldwide web at nwrel.org/scpd/catalog.

- The Accelerated Schools model was developed by Henry Levin, at Stamford University, in 1986. Its implementation involves a participatory process to achieve whole-school transformation. Its three guiding principles are unity of purpose, empowerment plus responsibility, and building on strengths. The transformation is a guided process that begins with "taking stock" of the current school conditions, developing a shared vision of what the school should be, identifying challenge and priority areas, analyzing problems through an inquiry process, implementing solutions to the challenges and assessing results. Each classroom is transformed into a powerful learning environment with high expectations and a rigorous curriculum. Instructional methods traditionally used to teach gifted and talented students are employed in all instruction. Bloom et al. evaluated this model and found a correlation between early implementation and improved student achievement (Bloom, Ham, Melton & O'Brien, 2001). This model may be funded through use of federal comprehensive school reform grant funds. Further information is provided on the worldwide web at nwrel.org/catalog, at accelerated-schools.net, at Stanford.edu/group/ASP and at uconn.edu/asp/Accelerated_Schools.

- The Integrated Thematic Instruction model, founded by Susan Kovalik in 1982, relies on current brain research to optimize student outcomes by creating a "body/brain compatible" learning environment that embodies eight principles; absence of threat; meaningful content, choice that meets individual needs, adequate and flexible time, enriched environment filled with real world objects, collaboration among students, immediate feedback from teachers, application of skills mastered, and movement activities that activate the body and brain systems for learning. The integrated curriculum revolves around a yearlong theme, which provides the structure for concept development, patterning and connecting facts and ideas (Northwest Regional Lab, 1999). This model may be funded through use of federal comprehensive school reform grant funds. Further information is provided on the worldwide web at nwrel.org/catalog.

- The Core Knowledge model, founded by E.D. Hirsch, Jr. in 1986, is a K-8 sequential program that focuses on a core knowledge sequence of concepts, including vocabulary and comprehension, found in the Core Knowledge Sequence Content Guidelines for Preschool through Grade Eight. Fifty percent of the curriculum is a progression of specific grade-by-grade content standards in language arts, mathematics, science, history, geography, music and fine arts. The rest of the curriculum is tailored to meet school and state standards. Parental involvement is critical; parents take part in planning, consensus building and development of the yearlong plan (Northwest Regional Lab, 1999). This model may be funded through use of federal comprehensive school reform grant funds. Further information is provided on the worldwide web at nwrel.org/catalog.

- The Talent Development High School with Career Academies model was developed for grades 9-12 at the Center for Research on the Education of Students

Placed At Risk, Johns Hopkins and Howard Universities in 1995 (Northwest Regional Lab, 1999). It was designed as a reform model for urban high schools with low attendance rates, discipline problems, low achievement scores and high dropout rates. Ninth graders participate in a success academy, with interdisciplinary teams of teachers sharing a block schedule and common planning time, and are offered extra math and English courses. Career Academies for grades 10, 11 and 12 offer separate academies for 250-350 students with a common core of academic subjects and differentiated career applications. Each academy features a core academic curriculum organized within four ninety-minute class periods. For those students with attendance or discipline problems, a twilight school offers an alternate after-hours program. This model may be funded through use of federal comprehensive school reform grant funds. Further information is provided on the worldwide web at nwrel.org/catalog.

- The Coalition of Essential Schools, in collaboration with the Educational Development Center, Project Zero and the School Development Program, developed the ATLAS Communities model (Northwest Regional Lab, 1999) in 1992 for preK-grade 12 students. Five interrelated elements (teaching and learning, assessment, professional development, family and community, and management and decision making) combine to form a pathway of curriculum, instruction and assessment aligned with state standards. This is accomplished through a systematic, data-driven school planning process that sets goals, identifies content, and determines an instructional focus. This model may be funded through use of federal comprehensive school reform grant funds. Further information is provided on the worldwide web at nwrel.org/catalog.

- The Different Ways of Knowing model was developed by Andrew G. Galef and Bronya Pereira Galef in 1989. It is a preK-8 model that uses multiple intelligences theory and a standards-based, interdisciplinary arts-infused curriculum. Year-long curriculum models integrate social studies and history with language arts, mathematics, science and the visual, performing and media arts, which are taught using inquiry-based instructional strategies (Education Week on the Web, 1999). Catterall reported positive impacts on both students and teachers participating in this model (Catterall, 1995), which may be funded through use of federal comprehensive school reform grant funds. Further information is provided on the worldwide web at nwrel.org/catalog.

- The High Schools That Work model, developed in 1987 by the Southern Regional Education Board in Atlanta, Georgia, focuses on improving achievement for career-bound students by combining traditional college preparatory coursework with career-related and technical courses in a personalized learning environment. Teamwork, applied learning and project-based instruction are used. The following key practices provide an environment for reform: an upgraded academic core, high expectations, challenging vocational studies, academic studies that include four years of English, three years of math, and three years of science, work-based learning, individual advisors, extra help, assessment to ensure continuous improvement, active engagement of students, and collaboration among academic and vocational teachers. Instructional time is provided in large blocks for continuity. It has been found that linking High Schools That Work practices with a strong career/technical program can give career-oriented students the academic core preparation necessary for post-secondary education and employment (Bottom, Presson and Han, 2004). This model may be funded through use of federal comprehensive school reform grant funds. Further information is provided on the worldwide web at nwrel.org/catalog.

School climate

School climate is a combination of factors, including relationships that are formed within the school arena and contribute to the creation of a safe, secure, orderly, disciplined, caring environment that is also conducive to learning; it is the social atmosphere in which the processes of teaching and learning take place. A shared sense of mission, teacher and student satisfaction, caring teachers, parental involvement, small class size, and a diverse student body composition all contribute to a positive school climate (Rosenholtz, 1991). Other important factors that affect school climate include school size, racial mix and achievement mix (high, average, low). Unchecked behavior problems, lack of enforcement of clearly defined rules and standards for student behavior, unsafe practices such as drug and alcohol abuse and violence, and disrespect for teachers and students are likely to create an atmosphere that impedes learning and leads to poor school climate.

A school climate that emphasizes discipline is associated with enhanced student learning. Class size is another indicator of school climate that affects students' achievement; the greatest achievement is found in classes of 13-20 students (Mayer, Mullins and Moore, 2001). Student body composition also contributes to a positive school climate and enhanced achievement. For example, Summers and Wolfe (1975) found that elementary students perform better when the proportion of African-American students range from forty to sixty percent, while junior high students perform better when the proportion is fifty percent. They also found that high achievers are not affected by the presence of low achievers, that African-American and low achieving high school students do best in small schools, that low achieving students in elementary schools achieve best when class size is less than 28 students, that the academic growth of students in junior high school decreases with a class size of more than 32 students, and that students in high school who are high achievers do best with a class size of less than 26. These factors are considered when placing student in magnet school classes.

Funding

There are several funding sources for magnet school projects. Federal, state and local options are described below.

A. Federal funding:

Magnet School Assistance Program: Because Congress has found that magnet schools are a significant part of the nation's effort to achieve voluntary desegregation in its schools, it created the federal Magnet School Assistance Program in 1985 (CFDA 84.165A, Title V, Part C, Section 5301). This grant, awarded to school districts on a competitive basis, supports the planning, development and implementation of magnet schools that assist in the desegregation of schools served by LEAs, as part of an approved desegregation plan, by:

1. Eliminating, reducing or preventing minority group isolation in elementary and secondary schools with substantial proportions of minority students;
2. Developing and implementing programs that will assist LEAs in achieving systemic reforms and providing all students the opportunity to meet challenging State academic content standards and student academic achievement standards;
3. Developing and designing innovating educational methods and practices that promote diversity and increase choices in public elementary and secondary schools;
4. Designing courses of instruction within magnet schools that will substantially strengthen the knowledge of academic subjects and the attainment of tangible and marketable vocational, technological, and professional skills of students attending such schools;
5. Improving the capacity of LEAs including, through professional development, to continue operating magnet schools at a high level of performance after federal funding is terminated; and
6. Ensuring that all students enrolled in magnet school programs have equitable access to high quality education that will enable them to succeed academically and continue with postsecondary education or productive employment.

The purposes of the grant are aligned with those of the No Child Left Behind Act: desegregation and choice; building capacity; and academic achievement of students. Funds may be used to accomplish the goals of the Elementary and Secondary Education Act, which was reauthorized as the No Child Left Behind Act of 2001, and requires that all students achieve to high standards and holds schools responsible for ensuring that they do so. Funds may be used for: planning and promotional activities directly related to the development, expansion, continuation, or enhancement of academic programs and services offered at magnet schools; acquisition of books, materials and equipment used to conduct programs; compensation of highly qualified teachers and instructional staff; activities, including professional development, that build capacity to operate the magnet program upon cessation of the federal funds; flexibility in designing magnet schools for students in all grades; and making available the special curriculum to students enrolled in a school in which the magnet program is located.

The Comprehensive School Reform Demonstration Program (USDE, 2003): Comprehensive school reform calls for a "whole-school" and coordinated approach to improve schools. The strategy differs from piecemeal and fragmented efforts in the past that seemed only to lead to short-lived changes. To stimulate whole-school reform across the country, Congress appropriated funds in FY1998 for the U.S. Department of Education to start the Comprehensive School Reform Demonstration (CSRD) Program. The Department allocated the funds on a formula basis to states, who made awards to support 1,840 mostly Title I schools in need of substantially improving their performance. Subsequent rounds of annual awards to support additional schools have continued through FY2003. In applying for and accepting these funds, schools were expected to implement nine components, which are aimed at improving student achievement:

1. Effective, research-based methods and strategies;
2. Comprehensive design with aligned components;
3. Professional development;
4. Measurable goals and benchmarks;
5. Support within the school;
6. Parental and community involvement;
7. External technical support and assistance;
8. Evaluation strategies; and
9. Coordination of resources.

The No Child Left Behind Act: The Elementary and Secondary Education Act of 1965, Title V, Part C was amended by the No Child Left Behind Act of 2001 and signed into law on January 2, 2002 by President George W. Bush. It is an educational reform plan that outlines four goals for all secondary and elementary students and requires each state to describe standards and monitor student achievement to ensure that these standards are met. It is based on the following four principles:

1. Accountability for results: each state is required to create standards for what a child should know and be able to do and align tests to these standards. Each district is required to test students' progress toward meeting these standards, in grades 3-8 in math, reading and science. Each state, school district and school must make adequate yearly progress (AYP) toward meeting the standards, and if they do not, sanctions will be imposed. The district and school must report performance results in state and local report cards. The law is specific in including all students, including those who are economically disadvantaged, have disabilities or limited English proficiency, or are from racial/ethnic minority groups;

2. Flexibility and local control: program requirements have been simplified and consolidated to make implementation less bureaucratic. The use of funds by states and districts is more flexible. There are no national standards or assessments; each state may develop its own;

3. Parent choice: parents of students in failing schools have the option of transferring their child to a higher performing school. Funds are allocated for the purpose of providing supplemental education services (tutoring, summer school, after-school). Funds are also allocated for the purpose of creating magnet and charter schools; and

4. Successful teaching practices: the implementation of research-based programs and methods are required for funded districts. Among the programs specifically targeted are: Reading First; comprehensive school reform; Early Reading First; interventions for beginning read-

ers; curriculum-based intervention for increasing K-12 math achievement; preventing high school drop-outs and increasing adult literacy; interventions to reduce delinquent, disorderly and violent behaviors; character education interventions; and peer-assisted learning in reading, math and science.

The following funding sources from the NCLBA may be allocated to qualifying magnet school programs. It is a useful reference for those readers wishing to pursue implementation of a magnet school, or to fund other program options that qualify.

1. Title I, Part A, Subpart 1, Sections 1114-1115: These formula-based funds may be used in eligible LEA schools to upgrade the entire educational program (for those schools qualifying as school-wide programs), to provide students with the opportunity to meet the State's challenging student academic achievement standards (for those students in targeted assistance schools), to develop an accelerated, high-quality curriculum, to provide professional development opportunities, to develop strategies to increase parental involvement, and to use effective methods and instructional strategies;

2. Title I, Part B, Subpart 1, Section 1201: These formula-based funds may be used by LEAs to establish reading programs for grades K-3 students that are based on scientifically-based research, to prepare teachers to identify specific reading barriers, to select or administer screening, diagnostic, and classroom-based instructional reading assessments, and to select and develop effective instructional materials;

3. Title II, Part A, Section 2101: These formula-based funds may be used to improve principal and teacher quality and increase the number of highly qualified teachers; and

4. Title IV, Part A, Subpart 1, Section 4002: These formula-based funds may be used to support programs that: prevent violence in and around school; prevent the illegal use of alcohol, tobacco, and drugs; involve parents and communities; and coordinate with related fed-

eral, state, school, and community efforts and resources to foster a safe and drug-free learning environment that support student academic achievement (NCLBA, Section 4002).

B. State funding

Capital Expenditures: In many states, the facility costs and costs of renovation are entirely or partially, through a reimbursement formula, covered by the state, either through a direct appropriation in the general fund or though issuance of bonds.

Per pupil reimbursement: There are several approaches to provide funding for students in magnet schools. Some districts assume the full cost of operation within their local school district budget. Some states provide reimbursement in the form of a per-enrolled student grant formula, and distribute the funds proportionately based on the percent of students from any given district to the population of the school as a whole (Connecticut General Statutes, Subsection (c) of Section 10-2641). Allowable funding expenditures include personnel and fringe (usually the highest cost), equipment and supplies (usually the second highest cost), travel, contractual, construction, training stipends, indirect costs, and other direct costs.

LEA tuition: In states with regional magnet schools, the sending LEA subsidizes the per-pupil cost through tuition.

The following information provides an outline for readers to use when designing and implementing a magnet school, but it also useful in demonstrating the systemic nature of the magnet school design. It includes enrollment (how to conduct marketing activities and how to recruit and admit students), transportation, instructional practices, assessment (Table 4 provides an outline for assessing achievement of each of the five goals), technology, and facility. The conceptual discussion continues with the section on the application of contemporary reform strategies.

Enrollment: Magnet schools differ in the manner in which they structure enrollment in their programs. Some schools offer a magnet program to all students in the school who are in the grades at which the program operates. These are referred to as *whole school* magnet programs. They are distinguished from *programs within schools* that offer magnet curricula to some, but not all, of the students in the school.

Recruitment: Magnet school programs have extensive marketing strategies to recruit students by informing parents of the choices available for their children. These strategies include press releases, focus groups, town meetings, open houses and tours, informational sessions for guidance personnel, discussions at PTA meetings, direct mailing of brochures, orientation sessions, radio and television ads, information distributed to students, tours of schools with transportation provided, media advertisements, advertising at fairs or other forums, presentations at other schools, information mailed to all parents or to parents that request it, and telephone calls to parents to explain the program. In addition, babysitters are provided for school events, presentations are made at community/church meetings, an internet site is developed, home visits are made to parents/students, magnet teachers make visits to other schools, parents make presentations and phone calls to other parents, and principals organize schools tours. In some cases, a full time staff is hired to assume responsibility for recruitment and admission; in other cases, a combination of magnet staff, students and parents conduct outreach activities.

Admission: There are several methods to determine student admission to a magnet school: controlled choice, percent set-aside, lottery, race-neutral lottery and first-come, first-served, or a combination of methods. In an effort to meet desegregation goals, some districts target particular groups of students. Others recruit students from the entire district, and some seek students from other districts.

Under the No Child Left Behind Act, LEAs cannot disregard entrance requirements, such as evidence of specific academic ability or other skills, when identifying transfer options for students choosing magnet schools over attendance at a low performing school. For example, students wishing to transfer to a fine arts magnet school or to a school for gifted students would still need to meet the requirements to attend those schools (Yecke & Lazo, 2002).

- Controlled choice method: This method enables parents to select any public school for their child to attend, subject to "controls" to maintain desegregation guidelines. For example, the Indianapolis Schools, under a 1979 court-ordered desegregation plan, implemented a Select Schools Plan, which involved a controlled choice method of assigning students. Parents were allowed choice as long as the guidelines of thirty-five/sixty-five percent minority/non-minority enrollment and space availability were met. In January 1997, the court abandoned this method and initiated an assignment plan based on attendance boundaries, within which parents could choose a school.
- Percent set-aside method: This method determines the proportion of minority and non-minority students and "sets aside" a designated number of seats according to pre-determined ratios.
- Lottery: This method creates a race-neutral, unbiased method of selecting students for admission. Student names are chosen, one-by-one, at random, either drawn from a pool of names, or selected by computer. Some schools allow siblings of selected students to attend the magnet school, even if they are not chosen through the lottery process.
- First-come, first-served method: This method encourages an open enrollment period, in which parents may apply for admission on behalf of their children. Students are selected based on the date of their application.

Transportation: Under usual circumstances, the costs of transportations for students in the regular public school are in the school budget and are reimbursable by the state. In the case of inter-district magnet schools, transportation becomes an issue and can be a burdensome expenditure for the sending district. Transportation usually is provided for students in intra-district magnet schools within the district budget, but practices vary from state to state.

Instructional Practices: Magnet school teachers strive to improve instructional practices to ensure that the needs of all students are met. Good practice includes: adding advanced work; adding new topics; changing teaching methods; changing assessment methods; increasing the use of technology; integrating the curriculum; providing application of the theory learned; and fostering higher order thinking skills (talking about what is read; writing about it; discussing interpretations; explaining and supporting understanding; comparing what is read to other works and other applications; and developing open-ended projects and presentations). Specialized curriculum that focuses on unique instructional practices was discussed earlier in this chapter.

Assessment: Magnet schools implement a comprehensive evaluation plan that produces results that determine how successful the program is in meeting its intended outcomes: improving student achievement; reducing racial isolation; improving school climate; improving instructional practices; and supporting systemic reform by implementing mechanisms for change. For each outcome, the plan proposes a series of research questions that form the framework and guide for the evaluation. Objectives that further break down the goals into discrete, obtainable, measurable units are delineated. For each objective, performance indicators are determined; these indicators measure the extent to which the goal is attained. The evaluation methods are objective, appropriate for the project, and able to produce data that are quantifiable. Both summative evaluation and formative assessment methods are useful in providing a complete picture of the attainment of the outcomes. Formative, or ongoing and continuous assessment, identifies areas of strength and weakness, monitors program implementation and enables the project director to modify or adjust the program based on areas identified for improvement. A summative evaluation, or summary assessment, provides information about meeting project goals and objectives. There is a plan for collecting and analyzing the data. The use of multiple methods (triangulation) includes standardized tests, student/parent/teacher surveys, student records, enrollment records, classroom observations, interviews, workshop evaluations, etc. and controls for bias and measurement error. A timetable indicating how, when and by whom the data will be collected is compiled. It is common to hire an outside evaluator to design and conduct the evaluation, in order to ensure neutrality and integrity throughout the process.

Tables 11.4-11.8 provide an outline for a sample evaluation plan of a magnet school. Each table, based on one of the five goals, includes framing questions, objectives, performance indicators and assessment instruments. A comprehensive evaluation plan would also include benchmarks, indicating intermediate progress toward meeting the goal.

Goal 1: To improve student achievement
Improving student achievement is the cornerstone of all education. It is the primary reason for the existence of schools. Student achievement includes mastering standards at a proficient level in reading, language arts, mathematics and science, at a minimum. Students who achieve are able to pursue lifelong learning, find employment, contribute to society as productive consumers and producers, and enjoy mental and physical health and well being.

TABLE 11.4: GOAL 1-IMPROVE STUDENT ACHIEVEMENT

FRAMING QUESTIONS (MSAP Evaluation, Appendix 3, Exhibit A-III-44, 196-203)	OBJECTIVES	PERFORMANCE INDICATORS	ASSESSMENT INSTRUMENTS
Has the magnet school produced a positive impact upon students and have all types of students benefited equally	All students will meet or exceed the state standards in reading/language arts, math, and science, and improve individual student achievement	The percentage of students who meet or exceed the proficient level on the state's assessments	State-level standardized assessments[2] Alternate assessments NAEP[3] Performance-based assessments Multiple choice tests

from the program?	(state goal required under the No Child Left Behind Act)		Grades SAT[4] Individual/group projects Individual/group presentations
To what degree does student achievement improve in the magnet schools as compared to the feeder schools?	All students will graduate from high school (state goal required under the No Child Left Behind Act)	The percentage of students in each minority subgroup who meet or exceed the proficient level on the state's assessments	Reading portfolio Math portfolio Essays
How does the performance of magnet school students compare to other students in the district?	All limited English proficient (LEP) students will become proficient in English and reach high academic standards, attaining proficiency in reading/language arts and math (required under the No Child Left Behind Act)	The percentage of students from each major racial and ethnic group who meet or exceed the state's adequate yearly progress standard	Graduate follow-up studies
To what extent does the special curriculum impact on student achievement?		The percentage of students who make adequate yearly progress The decrease in the achievement gap between minority and non-minority subgroups	LEP assessments State assessments
Are support services adequate to	All students will participate in the	The percentage	SAT partici-

ensure that students succeed? To what extent are students in the magnet school participating in the SATs? Are they performing at the same level as compared to the feeder schools? Compared to the state average? To what extent are students applying to and gaining admission to college? To what extent are students not wishing to pursue post-secondary education	SAT exam and meet the district and state average All students will improve career awareness skills All students will enroll in post-secondary education or find employment upon graduation from high school	of students who graduate from high school each year with a regular diploma The percentage of students who drop out of school The percentage of LEP students who have attained English proficiency by the end of the school year The percentage of LEP students who are at or above the proficient level in reading/language arts and math on the state's assessments The percentage of students participating in the SAT The percentage of students who meet the district and state average	pation rates SAT scores Log of school-to-career activities Employability performance assessments Graduate follow-up studies

finding employment? To what extent do they have the requisite skills? To what extent are students graduating from high school?		The percentage of students who participate in school-to-career courses and can demonstrate proficiency in employability skills The percentage of students who enroll in college or are employed	

Goal 2: To eliminate, reduce or prevent minority group isolation in the targeted school

Minority group isolation (MGI) refers to schools in which minority group students constitute more than fifty percent of school enrollment. The reduction of minority group isolation is one of the key purposes of the creation of magnet schools. It is for this reason that it is critical to collect, analyze and monitor data and adjust recruitment and admission practices, as well as the curriculum and classroom grouping practices, accordingly. Isolation should be reduced both in the magnet school setting and in the feeder schools from which students are sent. Data regarding the number and percent of minority students as compared to the number and percent of non-minority students in each grade level should be collected at the LEA level, the feeder school level, and the magnet school level.

TABLE 11.5: GOAL 2-REDUCE MINORITY GROUP ISOLATION

FRAMING QUESTIONS (MSAP Evaluation, Appendix 3, Exhibit A-III-44, 196-203)	OBJECTIVES	PERFORM-ANCE INDI-CATORS	ASSESS-MENT IN-STRU-MENTS
How will the magnet school ultimately impact student enrollment at the magnet school itself, at the feeder school and in the district as a whole?	Each applicant pool will include sufficient numbers of students of racial and ethnic diversity to ensure that enrolled students reflect such diversity	The percentage of students in the applicant pool	Data collection instruments
To what extent will the magnet school, the feeder schools and the district as a whole improve the racial and ethnic balance of the student body?	Minority group isolation will be reduced in the magnet school and the feeder schools.	The percentage of minority and non-minority students in the magnet and feeder schools	Classroom observations
To what extent does the criteria selected for ad-	All curricular activities will reflect the minority-non-mi-	The percentage of minority and non-minority stu-	Data collection instruments

mission im-pact the racial and ethnic balance of the student body?	nority distri-bution in the school	dents partici-pating in cur-ricular activi-ties at the classroom level	
Do recruit-ment proce-dures attract students from a cross-sec-tion of racial-ethnic/social groups?			Data col-lection in-struments
To what ex-tent will pro-fessional de-velopment be provided in the area of diversity and multicultur-alism?			

Goal 3: To improve the climate of the school

In order to evaluate the school climate, it is necessary to solicit, compile and analyze the opinions of parents, students and teachers in the school. This is most easily accomplished by the use of a written survey or needs assessment instrument that is widely dis-tributed and easily accessible. For example, the Connecticut State Board of Education developed a series of surveys for this purpose, as part of its magnet school evaluation plan (Connecticut State Board of Education Report, 2003, Appendix A: Parent and Guard-ian Survey). The parent survey focused on parent involvement, school climate, program quality, adequacy of resources, diversity, and student performance; the teacher survey focused on mission, curriculum and expectations for learning, resources supporting the instructional program, instruction and student assessment, parental involvement, school climate, diversity, leadership and satisfaction; and the student survey focused on adequacy of resources, teacher expectations, safety, diversity, comfort level, student activities, academic progress, parental involvement, teacher attitudes, grading, and behavior.

TABLE 11.6: GOAL 3-IMPROVE SCHOOL CLIMATE

FRAMING QUESTIONS (MSAP Evaluation, Appendix 3, Exhibit A-III-44, 196-203)	OBJECTIVES	PERFORMANCE INDICATORS	ASSESSMENT INSTRUMENTS
To what extent does the school provide a safe environment conducive to learning? To what extent do students feel safe within the school? To what extent do they feel welcome? To what extent does the school define its standards for appropriate student behavior? To what extent	All students will be educated in learning environments that are safe, drug free and conducive to learning (state goal required under the No Child Left Behind Act)	Specific reductions in the prevalence of identified risk factors Specific increases in the prevalence of protective factors, buffers or assets The classification of the school as persistently dangerous The number of prevention activities created to	Surveys (parent, student, teacher, administrator, board of education members) Needs assessment (No Child Left Behind Act, Title IV, Part A, Section 4113(a)(9) - Incidence and prevalence of illegal drug use and violence

do students adhere to student behaviors? To what extent are rules for enforcing positive student behaviors consistently enforced? To what extent are students disengaged in learning through tardiness, absenteeism, class cutting, apathy, lack of parental involvement, poverty, dropping out, poor health, nonpreparedness to learn? To what extent are there student behavior problems (physical conflicts, robbery, theft, vandalism, verbal and physical abuse of teachers, and disrespect for teachers)?		enable a safe, disciplined and drug-free environment, including consultation among teachers and parents to identify early warning signs of drug use and violence The number of programs developed to foster a safe and drug-free learning environment The number of parent and teacher training workshops in early prevention, intervention, rehabilitation and mentoring The number of incidences of violations of the student conduct policy code and the number	- Prevalence of risk factors associated with child abuse/domestic violence - Prevalence of protective factors, buffers, or assets - Truancy rates - Drug-related incidences resulting in suspensions and expulsions Log of parent activities

To what extent are students engaging in unsafe behaviors (use of alcohol, drug abuse, possession of weapons)?		of interventions by staff in accordance with the crisis management plan	
To what extent are students satisfied with school activities?		The number of students, parents, teachers and administrators who report satisfaction with the school	
To what extent do students feel comfortable talking with school staff to discuss problems?		The number of activities in which parents are involved	
What do parents think of the magnet program?			
Do parents feel their child is more successful in the magnet school than he/she would have been in the feeder school?			
Are parents encouraged to give			

input, voice their opinion, volunteer, visit classrooms?			
To what extent are parents involved in special events (open house, parent-teacher conferences, workshops, etc)?			
To what extent are parents involved in school governance (budget decisions, serving on governing board, instructional planning)?			
Are there mechanisms for teachers and parents to communicate?			
Do most teachers share beliefs about the mission?			
Do teachers care about students?			

Are teachers satisfied in their job?			
Are most teachers willing to put in extra hours?			
Do ethnic differences among staff create tensions?			
Do staff members support each other?			
Is there mutual respect between students and teachers, teachers and administrators, among students?			
Do administrators and teachers collaborate?			
Does the principal have confidence in the expertise of teachers?			
Does the principal look for-			

ward to working each day?			
Is the principal viewed as an instructional leader?			
Does the board of education support the professional staff? Does the school community feel like a family?			

Goal 4: To improve program quality

Program quality includes the design of the program, the extent to which characteristics of effective schools are modeled, the use of innovative instructional strategies, the suitability of the facility, the adequacy of resources, the size of the classes, the availability of technology, the strength of the leadership, the inclusion of higher order skills in the curriculum, and the degree of commitment of the staff.

TABLE 11.7: GOAL 4-IMPROVE PROGRAM QUALITY

FRAMING QUESTIONS (MSAP Evaluation, Appendix 3, Exhibit A-III-44, 196-203)	OBJECTIVES	PERFORMANCE INDICATORS	ASSESSMENT INSTRUMENTS

Do teachers use a variety of instructional strategies?	All students will be taught by highly qualified teachers (state goal required under the No Child Left Behind Act)	The number of certified, licensed and experienced teachers	Documentation of certification/licensure
Do teachers seek new ideas to infuse in their curriculum?		The percentage of paraprofessionals who are highly qualified	Documentation of coursework/Associate Degree of paraprofessionals
Does the school encourage and support innovation?			
To what extent are these practices implemented in grades K-5?	Innovative educational practices and methods that promote learning will be infused across the curriculum	The percentage of teachers who incorporate the designated innovative practices	Review of lesson plans
			Documentation of student portfolios/ products
-One hour of instructional time devoted to reading daily	High quality professional development that supports a professional learning community on the use of innovative instructional materials and multiple assessments will be provided for all	The number of teachers who participate in training and demonstrate proficiency in the designated practices and assessments	Log of professional development sessions
-One hour of instructional time devoted to math daily			
-Three hours of instructional time devoted to science weekly			

-A required number of books/pages to be read weekly -A required oral presentation at regular intervals -A required amount of homework to be completed each day -Completion of a portfolio of work in at least one subject To what extent are these practices implemented in middle and high school? -A required project -A required number of books read each month -A required amount of writing to	staff The listed practices will be implemented in all K-5 classrooms The listed practices will be implemented in all middle and high school classrooms All teachers will infuse higher order thinking skills into their curriculum materials Current and motivational textbooks and instructional materials related to the unique theme will be used The program will be housed in a	The number of practices implemented by each teacher The number of practices implemented by each teacher The number of curriculum objectives that incorporate higher order thinking skills The number of textbooks that meet the criteria set for the characteristics of "current and motivational"	Classroom observation Review of student work/portfolios Teacher evaluation Classroom observation Review of student work/portfolios Teacher evaluation Review of lessons plans and curriculum objectives Review of textbooks and curriculum materials

be com-pleted each week -A required oral pres-entation at regular in-tervals -A required amount of minimum homework to be com-pleted each day -Completion of a portfo-lio of work -Completion of an indi-vidual or small group project dur-ing the year To what ex-tent are teachers us-ing instruc-tional meth-ods that emphasize higher order thinking skills (read, write, pre-sent, ana-lyze, inter-pret, support understand,	state-of-the-art facility that accom-modates the theme Triangulated assessments will be used to test mas-tery of skills Class size will be lim-ited to no more than sixteen stu-dents Sufficient re-sources will be allocated to each school Each student and teacher will have a lap top com-puter that is linked to the World Wide Web	The adequacy of the facility The quality and quantity of assessment instruments The number of students in each class The per pupil expenditures The number of teachers and students with a laptop computer and access to the Internet and on-line data-bases	Facility evaluation Assessment tools Student roster School budget Laptop pur-chase orders and assignment to students and teachers

assimilate, think conceptually, solve complex problems, communicate ideas)?			
Are textbooks and instructional materials related to the theme? Are they current and motivational?			
Is the facility suited for the program?			
Do teachers use a variety of assessment tools?			
Are classes small enough to provide individual attention?			
Are there sufficient resources?			
Do teachers and students have access to computers?			

Goal 5: To implement systemic reforms and mechanisms for change

The magnet school model validates Sarason's approach (Sarason, 1972) to institutional change (as noted in Chapter 10), which is to avoid piecemeal change in an existing setting and create an entirely new alternative setting. The premise is that when an institution (the regular public school) is not adequately meeting the needs of a group of people (the students), changing the existing institution is often not effective. Creating a new environment (the magnet school) will be more effective in meeting the stakeholders' needs, creating a sense of community and embracing a shared mission.

The magnet school's well-being is directly related to the ability of the throughputs to reach the intended outcome. A thorough diagnosis of the problem is necessary in order to determine the nature of the interventions: personal, interpersonal or institutional. First, assessing the answers to the framing questions and analyzing the results of the assessment of goals one through five will determine the type of deficiency. Based upon the identified deficiency, research is conducted to determine proven and persuasive remedies and a prescription is detailed. It contains the goals and objectives of the intervention, programmatic modifications and a strategy for buy-in. In some cases, drastic measures may be necessary to evoke change; these include change in personnel, retraining of staff, counseling, teambuilding, changing the administrator, reconstituting the school, or closing the school. The prescription is implemented and the cycle begins again.

The No Child Left Behind Act is the current and prevailing reform movement in education. Its implementation demands accountability for student achievement by aligning state assessments to rigorous performance standards, reporting the results of those assessments and then realigning the throughputs to ensure achievement of the outcomes. Magnet schools use the state standards to develop themes and programmatic goals, provide for coordination among staff members of different disciplines to uniformly apply the standards, and develop sanctions for poor student achievement. They serve as a model for change by implementing innovative instructional practices and sharing the results with the district, in order that other staff may replicate those practices that impact positively on the achievement of students.

TABLE 11.8: GOAL 5- TO IMPLEMENT SYSTEMIC REFORMS AND MECHANISMS FOR CHANGE

FRAMING QUESTIONS (MSAP Evaluation, Appendix 3, Exhibit A-III-44, 196-203)	OBJEC-TIVES	PER-FORM-ANCE INDICA-TORS	ASSESS-MENT INSTRU-MENTS
To what extent have the state frameworks (content and performance standards) and assessments influenced the themes and goals of the magnet school? Are there interaction, communication and planning among the senior staff (coordinators of curriculum, professional development, Title I, etc.) and the magnet coordinator? Are there sanctions for poor student achieve-	The magnet school will coordinate and integrate all state, federal and local educational reform efforts

All curriculum will be aligned with state and district standards and assessments

Upon review of assessment results, | The degree of staff interaction and coordination, for planning curriculum, writing grants, etc.

The number of curriculums aligned with state standards

The num- | Comprehensive, coordinated grant applications

Revised curriculum guides

Log of sanctions and corrective action plan |

ment (principal reassigned, teaching staff reconstituted, takeover by a new governing body, etc.)?	sanctions will be implemented for poor student achievement	ber of related sanctions imposed	Report on practices implemented
Is technical assistance/professional development provided in the areas of reviewing state standards, student performance assessment, addressing the needs of LEP and special needs' students, addressing the needs of students from different cultural backgrounds, designing/selecting curriculum, developing theme-related activities, budgeting and resource allocation, parental involvement, motivating teachers?	Successful instructional practices will be identified and shared with staff in the regular public school setting

Professional development will be held and teachers will demonstrate proficiency in designated innovative instructional practices | The number of instructional practices successfully duplicated in the regular public school setting

The number of professional development workshops and the number of teachers proficient | Log of professional development activities and attendance

Outside evaluation |
| What curricular and instructional practices offered in the magnet | An annual analysis of all assess- | | Student assessments |

school can be duplicated in other public schools? -Are all tasks accomplished? -Are the goals clear, appropriate, measurable, achievable and embraced by all stakeholders? -Are all the energies (synergy) of school staff directed toward the accomplishment of the objectives? -What is the process by which success toward achieving goals is measured? Is there internal integration? -To what degree is staff utilized? -To what degree does staff feel they are a part of the organization? Does the school have the ability to grow and change? -Does the school monitor external	ment results will be conducted by an external evaluator to determine the diagnosis and prescription for change The school will employ school-wide reform strategies that are scientifically-based to strengthen the core academic program, increase the amount and quality of learning time, and address the needs of low-performing students	The number of prescriptive changes aligned with deficiencies noted in the analysis The number and quality of reform strategies and their impact on student achievement	

| changes?
- Does the school monitor its planning process?
- Does the school monitor its willingness to innovate?
- Which struc-tures, policies or staff inhibits change?			

Technology

Most magnet schools incorporate technology into daily in-struction, as well as a stand-alone activity. Computers are used for mastering academic skills, remediating unlearned skills, develop-ing written expression skills, communicating, finding information, analyzing information, presenting information, improving the use of the computer itself, completing internet research projects, com-pleting math and science simulations, and mastering software. Stu-dents learn more when computers are used to teach discrete skills (Mayer, Mullins and Moore, 2001). Staff development in the tech-nological competence and application is provided. Teachers often use the computer as an instructional tool, enabling students to complete research projects, workplace software, lab simulations in math and science, etc.

Facilities

Many magnet schools have either renovated or new state-of-the-art facilities to accommodate the rigorous and theme-based curriculum. The size of the school, the quantity and quality of laboratories, the size of the classrooms, the wiring accommoda-tions for the latest generation of computers, software and theme-related equipment, the inclusion of a gymnasium, thea-tre/auditorium, cafeteria, etc. and any theme-based needs are all considerations when planning to equip technologically a magnet. Each state has specific rules governing funding and building codes.

Outputs

Outputs are related to the productivity of the system, the yield, the impact of the combination of the throughputs. In order to determine the quality and success of the outputs, they need to be assessed in an orderly, systematic and objective way, relying minimally on conflicting stakeholders' views and politics. The attainment of each of the goals needs to be assessed in order to determine how well the system is performing and to determine necessary interventions for improvement and well being of the system.

Evaluation results from the Evaluation of the Magnet Schools Assistance Program (MSAP), 1998 Grantees: Final Report (USDE, 2002) are provided in this section to complete the picture of the evaluation process and provide sample outputs for each of the five goals. While these results are reported for a specific set of program implementers in a particular grant program, generalizations about the success of the throughputs in meeting each of the goals may be drawn. They will enable the reader to understand how these results should be reported and used to develop a prescription for change.

- MSAP Findings for Goal 1: Student progress
    a. MSAP-supported schools were most successful in meeting or making progress toward the student achievement goals they had set out for the first year of magnet program operation, but continued improvement over longer tine periods proved more difficult. MSAP-supported elementary magnets made noticeable progress in reading and mathematics during the grant period. However, when the analysis controlled for changed in the demographic composition of the schools, the gains exhibited . . . were not significantly different from those exhibited by non-MSAP schools with similar characteristics.
    b. One explanation for the modest improvement in achievement in MSAP schools may be that magnet programs in many schools were not fully implemented or not implemented early enough for achievement effects to be manifested during the

grant period. Several factors may have influenced the progress schools made in implementing MSAP programs: turnover in district and school leadership, tension between MSAP projects and other reform efforts, the absence of sufficient time to implement new programs, the need to revise themes to attract students; and teacher resistance to changes being implemented.

c. The measure most strongly associated with achievement growth in both reading and mathematics in MSAP-supported magnet schools was the overall strength of the professional community of the school. Greater progress in reading was associated with professional development related to standards-based reform and in mathematics with the schools in which state or district standards and frameworks reportedly had a strong influence on curriculum and instruction decisions, and with programs in schools whose magnet programs were in operation prior to the 1998 grant award.

- MSAP Findings for Goal 2: Reduction of isolation
  a. The impact of MSAP-supported programs on school desegregation was modest. Adjusting for district-wide demographic trends in minority enrollment, 57 percent of the desegregation-targeted schools succeeded in preventing, eliminating, or reducing minority group isolation, while 43 percent did not succeed.
  b. Schools are more likely to experience decreasing minority isolation when they have a racially and ethnically mixed group of minority students and when parents are involved in school events and activities. On the other hand, schools with larger numbers of students per teacher are more likely than those with lower student to teacher ratios to experience increases in minority group isolation.
  c. Some of the challenges facing the MSAP projects may explain the modest impact that MSAP magnet

programs have had on minority group isolation. These factors include decreasing number of non-minority students in many districts, a need for more effective recruitment, the need to support parents and retain students, limitations on factors that are used in the selection of students, and delays in re-cruitment efforts related to the timing of grant awards. The case study data suggest that districts are experimenting with strategies to address some of these challenges.

d. While on average minority students represent a lar-ger percentage of students in a district's MSAP schools (73 percent) than in the non-MSAP schools (63 percent), the average in both exceeds the mi-nority enrollment threshold by which the federal government defines minority group isolation. Available data indicate that on average, students in MSAP and non-MSAP schools within a district are similar in terms of the proportions who are eligible for free and reduced price lunches (60 vs. 58 per-cent), of Limited English Proficiency (14 vs. 12 percent), and who have Individualized Education Programs (13 vs. 12 percent). However, a larger proportion of MSAP-supported schools operate Ti-tle I programs.

e. Schools are more likely to experience decreasing minority isolation when the school has a racially and ethnically mixed group of minority students and when parents are involved in school events and ac-tivities.

- MSAP Finding for Goal 3: School Climate
  a. MSAP schools differ from non-MSAP schools serv-ing similar students in several key supports for teaching and learning. In particular, they have somewhat more positive school climates and a somewhat stronger sense of professional commu-nity among staff. There is some evidence that these supports for teaching and learning improved during

the three years of program support. For example, MSAP elementary schools reported that their professional community improved between 1999-2000 and 2001-2002, and both elementary and middle MSAP schools reported improvements in school climate.

b. MSAP schools differ from non-MSAP schools serving similar students in several key supports for teaching and learning. In particular, they have somewhat more positive school climates and a somewhat stronger sense of professional community among staff. There is some evidence that these supports for teaching and learning improved during the three years of program support. For example, MSAP elementary schools reported that their professional community improved between 1999-2000 and 2002.

c. Principals are also more likely to report that administrators and teachers collaborate to help make the school run effectively than are principals in non-MSAP schools. MSAP schools also have a somewhat more positive school climate (i.e., fewer student disengagement and behavior problems), although there is considerable variation among schools.

- MSAP Findings for Goal 4: Program Quality
    a. Teachers in MSAP schools are more likely than teachers in non-MSAP schools to use teaching methods that focus on higher-order thinking skills, such as project-based learning. MSAP teachers also make more use of technology in instruction in ways that support higher-order thinking, and make more use of varied assessment strategies.
    b. MSAP schools adopted a variety of themes and innovative practices, focusing especially on technology and science, and they differed from comparison non-magnet schools in their districts in several ways. In particular, a higher proportion of

MSAP than comparison schools adopted comprehensive school reform models; they had somewhat more positive school climates; and teachers reported giving more emphasis to higher-order thinking skills.

c. MSAP schools have adopted a diverse set of themes. Over a third of MSAP schools included technology among their themes, and more than a quarter of MSAP magnet schools included a science theme. Arts, communication, and mathematics were also common themes. Survey data indicate that the programs adopted in MSAP schools include specialized elective courses and added program requirements in secondary schools. The magnet programs have led to changes in English and language arts and mathematics instruction in both elementary and secondary schools.

d. MSAP principals report a high degree of familiarity with state standards and assessments, and they indicate that the content of state standards and assessments guided decisions regarding curriculum and instruction in their magnet programs.

e. According to teacher survey responses, MSAP schools make somewhat more use of technology in instruction than do comparable schools, and place more emphasis on instructional methods designed to elicit higher-order thinking skills, such as open-ended projects and presentations.

- MSAP Findings for Goal 5: Systemic Reform and Mechanisms for Change
  a. Principals report a high degree of familiarity with standards and assessments, and indicate that the content of state standards and assessments match the goals of their magnet programs.
  b. Magnet themes are generally consistent with the content emphasized in state standards.
  c. There is some evidence of tension between the goals of innovative instruction and systemic reform.

Staff in some MSAP schools reported feeling pressured to learn how to teach a new theme/curriculum while simultaneously being mindful of state content standards and assessments. It also appears that some MSAP schools altered their initial plans in order to bring the curriculum more in line with standards and assessments, or reduced their emphasis on novel programs to increase the time for work more directly related to state standards and assessments.

d. More than half of the MSAP schools have adopted comprehensive school reform models, such as Success for All. This is a substantially higher proportion than is observed among the full national population of Title I schools. It is also higher than among comparable non-MSAP schools in the MSAP districts.

APPLICATION OF CONTEMPORARY REFORM STRATEGIES

The Use Of Action Research In Magnet Schools

The magnet school delivery system mirrors Lewin's three-step action research process, as described in Chapter 2 (Lewin, 1947). The problems of poor achievement and segregation were identified; they needed improvement, were interesting enough to warrant further study, and were within the stakeholders' influence.

The research and literature were reviewed and the knowledge compiled. Purposeful change of the traditional throughputs was implemented and, based on triangulated assessment of these throughputs, the curriculum, setting and instructional strategies were altered; hence, an "action" was taken. And finally, an ongoing assessment of the success of this educational delivery modality was incorporated. As a learning organization, magnet schools require: direct and active involvement of all stakeholders; a focus on the teaching and learning process; use of sound assessment tools; and an ongoing planning/implementation cycle, tied directly to program and student assessment and evaluation. Through a strong accountability system, there is a collaborative engagement in learning, built-in corrective analysis and continuous change.

The Use Of Assessment And Evaluation In Magnet Schools

The power of assessment as an integral component of the teaching and learning process, as discussed in Chapter 3, is clearly evident in the magnet school design. Assessments are used to measure the student's construction of knowledge and to monitor student learning. Multi-faceted, multi-dimensional and inclusive assessments are related to the unique theme and curriculum. Many magnets employ a variety of assessments, using students' products and portfolios, performance-based demonstration of the skills learned, formal rubrics and checklists, observation and teacher feedback exercises. These assessments inform future teaching activities and monitor progress toward mastery of student goals.

For better or worse and largely in response to state and federal mandates and societal habit, magnet schools also engage in summative evaluations: report cards; state mastery tests; national norm-referenced tests, etc. Unfortunately, despite the high stakes' nature of these evaluations, their questionable reliability, validity, fairness and the way they are reported (averaging grades, cut scores, etc.), they are politically powerful and impossible to vanquish, despite evidence to disclaim their usefulness. Their niche in education is well grounded and will require major reform. Perhaps it is the magnet school that holds the most promise for winning the debate on the usefulness of assessment, and the inequity of evaluation, to promote the evolution of the educational system at-large.

The Importance Of Cultural Diversity In Magnet Schools

There is no educational setting more attuned to cultural diversity than the magnet school. Not only do magnet schools have as their mission the infusion of multicultural teachings, as described in Chapter 4, they embrace its deeper meaning as the basis for all learning. Magnet schools promote multiculturalism by utilizing Gay's systematic approach (Gay, 1993): curricular goals and objectives incorporate multicultural themes; examples from a variety of ethnicities provide explanation of concepts, facts, etc.; multicultural content intersects with subject-specific standards; and cross-cultural curriculum materials and activities represent a variety of ethnic groups.

Magnet schools reflect the philosophy of the National Association of State Boards of Education (NASBE), which encourages boards of education to adopt policies and programs that infuse multicultural education into every facet of the curriculum. Since these programs foster respect for diverse populations and mitigate mollify racial and cultural intolerance, equity is infused and desegregation maintained (NASBE, N.D.) It is in this manner that the vision of magnet schools is realized.

Inclusion In Magnet Schools

Magnet schools support the concept of inclusive education, as described in Chapter 5. The Stainbacks' notion that everyone belongs, is accepted, supports and is supported by his or her peers and other members of the school community in having his or her educational needs met (Stainback & Stainback, 1990) is an underlying principle of the magnet school vision. For all magnet school students, including those with special learning needs, comprehensive planning, adequate resources, individual student goals, support services and a focus on the best interests of each student foster both equity and excellence, despite diversity in background, aptitude, interests and goals.

Evidence indicates that choice strongly benefits all children, including the disadvantaged (Hill, 1996). And research shows that families of students with disabilities and parents of gifted and talented students tend to be satisfied with or favor school choice (Ysseldyke et al.,1991).

Students with special learning needs who apply and are admitted to magnet schools often encounter problems, and as a result, the courts and the Office of Civil Rights (OCR) have had to determine the appropriate application of the laws safeguarding their rights. Their rulings should serve as a guide when determining admission procedures, the appropriateness of the placement, the required accommodations and the design of the program. A summary of some of these rulings and references to the law, as reported in LRP SmartStart: Placement/Magnets, follows.

- Use of lottery system to determine admission: An admissions system that employs a lottery approach to selecting candidates for limited seats in magnet programs is almost always going to be problematic when it comes to students with disabilities. It is recommended that school districts refrain from using this approach. Leaving the admissions process up to chance is likely to be discriminatory under Section 504 or will constitute a denial of a free and appropriate public education (FAPE) under the IDEA because any denial of admission must be based on an individual inquiry into the appropriateness of the proposed program for the child with disabilities. This individualized inquiry must take into consideration whether, through the use of special education and related services available at the school, the child will be expected to receive reasonable educational benefit from placement there. Such an inquiry cannot be achieved by statistical weighing of applicants to create a sub-pool of students with disabilities. Where an individualized selection process for admission to magnet schools has been used, it has generally been upheld when challenged. *Little Rock (AR) School District*, 353 IDELR 214 (OCR 1986).

- Placement: When a district contemplates a magnet school placement, it must convene an Individualized Education Program (IEP) team to determine whether the placement is appropriate. The IEP team must consider whether the student will benefit from the instructional program, with supplemental aids and services, as may be necessary, offered at these specialty schools. If so, the team can then assist in planning for the appropriate delivery of services at the school (34 CFR, Section 300.552).

- Accommodations: Students with disabilities must be provided with reasonable accommodations necessary to attend magnet schools if they are otherwise qualified and meet the essential eligibility requirements for participation in magnet school programs. Magnet schools with a specific focus and emphasis, such as the arts, can assess whether the student would benefit from the curriculum, consistent with the obligations imposed under Section 504, which require schools to provide an appropriate education in consideration of a student's disability-related needs. *Portland (OR) School District. 1J*, 1 ECLPR 236 (OCR Region X 1992)). School districts are not required by Section 504 to alter the basic nature of a specialized program in order to provide some or more participation by students with disabilities. *Milwaukee (WI) Public Schools*, 22 IDELR 669 (OCR Region V 1987).

- Methods for providing special education services: There are several ways to provide services for students with disabilities in the magnet school setting. The services can be incorporated directly into the magnet school curriculum, or the school can offer certain services elsewhere in the school system. *Dougherty County (GA) School District*, 23 IDELR 843 (OCR Region IV 1995). Students with disabilities cannot be required to "waive" special education services as a condition of attendance or placement in a magnet school. *Chattanooga (TN) Public School District*, 20 IDELR 999 (OCR Region IV 1993).

Parent Involvement In Magnet Schools

As described in Chapter 6, parent involvement and communication has a direct and positive impact on student achievement. Parents of students in magnet schools play a critical role in the education of their children, from their initial selection of a magnet school to their active engagement in the learning process. Epstein's model for parent involvement (Epstein et al., 2002) is well established in the magnet environment.

Parents of magnet students are often highly motivated, work harder to make the educational system work, and are willing to expose their children to multiracial, multiethnic, multicultural experiences (Ross, 1994). Because magnet schools offer an attractive, specialized learning environment, parents of all races and ethnicities want to enroll their children. The challenging academic program, the high quality of professional staff and the high quality of the academic program are their primary reasons for selecting a magnet school. Parents think magnet schools are safe and secure, have adequate supports and resources and encourage mutual respect between teachers and students, and among students (Connecticut State Board of Education Report, 2003).

According to the Education Commission of the States (ECS, 1998), parents, in general:

1. Want to choose the schools their children attend;
2. Are more interested in good schools than theme schools;
3. Are more likely to choose schools based on the education philosophy and safety of the school than the school's location;
4. Choose schools in districts with higher levels of parent education, higher levels of student achievement, and higher per-pupil spending than their original district;
5. Are more satisfied with and more involved in the schools than parents who do not choose their child's school; and
6. Are more likely to choose another public school (African-American and Hispanic families), or a private school (Caucasian and Asian families) if they are unhappy with their neighborhood school.

And so it is that many parents choose the magnet school: they are safe, hold the promise of high student achievement, often have a higher per-pupil allocation and are considered to be "good" schools. Due to these factors, parents of students in magnet schools encourage open communication and active involvement in all aspects of the school; they engage routinely in the activities described earlier in this chapter and consider themselves partners in the educational process. It will be interesting to continue to track the data to determine the degree of the impact on student achievement, due to the strong parent component in magnet schools.

Technology And Distance Learning In Magnet Schools

As new, state-of-the-art magnet buildings are constructed, and older building are refurbished and brought up to code, the interface of technology and learning is clearly established. It is commonplace for the entire magnet school community to use technology in the day-to-day operation of the school: in scheduling and record keeping, in classroom activities, in homework assignments, and in communicating with parents. Technology training, as described in

Chapter 7, is embedded in content specific staff development, and includes collegial sharing and on-going support/follow-up. Students are required to use technology applications through independent learning activities, multi-media presentations, web site exploration, topical research, and distance learning (as discussed in Chapter 8). Some magnet schools provide a laptop computer to each student, conduct computer literacy training for parents, and offer on-line courses. Other magnets use technology as their unique curriculum focus. Since technology expands learning well beyond the traditional classroom, magnet schools optimize its use as an instructional strategy.

Mental Health Supports In The Magnet School

The mental health of students is one of the key variables that impacts learning, and poor mental health has been shown to be a barrier to learning. For this reason, many school districts are collaborating with community mental health professionals to provide prevention services in the school itself, as described in Chapter 9. Magnet schools, as part of their comprehensive systems approach to education, incorporate mental health support and prevention in their menu of services. Some magnet schools, in fact, have social responsibility or wellness as their unique curricular focus; others incorporate prevention programs, such as Primary Mental Health, Family Resource Centers or school-based health clinics. Magnet schools are eligible for state and national funding targeted to implement mental health programs.

The Magnet School As A Strategy For Change

The development of the magnet school movement relied on the strategies for educational change outlined in Chapter 10. A description of the problem— the segregation of large numbers of minority children and their poor achievement— was framed by the courts, who found it was a violation of the Constitution to separate children of color from the rest of the population for purposes of schooling them. Their description was based on supportive data, research and the values of stakeholders. These political views and values were identified as: a respect for cultural diversity and the values and traditions of different racial and ethnic groups; a focus on empowering the parents of these children to choose the type of education they believe to be beneficial to their children; and the importance of the psychological well being of children, which must be enhanced in a school environment that is safe, orderly and conducive to learning. The public school system required personal, interpersonal and institutional changes. Its well-being was in jeopardy and its task accomplishment, internal integration and ability to grow and change were in question. The decree from a high authority was issued; research and supporting data provided; and a prescription determined. The concept of the magnet school seemed a worthwhile remedy or prescription for the change agent to pursue. And so the implementation of the magnet school demonstration project was created and its success as a solution is being carefully studied.

Implementing The Magnet School Demonstration Project

When planning to design a magnet school, it is important to check the state law in which the school will operate for guidance about the parameters of implementation and the regulatory restrictions. Most states have an application package, which provides information about timelines, requirements, scoring and the review process. Magnet Schools of America, in its document "Needs Assessment Survey", (Magnet Schools of America, N.D.) outlines the following list of pre-planning activities, which serve as a checklist for implementation: establish a leadership group; complete a written mission statement; develop a school plan and budget; develop a written proposal; identify thematic instructional models; develop a vision statement; create an organizational structure; adopt policies and procedures; plan thematic instructional strategies; identify teaching and learning outcomes; align curriculum with the school's vision; develop student assessment and evaluation procedures; develop program evaluation; align policies with the organizational structure; establish a personnel policies/procedures handbook; create a student and parent handbook/policy manual; establish a parent involvement structure; establish a marketing plan; develop recruitment materials; develop a plan for communication with parents, community and the school board; and ensure compliance with federal, state and local statutory requirements, including civil rights issues.

Table 11.9 provides an outline for developing a plan of operation for a magnet school. A planning committee, comprised of members of each constituency group (superintendents, principals, teachers, parents, community members, etc, from feeder schools/ participating districts), is convened. The planning committee's role is to conduct interviews and focus groups, develop and administer surveys, obtain letters of support from all stakeholder groups, create a timetable that clearly delineates when major activities begin and end, and assign responsibility for the implementation of the tasks.

TABLE 11.9: MAGNET SCHOOL IMPLEMENTATION TIMETABLE

TASK LIST	
Administration/governance	Determine governing board membership
	Determine the management structure
	Create a job description for the director/principal
	Describe experience, education and duties of key administrative and teaching personnel, including those skills related to magnet school operation, desegregation and implementing the special curriculum
	Delineate reporting relationships
	Define the school calendar, hours of operation, daily schedule
	Determine the number of students and the grades to be served
	Create a school management/advisory team-
	Determine staff to student ratio
	Create student policies (discipline, attendance, equal access) and student handbook
	Create staff policies (non-discrimination in hiring, affirmative action, salary/benefit package, dismissal, etc.
	Determine strategies for parent communication and involvement

Admissions	Determine student admission criteria
	Create an admissions policy that ensures equal access and treatment of groups that are traditionally underrepresented
	Determine special exceptions to the admission policy (sibling preference, etc.)
	Outline the process and timetable for admitting students
	Outline strategies that will ensure equal access to and treatment of underrepresented populations
Facility	Determine building options and a timetable for securing a new, or renovating an existing, facility
	Contract with an architect and builder
	Determine construction costs and create a budget
	Determine code compliance issues for renovations
	Secure land
	Ensure that the building supports the theme
	Ensure that the building provides sufficient space for the number of students to be served, the special curriculum, space requirements, storage, wiring for technology, etc.
	Create construction plan with timelines and submit to appropriate agency for approval
Education plan	Describe the mission and underlying philosophy
	Research and select special curriculum and create a detailed overview of its tenets
	Determine measurable and quantifiable goals and objectives that are useful for determining progress toward measuring reduction of isolation, ensuring diversity and improving student achievement
	Outline the academic program, including

	core content (reading, mathematics, etc), vocational skills, technological skills, support services, community service, independent projects, electives, work experience, etc. Outline the teaching methods of specialized instruction List partners in providing the chosen approach (business, community services, etc.) Describe how the curriculum will include multicultural materials Describe the strategies to ensure interaction among students from different backgrounds Assign responsibility for achieving the objectives to specific staff Create performance standards that describe what students know and are able to demonstrate and to what extent (advanced, proficient, deficient) Create performance indicators to measure how well a program meets its goals and objectives Create content standards that describe what should be included in the curriculum of all subjects at each grade level
Student assessment	Create a plan to assess initially the educational needs of the students Describe the methods and the process for assessing goals Develop performance measures, benchmarks and a plan that outlines when, where and by whom data is collected, analyzed and reported
Special populations	Determine accommodations and supports needed for students with special needs, English language learners, students in need of remedial assistance, etc.
Transportation	Determine the cost of transporting students

	and assign responsibility for these costs
Funding	Create a budget that includes personnel (administrative/teaching/aides/clerical/tutors/other), fringe benefits, contractual (professional development, maintenance), travel, equipment, supplies (instructional/administrative), construction, property (land lease/purchase), student transportation, communications/marketing, other, indirect costs and total costs
	Determine funding streams (local, state, federal, tuition, parent contributions, endowment, contributions, etc.)
	Ensure that project costs are adequate and reasonable in relation to the objectives.

CONCLUSION

Magnet schools are not the perfect solution to reforming the educational system, but provide a fertile ground for observing systemic reform. The reader should be reminded that magnet schools are an experiment in using research-based practices and pedagogy to inform the teaching and learning process in an atmosphere that embraces diversity. Current research results are insufficient to determine definitively if minority group isolation is reduced or if students achieve better outcomes if they attend magnet schools; however, the preliminary evidence suggests this to be true. The magnet school comes closest to providing what is known to be successful practice—a challenging, interesting, motivating knowledge base in a state-of-the-art facility with students of diverse backgrounds, taught in a variety of ways using theme-based, integrated curriculum materials, by staff who are motivated, professional and dedicated to their art, supported by families and the community, with adequate resources, in an environment rich with technology, according to a detailed plan embraced by all stakeholders. Time will tell whether this experiment is worth replicating, but who would want less for their child than such an environment in which to learn.

DISCUSSION QUESTIONS

1. How is the magnet school an example of a social system?

2. How are magnet schools an effective district-wide and statewide desegregation strategy? How are they an effective strategy to improve student achievement? What are the impediments, if any, and how would you diminish them?

3. How do the inputs, outputs and throughputs of a magnet school differ from those in a traditional public school?

4. Are there greater, lesser, or equal educational benefits in a magnet school as compared to a traditional public school setting?

5. Why are states, school districts, businesses and the federal government interested in investing in magnet schools?

6. From what you have learned in previous chapters, how do magnet schools foster the innovations/strategies regarding: a systems approach to change; action research; assessment; cultural diversity; inclusion; parent/teacher communication; technology; distance learning; mental health and well-being; and change strategies?

7. Which of the cited curricular models could be replicated successfully in the traditional public school setting? Why?

8. How would you market the magnet school strategy to a team of stakeholders? Describe the benefits, the process for implementation and the components.

9. How is the magnet school an example of systemic educational reform?

NOTES

1.   The term "minority" includes American Indian, Alaskan Native, Asian, Pacific Islander, Hispanic and black students. Federal regulations for the Magnet School Assistance Program identifies a school as minority group isolated if minority students comprise 50 percent or more of the school's enrollment (34 CFDA 84.165A, Federal Register, Section 280.4(b)).

2.   The No Child Left Behind Act of 2001, Part A, Subpart 1, Section 1111(C)(v)(II), requires districts to measure the achievement of students against the challenging state academic content and student academic achievement standards in each of grades 3-8 in mathematics and reading or language arts (Part A, Subpart 1, Section 1111(C)(vii)) and to measure the proficiency of all students in science not less than one time in grades three through five, six through nine, and ten through 12 (Part A, Subpart 1, Section 1111(C)(v)(II)).

3.   The No Child Left Behind Act of 2001, Part A, Subpart 1, Section 1111(c)(2), requires the state to participate in biennial State academic assessments of 4th and 8th reading and mathematics under the National Assessment of Educational Progress, under Section 411(b)(2) of the National Education Statistics Act of 1994.

4.   Developed by Educational Testing Service for the College Board, the SAT is a national test designed to measure those abilities of college bound students in grades 11 and 12 thought to have an impact on college academic performance. The SAT is one of two entrance exams accepted by four-year institutions. Advance registration and a registration fee are required, and the registration deadline is one month prior to test date. (The test is given in October, November, December, January, March, May and June). Registration materials are usually available in the school's Career Center. The critical reading section, formerly the verbal section, includes reading comprehension, sentence completion and passage-based reading. The math section includes numbers and operations, algebra and functions, geometry, statistics and data analysis. The writing section includes grammar, usage and word choice. Scores are mailed directly to the student.

Bibliography

Albee, G. W. (1996). Revolutions and counterrevolutions in prevention. *American Psychologist, 51,* 1130-1133.

Alinsky, S. D. (1972). *Rules for radicals.* NY: Vintage Books.

Allen, G., Chinsky, J., Larcen, S., Lockman, J., & Selinger, H. (1976). *Community psychology and the schools.* Hillsdale, NJ: Erlbaum.

Argyris, C. (1964). *Integrating the individual and the organization.* NY: Wiley.

Association for Supervision and Curriculum Development. (2004). *A lexicon of learning: What educators mean when they say magnet schools.* Retrieved on March 25, 2004 from the worldwide web at ascd.org.

Bacon, N.A., & Kischner, G.A. (2002). Shaping global classrooms. *Educational Leadership, 60* (2) 48-52.

Banks, J. A. (1972). Imperatives in ethnic minority education. In M. D. Gall & B. A. Ward (Eds.) *Critical issues in educational psychology.* Boston, MA: Little, Brown & Co.

Banks, J. A., Cookson, P., Gay, G., Hawley, W.D., Irvine, J.J., Nieto, S., Schofield, J. W., Stephan, W. G. (2001). Diversity within unity: Essential principles for teaching and learning in a multicultural society. *Phi Delta Kappan*, 196-203.

Banks, J. A., & Banks, C.A.M. (2002) *Handbook of research on multicultural education* (2nd ed.). San Francisco: Jossey-Bass

Banks, J. A. (1995). Multicultural education: Historical development, dimensions, and practice. In J. A. Banks and C. A. McGee (Eds.) *Handbook of research on multicultural education of young children* p 3-24. NY: Macmillian.

Banks, J. A. (1997). *Multicultural education: Characteristics and goals.* In J.A. Banks and C.E. McGee Banks (Eds) Multicultural Education: issues and perspectives, 3-31. Boston: Allyn & Bacon.

Barker, R. G. (1964). *Ecological psychology: Concepts and methods for studying the environment of human behavior.* Stanford, CA.: Stanford University Press.

Barker, R. G., & Gump, P. V. (1964). *Big school, small school.* Stanford, CA.: Stanford University Press.

Bateson, G. (1972). *Steps to ecology of mind.* NY: Chandler.

Battistih, V., Solomon, D., Kim, D., Watson, M., & Schaps, E. (1995). Schools as communities, poverty levels of student populations, and student's attitudes, motives, and performance: A multilevel analysis. American Educational Research Journal 32, 627-658.

Bennis, W. G. (1966). *Changing organizations.* NY.: McGraw Hill.

Berger, D. (1996). *An orientation to the grants process and proposal preparation.* Unpublished memo, Marist College, Poughkeepsie, NY.

Berreuta-Clement, J. R., Schweinhart, L. J., Barnett, M. W., Epstein, A. S., & Weikart, D. P. (1984). *Changed lives: The effects of the Perry Preschool Program on youth through age 19.* Ypsilanti, MI: High/Scope Educational Research Foundation.

Bertalannffy, L. von (1968). *General systems theory.* (Rev. ed.) NY: George Braziller.

Bessell, H. (1972). Human development in the elementary school classroom. In L. N. Solomon & B. Berzon (Eds.) *New perspectives in encounter groups.* San Francisco: Jossey-Bass.

Bickford, A. (2002). Finding the right fuel for learning: Emints, *Multimedia Schools, 9 (5), 18-25.*

Bigelow, B. (1999). Why standardized tests threaten multiculturalism, *Educational Leadership,* 56 (7), 37-40.

Black, P., & William, D. (1998). Inside the black box: Raising standards through classroom assessment. *Phi Delta Kappan*, October, 1998.

Blaschke, C. (2003). 10 technology funding sources in nclb, *T.H.E. Journal, 30 (10), 22 25.*

Bloom, B., Englehart, M., Furst, E., Hill, W., & Krathwohl, D. (1956). *Taxonomy of educational objectives: The classification of educational goals. Handbook 1: Cognitive domain.* NY: Longmans Green.

Bloom, H. S., Ham, S., Melton, L. & O'Brien, J. (2001). *Evaluating the accelerated schools approach: A look at early implementation and impact on student achievement in eight elementary schools.* NY: Manpower Demonstration Research Corporation.

Blue-Banning, M., Summers, J. A., Frankland, H. C., Nelson, L. L., and Beegle, G. (2004). Dimensions of family and professional partnerships: Constructive guidelines for collaboration. Council for Exceptional Children, 70, (2), 167-184.

Bolman, L. G., & Deal, T. E. (1997). *Reframing organizations: Artistry, choice and leadership.* San Francisco: Jossey-Bass.

Boocock, S. S. (1980). *Sociology of education: An introduction* (2nd ed.). Boston: Houghton-Mifflin.

Bortoft, H. (1996). *The wholeness of nature – Goethe's way toward a science of conscious participation in nature.* NY: Lindisfarne Press.

Boss, R. W. (1983). Team building and the problem of regression: The Personal Management Interview as an intervention. *The Journal of Applied Behavioral Science, 19,* 67-83.

Bossert, P. J. (2001). Lessons learned: An inside look at four of the top technology school districts in the nation, *T.H.E. Journal, 29* (4), 62-67.

Bottom, G., Presson, A. & Han, L. (2004). *Research brief – linking career/technical studies to broader high school reform: What can schools districts, states and the nation do to get more high schools to implement comprehensive school reform?* Southern Regional Education Board.

Bower, E. M. (1972). Education as a humanizing process and its relationship to other humanizing processes. In S. E. Golam & C. Eisdorfer (Eds.), *Handbook of community mental health.* NY: Appleton.

Brakas, N. J. & Pittman-Smith, S. (2005). *The cultural voices of children's literature: Web supported instruction to unify theme and content for curricular approaches,* The Language and Literacy Spectrum, 15, 3-21.

Brannon, R. F. & Essex, C. (2001). Synchronous and asynchronous communication tools in distance education: A survey for instructors. *Tech Trends*, 45, (1) 36-41.

Bricker, D.D. (1995). The challenge of inclusion. *Journal of Early Intervention*, 19, 179-194.

Brody-Ortmann, C. (2002). Teachers' perceptions of a professional development distance learning course: A qualitative case study. *Journal of Research on Technology in Education*, 35 (1), 107-116.

Bronfenbrenner, U. (1979). *The ecology of human development: Experiments by nature and design.* Cambridge, MA: Harvard University Press.

Brooks, J. G., & Brooks, M. G. (1993). *In search of understanding: A case for constructivist classrooms.* Alexandria, VA: Association for Supervision and Curriculum Development.

Brown, M. R., Higgins, K. & Hartley, K. (2001). Teachers and technology equity, *Teaching Exceptional Children*, 33 (4), 32-39.

Bryk, A. S., & Schneider, B. (2003). Trust in schools: A core resource for school reform. Educational Leadership, 60 (6) 41-44.

Bunch, G. (1997). From here to there: The passage of inclusion education. In G. Bunch & A. Velio (Eds.), *Inclusion: recent research*. Toronto, Ontario, Canada: Inclusion Press.

Burkhead, J. (1967). *Input and output in large city high schools.* Syracuse, NY: Syracuse Univ. Press.

Burrello, L., Lashley, C. & Beatty, E. (2001). *Educating all students together.* Thousand Oaks, California: Corwin Press, Inc.

Caine, R. N., & Caine, G. (1994). *Making connections: Teaching and the human brain.* NY: Addison Wesley.

Campbell, A. & Guisinger, M.L.(2003). Redefining teamwork: Collaboration within virtual walls, *Multimedia and Internet @ Schools*, 10 (6).

Campbell, D. T., & Stanley, J. C. (1963). Experimental and quasi-experimental design for research on teaching. In N. L. Sage (Ed.), *Handbook of research on teaching.*
Chicago: Rand Mc Nally.

Caplan, G. (1964). *Principles of preventive psychiatry.* NY: Basic Books.

Capra, F. (1996). *The web of life: A new scientific understanding of living systems.* NY: Anchor Books.

Carr, S. (2000). More states create virtual high schools, *Chronicle of Higher Education,* 47 (3), A40.

Catterall, J. S. (1995). *Different ways of knowing: 1991-1994 national longitudinal study, program effects on students, and teachers (final report).* Los Angeles, California: University of California, Graduate School of Education and Information Studies.

Caywood, K., & Duckett, J. (2003). Online vs. on-campus learning in teacher education, *Teacher Education and Special Education,* 26 (2), 98-105.

Checkland, P. (1997). Systems. In M. Warner (Ed.). *International encyclopedia of business and management,* 667-673. London: Thompson Business Press.

Cicirelli, V. G. (1969). *The impact of Head Start: An evaluation of the effects of Head Start on children's cognitive and affective development.* Washington, DC: National Bureau of Standard, Institute for Applied Technology.

Clauset, K., & Gaynor, A. (1982). Improving schools for low achieving children: A system dynamics policy study. Paper presented at the annual meeting of the American Educational Research Assn., NYC. (ERIC Document Reproductive Service No. 214 243).

Coleman, J. S. (1982, January – February). Public schools, private schools and the public interest. *American Education,* 17-22.

Coleman, J. S., Campbell, E. Q., Hobson, C. J., Mc Partland, J., Mood, A. M., Weinfield, F. D., & York, R. L. (1966). *Equality of educational opportunity.* (U. S. Department of Health, Education and Welfare, Office of Education). Washington, DC: U. S. Government Printing Office.

Connecticut State Board of Education. (2003). *Interdistrict magnet schools and magnet programs in Connecticut: An evaluation report.*

Cornell Empowerment Group. (1989). Empowerment and family support. *Networking Bulletin, 1,* 1-23.

Council of Chief State School Officers. (2003). *Comprehensive assessment systems for Title 1: Handbook for professional development in assessment literacy, Vermont version.* Montpelier, VT: VT Department of Education.

Covey, S. R. (1989). *The seven habits of highly effective people: restoring the character ethic.* NY: Simon and Schuster.

———— 1991). *Principle-centered leadership.* NY: Summit Books.

Cowen, E. L. (1996). The ontogenesis of primary prevention: Lengthy strides and stubbed toes. *American Journal of Community Psychology, 24*, 235-249.

Cowen, E., Hightower, A., Pedro-Carroll, J., & Work, W. (1989). School based models for primary prevention programming with children. *Prevention in Human Services, 7*, 133-160.

Criscuola, M. (1994). *Read, discuss, reread: Insights from the junior great books program.* Educational Leadership, 58.

Cromwell, R. R., & Scileppi, J. A. (1996). Without knowing how the systems work, even the whole village cannot improve education: A systems approach. *Resources in Education, 31* (7). ED392 151.

Cuipers, P. (2002). Peer-led and adult-led school drug prevention: A meta-analytic comparison. *Journal of Drug Education, 32,* 107-119.

Curwin, R. L., & Mendler, A. N. (2002). Preventing violence with values-based schools. *Journal of Emotional & Behavioral Problems, 9,* 41-44.

Cutwright, B., & Griffith, M. (2000). The Acadia advantage and a new vision for education in Canada, *Technology Source.*

Darling-Hammond, L. (1999). Target time toward, teachers, *Journal of Staff Development,* 20 (2), 31-36.

Darlington, R. B., Royce, J. M., Snipper, A. S., Murray, H. W., & Lazar, I. (1980). Preschool programs and later school competence of children from low-income families. *Science, 208*, 202-204.

Davis, M., & Gidycz, C. A. (2000). Child sexual abuse programs: A meta-analysis. *Journal of Clinical Child Psychology, 29*, 257-265.

Deal, T. (1990). Reframing reform. *Educational Leadership, 47* (8), 6-12.

Deno, E. (1970). Special education as developmental capital. *Exceptional Children*, 37, 229-237.

Delandshere, G. (2002). Assessment as inquiry [Electronic version]. *Teachers CollegeRecord*, 104 (7), 1461-1484.

Dewey, J. (1916). *Democracy and education*. NY: Macmillan.

Dillow, S. (2001, Fall). *Education Statistics Quarterly, 3* (3). Washington, DC: National Center for Education Statistics. Doran, H. C. (2003). Adding value to accountability. *Educational Leadership*. 61 (3), 57.

DuFour, R. (2004). What is a "professional learning community?" *Educational Leadership*. 61 (8), 6-11.

Dupre, A. P. (1998, Winter). Disability, deference, and the integrity of the academic enterprise. *Georgia Law Review*, 393-473.

Dyer, W. G. (1977). *Team building: Issues and alternatives*. Reading, MA: Arbor House.

Ebel, R. L. (1974). What are schools for? In M. D. Gall & B. A. Ward (Eds.) *Critical issues in educational psychology*. Boston: Little, Brown & Co.

Eddy, J. M., Reid, J. B. & Fetrow, R. A. (2000). An elementary school-based prevention program targeting modifiable antecedents of youth delinquency and violence: Linking the interests of families and teachers (LIFT*). Journal of Emotional & Behavioral Disorders, 8*, 165-177.

Edison Schools, Inc. (2004). *Edison Schools Sixth Annual Report on School Performance: 2002 – 2003.*

Education Commission of the States. (1998). *Choice.* Education Issue Document. Retrieved on March 25, 2002 from the worldwide web at ecs.org.clearinghouse.

Education Commission of the States. (2004*). Magnet schools: Frequently asked questions*. Retrieved on March 25, 2004 from the worldwide web at ecs.org/html/Issue Section.

Education Week on the Web. (1999). National education related articles and government policy. *The Galef institute: Different ways of knowing.*

Eisner, E. (May, 2003). Questionable assumptions about schooling. *Phi Delta Kappan, 84*(9), 648-657.

Englemann, S., Becker, W.C., Carnine, D. & Gersten, R. (1998). *The direct instruction follow through model: Design and outcomes.* Education and Treatment of Children, 111(4), 303-317.

Ennett, S. T., Ringwalt, C. L., Thorne, J., Rohrbach, L. A. Vincus, A., et al., (2003). A comparison of current practice in school-based substance use prevention programs with meta-analysis findings. *Prevention Science, 4,* 1-14.

Ennett, S. T., Tobler, N. S., Ringwalt, C. L, Flewelling, R. L. (1994). How effective is drug abuse resistance education? A meta-analysis of Project DARE outcome evaluations. *American Journal of Public Health, 84,* 1394-1401.

Epstein, J. L., & Clark Salinas, K. (2004). Partnering with families and communities. *Educational Leadership, 61* (8), 12-17.

Epstein, J. L., Salinas, K. C., & Van Voorhis, F. L. (2001). Teachers involve parents in schoolwork (TIPS) manuals and prototype activities for the elementary and middle grades. Baltimore: Center on School, Family and Community Partnerships, Johns Hopkins University.

Epstein, J. L., Sanders, M.G., Simon, B.S., Salinas, K.C., Jansorn, N.R., & Van Vooris, F. L. (2002). School, family, and community partnerships: Your handbook for action (2nd ed.). Thousand Oaks, CA: Corwin.

Fairweather, G. W., & Davidson, W. S. (1986). *An introduction to community experimentation.* NY: Mc Graw Hill.

Farley, R. P. (1999). A tale of two schools. *Educational Leadership, 56* (50), 39-42.

Feldman, S. (2003). Out of many, one. *Teaching Prek-8,* 34 (6) 6-7.

Festinger, L. (1957). *A theory of cognitive dissonance.* Stanford, CA: Stanford University Press.

Fiedler, F. E. (1967). *A theory of leadership effectiveness.* NY: McGraw-Hill. Field-based Graduate Program in Education.

Finn-Stevenson, M. & Zigler, E. (1999). *Schools of the 21st century: Linking child care and education (renewing American schools).* Westview Press.

Flaxman, E., Guerrero, A., & Gretchen, D. (1999). *Career development effects of career magnets versus comprehensive schools: The educational benefits of magnet schools.* Berkeley: National Center for Research in Vocational Education, University of California.

Follansbee, S. (1997). Can online communications improve student performance? Results of a controlled study, *ERS Spectrum,* 15 (1), 15-26.

Fuchs, D., & L. S. Fuchs (1995). Counterpoint – special education – ineffective? Immoral? *Exceptional Children, 61,* 303-305.

Fullan, M. (1993). *Change forces: Probing the depths of educational reform.* NY: Falmer Press.

. . . (2000). The three stories of education reform. *Phi Delta Kappa, 81*(8), 581.

Fullan, M. & Hargreaves, A. (1991). *What's worth Fighting For? Fighting Together for Your School.* New York: Teachers College Press.

Fuller, R. B. (1963). *Operating manual for spaceship earth.* NY: E. P.

Futrell, M.H., Gomez, J., & Bedden, D. (2003). Teaching the children of a new America: The challenge of diversity. *Phi Delta Kappan* 84, (5) 381-390.

Gardner, H. (1983). *Frames of mind.* NY: Basic.

———— (1999). *Intelligence reframed: Multiple intelligences for the 21st century.* Basic Books.

Garratt, B. (1987). *The learning organization.* London: Fontana/Collins.

Gay, G. (2003). The importance of multicultural education, *Educational Leadership,* 61 (4), 30-35.

George, M., & George, N. (1993). Planning vision and descriptions. In N. B. Billingsley (Ed.), *Program leadership for serving schools with disabilities* (pp. 21-54). Richmond, VA: Virginia Department of Education.

Gergin, K. J. (1973). Social psychology as history. *Journal of Personality and Social Psychology, 26,* 309-320.

Gibson, M. (1976). Approaches to multi-cultural education in the united states: Some concepts and assumptions, *Anthropology and Education Quarterly,* 7 (4), 7-18.

Gilhool, T. (1976). Changing public policies: Roots and forces. In M. Reynolds (Ed.), *Mainstreaming: Origins and implications* (pp. 8-13). Reston, VA: Council for Exceptional Children.

Glazer, N. (1995). A new word for an old problem: Multicultural "school wars" date to the 1840s. *Annual Editions: Multicultural Education*, 74-77.

Gleik, J. (1987). *Chaos: making a new science*. NY: Penguin Books.

Golding, W. (1978). *Lord of the flies*. NY: Putnam.

Golley, F. B. (1993). *A history of the ecosystem concept in ecology: More than the sum of the parts*. New Haven, CT: Yale University Press.

Gollnick, Donna M. (1995). National and State Initiatives for Multicultural Education, Handbook *of Research on Multicultural Education*, New York: Simon and Schuster Macmillan. 44-64.

Good, T. L., & Weinstein, R. S. (1986). Schools make a difference: Evidence, criticism and new directions. *American Psychologist*, 41, 1090-1097.

Goodlad, J. (1984). *A place called school: Prospects for the future*. NY: McGraw-Hill.

Grant, C. (1994). Best practices in teacher preparation for urban schools: Lessons from the multicultural teacher education literature, *Action in Teacher Education*, 16, 1-18.

Great Books Foundation. (1993). *Our evaluation study*. Chicago, Illinois: The Great Books Foundation.

Grunwald Associates. (2002). Children, families, and the internet 2000. San Mateo: CA: Author. Available: http://grunwald.com

Guastello, E. F. (2004). A village of learners. Educational Leadership, 61 (8), 79-83.

Gullotta, T. P., & Bloom, M. (Eds.). (2003). *The encyclopedia of primary prevention and health promotion*. NY: Kluwer/Academic.

Gutknecht, B., & Gutknecht, C. (2001). Connecting at-risk children and teacher prep students virtually: Applications of synchronous distance education technologies, *Reading Improvement, 38 (3), 99-105.*

Hadley, R.G., & Browdin, M.G. (1988). *Language about people with disabilities,* Journal of Counseling and Development, 67 (3) 147-149.

Haggard, E. A. (1954). Social status of intelligence. *Genetic Psychology Monographs, 49,* 141-186.

Hall, M.E. (1999). Training key to understanding technology's value. *Thrust for Educational Leadership,* 29 (2) 15-19.

Hallahan, D., & Kauffman, J. (1988). *Exceptional Children: An introduction to special education.* Englewood Cliffs, New Jersey: Simon & Schuster.

Hamel, G., & Prahalad, C. K. (1994). *Competing for the future.* Boston: Harvard Business School Press.

Hardman, M., Drew, C. & Egan, M. W. (1996). *Human exceptionality.* Needham Heights, MA: Allyn & Bacon.

Hargreaves, A., & Fink, D. (2003). Sustaining leadership. Phi Delta Kappan, 84(9), 693-700.

Harris, J. (2002). Wherefore art thou, telecollaboration? Learning and Leading with Technology, 29 (6), 54-59.

Havelock, R., & Hamilton, J. (2004). *Guiding change in special education.* Thousand Oaks, CA: Corwin Press.

Hawken, P. (1993). *The ecology of commerce: A declaration of sustainability.* NY: HarperCollins.

Hawkins, J. D., Catalano, R. F., Kosterman, R., Abbott, R. & Hill, K. G. (1999). Preventing adolescent health risk behaviors by strengthening protection during childhood. *Archives of Pediatric Adolescent Medicine, 153,* 226-234.

Hearn, G. (1969). *The general system approach: Contributions toward a holistic conception of social work.* New York: Council on Social Work Education.

Herman, J. L., Aschbacher, P. R. & Winters, L. (1992). *A practical guide to alternative assessment.* Alexandria, VA: Association for Supervision and Curriculum Development.

Herzog, M. (1997). *Inside learning network schools.* Richard C. Owen Publishers, Inc.

Hill, P. (1996). *The educational consequences of school choice.* Phi Delta Kappan, Vol. 77, No. 10.

Hiltz, S. R. (1994). *The virtual classroom: Learning without limits via computer networks. New Jersey:* Albex Publishing.

Hobbie, F. R. (2001). Goals 2000 revisited: Goal # 1. *The Educational Forum, 66* (1), 50-57.

Hovland, C. J., Janis, I. & Kelly, H. H. (1953). Communication and persuasion. New Haven: Yale University Press.

Huey, S. J., & Henggeler, S. W. (2001). Effective community-based interventions for antisocial and delinquent adolescents. In Jan N Hughes & A. M. La Greca (Eds.) *Handbook of psychological services for children and adolescents.* London: Oxford Univ. Press.

Hughes, J. N., & Hasbrouk, J.E. (1997). Television violence: Implications for violence prevention. *School Psychology Review, 25(2),* 134-151.

Inclusion – Where are we today? (1996). *Council for Exceptional Children Today 1*(1), 5-15.

Jackson, P. (1968). *Life in classrooms.* NY: Holt, Rinehart & Winston.

Jacobs, H. H. (1997). *Mapping the big picture: Integrating curriculum and assessment, K-12.* Alexandria, VA: Association for Supervision and Curriculum Development.

Jacobsen, W. (1999). Why common ground thinking works. Educational Leadership 57, (4), 76-80.

Jasparro, R. J. (1998). Applying systems thinking to curriculum evaluation. *NASSP Bulletin, 82* (598), 80-86.

Jensen, A. R. (1969). How much can we boost IQ and scholastic achievement? *Harvard Educational Review, 39,* 1-123.

Jobs for the Future. (2001). *National partnership announces new schools: Initiative seeks to improve access to college.* Retrieved on April 29, 2004 from the worldwide web at early-colleges.org/Media

Jobs for the Future. (N.D.). T*he early college high school initiative at a glance.* Retrieved on April 29, 2004 from the worldwide web at earlycolleges.org

Johnson, D. W. (1970). *The social psychology of education.* NY: Holt, Rinehart and Winston.

Johnston, P. (1989). Constructive evaluation and improvement of teaching and learning. *Teachers College Record*, 90 (4), 509-528.

Kamin, L. J. (1979). Psychology as social science: The Jensen affair, ten years after. Presidential Address, Eastern Psychological Association.

Kamins, J. (1992, October 23). *Prognostications regarding the future directions of school psychology.* Presentation at the Daniel Kirk Annual Lecture, Marist College, Poughkeepsie, NY.

Kamps, D., Kravitz, T., Rauch, J., Kamps, J. L. & Chung, N. (2000). A prevention program for students with or at risk for ED: Moderating effects of variation in treatment and classroom structure. *Journal of Emotional and Behavioral Disorders, 8,* 141-156.

Katz, D., & Kahn, R. C. (1966). *The social psychology of organizations.* NY: Wiley.

Kaufman, J. M., McGee, K. & Brigham, M. (2004, April). Enabling or Disabling? Observations on changes in special education. *Phi Delta Kappan (85)* 8, 613-620.

Kelly, J. G. (1966). Ecological constraints on mental health services. *American Psychologist, 21,* 535 – 539.

Kelly, J. G., Ryan, A. M., Altman, B. E., & Stelzman, S. P. (2000). Understanding and changing social systems. In Rappaport, J. & Seidman, E. (Eds.), *Handbook of community psychology.* NY: Plenum.

Klauke, A. (2000). *Magnet schools.* ERIC Digest Series Number EA26. Retrieved on March 25, 2004 from the worldwide web at ericfacility.net/eric digests/ed293225.

Ko, S. F., & Cosden, M. A. (2001). Do elementary school-based child abuse prevention programs work? A high school follow-up. *Psychology in the Schools, 38,* 57-66.

Kohn, A. (2000). *The case against standardized testing: Raising the scores, ruining the schools.* Westport, CT: Heinemann.

Koret Task Force on K-12 Education (2003, March). Our schools and our future: Are we still at risk? *Education Next, 3* (2), 9-10

Kriss, J. (1996). Technology requirements of today's learners and educators, *Media & Methods,* 32, 1-3.

Kuhn, T. (1970). *The structure of scientific revolutions* (2nd ed.). Chicago: University of Chicago Press.

Langer, G. M., Colton, A. B., & Goff, L. S. (2003). *Collaborative analysis of student work: Improving teaching and learning.* Alexandria, VA: Association for *Leadership, 42*(6), 67-74.

Leitch, M. L., & Tangri, S.S. (1988). Barriers to home-school collaboration. Educational Horizons, 66 (2): 70-74.

Levin, B., & Wiens, J. (2003). There is another way: a different approach to education reform. *Phi Delta Kappan, 84*(9), 658-664.

Levine, M., & Perkins, D. V. (1987). Principles of community psychology: Perspectives and applications. NY: Oxford University Press.

Lewin, K. (1948). *Resolving social conflicts; selected papers on group dynamics.*

. . . (1951). *Field theory in social science.* NY: Harper.

Lewis, C., Perry, R., & Hurd, J. (2004). A deeper look at lesson study. *Educational Leadership.* 61 (5), 18-22.

Lickona, T. (1991). *Educating for character: How our schools can teach respect and responsibility.* NY: Bantam Books.

———— (2001). What is good character? And how can we develop it in our children? *Reclaiming Children & Youth, 9* (4), 239-51.

Lillard, P. (1996). *Montessori today: A comprehensive approach to education from birth to adulthood.* NY: Schocken Publishers.

Linn, R. L., Baker, E. L. & Betebenner, D. W. (2002). Accountability systems: Implications of requirements of the No Child Left Behind Act of 2001. *Educational Researcher, 31* (6), 3-16.

Lipsky, D. K., & Gartner, A. (1997). *Inclusion and school reform: Transforming America's classrooms.* Baltimore, MD: Brookes.

Losel, F. & Beelmann, A. (2003). Effects of child skills training in preventing antisocial behavior: A systematic review of randomized evaluations. *Annals of the American Academy of Political & Social Science, 587*, 84-109.

Love, J. M., Kisker, E. E., Ross, C. M., Schocket, P. Z., Brooks-Gunn, J., Paulsell, D., Boller, K., Constantine, J., Vogel, C., Fuligni, A.S., & Brady-Smith, C. (2002). *Making a difference in the lives of infants and toddlers and their families: The impacts of Early Head Start.* Washington, DC: Department of Health and Human Services.

Luke, C. (2000). New literacies in teacher education, *Journal of Adolescent and Adult Literacy,* 43 (5), 424- 435.

Magnet Schools of America. (N.D.). *Needs assessment survey of magnet schools.* Retrieved from the worldwide web on March 25, 2004 at fgse.nova.edu/nieo/MSA.

Maira, A., & Scott-Morgan, P. (1997). *The accelerating organization.* NY: McGraw Hill.

Maister, D. (1993). Managing the professional service firm. NY: Simon & Schuster.

Manathunga, C. (2002). Designing online learning modules: An Australian example in teacher education, *International Journal of Instructional Media,* 29 (2), 185-195.

Manning, M. L., &Lee, G.L. (2001). Working with parents- cultural and linguistic considerations. Kappa Delta Phi Record, 160-163.

Mapp, K. (1997). Making family-school connections work. *Education Digest, 63*(36), 9.

Marks, M. L. (1986, March). The question of quality circles. *Psychology Today*, p. 36-46.

Marland, S. P. (1974). Career education: Every student headed for a goal. In M. D. Gall & B. A. Ward (Eds.), *Critical issues in educational psychology.* Boston: Little, Brown Co.

Marshall, P. L. (2002). *Cultural diversity in our schools*, Belmont, CA: Wadsworth.

Marzano, R. J. (2000). *Transforming Classroom Grading.* Alexandria, VA: Association for Supervision and Curriculum Development.

Marzano, R. J., Pickering, D. J. & McTighe, J. (1993). *Assessing student outcomes: Performance assessment using the di-*

mensions of learning model. Alexandria, VA: Association for Supervision and Curriculum Development.

Mayer, D. B., Mullins, J. E. & Moore, M. T. (2001). Monitoring school quality: An indicators report. *Education Statistics Quarterly, 3,* 38-44.

McArdle, P., Moseley, D., Quibell, T., Johnson, R., Allen, A., Hammal, D., et al. (2002). School-based indicated prevention: A randomized trial of group therapy. *Journal of Child Psychology & Psychiatry & Allied Disciplines, 43,* 705-712.

McConaughy, S. H., Kay, P. J. & Fitzgerald, M. (2000). How long is long enough? Outcomes for a school-based prevention program. *Exceptional Children, 67,* 21-34.

McDonnell, L. M., McLaughlin, M. J. and Morison, P. (Eds.). (1997). *Educating one and all: Students with disabilities and standards-based reform.* Washington, DC: National Academy Press.

McFadden, S., & Perlman, B. (1989). Faculty recruitment and excellent undergraduate teaching, *Teaching of Psychology,* 16 (4), 195-198.

McGoogan, G. (2002). Around the world in 24 hours, *Educational Leadership,* 60 (2), 44-46.

McKenzie, J. (2000). Beyond *technology: Questioning technology and the information literate tool.* Bellingham, Washington: FNO Press.

McKimm, J., Jolie, C., & Cantillion, P. (2003). ABC of learning and teaching web based learning, *British Medical Journal,* 326, 870-873.

McLaughlin, M., & Henderson, K. (2000). Defining U.S. special education into the twenty-first century. In M. Winzer & K. Mazurek, (Ed). *Special education in the 21st century: Issues of inclusion and reform.* Washington, DC: Gallaudet University.

McLaughlin, M., & Warren, S. (1993). *Do inclusionary practices cost more?   Impressions of special education at eleven sites.* Unpublished manuscript, University of Maryland.

Meier, D. (2002). *The power of their ideas: Lessons from America from a small school in Harlem.* Boston: Beacon Press.

Melan, E. H. (2003). Towards a contingency framework of intervention using systems-based methods. Unpublished doctoral dissertation, The management School at Lancaster University, England.

Menkart, D. J. (1999). Deepening the meaning of heritage months, *Educational Leadership,* 56 (7), 19-21.

Meyer, S. R., & Crawford, V. A. (1994). Distance learning: Multimedia equipment at work. *Media & Methods, 1, 14-15.*

Mid-Atlantic Equity Consortium. (2004). *Magnet schools.* Retrieved on March 25, 2004 from the worldwide web at maec.org/mag-schl.html.

Miles, M. B. (1964). Innovation in education: Some generalizations. In M. B. Miles (Ed.) *Innovation in Education.* NY: Teachers College Press, Columbia University, 631-663.

Moeller, G. H. (1964). Bureaucracy and teacher's sense of power. *School Review, 72,* 137-157.

Moffett, C. A. (2002). Voices from the field: Using Peace Corps Literature, *Educational Leadership,* 60 (2) 26-30.

Montessori, M. (2002). *Montessori method.* Dover Publications, Inc.

Montgomery Halford, J. (1999). A different mirror: A conversation with Ronald Takaki, *Educational Leadership,* 56 (7), 8-13.

Moore, P. (1996). Multicultural education: Another look. *Update on Law-Related Education, 22, 22-25.*

Moynahan, M. J. P. (1981). *Staff Development: the key to successful desegregation / integration implementation.* (ERIC Document Reproduction Service No. ED 207 156).

Moynihan, D. P. (1969*). Maximum feasible misunderstanding: Community action and the war on poverty.* NY: Free Press.

Mrazek, P. J., & Haggerty, R. J. (Eds.) (1994). *Reducing Risks for Mental Disorders: Frontiers for Preventive Intervention Research.* Washington, DC: National Academy Press.

Munoz, R. F., Mrazek, P. J., & Haggerty, R. J. (1996). Institute of Medicine report on prevention of mental disorders: Summary and commentary. *American Psychologist, 51,* 1116-1122.

Murrell, S. A. (1973). *Community psychology and social systems.* NY: Behavioral Publications.

Nation, M., Crusto, C., Wandersman, A., Kumpfer, K. L., Seybolt, D., Morrissey-Kane, E. & Davino, K. (2003). What works in prevention: Principles of effective prevention programs. *American Psychologist, 58*, 449-456.

National Association of State Boards of Education. (N.D.). *Desegregation in an era of standard-based reform.* NASBE Policy Update, Vol. 4, No. 11.

National Commission on Excellence in Education (1983). *A nation at risk: The imperative of educational reform.* Washington, DC: Author

National Commission on Excellence in Education (1983). *A nation at risk: The imperative for educational reform.* Washington, DC: National Commission on Excellence in Education.

National Education Goals Panel (1999, Dec.). *National education goals: Lessons learned, Challenges ahead.* Washington, DC: Author.

National Highway Traffic Safety Administration. (1998). *Air Bags & On-Off Switches: Information for an Informed Decision.* DOT HS 808 629. Washington, DC: U.S. Department of Transportation.

National Institutes of Mental Health Prevention Research Steering Committee. (1994). *The Prevention of Mental Disorders: A national research agenda.* Washington DC: Author.

National Telecommunication and Information Administration (NTIA). (1999). Falling through the net: Defining the digital divide. [Online]. Available: www.ntia.doc.gov/ntiahome/digitaldivide.

Netday (2001). 84% of teachers say internet improves quality of education [Online]. Available: www.netday.org/news_survey.htm.

Nieto, S. (2000). Affirming diversity [book review]. *Multicultural Education, 7* (4), 44.

Northwest Regional Educational Laboratory, The National Clearinghouse for Comprehensive School Reform. (1999). *The catalog of school reform models.* Retrieved on March 26, 2004 from the worldwide web at nwrel.org/scpd/catalog.

O'Donnell - Dooling, J. (2000). What students want to learn about computers, *Educational Leadership, 58* (2), 20-24.

O'Neill, J. (1995). On lasting school reform: A conversation with Ted Sizer. *Educational Leadership, 52* (5), 4-9.

Office of Special Education. (1980). *Second Annual Report to Congress on the Implementation of PL 94:142: The Education for All Handicapped Children Act.* Washington, DC: U.S. Department of Education.

Ohler, J. (2000). A primer on taming the beast: Using technology effectively, creatively, wisely, *Independent School, 59* (2), 64-69.

Olsen, L. (1998). The unz/tuchman "English for children" initiative: A new attack on immigrant children and the schools, *Multicultural Education, 5* (3), 11-13.
Ontario: Ontario Public School Teachers' Federation; Andover, MA

Osborne, A. G. and DiMattia, P. (1994). The IDEA's least restrictive environment mandate: Legal implications. *Exceptional Children, 61,* 6-14.

Patterson, J. L. (1993). *Leadership for tomorrow's schools.* Alexandria, VA: Association for Supervision and Curriculum Development.

Payne, C. R., & Welsh, B.H. (2000). The progressive development of multicultural education before and after the 1960s: A theoretical framework, *The Teacher Educator, 36* (1), 29-48.

Penuel, W. R., Means, B., & Simkins, M. (2000). The multimedia challenge, *Educational Leadership, 58 (2), 34-38.*

Perkins, D. D. (1995). Speaking truth to power: empowerment ideology as social intervention and policy. *American Journal of Community Psychology, 23(5),* 765-795.

Perkins, D. D., & Zimmerman, M.A. (1995). Empowerment theory, research and application. *American Journal of Community Psychology, 23(5),* 569-580.

Perkins-Gough, D. (2004, January). Creating a timely curriculum: A conversation with Heidi Hayes Jacobs. *Educational Leadership, 61,* (4), 12-17.

Peters, T. (1987). *Thriving on chaos: Handbook for the management revolution.* NY: Knopf.

Peterson, A. D. (2003). *Schools across frontiers: The story of the international baccalaureate and the united world colleges.* Open Court Publishing Company.

Peterson, C., Maier, S. F., & Seligman, M. E. P. (1993). *Learned helplessness: A theory for the age of personal control.* NY: Oxford University Press.

Pinar, W., Reynolds, W., Slattery, P. & Taubman, P. (1996). *Understanding curriculum.* NY: Peter Lang.

Podmolik, M. E. (2000). LA's college hits the books in a turn-around, *Crain's Chicago Business,* 23 (25), 69-70.

Pong, S. L. (1997). Family structure, school context, and eight-grade math and reading achievement. Journal of Marriage & Family, 59 (3), 734-747

Pope, K. S. (1990). Identifying and implementing ethical standards for primary prevention. *Prevention in Human Services, 8,* 43-64.

Ramsden, P. (1992). *Learning to teach in higher education.* London & NY: Routledge.

Rappaport, J. (1977). *Community Psychology: Values, research, and action.* Chicago: Holt Rinehart and Winston.

———— (1987). Terms of empowerment/exemplars of prevention: Toward a theory for community psychology. *American Journal of Community Psychology, 15* (2), 121-148.

———— (1995). Empowerment meets narrative: listening to stories and creating settings. *American Journal of Community Psychology, 23(5),* 795-808.

Ravitch, D. (2002). September 11: Seven lessons for the schools, *Educational Leadership,* 60 (2), 6-9.

Reeves, D. B. (2000). *Accountability in action: A blueprint for learning organizations.* Denver, CO: Advanced Learning Press.

———— (2004). *Accountability for learning: How teachers and school leaders can take charge.* Alexandria, VA: Association for Supervision and Curriculum Development.

Resnick, D., & Resnick, L. (1985). Standards, curriculum, and performance: A historical and comparative perspective. *Educational Researcher,* 14 (4), 5-21.

Revenaugh, M. (2000). Toward 24/7 learning community, *Educational Leadership, 58 (2), 25-28.*

Richmond, G. H. (1973). *The micro-society school: a real world in miniature.* Harper and Row.

Richmond, G. H., Richmond, C. K., Schweber, L. & Kharfen, R. (1996). *Microsociety handbook.* Microsociety, Inc.

Riegal, K. F. (1972). Influence of economic and political ideologies on the development of developmental psychology. *Psychological Bulletin, 78,* 129-141.

Riley, W. R. (1994). Ingredient for success: Family involvement, *Teaching preK-8, 25,* 12-14.

Ripple, C. H. & Zigler, E. (2003). Research, policy, and the federal role in prevention initiatives for children. *American Psychologist, 58,* 482-490.

Rokeach, M. (1968). *Beliefs, attitudes and values: A theory of organization and change.* San Francisco: Jossey Boss.

Rose, M. (2001). Bridging the digital divide, *American Teacher* 85, no. 5, 10-14.

Rosenholtz, S. J. (1991). *Teachers' workplace: The organizational context of schooling.* NY: Teachers College Press.

Ross, R. (1994, March 30). *Magnet Schools and Cultural Understanding.* Education Week.

Rothenstein-Fisch, C., Grcenfield, P.M., and Trumbull, E. (1999). Bridging cultures with classroom strategies. Educational Leadership, 56 (7), 64-67.

Ryan, W. (1971). *Blaming the victim.* NY: Random House.

Sadker, D., & Zittleman, K. (2004). Test anxiety: Are students failing tests – or are tests failing students? *Phi Delta Kappan.* 85 (10), 741.

Sagor, R. (2000). *Guiding school improvement with action research.* Alexandria, VA: Association for Supervision and Curriculum Development.

————— (1992). *How to conduct collaborative action research.* Alexandria, Virginia: Association for Supervision and Curriculum Development.

Salend, S. J., Duhaney, D., Anderson, D. J., & Gottschalk, C. Using the internet to improve homework communication and completion, *TEACHING Exceptional Children,* 36 (3), 64-73.

Saphier, J., & M. King. (1985). Good seeds grow in strong cultures. *Educational   Psychologist, 21, 535-539.*

Sarason, S. B. (1972). *The creation of settings and the future societie* San Francisco: Jossey Boss.

Satcher, D. (2000). Mental health: A Report of the Surgeon General: Executive summary. *Professional Psychology: Research and Practice, 31,* 5-13.

Schmoker, M. (1999). *Results: The key to continuous school improvement.* Alexandria, VA: Association for Supervision and Curriculum Development.

Schweinhart, L. J., & Weikart, D. P. (1989). The High/Scope Perry Preschool study: Implications for early childhood care and education. *Prevention in Human Services, 7,* 109-131.

Schweinhart, L. J., Barnes, H. V., & Weikart, D. P. (1993*). Significant benefits: The High/Scope Perry Preschool study through age 27.* Ypsilanti, MI.: High Scope Press.

Scileppi, J. A. (1988). *A systems view of education: A model of change.* Lanham, MD: University Press of America.

Scileppi, J. A., Teed, E. L. & Torres, R. D. (2000). *Community psychology: A common sense approach to mental health.* Upper Saddle River, NJ: Prentice Hall.

Seline, A. M. (1996). The shift away from need *Black Issues in Higher Education, 13,* 38-41.

Senge, P. (1990). *The fifth discipline.* NY: Doubleday Publishers.

———— (1994). The fifth discipline: *The act and practice of the learning organization.* NY: Doubleday.

Senge, P., Cambron-McCabe, N., Lucas, T., Smith, B., Dutton, J. & Kleiner, A. (2000). *Schools that learn: A fifth discipline resource.* NY: Doubleday Dell.

Shaps, E. (2003). Creating a school community. *Educational Leadership,* 60 (6) 31-33.

Shaw, D. (1999). Classrooms without walls, *Curriculum Administrator, 35* (2), 28-36.

Sherif, C., Sherif, M., & Nebergall, R. (1965). *Attitude and attitude change.* Philadelphia: Saunders.

Shinn, K. (2002). Luring high school parents onto our turf. The Education Digest 67, (2) 34-36.

Simonson, M. (1999). Equivalence theory and distance education, *Tech Trends* ,43 (5), 5-8.

Simonson, M., & Sparks, K. (2001). Learning at a distance in South Dakota: Evaluation of the process, *Tech Trends,* 45 (3), 38-43.

Simonson, M., Smaldino, S. Albright, M., & Zvacek, S. (2000). *Teaching and learning at a distance: Foundations of distance education.* Upper Saddle River, NJ: Merrill/Prentice Hall.

Skelding, M. (2000). *Lasting results: Rediscovering the promise of standards through assessment-based instruction.* Montpelier, VT: Common Roots Press.

Skelton, M., Wigford, A., Harper, P.& Reeves, G. (2002). Beyond food, festivals, and flags, *Educational Leadership,* 60 (2), 52-55.

Skinner, B. F. (1958). Teaching machines. *Science, 128*, 969-977.

Slavin, R.E. & Madden, N.A. (2003). *Success for all/roots and wings: 2003 summary of research on achievement outcomes.* Johns Hopkins University, Center for Research on the Education of Students Placed At Risk. Baltimore, MD.

Slavin, R.E., Madden, N.A. and Colleagues. (2000). *Success for all brochure.* John Hopkins University. Success for All Foundation, Inc. Baltimore, MD.

Smith, F. (1995). Let's declare education a disaster and get on with our lives. *Phi Delta Kappan, 76* (8), 584-590.

Smith, S. (2002).Teacher mentoring and collaboration, *Journal of Special Education and Technology,* 17 (1), 45-48.

Speaker, K. M. & Peterson, G. J. (2000). School violence and adolescent suicide: Strategies for effective intervention. *Educational Review, 52*, 65-73.

Speer, P.W., & Hughey, J. (1995). Community organizing: an ecological route to empowerment and power. *American Journal of Community Psychology, 23(5)*, 729-748.

Stainback, W. & Stainback, S. (Eds.). (1990). *Support networks for inclusive schooling: Interdependent integrated education.* Baltimore, MD: Brookes.

Stefanikis, E. H. (2002). *Multiple intelligences portfolios: A window into the learner's mind.* Portsmouth, New Hampshire: Heinemann.

Stein, M. R. S., & Thorkildsen, R. J. (1999). *Parent involvement in education: Insights and applications from the research.* Bloomington, IN: Phi Delta Kappa International.

Steinwachs, B. & Thiagarajan, S. (1990). Barnga. Yarmouth, ME: Intercultural Press.

Stiggins, R. J. (1997). *Student-centered classroom assessment.* Upper Saddle River, NJ: Prentice Hall.

Summers, A. A., & Wolfe, B. L. (1975). Equality of educational opportunity quantified: A production function approach. Paper presented at the winter meeting, Economic Society, Philadelphia.

Sun, L., Bender, W. N., & Fore, C. (2003). Web-based certification course: The future of teacher preparation in special education? *Teacher Education and Special Education,* 26 (2), 87-97.

Swain, C., & Pearson, T. (2002). Educators and technology standards: Influencing the digital divide, *Journal of Research on Technology in Education,* 34 (3), 326-335.

Symes, C. (1996). Selling futures: A new image for Australian universities, *Studies in Higher Education,* 21 (2), 133-147.

Tebes, J. K., Kaufman, E. & Watts, J. S. (2002). Introduction: System development and system change. *The Community Psychologist, 35* (2), 13.

Tell, C. (2000). The i-generation- from toddlers to teenagers: A conversation with Jane M. Healy, *Educational Leadership, 58 (2), 8-13.*

Thoreau Society. (1999). *Uncommon learning: Thoreau on education* (Ed. Martin Bickman). Boston, MA: Houghton Mifflin Company.

Tobler, N. S. (2000). Lessons learned. *Journal of Primary Prevention, 20,* 261-274.

Tobler, N. S., Lessard, T., Marshall, D., Ochshorn, P. & Roona, M. (1999). Effectiveness of school-based drug prevention programs for marijuana use. *School Psychology International, 20,* 105-137.

Tobler, N. S., Roona, M. R., Ochshorn, P., Marshall, D. G., Streke, A. V. & Stackpole, K. M. (2000). School-based adolescent drug prevention programs: 1998 meta-analysis. *Journal of Primary Prevention, 20*, 275-336.

Tobler, N. S., & Stratton, H. H. (1997). Effectiveness of school-based drug prevention programs: Ameta-analysis of the research. *Journal of Primary Prevention, 18*, 71-128.

Toch, T. (1991). *In the name of excellence: The struggle to reform the nation's schools, why it's failing, and what should be done.* NY: Oxford University Press.

Tokeshi, M. (1999). *Species coexistence: Ecological and evolutionary perspectives.* Malden, MA: Blackwell Science, Ltd.

Tubin, D., & Chen, D. (2002). School-based staff development for teaching within computerized learning environments, *Journal of Research on Technology in Education, 34* (4), 517-529.

Turner, J. (2000). *Parent involvement: What can we learn from research?* Montessori LIFE, 37-39.

U.S. Department of Education (1997, December). A compact for learning: An action handbook for family – school – community partnerships. Retrieved on May 26, 2004 from the worldwide web at cd.gov/pubs/compact.htm.

U.S. Department of Education, National Center for Education Statistics. (2001-2002*). Public elementary/secondary school universe study: Table 9.* Common Core of Data.

U.S. Department of Education, National Center for Education Statistics. (2001-2002). *Characteristics of the 100 largest public elementary and secondary school districts in the United States. Table 6.* Common Core of Data.

U.S. Department of Education, National Center for Education Statistics. (1993-1999). *Summary and conclusions: Trends in the use of school choice – statistical analysis report.* National Household Education Surveys Program.

U.S. Department of Education, Office of Educational Research and Improvement, Early Childhood Institute. (1999). *Yale Bush Center in child development and social policy three-year national evaluation of the 21C model.*

U.S. Department of Health and Human Services. (1999). Mental health: A report of the Surgeon General. Rockville, MD: U.S. Department of Health and Human Services, National Institute of Mental Health.

U.S. Department of Education. (2002). *Evaluation of the magnet schools assistance program, 1998 grantees: Final report.* American Institute for Research.

U.S. Department of Education. (1997). *To assure the free appropriate public education of all children with disabilities: Nineteenth annual report to Congress on the implementation of the Individuals with Disabilities Education Act.* Washington, DC: Office of Special Education Programs.

U.S. Department of Education. (2002, July 11). Fact sheet: The No Child Left Behind Act of 2001. Retrieved on March 15, 2004 from the worldwide web at ed.gov/offices/OESE/esea/factsheet.htm.

U.S. Department of Education. (2003). *Executive summary, volume I: Final report – field focused study of the comprehensive school reform demonstration program.*

U.S. Department of Education. (2004). CFDA 84.165A Federal Register, Vol.69. No. 21. *Magnet school assistance program: Notice inviting applications for new awards for fiscal year (FY) 2004, notice and final rule.*

U.S. General Accounting Office. (1997*). Head Start: Research provides little information on impact of current program* (GAO No. GAO/HEHS-97-59). Washington, DC: Author.

Vassalo, P. (2000). *More than grades: How choice boosts parental involvement and benefits children.* Policy Analysis No. 383, October 26, 2000. Washington, DC: Cato Institute,

Vojtek, B., & Vojtek, R. (1997). Are schools ready for the technology age? *Journal of Staff Development,* 18, 60-61.

———— (1997). Connecting the human infrastructure, *Journal of Staff Development,* 18, 42-43.

Wagner, M., Blackorby, J., Cameto, R., Hebbeler, K., and Newman, L. (1993). *The transition experiences of young people with disabilities. A summary of findings from the national longitudinal transition study of special education students.* Menlo Park, CA: SRI International.

Waldrip, D. (N.D.). *A brief history and philosophy of magnet schools: Magnet schools of   America.* Retrieved on March 30, 2004 from the worldwide web at magnet.edu.

Walter-Thomas, C., Korinek, L., McLaughlin, V. & Williams, B.T. (2000). *Collaboration for inclusive education.* Needham Heights, MA: Allyn and Bacon.

Wanderman, R. (2003). Tools and dyslexia: Issues and ideas, *IDA Perspectives.*

Watzlawick, P., Weakland, J. H., & Fisch, R. (1974). *Change: Principles of problem formation and problem resolution.* NY: Norton.

Weissberg, R. P., Gullotta, T. P., Adams, G. R., Hampton, R. L., & Ryan, B. A. (Eds.) (1997a). *Healthy Children 2010: Enhancing Children's Wellness.* Thousand Oaks, CA: Sage.

——— (1997b). *Healthy Children 2010: Establishing Preventive Services.* Thousand Oaks, CA: Sage.

Weissberg, R. P., Kumpfer, K. L. & Seligman, M. E. P. (2003). Prevention that works for children and youth. *American Psychologist, 58,* 425-432.

Wiener, N. (1961). *Cybernetics: Or control and communication in the animal and the machine,* (2nd ed.). Cambridge, MA: MIT Press.

Wiggins, G. (1998). *Educative assessment: Designing assessment to inform and improve performance.* San Francisco, CA: Jossey-Bass.

Wilson, D. B., Gottfredson, D. C. & Najaka, S. S. (2001). School-based prevention of problem behaviors: A meta-analysis. *Journal of Quantitative Criminality,* 17, 247-272.

Wilson, E. O. (1992). *The diversity of life.* Boston, MA: Belknap Press.

Winzer, M. & Mazurek, K. (Ed). (2000). *Special education in the 21st century: Issues of inclusion and reform.* Washington, DC: Gallaudet University.

Wolfensberger, W. (1973). *Normalization.* Toronto, Canada: National Institute on Mental Retardation.

Wong, H. K. (2003). *Collaborating with colleagues to improve student learning,* 11 (6). Retrieved on July 8, 2004, from www.ENC.Focus.org

Woods, L. (2001). Get credit for surfing the web. *Kiplinger's Personal Finance Magazine. 55,* (2) p. 26.

Worster, D. (1994). *Nature's economy: A history of ecological ideas,* (2nd ed.). NY: Cambridge University Press.

Wurtz, E. (2000). Promising practices: Progress toward the Goals 2000: Lessons from the states. ERIC Document Reproduction services No. ED455 590.

Yecke, C. P., & Lazo, L. O. (2002). *Choice provisions in no child left behind.* Special Ed Connection, Federal Policy and Guidance: No Child Left Behind.

Yonezawa, S. & Oakes, J. (1999). Making parents partners in the placement process. Educational Leadership, 56 (7), 33-36.

Ysseldyke, J. E., Lange, C. M., & Algozzine, B. (1991). *Public school choice: What about students with disabilities?* Minneapolis, Minnesota: University of Minnesota

Yukl, G. (1998). *Leadership in Organizations,* (4th ed.). Upper Saddle River, NJ: Prentice Hall.

Zerillo, V. (1999). *In the name of action research.* Burlington, Vermont: Trinity College,

Zigler, E. & Child, I. L. (1969) Socialization. In G. Lindzey and E. Aronson (Eds.) *The handbook of social psychology,* (2nd ed.). *3.* Reading, MA: Addison-Wesley.

Zigler, E., & Valentine, J. (Eds.) (1979). *Project Head Start: A legacy on the wave of poverty.* NY: Free Press.

Zimmerman, M. A., Israel, B. A., Schultz, A. J. & Checkoway, B. (1992). Further explorations in empowerment theory: An empirical analysis of psychological empowerment. *American Journal of Community Psychology, 20* (6), 707-727.

Zimmerman, M.A. (1995). Psychological empowerment: issues and illustrations. *American Journal of Community Psychology, 23(5),* 581-590.

Zmuda, A., Kuklis, R. & Kline, E. (2004). *Transforming schools: Creating a culture of continuous improvement.* Alexandria, VA: Association for Supervision and Curriculum Development.

Name Index

Subject Index